Daily Life in the Middle Ages

Daily Life in
the Middle Ages

by PAUL B. NEWMAN

McFarland & Company, Inc., Publishers
Jefferson, North Carolina, and London

Library of Congress Cataloguing-in-Publication Data

Newman, Paul B., 1961–
    Daily life in the Middle Ages / by Paul B. Newman.
      p.   cm.
    Includes bibliographical references and index.
    ISBN 0-7864-0897-9 (softcover : 50# alkaline paper) ∞
    1. Civilization, Medieval.   2. Middle Ages.   3.   Europe —
Social life and customs.   4. Social history — Medieval, 500–
1500.   5. City and town life — Europe — History — To 1500.
6. Country life — Europe — History — To 1500.   I. Title.

CB353.N46   2001
940.1— dc21   00-52197

British Library cataloguing data are available

McFarland & Company, Inc., Publishers
  Box 611, Jefferson, North Carolina 28640
    www.mcfarlandpub.com

For my wife, Alice,
without whose endless patience and support
this book would never have been written.

CONTENTS

ACKNOWLEDGMENTS

I wish to thank all the people who helped me complete this book, especially Jane Walker for her excellent drawings, Dr. Robert G. Calkins for generously providing four photographs from his book *Medieval Architecture in Western Europe*, and the Walters Art Gallery and its Photographic Services Division for images of some of its extensive collection of medieval illuminations. I also would like to thank John Price, Ana Garcia, Matt Amt, Dr. Carolyn Miles, Geraldine and Robert Newman (my parents), and everyone else who took the time to read and comment on my manuscript. Finally, I thank my wife, Alice, for her assistance in reviewing and editing the text as well as for all her patience and other support.

INTRODUCTION

Life in the Middle Ages bore very little resemblance to its depictions in movies, novels, and the ever-growing number of Renaissance festivals featuring "medieval" entertainments. Though life in the Middle Ages was not as comfortable and safe as it is for most people in industrialized countries today, living in the Middle Ages was not as primitive and crude as it is so often portrayed. Though some parts of Europe temporarily lapsed into barbarism after the fall of Rome in A.D. 476, Roman institutions and public works were such an integral part of European civilization that they rarely disappeared completely. Even during the worst years of the centuries immediately following the fall of Rome, the so-called Dark Ages, the legacy of Roman civilization survived.

Besides any technological and cultural benefits inherited from the days of the Roman Empire, age-old practices such as weaving cloth, growing and preparing food, brewing beer, keeping clean, playing games, trading merchandise, and other fundamental human activities continued and evolved over the course of the Middle Ages. The fact that Romans no longer governed most of Europe had little if any impact on both the need for these activities and the ability of people to carry them out. Nor did the end of Roman rule mean an end to human imagination and creativity. The artistic and technical genius displayed in the great cathedrals, illuminated manuscripts, and other creations of medieval craftsmen proves this to be true.

It's easy to lose sight of what life was really like back then. After all, extremes of behavior, both high and low, are usually far more eye-catching than the day to day actions that keep a society running. So it's not surprising that the Middle Ages are typically thought of as a time when kings and queens lived in opulence in splendid but drafty castles, when knights rode about in glittering armor performing chivalrous deeds or engaging in brutal warfare, and when peasants subsisted as best they could. However, as is usually the case, the truth lies somewhere between the extremes and there was much more to living in the Middle Ages than these stereotypes present.

In this book, I've tried to present a sketch of the major activities that were part of everyday life in the Middle Ages. Admittedly, I have had to make some generalizations in trying to cover life across Europe over a span of almost a thousand years, from the fall of Rome to the beginning of the Renaissance around the end of the 1400s. Further, in keeping this book to a manageable length, I've focused more on the second half of the Middle Ages, from about A.D. 1000 to 1485. Still, I think you'll find that *real* medieval living was in many ways even more fascinating than some of the wildest fiction that's been created about the Middle Ages. For more detailed information on any of the topics, the reader may consult the books listed in the bibliography.

One final point, the term "Middle Ages" is actually a derogatory term. Historians long after the Middle Ages stuck this epoch of history with this label because they viewed these centuries as filler, a time in the *middle* between the great ages of classical Greco-Roman civilization and the Renaissance. But, as I hope this book and the many fine medieval studies now available prove, the Middle Ages were not a time of stagnation or decline. While its pace may have been less than steady, Western civilization continued to develop and progress during this time. Most of the highly touted achievements of the Renaissance did not appear spontaneously. Rather, they were based on groundwork built by artists, architects, engineers, intellectuals, writers, and other people of the Middle Ages, many of whose names and identities have been long forgotten. This book explains how those people lived.

EATING AND COOKING

Mentioning the foods and eating habits of the Middle Ages evokes a variety of vivid images, from the great feasts of the nobility to wretched meals of the peasantry. But permeating the popular idea of food in the Middle Ages are two persistent myths about medieval diet that reflect a deeper misunderstanding of how Europeans before, during, and after the Middle Ages lived. The first common myth is that spices were highly prized because they were instrumental in disguising the smell and flavor of the rotten meat that was a staple of the medieval diet. This myth is grounded in the assumption that the Europeans did not know how to preserve meat and therefore frequently had to eat spoiled meat. To support this myth, most people recall their grade school history lessons that taught that this need for exotic spices was one of the reasons that Columbus and other explorers set out on their hazardous voyages. The second common misperception is that the diet, even of the upper classes, was a poor one, poorly balanced with few or no vegetables. After all, the surviving menus for the great feasts indicate a preponderance of heavy meat dishes and some medieval church sermons as well as medical tracts warn against the potentially harmful effects of eating vegetables, especially raw ones. There are small grains of truth in both these myths, but let's examine them further and try to get a better picture of what food and diet were really like back then.

The Truth About Spices

Spices and other flavorings for food were certainly highly prized in the Middle Ages but the idea that any of them were routinely used to disguise the smell and taste of rotten meat is just silly. Once meat has spoiled, it is toxic and no amount of spices can make it safe to eat. Medieval Europeans were no more immune to food poisoning than we are today. So why were spices so sought after? To add more flavor and zest to the food. Medieval Europeans weren't that different from modern people. They had taste buds. They enjoyed different flavors and were willing to pay for them, much as modern restaurant patrons are every time some new cuisine appears. They also had some needs for spices which we generally don't have today: for use in mixtures for preserving foods and in preparing foods that had been preserved and reconstituted, losing much of their natural flavor in the process. Reconstituting meats preserved by dehydration, especially salting, required boiling or soaking to restore them to edible condition, not unlike with Smithfield ham or salt cod even today. Thus, spices helped make up for the loss of natural flavor incurred by the drying out and then rehydration of the meat.

Food Preservation

Refrigeration, one the most common means of food preservation in use today, was available only during the winter months when naturally cold conditions permitted the prolonged freezing of meat and fish. In some parts of Europe, most notably Scandinavia and Russia, the long winters made freezing an important means of preservation. For example, an Italian diplomat in 15th century Moscow marveled at the food market held on the city's frozen river where meat from whole skinned cows and pigs (some even positioned standing upright on their feet as though still alive!) was sold up to three or more months after the beasts had been slaughtered. Still, the use of natural refrigeration and freezing was very limited. Medieval Europeans lacked year-round refrigeration and some of the other food preservation techniques we enjoy today. But in this respect, they were no different from the classical Romans or the peoples of the Renaissance. No major innovations

in food preservation were made until the 19th century. Only then did people begin enjoying the benefits of more advanced food preservation methods and it was not until nearly the middle of the 20th century that many of these methods were perfected and made widely and easily available. For example, canning — the heating of fruits, vegetables, and other foodstuffs to high temperatures to kill bacteria and then packing the food in airtight containers, invented in the last years of the 18th century and developed extensively during the 19th century — has been perfected and created a reliable source of hundreds of varieties of ready-to-eat foods, from out of season fruits and vegetables to soups and stews. Mechanical and chemical refrigeration were developed during the 19th century but have swept the world only in the last fifty years when advances in cooling technology and increased availability of electricity have made them practical on a large scale. These methods of preservation have brought even more bounty to our tables through cooling or freezing foods to extend the time of their edibility. Then there are all the chemical stabilizers and preservatives, typically used in conjunction with another technique like canning or freezing but also used by themselves as in baked goods and other items to retard spoilage or simply to keep the product looking, if not tasting, fresh. All these methods of preservation are such an integral part of our day to day lives that it is difficult, if not impossible, to envisage life without them. Thus, it is easy to assume that life without them was unbearably primitive and rife with spoiled foods. And certainly life was much more difficult and unpleasant without these marvelous techniques for keeping food fresh and available all year round, but it was not as awful as it seems.

There are many ways to preserve food other than canning, freezing, or treating with modern chemical compounds. There's smoking, drying, salting (either dry or with brine, a solution of salt and water), pickling in vinegar, candying, and packing in oil or fat. All these techniques were known in Europe long before the Middle Ages and all of them were in use during the Middle Ages. In fact, though they may be less important now than in earlier times, all these techniques remain in use now, right alongside the more modern techniques. Let's look at the techniques, see how they work and the foods to which they were applied.

SMOKING, DRYING, AND DRY SALTING ANIMAL FLESH

Smoking, drying, and salting with dry salt (as opposed to wet salting with brine) were all methods of preserving foods by dehydration; that is, by the removal of as much water and other fluids as possible. By desiccating, or curing, foodstuffs, these methods retarded spoilage by removing watery tissue fluids which could readily serve as a medium for bacteria. Since bacteria would remain undiscovered until the invention of the microscope in the 17th century and the harmful effect of some bacteria would not be proven until the 19th century, it can only be assumed that this method of preservation was discovered empirically: old, dried out meats, though tough, could be eaten without making the diner ill, while old meat that had been left moist smelled bad and made a person sick if he or she ate it. Regardless of how or when it was discovered, dehydration was well known by the beginning of the Middle Ages and was widely practiced using one or a combination of these three methods.

The choice of methods depended on the food to be preserved and the resources available. Let's examine the preservation of meats and fish first since all three methods were used either separately or in combination to preserve them. Smoking meat or fish accelerated the curing process since the heat of the smoking fire dries the air, speeding up evaporation of fluids in the flesh thereby reducing the chance that the oils in the meat would go rancid before the meat was thoroughly dried. It also imparted a pleasant taste to the smoked flesh, something we enjoy even today in items like smoked salmon, kippered herring, or "hickory smoked" bacon or ham. But smoking required wood for fuel, something that may have been very scarce in certain locales. Besides firewood, it also required a smokehouse or shed in which to hang the flesh and contain the smoke as well as someone to watch and tend the fire. Drying was a cheaper alternative, particularly suited for fish which could simply be spread out on the rocks or beach near where they were brought ashore. But this was a less reliable method. It required several days of good, clear sunny weather with warm or hot temperatures and even then there was a substantial risk of the flesh decaying before it was thoroughly cured. Given the limitations of smoking and drying, the most common method was salting: typically combining some preliminary drying, either with or without smoking, with packing in dry salt or a mixture of salt and spices to draw out the remaining moisture.

This explains the importance of salt in the Middle Ages. Just as in classical times, when salt had been such an important commodity that Roman soldiers received a special pay allotment for salt (from which the word "salary" is derived), salt was more than just a food flavoring, it was a vital element for maintaining life both as a nutritional mineral and as a preservative for foodstuffs and so was valuable and highly sought after. The salt industry was highly developed in the Middle Ages. Salt was obtained in several ways. The most common, but lowest grade of salt was sea salt, produced by flooding specially constructed fields near marshes or other low, flat plains bordering the sea. These fields had low earthen walls to contain the water which was gradually evaporated by the sun, leaving the precious, though coarse, salt behind. While effective for producing salt on a relatively large scale, the resulting salt usually had grit and other impurities mixed in. Despite its grittiness, sea salt was commonly used because it was cheap, typically selling for less than half the price of better quality, cleaner salt. Though it may have sometimes lacked the iodine, magnesium, and other important trace elements found in sea salt, consumers preferred salt that was more pure and tasted cleaner, such as that obtained from natural springs that flowed through salt deposits on their way to the surface. This salt was more expensive to produce than salt evaporated from seawater by the sun. Manuscript illustrations show water being piped from these springs into massive kettles where the water was boiled away to obtain the pure salt. Finally, as with other valuable minerals, salt deposits were mined. The significance of these mining operations is reflected in place names, such as Salzburg, in Austria, named so because of the numerous salt mines in the vicinity. Though all mining was dangerous and involved significant health hazards from dusts or gases in the mines, salt mining was notably pernicious because of the respiratory problems caused by inhaling the fine crystals of salt as well as the general irritation of the eyes, nose, and mouth caused by the dehydrating effect of the salt. This is probably why even today we refer to performing unpleasant work as "another day in the salt mines." Despite the difficulties in obtaining it, salt was highly valued because it was an essential element both for good health and for preserving those

dietary staples and main sources of protein: meat and fish.

Preserving meats and fish was a year-round activity. Trade in foodstuffs involved shipping items long distances using slow means, such as wagons or barges. Thus, fish from coastal ports had to be preserved immediately so that it could be shipped to consumers inland as well as to save large catches for later consumption locally. Livestock, such as cows, sheep, and goats, were raised throughout Europe and, for much of the year, could be slaughtered as needed, reducing some of the need for preservation. However, some areas were obviously better suited for livestock grazing and produced surpluses that could be sold to distant customers. And transporting these surpluses in the form of salted joints of beef or mutton was far easier than trying to herd live animals long distances, a process which had significant risks of disease, injury, or just weight loss from physical exertion, all of which could diminish or entirely destroy the animals' value. Livestock production was also tied to an annual cycle of procreation, grazing, and slaughter. Pasturage was plentiful in the late spring into the fall until frosts and cold weather ended the open grazing season. Unlike modern livestock farmers, medieval farmers did not have the resources to produce and store the amounts of fodder necessary to keep large numbers of animals alive through the winter. Thus, while a few animals were carefully kept alive for breeding, most livestock was slaughtered and butchered over the course of the late fall and early winter as the grazing ran out and so this was the traditional season for preserving meats on a large scale.

Before moving on to other foods, one last point about meat preservation and the salt and spice mixtures mentioned earlier. These mixtures could include clove, black pepper, and other powdered spices. Besides flavoring the meat, these seasonings contributed to the desiccating action of the mixture and also served to repel insects and other pests while the meat was curing and afterwards while it was stored awaiting use. It may have been this use of spices that was later mistaken as being a means of hiding the smell and taste of rotting meats.

DRYING OTHER FOODS

Smoking, drying, and salting weren't applied only to animal flesh. Cheese was made with salt to dry it out and make it less prone to spoilage. It could also be smoked both to flavor it and to further desiccate it to extend its useful life. Butter, another common dairy product, was also salted to preserve it.

Whereas meats or fish could easily spoil before thoroughly drying out without the aid of smoking, simple drying was a useful technique for preserving fruits since fruits were relatively small or could be sliced up to increase the amount of surface area exposed, facilitating fast and thorough dehydration. Further, they did not contain the fats and oils that accelerated spoilage in meats and fish. Drying was accomplished by placing the fruit on open wooden racks that allowed air to circulate freely around the fruit. Such drying was best performed outdoors under direct sun but could also be done indoors in well-ventilated areas. Besides apricots, raisins, dates, figs, and prunes which are still common foods today, medieval Europeans also routinely dried pears, apples, peaches, cherries, and many other fruits which have only recently begun to be enjoyed again in dried form today as "health food." Like meat and fish, fruits were dried for a variety of reasons. Obviously, fruits typically have a very short "shelf life" and spoil quickly if not promptly preserved. Thus, to provide a tasty and nutritious element to

the diet year-round, fruits were preserved as they came into season and were stored for later use, especially for the long, fruitless winters. Also, fruit production was more specialized and localized than livestock cultivation. Not all fruits could be grown in all parts of Europe or, in some cases, any part of Europe. So, dates and figs from Syria found their way to consumers throughout Europe along with raisins and other fruits from the sunny climes of the Mediterranean's northern shores. Dried fruit was ideally suited for the long, slow trips to those countries further north where these delicacies could not be grown.

Most vegetables were unsuited to preserving by dehydration, with the notable exceptions of legumes including peas, beans and lentils which, then as now, were harvested and dried for later use. Fortunately, many vegetables, such as root vegetables like carrots, turnips, and parsnips, were relatively durable and could be kept edible for weeks after harvesting if stored in a cool, dry place. Most other vegetables simply had to be prepared and consumed as they became ripe.

Herbs were also dried to provide a year-round source of flavoring. Parsley, sage, rosemary, and many other herbs were routinely grown in most "kitchen gardens" whether on the farm or in town. Most could simply be trimmed off, tied up in a small bundle, and then hung on the rafters or other beams inside the house until they were dry. Often, they were hung near to the hearth to speed drying but also to keep them at hand for use in cooking.

OTHER METHODS OF PRESERVATION

Wet Salting

Dehydration by smoking, drying, or salting was not suitable for all foods. Even for some meats and fish, the drying process could destroy their texture leaving them virtually inedible. One alternative that kept the flesh moist and thus better preserved its texture was to pack it in brine, a solution of fresh water mixed with salt. This method was used on meats, such as beef to turn it into "corned" beef, and on many varieties of fish. The salt in the brine saturated the flesh, arresting the growth of bacteria, and the brine solution itself shielded the preserved flesh from further contact with airborne contaminants. But, despite its merits, packing in brine had some practical limitations that restrained its use. Brined foodstuffs had to remain covered in brine or they would spoil so they had to be stored and transported in watertight barrels. While dried foods were often stored in barrels too, it was absolutely critical for brined foods that these barrels were kept well sealed to prevent leakage or evaporation of the brine. Brining also had the disadvantage of producing a heavier "package" than dehydration. Dehydration reduced the weight of the flesh being preserved by removing most of the water but brining saturated and surrounded the flesh with a solution that weighed over eight pounds per gallon. So a relatively small barrel with a capacity of 15 gallons would weigh over a hundred pounds when filled with fish and brine, making it very cumbersome to transport. These drawbacks limited the usefulness of brining. Thus, it was typically reserved for preserving fish for wealthy consumers inland or for local consumption where transportation was far less a problem.

Packing in Wine, Vinegar, and Oil

Another liquid-based method of preserving foods was to pickle them in a solution of brine mixed with wine or vinegar, often with spices added for flavor. The acidity of the wine or vinegar, combined with the salt of the brine, was highly effective in preventing bacteria growth. This process would turn ordinary vegetables into pickles and relishes and so was a form of food preparation as well as a preservation technique. Alternatively, the wine could be sugared, turning it into syrup, and used to pack fruits. The expense of wine and sugar ensured that this method was applied to only those delicacies that were worth the cost.

Similar to packing in wine, foodstuffs could be packed in oil. The primary products packed in this manner were olives with olive oil being used as the packing solution. Again, spices could be added to marinate and flavor the olives while they were stored. While vegetable oils in general do not turn rancid as quickly as oils from animals, olive oil is particularly well-suited for preserving food since it is a monounsaturated fat and contains antioxidants. This combination of factors makes olive oil much less likely to go rancid than other oils.

Candying

Small whole fruits or slices of fruits were dried and coated in dry sugar or syrup and then dried again. The sugar coating sealed the fruit, preventing moisture from getting back in. If they were transported and stored in dry containers, such candied fruits could be shipped long distances and still stay edible for months, as the presence of sugared Syrian figs and dates on medieval banquet tables attests.

Packing in Gelatin or Fats

One preservation technique used in the Middle Ages which is now alien to most cooks is preserving cooked foods using gelatin or fat. This method involved a form of dehydration combined with a protective coating. First, the food, usually meat, was cooked, thus reducing its moisture content and thereby slowing spoilage by decreasing the amount of watery medium in which bacteria could grow. After cooking, the food was immersed in either gelatin (usually obtained from the boiled hooves and feet of calves and cows) or rendered animal fat which then congealed, forming a coating that protected the cooked meat from airborne bacteria and other contaminants. This method was commonly used on meats and fish and worked best when the combined flesh/gelatin or flesh/fat mixture could be stored in crocks or other sealed containers placed in a cool dry location. The use of fat may not seem practical, given that animal fats will go rancid. However, fats and oils that have been rendered — that is, have had the water cooked out of them — will actually stay fresh and edible for several weeks or months if stored in a cool, dry location, as can be seen today with shortening and lard. And as long as the fat or gelatin remained untainted, the food inside would generally remain edible as well. These techniques worked best when the mixture was stored at temperatures of forty degrees Fahrenheit or below. While refrigerators did not exist in the Middle Ages, the naturally cool temperatures of the late fall and winter created ideal conditions for these methods of preservation. The requirement for cool temperatures meant that these techniques could be used, along with smoking, salting, and other methods, to preserve the yield from the large scale slaughtering of livestock that also occurred in the late fall and early winter, providing a useful supplement to the other techniques for short-term storage of ready to eat meat.

Food Availability and Choices

The list of foods introduced from the New World to Europe after the voyages of discovery is well known. Tomatoes, potatoes, peanuts, bell peppers, cocoa, and corn have transformed diets around the world in the last 500 years, while some other items like pasta were only introduced to Europe from Asia in the 13th century. It's very difficult to imagine the Spanish cooking without tomatoes and bell peppers or the Italians cooking without tomatoes and pasta but all the Europeans, just as the Greeks and Romans did before them, created a widely varied cuisine from the myriad ingredients that were at hand. While they lacked tomatoes, corn, and potatoes, they had beans, peas, onions, cauliflower, asparagus, summer and winter squashes, leaf vegetables like lettuce and spinach, celery, turnips, carrots, cabbages, parsnips, and many more. Fungi were also eaten in much of Europe. Just as they are today, wild mushrooms were hunted and gathered to provide tasty treats, despite the risks of accidental poisoning from misidentified mushrooms. As for fruit, though some of the varieties we enjoy today were not yet hybridized, they did grow most of the fruits we are familiar with today, except, of course, for some of the exotic tropical fruits like banana and pineapple. From pictorial evidence, excavation of cesspits (which contain the indigestible seeds that passed through the digestive tracts of medieval consumers), and other records, we know they had many varieties of grapes, plums, apples, and pears as well as peaches, strawberries, blueberries, raspberries, apricots, and cherries. By the late 13th and early 14th centuries, even oranges and lemons were being exported from Spain to the rest of Europe.

For meat dishes, beef, veal, mutton, lamb, pork, and goat were routinely available. Game meats included boar, stag, deer, hare, rabbit, and bear. Even the now rare European beaver didn't escape the kitchen and dining table. Poultry included both domestic and wild birds like ducks, geese, chickens, pheasants, pigeons, partridges, and all the other species we eat today (except turkey, a bird native to North America). They also prepared and ate many other varieties of game birds which, regardless of whether or not they are on the endangered species, most of us wouldn't dream of eating today, like swans, sparrows, herons, cranes, bitterns, spoonbills, eagles, curlews, and the European bustard (a large, ungainly bird). The eggs of these birds were also eaten. Like birds, great varieties of fresh and saltwater fish, finfish and shellfish were harvested for the tables of medieval Europe. Lobster, crab, crayfish, clams, oysters, mussels, squid, octopus, eel, mackerel, pike, herring, trout, bream, tench, perch, salmon, the fish formerly known as dolphin (now called "mahi-mahi" on most menus to avoid any confusion with the sea mammal of the same name), sole, flounder, halibut, and many more species were caught and sold to eager consumers. While most were netted from rivers or the open seas, some varieties of freshwater fish (primarily carp, eel, and pike) were reared in stock ponds on noble estates or monastic manors. These man-made ponds were relatively small and the fish were easily netted by men standing on the banks. This technique provided a reliable source of fresh fish and was basically the same as current "aquaculture" in which catfish, salmon, and even shrimp are raised in pools or ponds under controlled conditions and then harvested for market. Fish weren't the only marine animals used for food. Seals, porpoises, and several species of whales were also hunted for their meat, oils, and other valuable products, including tusks from narwhals that were usually sold as "horns of unicorns," and "whalebone" (more accurately called baleen, a flexible, plastic-like material) from the mouths of whales that feed by filtering plankton from sea water. Whales and porpoises were considered "royal" animals in much of Europe

and any caught or found beached were technically the property of the crown and could not be disposed of without the permission of the king or his representative. This raises another issue about the availability of all these various meats: not all of them were available to the general public. Economics and social strictures dictated that only the nobility really had access to all these birds, fish, and other animals, especially wild game. Still, many types of animals in each group were available to all and found their way onto even some of the humblest tables.

What about nuts? They were a common source of protein and oils, widely cultivated and marketed. They included walnuts, chestnuts, hazelnuts (or filberts), pistachios, pine-nuts, and, most importantly, almonds. (We'll discuss why almonds were so important later.) And we shouldn't forget dairy products: cheeses, yogurts, butter, and milk. Then there were the grains too, which Europeans still refer to as "corn." (Remember, corn as in "corn on the cob" or "maize" wasn't introduced to Europe until after 1492. Germans still call multi-grain flour "multikorn" and many cities in the rural heartland of England had "corn markets" where grains were brought for sale.) These grains included wheat, spelt, oats, barley, rye, and — from around the Mediterranean — rice. They were used for making bread and other baked goods as well as pottages (dishes of boiled grain that could be served either as a side dish or main dish) depending on the occasion and the wealth of the household.

This list of foods is by no means exhaustive. Listing all the foods available for consumption in medieval Europe could fill most of a book (if you don't believe me, just look at some of the books in the bibliography for this chapter). The purpose of this partial list is to give some idea of the range of items available and to prove that medieval Europeans had a broad and varied basis for their diets. Does this mean that all of them enjoyed richly varied diets all the time? No, but it shows that they didn't just eat roast meat and gruel either. Their diets were limited by personal taste in food, economics, religious strictures, geography, and social status. But this is not unique to the Europeans of the Middle Ages. In differing degrees, these same factors still limit our diets today. Even with the modern convenience of food from every corner of the globe being available year-round in the nearest grocery store, many people choose to subsist on diets of fast-food hamburgers and take-out pizzas. Others have their choices severely limited by their incomes. Still, even with these common limitations, we do not characterize the current era as a time of dull, mediocre, monotonous diets. But, apart from the feasts of the very wealthy, that is precisely the inaccurate image commonly evoked by the phrase "food in the Middle Ages." Feasting was part of life in the Middle Ages for a select few and will be examined later in this chapter, but let's turn to everyday food preparation and eating for all levels of society.

Obtaining Food

People of the Middle Ages cultivated their own foods as much as possible. This was certainly most common for farmers and village dwellers out in the country, but even in towns and cities people often kept kitchen gardens for cultivating fresh herbs and vegetables as well as keeping a few chickens for fresh eggs and the occasional chicken for the table. Those foods which they could not grow themselves, they obtained through barter or purchase. While barter was probably common in rural areas where farmers and villagers would trade amongst themselves, recent

studies of medieval societies and their economies indicate that they were more developed economically than was thought in the past. For most of the Middle Ages, cash-based trade was quite common except during shortages of silver when the supply of coinage was restricted. This position is also supported by the many regulations on the foods trade in cities and towns throughout Europe. These regulations, some of which date back to the early 13th century, specify qualities, weights, and prices (down to the fraction of a penny, though the silver penny was the largest denomination of coin ever owned by many consumers) for bread and other staples. Thus, many transactions, for food as well as other items, were probably on a cash basis rather than barter. So, from street vendors, markets, or established shops, medieval consumers could easily buy the food items they needed for their meals: vegetables and fruits from market stalls, bread from a bakery, meat from a butcher shop, fish from the basket of a wandering fish-monger, and so on. And, while the strolling vendors have disappeared, shopping for groceries like this can still be done in many European towns and cities on market days.

And not just the raw ingredients for meals were available. We may think that convenience foods are a modern creation but they can be traced back to at least the Middle Ages, if not earlier. In any major town or city in medieval Europe, a range of ready to eat meals were available from cooks such as piemakers and roasters who specialized in producing only certain types of foods. From these cooks, one could obtain foods ranging from small pastries filled with meat for the person on the go up to fully prepared roast chicken or goose dinners with all the sauces and side dishes to feed a whole family or dinner party.

Still, whether for raw ingredients or finished dishes, all these sources were limited to those foods (either fresh or preserved) which were grown in the immediate area or which were produced in another region, preserved, and shipped in. Limitations in preserving techniques and in speed of transportation certainly limited the variety and availability of foods but the medieval Europeans did the best they could, taking full advantage of what they did obtain.

Selecting Foods

As mentioned above, numerous factors guided (or limited) medieval consumers in their selection of foods. Some of these we can readily identify with today, like economics (Can I afford lobster and steak this week?) or personal taste (I don't care how reasonably priced or good for me the brussels sprouts are, I'm not getting them!). Others, like geography (distance from where the item is grown to where it is consumed) and the season of the year (whether a fruit or vegetable is available at all), are increasingly irrelevant to modern consumers who, if they can afford it, can enjoy fresh foods shipped hundreds of miles (like fresh seafood served in the landlocked heart of a continent) or even thousands of miles (as with fresh summer fruits and vegetables served in the dead of winter). Thus, living in an age where New Zealand "spring" lamb, Chilean berries, South African apples, and hundreds of other foods are shipped from frost-free zones or even other hemispheres to provide year-round availability of a tremendous variety of foodstuffs, it may be difficult to understand the limitations imposed by having access to only locally or regionally grown foods and a few imported, mainly preserved items.

Certainly the limitations of not being able to ship fresh fruits and vegetables in

from distant lands that enjoyed frost-free weather or other variations in climate that produced different growing seasons meant that most Europeans had no access to these nutritious foods except when they were ripe within the immediate vicinity. Thus, from the late fall through early spring, many people during the Middle Ages endured monotonous diets, largely devoid of fruits and vegetables, and likely suffered some form of malnutrition, such as scurvy from lack of vitamin C. But it must be emphasized that these nutritional deficiencies were the result of the natural growing cycle and were not caused by ignorance or by any superstitious bias against consuming fruits and vegetables. In fact, some evidence, such as the repetition of stern warnings against overconsumption of fruits and vegetables in heath and diet manuals throughout the period, suggests that medieval Europeans did not generally have any such bias and were prone to overindulging in eating fruits and vegetables, particularly raw ones, when they were in season. For example, Frankish records from the ninth century include complaints from orchard owners near monasteries with schools that schoolboys were raiding the orchards and stealing fruit. This behavior is quite understandable in view of the months these people went without such tasty and nutritious foods. Their bodies must have craved the vital minerals and vitamins these foods contained and their palates yearned for the simple but pleasing taste of a nice, juicy plum or a crisp, sweet apple. Yet, the warnings about the dangers of this behavior are also understandable. These warnings, which are often incorrectly cited as reflecting an absurd, unhealthy bias against eating *any* fruits and vegetables, were likely the product of practical observations of the impact of flooding the human digestive system with food rich in nutrients and fiber after prolonged periods of dietary deprivation. Cramps, diarrhea, and other illnesses must have often been the outcome. These problems are not unlike those encountered this century in the course of rescue operations to aid starving populations. In these operations, aid workers are given guidance comparable to the medieval warnings: Do not feed starvation victims rich foods, such as MREs (MREs are "Meals-Ready-to-Eat," U.S. military food rations dense in nutrients and designed to sustain physically fit people engaged in strenuous activities), because the sudden reintroduction of such food can actually make them more ill, to the point of causing death, as their digestive systems struggle to break down and assimilate the sudden flood of nutrients. So care must taken in accepting traditional views about life in the Middle Ages as well as in taking some written evidence at face value. Yes, some medieval health manuals warned against consuming fruits and vegetables but this was usually in the context of warning against *excessive* consumption, particularly at certain times of the year, or against eating foods that were out of season and which were thus likely to be either unripe or past their prime. But these warnings were *not* flat prohibitions against *all* consumption and at *all* times. And yes, medieval diets may have been monotonous and nutritionally lacking at times but not because the medieval Europeans irrationally chose to reject better dietary options, but because their food choices were restricted by seasonal and regional limitations in food production. And in this respect, the peoples of medieval Europe were the same as the rest of the world's inhabitants up until recent times, when the advent of improved shipping and preservation have benefited diets around the globe. Further, while their diets varied in accordance with the season and region far more than most modern diets, the section below on food preparation shows that they didn't lack creativity in the kitchen and

that all diets were not monotonous year round.

Besides the physical restrictions that season and location imposed on food availability and selection, a final and important limitation was that imposed by religious strictures. For Jews, these included the traditional requirements for the preparation and consumption of kosher foods. For Christians, a complex calendar evolved during the Middle Ages that dictated the days and times of the years, such as Lent and Advent, when meat and related foods were permitted or prohibited and a few days when complete fasting was required. These restrictions, which varied widely over the course of the Middle Ages and from region to region, were often hotly debated by religious scholars, both in earnest and in jest. Under the strictest interpretation of the Church's requirements, there were twelve fast days a year when no substantial food was to be eaten. Further, meat from any animals (four-legged or fowl) and any foods derived from them (eggs, milk, cheese, fats, and oils) were prohibited on Mondays, Wednesdays, Fridays, Saturdays, as well as on every day during Advent and Lent. Though most interpretations of the requirements for abstaining from meat were likely less severe, both in terms of the numbers of days and the range of items to which they applied, there were still several days a week and the forty days of Lent when the only flesh permitted good Christians was fish. These limits gave fish an additional significance within the diet of medieval Christians, or at least of those who had access to and could afford fish to substitute for animal flesh. The restrictions against eating milk, butter and animal fats led to the use of vegetable based substitutes on the days affected. Unlike kosher food preparation, little remains today of the Christian dietary laws, except a few survivals like the observance by traditional Catholics of two days of fasting a year and abstaining from meat on Fridays. Thus, for the Christian population of Europe from the highest kings to lowliest of peasants, some components of the diet alternated from day to day as the Church dictated. Mind you, this does not appear to have created too great a hardship. Surviving recipes and menus for noble households reflect the ingenuity of their chefs in preparing fish dishes every bit as sumptuous as their meat dishes. For the lower classes, meat was scarce for most households, so the restrictions against eating meat were probably not difficult to comply with. However, for those of middling means in inland communities, the expense of obtaining fish was likely problematic. In fact, correspondence surviving from the early 15th century include records of families and business associates advising each other to lay in supplies of preserved fish well in advance of Lent or Advent, before the prices went up.

The religious injunctions against consuming animal flesh on certain days as an act of faith and personal denial produced some odd results. Even with the broad variety of fish available, by the late Middle Ages, some epicurean clerics had managed to add several species of seagoing birds as well as some mammals to the list of animals that could be consumed on fish days. Given that they lived at sea like fish and were caught like fish, it's easy to understand that marine mammals like whales, porpoises, and seals were considered "fish." But it is more difficult to accept the reasoning in the case of beavers which were also classed as fish because they were aquatic and had fish-like tails. This classification had the unfortunate result of contributing to the decimation of European beavers since they were hunted to provide one more fish day delicacy, beaver tail, for the wealthy. The classification of birds as "fish" seems similarly absurd, yet puffins and a type of goose called the "barnacle goose" were among those birds classed as "fish" because they were believed to reproduce at sea, not unlike fish.

Preparing Food

Food preparation was as varied as it is today. The people of the Middle Ages used the same methods available to us today: broiling, grilling, baking, roasting, boiling, poaching, and frying. Despite having the same range of cooking methods, much medieval cooking seems very alien with some dishes appearing unpalatable and a few being outright disgusting to most modern diners. This is particularly true of the foods prepared for the nobility. Examining these dishes, medieval cooks seem more daring and creative than the average modern cook in their unusual combinations of ingredients and styles of presentation. But, as we'll see below, these cooks were highly trained professionals and their specialized cookery was no more characteristic of the typical cuisine of their time than modern, cutting edge cuisines are representative of what people usually eat today. So, first the basics.

GRAINS

The varied uses that grains could be put to, their nutritional value, their durability (grains, either in whole form or processed into flour, remained edible for prolonged periods if kept dry), and that two crops of grains could be planted and harvested in a single year assured grains an important place in the medieval diet. Cereal crops of wheat, barley, rye, and spelt were grown throughout Europe and were the raw ingredients in three foods that formed the basis for the medieval diet: bread, pottage, and beer.

Bread

Bread was the most basic component of the medieval diet but virtually no recipes for bread survive from the Middle Ages. This lack of recipes, even in encyclopedic collections from grand households, may be attributable to the fact that baking bread was performed by bakers instead of chefs and were thus omitted from the recipe collections since they were composed by the chefs, not by the bakers. However, recipes for bread are also absent in other documents such as a comprehensive book on household management and home economics by the "Menagier de Paris," a late medieval book written by an older upper-middle class husband for his new, young wife. But despite this lack of written evidence on how to make it, countless illustrations and written accounts of meals show that bread, in varying forms, was consumed throughout Europe by all classes of society. So the lack of surviving recipes could be just bad luck or it could be that bread baking was so common that recipes were passed down orally and by direct experience from one generation to the next, making the recording of bread recipes as useful as writing down the recipe for boiling water.

Whatever the recipe, the basic ingredients for bread have remained the same: a powdered starch (usually a flour made from wheat, spelt, rye, barley, or other grain), a liquid (water or milk), salt, and a rising agent. By far, yeast was the most common leavening for bread but easy to use dry yeasts like we have today did not exist. Instead, old dough (which is still used in traditional "sour dough" bread) or "barm" (a liquid yeast produced in the process of fermenting grain mash into beer) were used to start bread dough rising. Besides the basic ingredients, oats, nuts, dried fruits, and even beans and lentils were sometimes added in for flavor and texture or to act as fillers when grain

was in short supply. Bean breads were usually served to horses but people would eat them as well if no better bread was available.

Even without the addition of oats and beans, most bread was rather coarse (and probably a bit tough and chewy) since whole grain flour of varying quality was usually used. But the nobility and other well-off people could afford finer bread made of white flour from which the bran and germ had been removed by sifting the flour through fabric called *bolting cloth*. To produce very fine flour, the flour was re-sifted two or three times. This fine sifting required additional labor and wasted some of the flour, making white flour far more expensive than whole grain flour. This sifted flour produced lighter, more delicate breads but, as modern dieticians are quick to point out, these breads lacked the fiber and nutrition provided by the bran and germ. However, medieval white flour was not the bleached and bromated white flour common today. Since it did not undergo the rigorous mechanical and chemical treatments commonly used in modern flour refining, it probably retained more of its natural nutritional value. Additionally, the reduction in fiber content may not have been a bad thing. Recent studies of medieval diet indicate that most people during the Middle Ages had diets rich in fiber from beans, peas, and other legumes as well as bread and so few suffered from low fiber intake. In fact, hypothetical reconstructions of "average" medieval diets suggest they may have often contained excessive levels of fiber, to the point that the digestive tract was so overloaded with fiber that it prevented proper absorption of nutrients. So, the elite's consumption of bread made from white flour likely had little adverse impact on their health and may have actually been healthier for them.

Large institutions, such as monasteries, castles, or palaces maintained their own ovens for their own bread baking needs but most people did not have ovens in their homes and had to take their bread to communal ovens for baking — in villages or manors at ovens directly owned or licensed by the local lords, or in towns and cities at commercial bakeries. In an age when ovens, and even bread machines, are common household appliances, it may be difficult to understand why communal ovens were the norm but in the Middle Ages ovens were typically large, domed structures, several feet in height and sometimes up to six feet or more in diameter and made of stone, clay, and brick. A single family could rarely afford to build an oven for private use. Further, the expense of maintaining it and keeping it supplied with wood for its fire were also prohibitive. Additionally, there was an economy of scale in using communal ovens. Heating an oven to a baking temperature took considerable time and fuel, so it was highly impractical to fire up an oven just to bake a single day's worth of a bread for one family. It was far more economical to have an oven to which many households could bring their breads and other pastries to be baked and then share the expense by paying a fee to the person who owned and maintained the oven. Admittedly, when lords prohibited the building of other ovens in order to protect their own monopolies and income, this did not mean that the fee was always fair. And there was another peril — unscrupulous commercial bakers! Legal records of actions against bakers in 14th century London include cases in which bakers stole small amounts of dough out of the breads brought to them for baking. Some of the techniques were so ingenious that only the most watchful of customers could detect them. Still, despite these drawbacks, the communal oven was probably the best means of providing baking services for the average consumer, given the resources and technology available. And, in crowded towns and cities filled with timber buildings, the use of communal ovens may have also reduced the risk of catastrophic fires by limiting the number of places where large fires were kept burning for prolonged periods.

Pottage

This dish is unfamiliar to most modern diners, at least by this name. Pottage, also known as porridge, was made by boiling grain in water or stock, causing the grains to plump up and soften. Depending on the exact method of preparation and ingredients, results varied from just having the grains expand, soften slightly, and remain separate (tasting rather nut-like, akin to the flavor and texture of wild rice) to having the grains become very soft and mushy, releasing much of their starch, and thickening the water or stock into a sticky paste. This may not sound too appetizing and may call to mind another name for pottage — gruel, that thick, grey, tasteless muck that Oliver Twist and the rest of the workhouse orphans were fed. But, despite the unpleasant images and associations that have grown up around this dish over the centuries, properly prepared pottage was quite savory and could be like a rich cream soup, only much thicker. Pottage was served as a main or side dish. Herbs, spices, and vegetables like onions, leeks, carrots, and leafy greens like chard or spinach were often added to pottage, improving both its flavor and nutritional content. Pottage was also made with beans, peas, or other legumes. Legumes and grain are complementary proteins which, when consumed together, provide the same essential amino acids as meat or fish. Meat and fish were sometimes scarce during the Middle Ages, especially for the poorer people, so this combination of legumes with grains was a valuable source of protein in many people's diets.

Finer ingredients than just barley or wheat could also be used in pottages. Recipes survive for semolina pottages that are reminiscent of modern *couscous*. Rich, creamy pottages of rice or grain could also be served as a dessert. Prepared with milk, either animal milk or "milk of almonds" (a mixture of water and powdered almond) instead of water or stock and sweetened with honey or, for those who could afford it, sugar, such pottages were sort of like rice pudding.

The popularity of pottages can also be attributed to their ease of preparation. Boiling up water in a pot, then adding ingredients and letting them simmer is one of the easiest, most straightforward ways of cooking. It is also one of the most energy efficient forms of cooking, requiring much less than for heating an oven for baking or roasting, which was an important consideration in an age when fuel had to be carefully gathered and conserved to meet all the heating and cooking needs of the household.

Beer

Beer brewing has been traced back to Egyptians who were making beer at least as early as 2000 B.C. Knowledge of this process survived through the centuries and migrated around the Mediterranean Sea. The Greeks and Romans produced fermented grain drinks as well, though wine, by far, appears to have been their beverage of choice. In any event, by the dawn of the Middle Ages, beer making was a well-known art in every region of Europe where cereal crops were cultivated — in short, everywhere.

Beer was a far more hygienic beverage than water during the Middle Ages because of the lack of technology for purifying drinking water. The fermentation process rendered water more safe to drink by producing alcohol which killed much if not all the harmful bacteria in the water.

While beer was produced everywhere, consumption and the scale of production varied widely by region. In England, the Low Countries, and the Germanic countries, beer was the primary beverage of the common man and even the nobility of these countries who consumed significant quantities of wine certainly did not spurn good beer. The pervasiveness of beer in these countries was reflected in many records throughout the Middle Ages, from rules for monastic houses that specify the amounts of beer the brothers are to receive each day to German labor regulations that mandated beer rations of certain fixed sizes as part of daily compensation for some classes of workers. Though beer was produced in France, Spain, and Italy, these countries were far larger producers of wine and so, for all levels of their societies, wine was the more typical beverage in these countries. Thus, per capita beer production (and consumption) appears to have been higher in the northern countries like England where viniculture was poor or nonexistent than in those countries that produced grapes as well as grain.

Like all other industries during the Middle Ages, beer production was done on a small scale. As with bakeries, monasteries and noble households maintained their own brewing facilities to meet the needs of their communities, while commercial breweries served the general public. We may have "micro-breweries" today but most of them would be giants compared to the commercial breweries of the Middle Ages. Medieval breweries ranged from the goodwife who made home brew for her own family with enough to spare to sell to a few neighbors, to taverners who brewed their own merchandise, up to businesses that brewed beer and sold it both directly to consumers to take home as well as to inns and taverns for resale to their customers. But to make up for the small scale of production and meet the demand, there were staggering numbers of brewers in every German, Low Country, or English city and town of any significant size. In some cases, the ratio of brewers to inhabitants appears to have run as high as one brewer per 100 citizens. Brewers were so numerous in the city of London that they sometimes constituted a threat to the public water supplies: Like the rest of the public, the brewers drew most of their water from the conduits that fed spring water through the city but they needed large quantities of water to make their product and so, if left unchecked, they tapped water at such a high volume and rate that they often left little or no water for other users. Thus, from as early as the first quarter of the 14th century, London's civic regulations included limits on the amount of water that brewers could draw, with fines and other penalties for excess usage.

MILK

Milk from cows, sheep, and goats was widely consumed in the Middle Ages but rarely in the plain liquid form we commonly enjoy today. Without refrigeration, liquid milk spoiled rapidly and so it had to be consumed soon after it was extracted, so that it could seldom reach market and be sold to a consumer before it became foul. There were other drawbacks to milk that further explain its unpopularity. In an age before pasteurization, tuberculosis and other communicable diseases could be transmitted from animals to people through consumption of the animals' milk. Because of these hazards of drinking raw milk, physicians and others discouraged its consumption as a beverage, particularly for the young.

But this did not mean that the medieval diet lacked dairy products. Milk can be processed into a variety of products and this processing limited or negated

much of raw milk's shortcomings, especially rapid spoilage and possible transmission of diseases. Butter, cheeses, and other dairy foods were all made and marketed throughout Europe. Butter was salted in the course of its manufacture. Salt may have been added as a flavoring but, more importantly, salt promoted curdling and retarded the growth of bacteria. Given the number of times that medieval cookbooks direct that butter must be clarified to remove the salt before use to avoid spoiling the flavor of dishes, butter was likely often heavily salted to preserve it. Some varieties of cheese (the harder varieties) were also smoked, or otherwise dried and occasionally encased in wax or wrapped in fabric to protect them from airborne contaminants. Thus, these items could be produced, transported, and sold to consumers while still in edible condition. Softer fermented milk products such as sour cream, *crème fraîche*, and yogurt were also common. As with cheese, the by-products of the bacteria culture that aided in the fermentation of these dairy products inhibited the growth of the harmful bacteria. Although these soft dairy products were not as durable as butter and hard cheese, they remained safe to eat longer than unrefrigerated liquid milk and so were a regular part of the diet for at least the households that produced them as well as for other households in the vicinity who traded for them.

Another measure taken by medieval cooks to make up for the shortcomings of animal milk was to use vegetable-based substitutes. Besides the practical problems of keeping fresh dairy liquid milk and butter on hand, these substitutions were needed because of the Christian dietary prohibitions against consuming any animal products on certain days of the weeks (Fridays through Sundays) and during certain times of the year (Lent and Advent). On the days dairy products were proscribed, cooks used vegetable oils for frying instead of butter. Olive and nut oils were also used but these were far more expensive since olive oil had to be imported, except in those areas immediately around the Mediterranean where olives could be grown, and nut oil was generally available only in small quantities because of the careful harvesting, shelling, and pressing required. In place of milk, medieval cooks substituted "nut milks" made from walnuts or, more commonly, almonds. Nut milk was the powdered milk of the Middle Ages. Nuts could be stored for many months or longer, either shelled or left in the shell, and remain edible and nutritious. To make nut milk, a cook ground the nuts into a fine powder and then mixed it with water. This mixture was usually simmered to more thoroughly suspend the nut solids in the water, making it more milk-like. While the resulting nut milk lacked the calcium and many of the other nutrients in animal milk, its flavor and consistency were close enough to real animal milk for most cooking purposes, such as in sauces and pottages. To make up for the differences between it and real milk, almond milk added a richness and subtle flavor, something enjoyed even today in many Indian dishes where powdered almond is added to thicken and delicately flavor sauces.

WATER

Water was a popular thirst quencher in the Middle Ages. However, as with liquid milk, medieval people were well aware of the health risks from exposure to water from contaminated sources. In fact, as discussed in Chapter IV, they had numerous sanitary regulations to protect water quality. Thus, as a serious health measure and not just as a fad or status symbol, spring water, cool and straight out of the ground, was recognized as the best possible water to use for drinking and cooking. Water from clear running streams was a poor second. Obviously, relatively few people had access to water from either of these preferred sources and had to make do with well water or river water. It may seem odd that well water was held in low esteem, but well water was often of low quality. With rare exceptions, such as at Dover Castle where the well was driven over 280 feet down through rock to guarantee the availability of water even during a siege, most medieval wells were shallow by modern standards. These shallow wells reached only the uppermost levels of the water-table and were very susceptible to ground water contamination from sewage and storm water run-off that carried bacteria, parasites, and other harmful impurities. Such contamination was especially common in densely populated areas or anywhere else cesspits were too close to wells. So, it's quite understandable why beer and wine were usually considered superior to water.

But beer and wine could not entirely replace water. Despite its sometimes dubious quality, water was still essential as a beverage and in the preparation of food. Dishes and cooking utensils still had to be washed. Ingredients like vegetables and freshly slaughtered livestock and poultry still needed to be rinsed. And broths and soups simply couldn't be made without water for the stock. So the only solution was for them to make do and use the purest water available to them, regardless of its source, just as their ancestors did and just as their descendants would do until water purification treatments were developed centuries later.

WINE

The basic process for turning grapes into wine during the Middle Ages was no different than that employed by the Greeks and Romans and by vintners today: grapes were crushed in vats, the juice collected, and poured into barrels to ferment. Judging from illuminations and tapestries depicting wine-making, grapes were often crushed by workers stomping them with their feet. While this method had been in use for millennia before the Middle Ages and continued in use for many centuries after the Middle Ages, its inefficiency as well as its detrimental effect on the quality of the resulting wine was long recognized. In fact, in the 8th century, Charlemagne had attempted to stamp out this method and required that wine produced on his own estates be made only with grapes that were pressed by machine. These presses also commonly appear in medieval depictions of wine-making, sometimes being shown right alongside tubs of grapes still being crushed by foot. The presses were in the form of vats of various shapes with thick, heavy lids. Grapes were placed in the vats and crushed as the lids were forced down into the vats by pushing with massive levers or by rotating a threaded wooden shaft fitted to the lid that screwed the lid down like a giant nut and bolt. The juice trickled out of spouts in the bottom of the vats and into tubs or buckets below.

Regardless of the method used to crush the grapes, wine production flourished throughout much of medieval Europe. Along with the traditional wine growing areas of France, Spain, and Italy, the Rhine and other river valleys in modern day Germany, Switzerland, and Austria were all long established wine growing regions by the start of the Middle Ages thanks to the Romans who routinely brought viniculture into the areas they conquered. Surviving landscape evidence of cultivation and contemporary documentation show that grapes for wine were grown even as far north as England during the Middle Ages, up through the long period of mild climate that lasted until the approximately the end of the 14th century, when weather conditions generally deteriorated with lower temperatures and increased dampness crippling agriculture across northern Europe. However, English wine production was never on as large a scale as in France or even Germany and most physical traces of its existence quickly disappeared. Further, by as early as the second half of the 12th century, England's ties to France through the Angevin dynasty had created a steady import trade in wine from France which continued to grow through the following centuries.

Then as now, the quality and flavor of wines varied greatly from one region to the next but some of the qualities that were highly sought after may seem odd now. For example, surviving import duty and price control regulations from England in the mid–14th century indicate that red wines, especially very sweet red wines, were the most highly valued. In household expenditure records and descriptions of banquets of English and French nobility, sweet red wines from Rhodes and Cyprus were often noted as being the most expensive and very desirable, particularly those varieties of wine that had leached some of the pine resin flavor from the casks they were made and shipped in (a flavor which is now enjoyed primarily by those devotees of Greek food who drink "retsina" with their meals). The high price of these wines reflected both the costs of shipping them in from eastern extremes of Christendom and the smaller harvests available for their production (compared to the great wine producing areas of France). Red wines from Spain appear to have been the next most popular, followed by the robust and plentiful wines of France. German wines were popular within Germany but were also exported to the Low Countries and England.

The fact that most German wines were white wines limited their appeal because most people of the Middle Ages seemed to have preferred red wines. Besides the possibility that medieval palates simply found red wines more pleasing than white wines, there were some other reasons that may have contributed to the popularity of red wines. First, for the nobility or those upper middle class people who could afford the ingredients, wines flavored with spices were very popular. Commonly called *hippocras* after the legendary Greek physician Hippocrates who was credited with inventing it, spiced or mulled wine was flavored with a variety of spices, including ginger, cinnamon, sugar, clove, and cardamom. While many households had their own preferred recipes, pre-mixed hippocras powder was also usually available from any well-stocked spice vendor. Though some surviving medieval recipes indicate that either red or white wines may be made into hippocras, based on the continued survival of sangria as well as other flavored red wine mixtures, red wines are far more suited to such adulteration than white wines. Second, under popular medieval medical theories, each food possessed "humors" which either complimented or opposed the humors found in people. These humors were characterized as a combination of four qualities: heat, cold, moistness, and dryness. Red wine was attributed the desirable characteristics of warmth and dryness. White wine was also considered dry but was deemed cooler than red wine and thus poorer in the positive qualities of wine. Admittedly, the impact of this medical theory was probably limited to those who could afford professional physicians to advise them on their diet but this would have been the same class of society that could afford to pick and choose their wine rather than just accepting what was cheap and available.

Regardless of its color, wine was widely consumed, even where it had to be imported. It was only beyond the reach of the very poor for most of the Middle Ages.

OTHER GRAPE PRODUCTS

Besides wine, grapes yielded three other liquids that were very important to food preparation during the Middle Ages, at least for the upper classes. These were vinegar, verjuice, and must. Vinegar, made from wine that had "turned" (that is, the wine was either intentionally or accidentally stored or treated so that its acid content rose to the point of turning the wine sour and undrinkable), was a common ingredient in medieval cooking, such as in sweet and sour sauces for meats and fish. Though very popular in the Middle Ages, verjuice has long disappeared from the European kitchen. The variety of descriptions of it given in medieval texts make it difficult to replicate with a high degree of certainty but verjuice was most likely the partially fermented juice of tart grapes, either under-ripe grapes or grapes specially selected and cultivated for their tartness. Surviving recipes indicate that verjuice provided a piquant flavor to sauces, sharp but far more subtle than vinegar. Supporting this estimation of the flavor, some of these recipes suggest that juice from bitter oranges or other tart fruits could be substituted if verjuice was not available. The third liquid was must, unfermented grape juice that was used to provide a light, fruity flavor to dishes.

HONEY

Sugar from sugar cane was an expensive commodity and was sometimes very difficult to obtain. Thus, honey was the most common sweetener in medieval kitchens. While beekeeping was practiced throughout Europe, the lands now within modern Spain, Russia, and Ukraine were leading producers of honey and exported it to markets in England and elsewhere. Besides being used as an ingredient in dishes, honey was also fermented to make mead. Mead was most common in Scandinavia, England, and Eastern Europe. Even in these areas, it was not an everyday drink. Mead was so expensive that it was typically consumed only by the nobility and even they reserved it for special occasions.

VEGETABLES

As mentioned previously, a variety of vegetables were available depending on the region and time of year. Vegetables were generally eaten in one of two forms: raw or boiled. Accounts of eating vegetables raw were recorded in medieval chronicles primarily in the context of illustrating desperate conditions during times of famine when many people were reduced to scavenging for whatever foods they could find, such as wild greens and roots. However, medieval health manuals indicate that some vegetables, including onions, lettuces, spinach, and other greens were commonly eaten raw by choice. One Italian book on health and diet even suggested serving lettuces with oil and vinegar — an early salad with dressing — as a light, nourishing dish.

All types of vegetables were also served boiled, either as ingredients in soups, pottages, meat stews and other dishes or as separate side dishes. Though most recipes indicate that the vegetables were reduced to soft mush, other recipes suggest parboiling that would have left them some texture for the diner to enjoy. The practice of boiling vegetables certainly lowered the amounts of vitamins and other nutrients that they con-

tained in their raw state. However, not all these nutrients were lost but were transferred to the broth which, in an era when soupspoons were seldom used, was usually sponged up with bread and eaten.

FRUITS

Like vegetables, fruits were eaten raw or cooked, though eating raw fruit seems to have been more common. The same Italian manual that recommended the green salad with oil and vinegar also mentioned that apples and pears are good, light foods suitable for starting meals. And those ninth century schoolboys mentioned before and all those who followed after them most likely ate the apples and other fruits they stole from the orchards and gardens raw. Still, cooked fruit was also popular whether in sauces for main-dishes or, quite commonly, as an ingredient in desserts, which ranged from baked pears or apples to elaborate fruit tarts, fritters, and puddings. Depending on the season and local availability, dried or candied fruits may have been substituted for fresh ones in some dessert dishes while some preserved fruits, like dates and figs, were often served uncooked as sweet snacks to cap the meal. Fruits were also crushed and fermented to create a variety of beverages. In addition to wine from grapes, cider from apples and perry from pears filled the cups on many tables during the Middle Ages.

LIVESTOCK

During the Middle Ages, meats of all types were relatively expensive. Raising livestock, like cows or sheep, required access to pasturage and the wealth necessary either to produce and store enough fodder to keep breeding animals alive through the winter or to buy new animals in the spring. Obviously, many people did not possess these resources. However, some animals were easier to maintain, pigs being the most notable example. Besides being able to survive on vegetable trimmings and other scraps, pigs could forage for their own food, such as acorns and edible roots in forest and brush lands. Yet the poor typically lacked even these resources and likely had little or no meat, apart from the occasional rabbit or trimmings from the slaughter of their neighbors' livestock. Thus, the poor had to rely on pottages of legumes and grains for their protein. However, for the middling classes meat was far more common, though conditions varied widely over the course of the Middle Ages and from region to region. For example, German labor regulations from the second half of the 15th century stated that craftsmen were to receive two meat dishes a day and studies of French towns in the 14th century indicate that middle class townspeople consumed an average of a hundred pounds of various meats per person in a year. Even if the regulation and estimates reflect ideal rather than actual conditions, these bits of evidence combined with records of food markets, laws regulating prices on raw and cooked meats, excavations of animal bones from medieval sites, and other clues to medieval food consumption prove that meat was readily available at prices that many people could afford, except during famines caused by wars, droughts, or other disasters. As for the nobility, their household records and accounts of their feasting leave little doubt as to their carnivorous tastes.

Stewing was probably the more common method of cooking meat since it required less fuel than roasting, grilling, or baking, but meat was prepared in a great variety of ways. Many illustrations and cookbooks from the Middle Ages describe meat being roasted on spits; pre-cooked (often parboiled) and then chopped fine, mixed with eggs, cheese, and seasonings and baked in pies (what would commonly be called "pot pies" today); cut into pieces, fried, and drenched in sauce; and made into sausages, meatballs studded with slivered almonds, meat "olives" of sliced meats wrapped around layers of ground, spiced meats; and any number of other dishes. Though many of these dishes graced only the tables of the elite, there was certainly more to most medieval cooking than just boiling it all up in a pot.

POULTRY

Their ability to survive in a wide variety of climates and environments made poultry, especially chickens, the most common food animals kept by people of all classes. Both their meat and eggs provided valuable protein. Chickens, like pigs, were maintained in both the town and farm and allowed to scavenge for their food, which was supplemented by the occasional handful of grain. Unlike pigs and larger livestock, chickens had the added advantage of being much easier to keep alive through the winter, though many undoubtedly met their ends as part of Christmas-time feasts. Though they required more care, geese were also popular. Besides meat and eggs, they provided fat for cooking as well as feathers for pillows, high quality beds, and fletching for arrows.

Poultry was cooked using many of same methods applied to meats of larger animals, except that the grilling or roasting of whole animals was far more often applied to birds than to cows or even pigs.

FISH

Besides the fact that they were tasty and nutritious, part of the popularity of fish in the medieval diet can be attributed to Christian dietary restrictions against consuming "animals" that applied several days a week as well as during Advent and Lent. Thus, fish was as important as meat in the medieval diet and was prepared in many of the same ways mentioned above, though traditional recipes for certain types of fish should be noted. For example, several sources state that eels and lamprey, though a delicacy, were dangerous to eat but could be made safer by, respectively, burying them in salt or drowning them in wine to kill them. They were then roasted. These precautions were dictated by the medical theories of the time. Under these theories, the warm and dry *humors* of the salt or wine and the cooking method counteracted the dangerously high levels of coldness and moisture that were characteristic of these fish. Despite this and some other odd warnings and measures to temper the dangerous humors, fish were common ingredients in many dishes and many recipes, such as those for meat-filled pies, were annotated to indicate that fish could be substituted for poultry or other flesh to make the dishes suitable for days of fasting. While fish was sometimes treated as being just another meat, there were also fish dishes that showcased the flavors and textures unique to fish. These included whole poached fish in aspic, smoked fish, and masterpieces in which larger fish, such as sturgeons or big pikes, were divided into thirds with each section prepared a different way (one roasted, one fried, and the last poached or boiled) and then reassembled for presentation to the diners. With dishes like these, we enter the realm of the great feasts of the nobility.

One Pot Cooking

Before moving on to feasting, one last word about basic foods and their prepara-

tion during the Middle Ages. The need to conserve fuel, at least for the lower and middle classes, has been mentioned as one reason why so many dishes were boiled or stewed but there was another technique in which several different dishes were cooked together inside a single pot, an economical method that may have been particularly popular in smaller households. Evidence for this method is very scarce, mainly just a few pottery crocks and some ambiguous illustrations, but it appears to have been a form of double-boiler cooking. It also resembles some traditional Asian cooking methods, such as Chinese dim sum, where a variety of dishes wrapped in individual packets are steamed or poached together using a single pot of boiling water.

Pottage, meat (usually chopped up into a paste, probably with seasonings added, and then formed into something like a very large meatball), and vegetables were wrapped in cloth as separate packets. These cloth packets were then stacked inside one or more clay pots. Broth was added to each pot. The packet of pottage was likely placed at the bottom so that it would boil in and absorb the broth while the other foods would poach or steam. The top of each pot was sealed with another piece of fabric (surviving cooking crocks typically have lips that would have allowed the fabric to be secured with a cord tied around the crock, under the lip) and then placed into a single, larger pot or cauldron of boiling water. The smaller pots were not immersed, their tops remained above the water level. The pots were then left to cook; the only tending needed was to keep the fire burning and to add water to the outer cauldron if too much water boiled away.

This method of cooking seems well suited to small households since, with a minimum of effort and fuel, it produced several different dishes comprising just enough food for immediate consumption (an important factor in an age when leftovers couldn't be refrigerated and eaten later). It had several other advantages as well. The use of double-boiling ensured that the food would not be burned or scorched, a common problem when cooking directly over open flame, which was in fact such a common problem in the Middle Ages that several cookbooks and the Menagier de Paris handbook contain suggestions on how to remove burned flavors from pottages cooked in saucepans. It also steamed or poached most of the foods in the pot so they weren't boiled to mush. The sealing of the pots may have also conserved herbs and precious spices by sealing in the cooking juices and ensuring that as much flavor as possible was retained in the dish, permeating the foods. It may have also had two other benefits of particular concern to peoples of the Middle Ages and other places and times where nutrition and sanitation were far from secure. First, the sealed pot method ensured that nutrients, especially the fats and oils of the broth and meat, were retained in the dish, likely absorbed into the pottage. This may not seem desirable today when reducing the fat and cholesterol in our diet is an obsession. However, the human body needs to take in some fats and oils for proper development and functioning and fats and oils were scarce in the Middle Ages compared to today — meat was much leaner, fried foods were far less common, and vegetable oils were not as available. The second benefit may have been that double-boiling minimized direct contact between the food being cooked in the pots and the water in the outer pot or cauldron. Besides preventing most of the food from being boiled, this separation should have lessened the risk of the prepared food being tainted by parasites or other contaminants in the water which were not killed or removed by the boiling. However, people of the Middle Ages had a limited understanding, at best, of the true nature and risks of water contamination and how to combat them. And water was certainly still the main ingredient in the ubiquitous stews and soups of the age. Thus, any hygienic benefits medieval people may have obtained from double-boiling were most likely fortuitous rather than the product of any conscious effort to lower the risk of contamination by physically separating the food to be eaten from the water cooking it.

Now that we've looked over the basic elements of diet during the Middle Ages, let's move on to the more elaborate cuisine of those conspicuous consumers — the nobility.

Food for the Nobility

Cookery for the aristocracy and cooking for the ordinary people were two completely different things. One of the most distinguishing elements of aristocratic dishes was the use of spices, including sugar which was considered a spice during the Middle Ages. These had to be brought great distances and so were very expensive, well beyond the reach of the peasant and barely within the reach of the upper-levels of the merchant class. Another obvious difference was the amount and variety of meats, fish, and fowl the dishes of the nobility usually contained. The nobility and their households were at the top of the medieval food chain and they didn't seem to hesitate at eating almost any creature, as the lengthy list of fish, birds, and other animals near the beginning of this chapter shows. A final difference was that aristocrats regularly used food and dining as part of elaborate ceremonies to mark significant personal and political events or simply to demonstrate and reinforce their status and bonds with their subordinates, peers, and superiors (if they admitted they had any) within their local or regional power structure.

From the late 14th century through the end of the Middle Ages, the eating habits and methods of food preparation of the nobility can be reconstructed with more certainty than those of the general public because of the significant number of illustrations of their feasts, recipes books compiled by their chefs, and physical remains of their dining halls and kitchens that have survived. These provide a fascinating glimpse of how the elite of medieval society ate, drank, and socialized. While these people were the most important social and political figures of their day — many were quite literally "history makers" — it must be remembered that they were only a very small and very privileged fraction of society. Their lifestyles and tastes no more reflected the experiences of the average person than the lifestyles and tastes enjoyed by celebrities and world figures do today. That said, on with the show! Stuffed peacocks, fountains that spout wine, and dishes with live animals inside await!

THE CAST

Chefs and Their Staffs

The production of meals for the nobility required trained specialists. Thus, the nobility employed professional chefs with support staffs to prepare their meals, both at home and while on the road, when touring their domains or traveling abroad. Depending on the size and importance of the household, the cooking staff could range from a cook, either alone or with a handful of assistants, up to a chef with dozens of subordinates from skilled pastry and sauce chefs down to lowly scullions and kitchen varlets (boys who scrubbed dishes, hauled water, and turned roasting spits).

The Table Servers

Besides the personnel that prepared the food, noble households also had staff to serve the food. These staffs included:

- The ewerer who held and poured water from the ewer or pitcher for washing hands before the meal.

- The panter or pantler (the man in charge of the bread or, in French — which was also the official language of the English court for much of the Middle Ages —*pain*) who kept the diners supplied with fine, white bread rolls through the meal, cut loaves of bread (fig. 1) into manageable pieces before they were served, and also trimmed loaves of stale, coarser bread into trenchers. Trenchers were disposable plates or shallow bowls of stale bread that absorbed sauces. They were rarely eaten at the feast and but were kept as leftovers for later snacking or, more typically, given away to the poor by the household's almoner who was responsible for overseeing the disbursement of his master's charity.

- The butler and or cellarer in charge of beverages, so named because he was responsible for the *butts* (barrels) of beer and wine stored in the cellar or *buttery*. He also oversaw the spicing and decanting of wines into jugs and bottles for serving. This use of bottles may have also given rise to the term *butler* but the similarity and shared roots of the words *butt* and *bottle* make it difficult to establish which word is the true root of *butler*.

- The cupbearer who took the jugs and bottles prepared by the butler and served beverages to the guests at the table.

- The carver who sliced up roasted fowl or meats into manageable portions for the diners. Carving was among the services that pages had to learn as part of their education as gentlemen and being allowed to carve for one's lord was a signal honor.

- The steward, the master of ceremonies who coordinated and directed the staff and was responsible for ensuring that all of them discharged their duties properly and that all dishes were presented correctly.

In households of minor size and prestige, several of these positions might be held by the same person but in the great houses each position would be filled by only one person, though he might have several assistants, while in the greatest of houses, those of kings and emperors, the people serving in these roles would be nobility themselves and would wait upon the host and his most important guests personally while ordinary servants or young noblemen in training attended to the other guests. Surviving illustrations show women cooking and serving meals only in domestic scenes of the middle and lower classes. For the nobility, written accounts and illustrations of feasts indicate that only men and boys served in the kitchens and at table of most households. Use of only males in table service at feasts was tied in part to the fact that feasts were often displays of political and social bonds. Thus, the key serving positions provided a highly visible opportunity for vassals (who were usually male) and their male children (who hoped to one day succeed to their fathers' positions and were currently serving as pages in the lord's household) to publicly serve their lords, symbolically acting out their political and social relationships. As for the kitchen, the few chefs whose names have survived, such as Chiquart and the internationally famous Taillevent, were men. Further, all references to lesser kitchen staff as well as all illustrations of preparations for feasts depict only males of various ages. This limited evidence does not mean that women never served as chefs or in other capacities on the cooking staffs of noble households but it does make it seem that these staffs were predominantly male, perhaps indicative that work in the large institutional kitchens of medieval courts was backbreaking work in a hot, smoky environment, not unlike a forge or smithy which were also home to male-dominated workforces.

The Settings

Kitchens

Kitchens evolved dramatically over the course of the Middle Ages. Initially, cooking was done over open fire pits in the dirt floors of buildings, with pits even being located in the center of the same hall in which the food was served and thus serving to heat the building as well. However, the risk of fire encouraged construction of kitchens as separate buildings, away from the primary residential structures. Covered walkways were often built with these kitchens so that the food could be kept warm and dry on its journey to the table. Further improvements in construction led to the development of hoods over the open pits and later on hearths with chimneys located along the outside walls of the building, improving ventilation and providing places to attach hooks and racks for suspending pots and pans over the cooking fire.

By the 14th century, kitchens were being constructed in stone as part of residential complexes at palaces and monastic houses. Some of the surviving kitchens are huge, reflecting the large numbers of people they fed. For example, the kitchens at the abbeys of Durham in England and Fontevrault in France are large octagons about forty feet across. Making them octagonal maximized the number of walls available for hearths (Fontevrault has five remaining today) and the overall rounded shape minimized the distance between any open hearths in the center of floor and additional flues located in the walls for venting their heat and smoke (the kitchen at Fontevrault has a chimney flue for each surviving hearth and over a dozen more placed at other locations around its circumference to provide additional ventilation). These kitchens also had high, tapering ceilings that lead up to an opening capped with an open work cupola that helped provide a fresh air intake for the building and improve air circulation. To further improve the airflow and provide some light other than just the glow from the hearths, these kitchens usually had many large windows fitted with louvered shutters. Some of these windows were also used as additional doorways to permit scullions and other workers to easily move large bulky items, such as bundles of wood for the fire or sides of beef, into the kitchen. Another interesting, labor-saving feature found in some kitchens were garbage chutes for rapidly and easily moving waste out of the kitchen. One notable example is at Fountains Abbey in England, where the kitchen was built spanning a small river and had a built-in garbage disposal in the form of floor grates that allowed kitchen waste to be dumped directly into the river and carried away downstream.

The Feasting Hall

Feasts were generally conducted in the great hall of a castle or palace. This hall was used for many functions besides feasting, typically serving as the facility's primary meeting room where the noble held court and administered justice. It was also often used as sleeping quarters for servants and other members of the household. Only in monasteries, where dining halls called refectories were constructed, was one likely to encounter a room dedicated only to eating.

To serve its various roles, the furnishings of the hall were kept very simple. Among the few permanent fixtures in the room was a wooden screen along one end of the hall, across the front of the main doors leading outside, usually including the door out to the kitchen. Despite its name, the screen was actually a rather solid wooden wall that stopped the draft from the outside doors from disturbing the hall. This space between the outer wall and the screen could also be used as a staging area where foods from the kitchen were inspected before either being taken through doors in the screen into the hall or passed through the serving hatch (a window in the screen) to waiting servants. Another permanent, though less massive feature was the sideboard or *aumbry*. This was a large piece of furniture like a china cabinet or Welsh dresser with open shelves where the host kept his finest platters, pitchers, goblets and other serving pieces for use and for display (during non-feasting times). During the feast, the butler or cellarer used the aumbry as a place to prepare flavored wines and to refill the wine jugs.

Additional tables, either permanent pieces or temporary ones constructed of boards on trestles, were used by the pantler to prepare the trenchers and by the chef or his staff for final dressing or saucing. At some feasts, dishes were brought out and placed on such tables just so the guests could be amazed by the variety and amounts of foods to which they had to look forward. On such occasions, these tables earned the name "groaning boards" from their creaking and groaning under the weight of the dishes. As for the rest of the fittings, dining tables were usually temporary, again constructed of boards and trestles, with one table often set up on a

Figure 1. Feast of St. Cecilia. Manuscript illumination from the late 13th century. This depiction of a feast illustrates many common attributes of formal medieval dining including the lack of forks and scarcity of other flatware, the sharing of drinking cups (see the couple in the upper right corner), and the slicing off of bread crusts before the bread is presented to the guests. Along the lower edge of the scene are the entertainers for the feast. From left to right, they include a psaltery player, a dancer, a portative organ player (who is playing the organ with his right hand while working the bellows with his left), and a musician playing a rebec or other violin-like instrument (courtesy of the Walters Art Gallery, Baltimore).

platform, making it the *high table* where the lord the most important guests and member of their retinues. (A high table is shown in fig. 1.) Additional tables were assembled as needed, typically in a "U" shape with parallel tables projecting down from either end of the high table. Seating was on long benches. For much of the first half of the Middle Ages, these benches were also used as beds by the servants and other members of the household who slept in the hall and were easily stacked along the side of the hall when not in use. Those seated at the high table used any chairs and stools available, preferably with cushions. However, illustrations indicate that even they often shared communal benches. Guests were seated according to their rank and importance, with the most important seated closest to the host and the least significant seated farthest away. Finally, beneath it all, the floor of the hall was covered in rushes, but these were not simply loose rushes strewn about the floor. Illuminations, such as those done for the Duke of Berry in the 15th century, show that the rushes were often woven into large mats that completely covered the floor of the hall, providing an absorbent and resilient, yet disposable, carpeting. (Besides their absorbency and slight cushioning effect, rushes were used because they were cheap and readily available since they grew as weeds along the edges of the many marshy areas that were common throughout Europe before organized programs of drainage turned the marshes into land for farming and building.)

The Ingredients

Though limited by what produce and other foodstuffs were in season in the area, chefs for the great households had access to broadest selections of ingredients possible, all the items available to the common people, including fruit (both fresh and preserved), vegetables, eggs, cheese, nuts, butter, wine, verjuice, fish, poultry, herbs, and livestock, and two more items that most distinguished meals of the nobility from those of lesser men: spices and game.

Spices

Mentioned before in the context of food preservation, spices were a key ingredient of fine cooking in the Middle Ages, particularly after the Frankish nobility and many others had gotten a taste for them either while on crusade in the Middle East or in the more cosmopolitan European courts that obtained the seasonings as part of the increased trade with that region that followed initial Christian victories. A few spices, such as saffron (which was as prized for its ability to turn food a golden color as it was for its taste), were grown around the Mediterranean in Italy and Spain. Many others, including black pepper, cardamom, and sugar, were grown in Asia Minor or the Middle East. Cinnamon, ginger, nutmeg, and others, though imported through the Middle East, were grown much further away in India and other parts of Asia. The distance these commodities had to be shipped as well as the small quantities in which they were produced ensured that they commanded a high price by the time they reached consumers in Europe. Difficulties in equating prices of several centuries ago to modern money make it impossible to state an exact price for spices that would be meaningful and accurate. However, based on studies of food, diet, and prices in late 13th century England, the relative expense of spices can be expressed as follows:

- Eight bushels of grain, referred to as a "quarter," was approximately enough to make the bread and pottage portion of one person's diet for a year.
- A quarter of grain usually sold for around six shillings.
- Prices for spices ranged from one to three shillings per pound, with especially rare spices like saffron commanding from 12 to 16 shillings per pound.

Though a pound was a large amount of spice, the comparatively high cost of spices is obvious.

Some attempts were made to find alternate sources for spices, particularly after the collapse of the Crusader states in the Middle East made direct trade with the region more difficult for a time. The biggest success in lessening dependence on foreign sources was the spread of the cultivation of sugar to Sicily, Cyprus, Malta, and Rhodes by the late 13th century, reducing the distance it had to be shipped to markets in the rest of Europe. However, the backbreaking labor required to harvest the cane, chop it, grind it, boil it, and repeatedly refine it to yield fine, white sugar kept prices high. Thus, most people continued to rely on honey for sweetening their foods while sugar remained a treat for the wealthy.

The cost and their medicinal properties, either real or imagined, meant that sugar and most other spices were sold by apothecaries, those forerunners of modern pharmacists, and some noble households employed their own apothecaries to whom the spices were entrusted. Records from one household show that the chef had to formally requisition spices from the apothecary for each meal, designating the specific amounts he needed. Clearly, spices were valued treasures. This tight control of spices also suggests that, despite the lack of measurements in most surviving recipes and the large numbers of different spices often used in preparing a single dish, medieval cooks were more sparing in their use of spices than was long thought. Besides securing and portioning out spices to the chef and the more traditional role of preparing any medications needed, the household apothecary was also responsible for making *dragees*, candies made of sugar mixed with spice that were served at the end of feasts to freshen the breath and provide a small, sweet treat to cap off the meal, not unlike modern after-dinner mints.

Game

As we all know from the stories of Robin Hood, deer, boars, bears, and other game animals were reserved exclusively for the sport of and consumption by the nobility. There were many motives for this strict regulation, most of which will be explored in the chapter on playing and relaxing, but only a few that concern us at the moment: medieval nobility enjoyed hunting and enjoyed the taste of the meat of game animals, so much so that sending gifts of freshly killed game was a common gesture of goodwill between neighboring nobility.

Game dishes included many that are enjoyed today, like venison steaks and roasted boar, as well as some showpieces like boar's head. But there were others that include some meals that would be quite unappetizing to most modern diners including bear paws; entrails and testicles of boar, stag, and a number of other animals; and a selection of other organ meats. (Though it should be noted that even today, "Rocky Mountain Oysters," the testicles of young male beef cattle removed to turn the animals into steers, are considered a delicacy in some circles.) However, game was not unique in providing such dishes — virtually every internal organ of the cow or calf, from brains and lungs down to stomachs and intestines, appeared on medieval dining tables at one time or another. In part, organ meat may have been a delicacy but its widespread consumption likely reflects the fact that people could not afford to routinely waste edible animal tissue, especially since the organs constituted a large part of the animal's total weight. So, despite its elevated status, game was usually prepared like any other meat, though its privileged consumers presumably appreciated that its flavor and texture was superior to those of the mundane, domestic meats. In fact, the survival of several recipes in the "Menagier de Paris" handbook and elsewhere for making "mock" game out of domestic animal meat indicate that medieval palates were quite able to discern between game and domestic animals and preferred the former.

THE PREPARATION

As mentioned previously, chefs in the Middle Ages used the same methods available to us today: broiling, grilling, baking, roasting, frying, boiling, and poaching. Some of the combinations of methods, and especially the combinations of ingredients and seasonings may seem alien but examining these dishes, particularly in light of many "foreign" cuisines that have swept the U.S. and the rest of the western world in recent years, shows that most of these foods were not as bizarre and vile tasting as they have long seemed to historians. For example, how about a chicken dish made with the chicken roasted or boiled, "smitten" and "hacked small," and then "seethed" and served in a sauce of "galingale," "grains of paradise," and "milk of almonds"? At first glance, not many of us might be eager to gulp this down but what if it were described as a delicately flavored "curry" with pieces of boneless or semiboneless chicken simmered in a rich sauce made from ginger, cardamom, and powdered almonds? Putting the archaic cooking instructions aside, that's what this dish translates to. "Galingale" was one of the names given to ginger in medieval Europe. The name may have been derived from "galangal," a spice related to ginger that is still used in Thai cooking. "Grains of paradise" is generally believed to have been a name for cardamom, which is an integral part of "curry" powder and many other elements of Indian cooking. Finally, "milk of almonds" is simply a liquid made by combining dried, ground almonds with water or milk. There are other elements of medieval cuisine suggestive of Asian cuisine as well, such as the common medieval spice mixture, *powdre douce*, which, though recipes varied slightly, usually contained cardamom, coriander, and ginger, not unlike many Indian curry powders. Thus, far from being either bland or a

distasteful hodgepodge of spices, it seems that some of the finest dishes in medieval cookery may have been subtly and complexly flavored, surprisingly delicious even to modern palates.

Another type of dish that was quite popular at feasts were pies. Most of these pies would be called "pot pies" today because they were filled with mixtures of meats, poultry, or fish and vegetables and cheese. They were made in a variety of sizes and part of their popularity may have been that they could be made in individual serving portions or were at least easy to cut up into manageable pieces.

Beyond just preparing food that tasted good by contemporary standards, chefs also had to make dishes that were eye-catching or even spectacular. Such dishes included swans or peacocks that were killed, skinned, cooked, and then redressed in their skins (feathers and all) and set up in a lifelike pose. One chef even took this further and redressed cooked geese inside the skins of peacocks to surprise and delight his master's guests. According to the chef's directions for this dish, part of the delight can be attributed to the fact that goose is more tasty and far more tender than peacock. A similar surprise dish was the "cockatrice" (a mythical hybrid of chicken and snake) made by attaching the upper half of a rooster to the hind end of a roast piglet.

There were even more outlandish "dishes" that were not meant to be eaten but to entertain instead. Typically presented between courses in the meal, these included pies made with pre-baked crusts into which songbirds (such as "four and twenty blackbirds") or other live animals were placed before the top crust was placed over them and sealed. Among other entertaining dishes were castles or complete dioramas made of painted pastry or almond paste. These dishes were sometimes taken to extremes. In the early 15th century, Chiquart, the same chef who dressed geese as peacocks, also recorded creating a large model castle, with animals that "breathed" real fire mounted in the castle's towers, and many other incredible features. The castle was so large, in fact, that it had room for four live musicians and their instruments. (Perhaps this was the origin of those oversized, inedible cakes that exotic dancers pop out of at stereotypical bachelor parties.)

Another noteworthy feature of Chiquart's castle was a fountain that pumped out rose-water and spiced wines. Fountains that produced flows of different wines, sometimes with the selection changing as the feast progressed to match the different foods being served, were especially popular in France and adjoining regions. Some were relatively simple, resembling large coffee urns with a raised tank that used gravity to supply the spigots below, but others actually shot the wine up and out through nozzles, like miniature garden fountains. These more complex fountains required concealed servants operating manual pumps to keep the wine flowing under pressure through small metal tubes from tanks containing reserves of wine to the fountain itself.

Fountains weren't the only decorative but functional objects found on medieval dining tables. Far more common and essential was the salt cellar. These containers, sometimes called *nefs*, were often highly ornamented and usually made in the shape of ships, perhaps symbolic of the sea, that most plentiful source of salt. (Additionally, the term *nef* appears to been derived from the Latin *navis*, meaning "ship.") Beyond its practical function of holding fine grain salt with which diners could season their food, salt cellars were used to denote the comparative ranks of the diners. The best quality salt cellars were of course placed on the high table. Additional salt cellars were placed on the

other dining tables that extended away from the high table. As mentioned before, guests were seated at these tables in descending order of importance, with the highest ranking being seated at or near the top end of the table nearest the high table. At these tables, guests, who though not important enough to merit a seat at the high table, were reassured of their host's esteem by having the salt cellars placed near them, between themselves and those inferior guests seated even farther away from the host. (This practice gave rise to using the term "below the salt" to describe a person of lower social standing.)

ETIQUETTE

As the seating arrangements and placement of salt cellars as symbolic dividers suggests, feasts were conducted with considerable formality. In western Europe, there are written guidelines for behavior at feasts dating as far back as the early 12th century, proving that conduct at these occasions was expected to conform to certain rules of etiquette. This is not to say that such rules were observed in the halls of Viking lords in earlier times or at peasant weddings, harvest festivals, and other celebrations at parish halls even during the late Middle Ages. Then as now, despite the existence of rules of etiquette, good manners were not always practiced. But it does mean that most of the aristocracy throughout Europe knew and observed certain rules about how to behave themselves during a feast. Among these rules were:

• Be sure your fingernails are clean before you go to the table. This admonition was particularly important since tableware was very limited and most foods were eaten by being picked up and directly held in the fingers.

(Guests usually brought their own knives for cutting food while spoons were relatively rare and, when available, were used only for soups. Forks did not begin come into common use until the Renaissance.) Further, since feasting was a communal activity, with even the most important guests often sharing a cup (see fig. 1) and other dishes with at least one other diner, the prospect of picking up a piece of meat in sauce from a bowl or plate which someone had just dipped his or her dirty fingernails into was no less unappetizing then than it is now.

• Wash your hands before the meal. Again, the limited tableware and intimate communal nature of feasting made this an important rule. Hand washing was sometimes performed ritualistically with the lord who was hosting the feast pouring the water for the most important of his guests. More commonly, the host's ewerer or another of his servants would pour the water, which was kept in a small ewer or pitcher and scented with flower petals and spices, when they were available. The water was caught in a small basin held below the guest's hands. Some of these pitchers and basins have survived. The pitchers (called *aquamaniles*) were often made in the shape of animals or people (such as lions or knights on horseback) with the mouth of the figure serving as the spout of the pitcher, reminiscent of those "dribbling cow" creamers found at truck stops and "country-style" restaurants across America's heartland.

• Chew with your mouth closed, don't talk with your mouth full, and don't let food in your mouth recirculate back out into the communal drinking cup.

• Don't handle a piece of food unless you are going to eat it.

• Accept the food placed in front of you and don't make a grab for seemingly better food in dishes placed before another guest.

Etiquette guides from the 13th and later centuries further refined the rules:

• Don't gorge. This may seem incredible given the numbers and amounts of foods served at many of the recorded feasts of the Middle Ages. However, gluttony was a sin and overindulgence is repellent. Besides just wanting to appear gracious, diners knew they would be inundated with food and so took and ate only small amounts of each dish, pacing themselves so they would have the room to enjoy the entire meal from beginning to end.

• Don't get drunk. Again, this may seem like an unavoidable consequence at meals where all the beverages contained alcohol. Yet, like the Romans before them, people of the Middle Ages routinely added water to their wine, diluting its alcohol content and allowing them to drink more without getting drunk. The water was taken from the purest sources available but adding water was obviously less hygienic than drinking pure wine. Presumably they thought that the wine adequately purified the water. The butler oversaw the diluting of wine served to most guests but the occupants of the high table were normally given undiluted wine with a jug of water so they could mix their own to suit their tastes.

• Don't pick your teeth, fingernails, or nose.

• Don't fidget, slouch, or rest your arms and elbows on the table.

• Don't pet dogs and cats during the meal. (Some medieval illustrations show dogs and the occasional cat begging for food and scrounging for stray scraps around dining tables. Dogs, for hunting and as just plain pets, as well as cats, for keeping mice and other vermin down, were common in most castles and palaces.)

- Don't curse or bring up any controversial topics or any distasteful ones, like diseases, operations, or off-color or ribald stories.
- Turn away from other diners if you need to sneeze or cough.
- Go the toilet before the meal, to purge your system and lessen the chance of embarrassingly passing gas at the table.
- Don't burp at the table.
- For men, be polite to the women present and don't gawk at them.

These are just some of the high points of what was considered good manners for feast-goers. Medieval feasts were certainly amazing spectacles but they don't appear to have been spitting, belching, wench-pinching, drunken free-for-alls. But this was reasonable given that feasts, despite their obvious festive aspects, were also in some respects "a business dinner with the boss" for most of those in attendance. Feasts were also an opportunity for the lord hosting the event to fully display his wealth and power through the magnitude of his hospitality and the splendor of his hall. Thus, feasts were both social events and ceremonial occasions at which political ties and other important social bonds were recognized and reinforced. Therefore, it should be no surprise that attendees tried to conduct themselves with dignity and decorum, to distinguish themselves and prove their worth to all present, especially their feudal lord and any guests of high rank who could advance their careers and fortunes. However, this depiction may be too strait-laced. The fact that guides on manners were often reissued and updated suggests that conduct at feasts may not have been uniformly genteel. Perhaps, with all that wine and good food, feast-goers had difficulty keeping themselves in check and engaged in regrettable behavior such as is seen even today at company picnics or office holiday parties when bosses and co-workers have a few too many drinks and, with reduced inhibitions, say or do inappropriate things.

ENTERTAINMENT

Besides the food which was often quite entertaining in itself, guests were treated to playlets performed by silent actors, tumbling by acrobats, juggling, and allegorical tableaux presented between courses or at the conclusion of the meal. Throughout the meal, musicians played (fig. 1), with suitable flourishes to draw attention to presentations of spectacular dishes or performances. They also provided music for any dancing the guests may have indulged in after the feast.

And they would have had time for dancing, games, and other less amusing activities, like meeting to discuss business or political matters, after the feast because most feasts were held in the middle of the day, not at night. Throughout Europe and all levels of medieval society, the midday meal was traditionally the big meal of the day. Breakfasts were small, simple meals, just enough to get you through until lunch. Evening meals were also relatively small, perhaps relying on leftovers from lunch for much of their content. Night feasts are recorded but the foods and numbers of courses listed indicate that they were usually much lighter, shorter affairs than the big noontime feasts. Also, night-time feasts were seldom held except as part of prolonged festivities when guests were staying for several days and so required entertaining and feeding during the evening as well. While feasting during the middle of the day may not line up with some modern ideas about the Middle Ages, it does make it more understandable how medieval nobility were able to withstand these marathon meals and remain awake to the end.

BUILDING AND HOUSING

Castles, cathedrals, and the "huts of the lowly peasants" are the buildings we most commonly associate with the Middle Ages but there were a great variety of other buildings constructed as well. Wharves, warehouses, workshops, and mills, as well as townhouses, farmhouses, and barns and public works such as bridges and city walls were all vital parts of medieval Europe. But the romantic appeal of castles and the awe-inspiring grandeur of the great cathedrals have assured those structures a prominent place in the modern view of the Middle Ages and its buildings. Besides the visual and emotional appeal of castles and cathedrals, another equally important factor that has shaped our image of medieval buildings is the passage of time and the toll it has taken on these buildings, especially on the more mundane ones. Many of those buildings have been demolished, disappearing without a trace except for the vestiges of their foundations or a glimpse provided by some old illustration. A few, though they have survived, have been used continuously, or nearly so, since they were

built and have been renovated and remodeled so many times and for so many different purposes that it is often very difficult to accurately discern their original shape and, in a few cases, purpose. Thus, the disproportionately high number of major edifices such as castles and cathedrals that have survived to the present relatively intact, combined with the near extinction of the other buildings, especially the houses of ordinary medieval citizens, have contributed to the misconceptions about medieval living.

For example, compared to the total number of houses that were built over the course of the Middle Ages, extremely few houses have survived to the present. Most houses were constructed primarily of wood and now all that is left of most of these buildings are tracings of foundations and the post holes (these are the holes that contained the wooden posts or beams that made up the foundation of the building). The lack of more substantial evidence has left us with an immense gap in our view of the Middle Ages, a gap which has all too often been filled by the worst imaginings of a landscape dotted with wretched huts and hovels and of towns and cities crowded with shanties and lean-tos of the shoddiest and most haphazard construction. Taking these imaginings for fact, some people have thus concluded that the bulk of the population during the Middle Ages lived in squalid dwellings that quickly disappeared without a trace. While some wretched houses certainly existed, the surviving examples and contemporary illustrations of medieval architecture suggest a different picture, one in which most houses and other buildings were solid and well built. As will be seen below, though some people in the Middle Ages were homeless or lived in abysmal conditions, many homes, while far from palatial, were sound and substantial buildings and quite fit for human habitation in their day.

As with houses, workshops, forges, kilns, and mills too have had a low survival rate, which contributes to a distorted view of medieval technology and commerce. While these industrial sites may not have been as large and productive as modern factories, they were still well developed production centers that provided a wide range of manufactured goods, including clay pots, wooden barrels, swords, armor, household cutlery, furniture, and cloth. Producing all these items required a sophisticated infrastructure to supply the necessary raw and finished materials to the specialized craftsmen who satisfied the varied needs of medieval consumers.

In this chapter, we'll look at both the well-known and well-loved structures that have survived as well as the ones which have disappeared and largely been forgotten despite the vital roles they served in the Middle Ages. First, though, let's examine the materials and techniques that went into creating all these buildings.

Construction Materials and Techniques

While building styles differed across medieval Europe and evolved over the course of the Middle Ages, the basic techniques and building materials were fairly uniform. This said, however, the difficulty of moving large volumes of construction materials, especially overland, meant that the abundance or scarcity of some building materials near the construction site often dictated which materials were used. As they had been for centuries before and would be for centuries after the Middle Ages, stone, mortar, wood, metal, and clay were the primary materials for constructing buildings. Reinforced and pre-stressed concrete, steel girder construction, and the host of synthetic materials now commonly in use did not begin appearing until the 19th century. Still, as the number of significant ruins as well as intact structures attest, medieval Europeans were quite as capable as the Romans of constructing beautiful and enduring buildings using and combining the basic elements available.

WOOD

Wood was the most common building material in the Middle Ages. With the exception of the lands immediately surrounding the Mediterranean, much of medieval Europe was covered in thick forests that provided a seemingly inexhaustible supply of timber, though population growth and centuries of building did deplete many forests — especially those nearest population centers. And all buildings used wood in some capacity. Many buildings were constructed almost entirely out of wood, from the framing for their walls and roofs to their siding and shingles. And even stone buildings required substantial wooden construction both while being built, in the form of scaffolding, ramps, and frames to support arches until the mortar hardened, and in their final forms for fixtures such as floors, roof beams, window frames, doors, and some interior walls.

The ready availability of wood in most locales (which also made it a rather cheap building material), the ease with which wood can be worked, and the speed with which a wooden building can be raised combined to make timber the material of choice for most buildings. Though building in stone became more popular over the course of the Middle Ages, even the wealthiest of builders, the Church and nobility, frequently continued to build wooden structures first and then later replace them with stone buildings. This practice was quite common during the early Middle Ages, especially when constructing defensive works such as town walls and castles. While all that usually remains of these wooden structures are the outlines in the earth of the holes that held the upright beams or posts that formed their foundations (called *post holes* as mentioned above), these fortified enclosures must have looked much like the stockade forts of the American Old West and served the same purpose of quickly providing a sturdy, defensible perimeter. Though the town walls may have looked like something out of American pioneer days, the houses, shops, and other structures within the palisades were generally comprised of wooden frame buildings and not made from rough-hewn tree trunks like log cabins. However, excavations, primarily in Russia, have found a few medieval buildings that were built of logs.

The perishable nature of wooden buildings has led to their being forgotten by later people. Properly maintained wooden structures can last centuries, as the "stave churches" of Norway attest. Built wholly of wood in the Middle Ages, a few of these churches have survived to the present and, despite some restoration and remodeling, retain most of their original form and even some of their original wooden components. However, few buildings have received such tender care and, either through neglect and abandonment or by intentional demolition to make way for newer buildings, most have been destroyed. This large-scale destruction of medieval wooden buildings leaves a very difficult task for the archaeologist and historian attempting to reconstruct such buildings. Often, the only evidence left is the post holes or, if the site sunk into damp ground or was later covered over by wet earth, perhaps a few feet of the base of the structure and any of the upper elements that collapsed in on the site. (A covering of very wet mud often preserves wood from complete decay by forming an anaerobic layer that cuts off the oxygen needed by the bacteria that consume the wood.) Accurately determining what a building looked like in its heyday based on such limited evidence is extremely difficult, if not impossible. See for yourself. Pretend to be an archaeologist a few centuries from now and try to imagine what will likely remain of most houses in existence today if their current residents abandoned them to the elements or if they were bulldozed to clear the property for new houses. In most cases, all that would be left would be a bare concrete foundation slab or basement and some scraps of the materials that made up the upper stories. Admittedly, the hypothetical future archaeologist might have more to work with, given the virtual indestructibility of vinyl and aluminum siding, Fiberglas insulation, and some other modern building materials, but how would he or she know how well a particular house had been built, let alone such details as whether it had been one-story or two? A split-level, a colonial, or a contemporary? Did it have a garage? Without illustrations or other independent evidence, it is impossible to reconstruct a particular building with a high degree of accuracy from such sparse physical evidence. With this point in mind, we should not jump to the conclusion that most houses and other wooden buildings from the Middle Ages were shoddily built hovels and shanties. Rather, the gaps in the evidence can be filled in to some degree by examining the few surviving examples of medieval architectural woodworking as well as contemporary illustrations of ongoing construction and of completed buildings. With this additional information, a different conclusion emerges: most medieval wooden buildings were solid and stout, raised by skilled workmen.

Working Wood

Fortunately, although most of the wooden buildings of the Middle Ages have long since vanished, there are still contemporary illustrations of buildings and other wooden structures both completed and under construction. For example, illustrations in bibles and prayer books depicting the construction of Noah's ark provide valuable insight into the construction of medieval wooden buildings since the ark was depicted more like a large barn than a large boat. These illustrations show carpenters busily at work with a great variety of tools, most of which are quite familiar to modern woodworkers: saws, augers, planes, adzes, mallets, chisels, and hammers as well as levels, squares, and measuring rods.

The basic component in wooden buildings was the beam, roughly square in section, and varying in length and thickness according to how it was to be used. Upright beams were sunk vertically into the leveled ground of the building site (becoming the "posts" found by later archaeologists) or were placed on top of stone pads or low walls, which protected the beam from some of the moisture in the ground and thus inhibited rot. Attached at right angles to the uprights and connecting them were the beams that formed the walls and floors of the building. For many buildings, the beams were likely cut from trunks of trees felled at or near the building site. The tree trunks were trimmed into beams by pairs of men using long, two-handled saws. The log was placed in a long frame that held the log several feet above the ground, though in many instances the frame was placed at ground level with a deep trench or narrow pit dug beneath it. One man was then positioned underneath the frame while another man stood on top of the frame supporting the log or atop the log itself. Together, placed above and below the log, the two sawyers pushed and pulled the large, two-handled saw up and down, slicing and trimming the logs into square beams and boards. This technique for sawing wood was still practiced well into the 18th century. More rarely, wood was cut at water-powered sawmills. These mills, which appear to have originated in the early 14th century, were not mills with big circular "buzz-saw" blades like we have today but instead had large, straight blades like those on the man-powered pit saws and, driven by systems of gears that converted the rotary motion of the millwheel into an up-and-down action, sliced the wood with the same sort of reciprocating stroke.

Regardless of the exact method of sawing, most beams and other wooden components, even of furniture, appear to have been cut directly from green wood, that is, wood which has been freshly cut down and not allowed to thoroughly dry out and season, as is the standard practice today. Though some shrinkage, twisting, and cracking occurred after construction as the pieces dried out, medieval carpen-

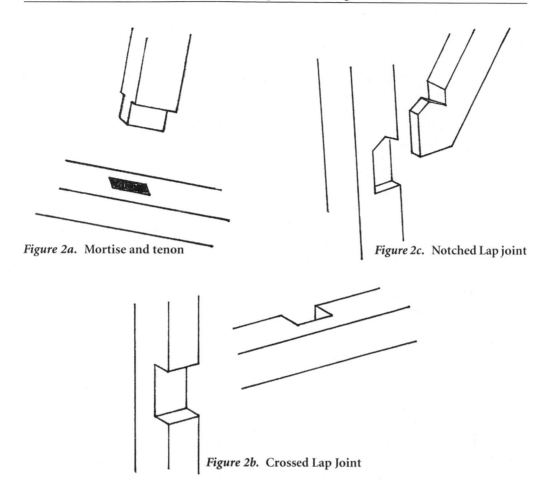

Figure 2a. Mortise and tenon

Figure 2c. Notched Lap joint

Figure 2b. Crossed Lap Joint

Figures 2a, 2b and 2c. Common joints used in wooden construction in the Middle Ages (drawings by author).

ters were familiar with their materials and produced surprisingly solid buildings. Their success in overcoming any subsequent distortion of the pieces may be attributable to the fact that, for the key joints of the buildings, they relied more on all wooden construction rather than metal fasteners, such as nails and screws (which, though very crudely threaded by modern standards, were available, manufactured by medieval ironsmiths). For example, a very common form of joint was the mortise and tenon (fig. 2a) in which one end of the beam is narrowed down to form a tab called a tenon and fitted into a rectangular slot, a mortise, in another beam.

Another common form was the crossed lap (fig. 2b) in which a slot was cut across the width of a beam, then a beam with a similar slot was fitted to the first beam so that the beams crossed and locked together at their matched, overlapping slots (like children's "Lincoln Logs"). When cross-braces were needed for additional strength and stability, slots were cut at angles across the beams to accommodate the braces. To tie the end of a cross-brace securely into a beam, medieval carpenters often used notched lap joints (fig. 2c) in which an angled recess was carved into the side of the beam and the end of the brace was cut to fit the recess tightly. All these joints were

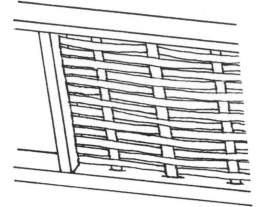

Figure 3. **Panel of wattle before daubing (drawing by author).**

typically secured with wedges or tapered wooden pegs that firmly locked all the pieces together, creating a strongly unified structure in which the distortion of any single piece of wood was resisted and countered by the rest of the structure.

Modern builders have discarded the use of wood-on-wood joints and trust almost exclusively in joints secured with metal plates, nails, or screws because they know that the seasoned, dried wood they use is not going to shrink or otherwise change its shape so much that it will pull loose from the metal fasteners. However, had the medieval builders relied more on metal fasteners, such as nails, spikes, and screws, many of their buildings would likely have soon torn themselves apart as they settled and dried out. Thus, they wisely used the materials at hand and limited their use of metal fasteners to attaching siding, fitting doors, and other uses less critical to the overall stability of the buildings.

Wedges, Pegs, Shingles, Wattle, and Lath

Besides being cut and trimmed into large beams and boards to make walls, roof beams, and door and window frames, wood was also fashioned into a number of other smaller pieces needed to finish a building. These included the wedges that were sometimes needed to tighten mortise and tenon and other joints as well as the slightly tapered pegs used to secure boards and beams. For roofing needs, blocks of wood were split into thin, relatively small, squarish pieces to form shingles. Wood, especially from saplings and willows, was also split into long, narrow lengths. These flexible but tough strips were woven basket-fashion around large sticks to make rectangular sheets of various sizes. Though perhaps most commonly associated with England, where this material is called *wattle*, it was used throughout much of Europe. Wattle (fig. 3) was used to make fences and pens for animals but it was also used to make walls for houses and other buildings. When used for houses and buildings, wattle was coated with other materials as described below under "Clay." Finally, lath, long pieces of wood but in the form of very thin and narrow planks rather than flexible strips, was used inside some buildings where it was nailed or pegged horizontally across the beams that formed the frame of the walls and then coated with plaster to create the finished surface of the interior walls.

Limits on Building with Wood

Despite its advantages, there were limits on building with wood. Wood's flammability rendered it inferior to stone for castles and other buildings that had to withstand attack and its vulnerability to rot encouraged builders who desired to build great, enduring edifices such as cathedrals to use stone. Still, even in the great Gothic cathedrals, wooden beams were still needed to support the roofs and, by the time these marvelous buildings were being raised, finding trees large enough to provide the beams was a difficult task since most of the best and biggest trees — the huge oaks, walnuts, and other fine hardwoods — nearest the towns and cities had long since been cut down for earlier building projects, fuel, and other needs. This shortage of trees forced some cathedral builders to ship in wood, in one case incurring transportation costs that were eight times the value of the wood itself!

Clay

Clay was used in a variety of ways in medieval construction. It was used to fill in cracks and gaps in wooden buildings to make them less drafty, in the same way that American pioneers filled the gaps and cracks in log cabins with clay or sod. Clay was also used to coat panels of wattle. The clay was usually mixed with other materials such as chopped straw and cow hairs to create a substance called *daub*. The coating of daub made the wattle more weather- and draft-proof and had the added incidental benefit of making the wattle slightly less vulnerable to fire, an important consideration when all heating, cooking, and artificial lighting was achieved by use of open flames. The daub was applied to the panels of wattle after the panels were constructed within the gridworks of beams that formed the walls of wooden buildings (fig. 3).

Clay was also formed and baked to create bricks, a popular building material throughout Europe, but especially in the Low Countries (modern day Belgium, Luxembourg, and the Netherlands) where stone suitable for building was in very short supply. In fact, this scarcity of stone caused the inhabitants of the Low Countries to be among the first Europeans to build castles almost entirely out of brick. Though somewhat less durable than many stone castles, these brick castles were as fireproof as stone ones.

Bricklayers cemented the bricks to-gether using mortar made of water, sand, and lime. Lime was made by heating limestone or seashells (the shells of oysters and clams were most commonly used since these mollusks were harvested and eaten in large numbers) and then crushing it into a powder. This lime powder was calcium oxide and it provided the adhesive element of the mortar. Besides being used as the primary material in some buildings, bricks were also used as supplementary material for the walls of buildings. For example, wattle wasn't the only material used to fill in the spaces left in gridworks of beams; bricks and mortar were also used. And, as discussed more below, bricks and mortar were also used to form the cores of the walls of many stone buildings as the Middle Ages progressed.

In addition to bricks, clay was also shaped and fired to make roofing and floor tiles. While roofing tiles were fairly common, floor tiles were more of a luxury item and were often quite ornate, decorated with stamped and painted designs or formed into shapes that created elaborate geometric patterns across the entire floor. Examples of all these types of tiles can be seen at Byland Abbey in North Yorkshire (fig. 4). Such tiles were used in churches, monasteries, and homes of the nobility and other wealthy individuals throughout the Middle Ages. Most people, however, appear to have made do with floors of earth or unfired clay, pounded flat to form a hard, level surface. As for roofing tiles, their durability and nonflammability made them popular in many parts of Europe. Just as today, roofing tiles were especially popular in southern Europe. Because of their light coloring, the pale red or tan tiles reflect away more of the sun's light and heat than darker roofing materials. Additionally, while the tiles absorb and store some of the heat, they gradually release that heat at night. Even in the Middle Ages, residents of the areas ringing the

Figure 4. **Floor tiles at Byland Abbey, North Yorkshire, England. These tiles date to the middle of the 13th century and include both square tiles with painted designs and tiles formed into shapes that create large geometric patterns (photograph by author).**

Mediterranean, a region famous for its intensely sunny days, likely understood the thermal properties of clay tile and used it to their advantage in heating and cooling their buildings.

STONE

Because of its durability, stone was the preferred building material. In many places, houses, churches, and other buildings were constructed of whatever types and sizes of stone was at hand, regardless of whether the stone was well suited for use in building or not. When using the stones gathered from around a building site and its immediate vicinity, stone masons used a technique called "random rubble" building in which they constructed the walls of the structure by carefully fitting and mortaring the rocks of random shape and size together (fig. 5). Some of the stones, such as those that formed window or door frames or the outside corners and edges of the building were dressed (that is, chiseled to make them flat and square) but most were left rough and irregularly shaped with no two looking the same; hence the name "random rubble."

While rubble construction had the advantage of being able to turn almost any type of stone into a building, it was a technique suitable only for relatively small structures. Because of the irregular shapes of most of its component rocks and reliance on mortar to fill in any odd gaps, rubble walls typically lacked the structural soundness required for very high walls or for other walls that had to bear a lot of weight. Thus, for castles, cathedrals, and other major works, medieval builders required vast numbers of dressed stones that could be fitted securely together, bearing the weight of the building and channeling the resulting stresses reliably and uniformly. The building stones also had to be made of a type of a stone that was hard enough to endure these pressures. Obviously, not all types of stone were suitable for building and the expense of obtaining good building stone was often prohibitive. Further, cutting and dressing stone was more difficult work than preparing and finishing other building materials such as wood or clay. This higher level of difficulty meant that stone construction was more expensive and often took much longer to complete than other types of construction. These factors generally placed construction in stone beyond the means of most people during the Middle Ages, leaving stone to be used by those with the requisite money and time: the Church and the secular nobility. The nobles and the Church also had the most need of durable stone buildings. Individual, common people did not need to build residences capable of withstanding a siege like a castle, much less homes large and durable enough to shelter scores of people like a monastery, or

Figure 5. Chapel at Pickering Castle, North Yorkshire, England. Built in the 13th century and subsequently modified and restored, this building is a good example of random rubble construction. The walls are made of stones of varying shapes and sizes which have been carefully arranged to create a solid wall. As is typical in random rubble construction, only large, fully finished stones appear at the edges such as at the corners and, as shown here, the windows. These windows are quite narrow, only about ten inches wide, and are fitted with wooden shutters that close from the inside. Like many windows in the Middle Ages, these windows were probably not fitted with glass. If they had any covering in addition to the shutters, it was likely made of either thin pieces of horn or oiled cloth mounted in a wooden frame within the stone window frame (photograph by author).

massive and beautiful enough that it could host services for hundreds, if not thousands, of the faithful in a suitably inspiring setting for generations like a cathedral. However, citizens in urban centers did

occasionally form groups and contracted for public works that required stonework, such as bridges, city walls, and embankments for harbors and riversides, and some wealthy individuals did have houses built in dressed stone for their protection as well as to reflect their high standing in the community. Thus, despite the advantages of building in stone, the expense and time required for raising such buildings limited their construction and meant that, as previously discussed under "Wood," these buildings represent only a fraction of the structures built in the Middle Ages, although it is a fraction that embodies some of the highest technological and artistic achievements of the day.

Working Stone

Stone construction began with leveling and stabilizing the site. Sometimes this meant sinking wooden pilings into the ground or clearing the earth away down to bare rock and cutting into the bedrock to provide a solid, level base for the foundations. In many cities and towns, medieval builders had the advantage of being able to build on top of the remains of Roman forums, temples, or other large, public buildings, as in York, England, where the cathedral or *minster* was built on the site of the former headquarters of the local detachment of the Roman army. Such sites were ideal since the Romans had already done most of the hard work. In many instances, all that later builders had to do was clear away any of the unwanted ruins that remained above the foundations.

The Roman ruins also provided another construction shortcut: a handy supply of building materials in the form of whatever stones were left from their buildings. Dressed building stones and brick from Roman structures were often salvaged to provide a ready-made source of building material, saving builders the expense and time of having to quarry and square off raw stone. If pre-dressed stones weren't available, then a source of suitable stone had to be located. Some quarries were well established and produced building stone noted for its quality for

centuries, such as the fine limestone from the quarries around Caen in France and marble from Carrara in Italy. Away from such well-known quarries, builders had to scour the countryside near the building site in hopes of finding either an existing quarry or, failing that, an outcropping of usable stone that could be quarried. Ideally, quarries were located near navigable rivers so that the stones could be shipped by barge to the construction site, an activity sometimes depicted in late medieval illuminations. If shipping by river wasn't feasible, the only other form of transportation available was carting the stones on heavy-duty wagons pulled by draft animals, typically those tractors of the Middle Ages: oxen. The slow pace of the animals and the generally poor condition of most roads meant that this was a time consuming process and often very costly as well.

At the quarry, laborers worked with hammers, chisels, wedges, crowbars, and pickaxes. Using only their own muscle power, these workers cut, pried, and lifted the stones from the bedrock. Without the aid of hardened carbon drills, hydraulic equipment, and explosives, this work must have been incredibly backbreaking.

While still at the quarry, masons began shaping the stones into their final forms. Many stones, particularly the basic rectangular "building-block" ones, would be finished at the quarry and shipped to the building site ready to use. By ensuring that the blocks were already either completely or nearly cut down to their desired finished shapes, this practice helped cut down on transportation costs by reducing the amount of stone that had to be shipped. As reflected in some late medieval building contracts, the shipping cost was no small matter. In one instance, shipping added more than 50 percent to the cost of the materials. Over the course of the Middle Ages, even the more intricately shaped stones for pillars and arches were increasingly finished, at least partially if not entirely, at the quarry. The masons at the quarry shaped these stones according to templates sent out by the master mason. Such stones would be carefully marked so that they could be properly identified for placement once at the building site. The individual masons who shaped the stones usually chiseled in their own personal identification mark as well. These marks were noted by an accounting assistant to the master mason who logged in the number of pieces produced by each mason so that the men could be paid according to their output. The marks also served a quality control purpose. If a stone failed during construction due to the poor workmanship of a mason who had dressed the stone, the mason responsible was identified according to his mark on the stone and fined.

Besides the quarrymen and the masons who cut the stones, there were many other laborers on medieval building sites: Excavators, using only wooden shovels, pickaxes and other manual tools, dug into the earth and stone of the site to provide the level, stable ground required for the foundations. Carpenters made the scaffolds and ramps needed to build the high walls as well as the forms needed to hold the stones of arches in place until the mortar hardened and the arches stood on their own. Mortar makers mixed water, sand, and lime in wooden troughs or in trenches dug at the site to produce the mortar (fig. 6).

Providing the muscle power to lift and place all the stones in their designated positions, as well as transporting the mortar and all the rest of the building materials, were scores of ordinary laborers. They carried hods of mortar (fig. 6), toted beams, and, working in pairs, lifted and carried stones on stretcher-like conveyances, sometimes with additional support of neck yokes. These workers must have welcomed the arrival of the wheelbarrow,

which was introduced to Europe from Asia some time in the 13th century.

The laborers often provided the motive power for cranes as well, though horses and mules were also used. Though simple pulleys with teams of men were also used to hoist stone up as the buildings rose, cranes, powered by treadmills, were more efficient and required fewer men to operate. As shown in figure 6, these early cranes were fitted with two large, spoked wheels that were connected with boards to form a giant drum or treadmill that turned on an axle. The crane's rope was attached to the axle and wound around the axle as it turned, forming a gigantic winch. These drums looked and operated much like gigantic versions of guinea pig or gerbil exercise wheels. To power the crane, men or draft animals entered the drum through its open sides and began walking the endless circuit of the inside wall of the drum, causing the drum to turn and wind the winch. When building towers or very high vaults, the cranes were disassembled and moved up as each succeeding level was completed until the crane was at the very top story. In some churches and cathedrals, the cranes were left in place in the top stories when their towers were completed and are still there today, as at Salisbury Cathedral in England and Beauvais Cathedral in France.

In addition to cranes, wooden ramps and scaffolding were essential in the construction of stone buildings (fig. 6). The gently inclined ramps allowed vast quantities of heavy building materials to be easily moved up to the ever-rising level of construction. These ramps were typically supported on one side by the rising walls of the building itself and rose right along with the building. In fact, the towers and walls of many castles still have the "putholes" which held the ends of the ramp supports during their construction. These holes are about six inches square and

several inches deep and were often simply left empty after construction was completed and the ramps dismantled.

As with many Roman stone structures, medieval stone buildings were often constructed with fine, fitted stone facades over the top of much rougher work. Especially for very thick walls, such as those for city walls and castles, only the outer few feet on each side of the wall were made of carefully fitted blocks. The cores of these walls, often several yards thick, were made of rubble; that is, miscellaneous, large stones and gravel dumped into the channel formed by the two finished faces of the wall and secured by cement poured over the rocks to bond them in place. While this process may sound like a sloppy method of building, the rubble was usually carefully compacted and wooden beams were placed to connect the opposing, finished faces. Or, in some instances, gridworks of beams were placed within the layers of rubble, providing additional stability to the wall and better bonding together of the rubble core with the finished faces. These techniques, combined with the external layers of fitted stone, resulted in strong, unified walls that were much stronger than the random rubble walls described at the beginning of this section.

By the late Middle Ages, surviving illuminations show that cores of brick had replaced rubble cores, at least in the fine Gothic cathedrals and other stone buildings whose walls were thinner and less massive than their predecessors. Some of these illuminations also depict another interesting practice used in stone construction: covering the tops of partially completed buildings with straw or sod. Raising a large stone building such as a cathedral often took many decades, both because of the difficulty of the construction and because of delays caused by funds running out, so there were often gaps of a year or more between the completion of a wall or set of pillars and the completion of the roof that permanently protected them from rain, snow, frost and other damaging weather. Thus, for the annual winter hiatus or other long breaks in construction, the workers covered the exposed tops of partially completed sections with sod and straw to help prevent moisture from seeping into the masonry and damaging it.

The Types of Stone Used

The types of stone used in construction depended primarily on which stones were most readily available in the vicinity

Opposite: Figure 6. **Construction of the Tower of Babel. Fifteenth century manuscript illumination. Though depicting a scene from the Old Testament, this illustration shows the Tower of Babel being built as though it was a castle or cathedral in the 15th century. At the base of the tower, one worker picks up a dressed stone while another mixes mortar. To the left of the tower, another laborer carries a basket filled with small lumps which could be either chunks of lime for making more mortar or rocks that would be used to fill in the core of the tower's thick walls. Half way up on the right side is a wooden scaffold, supported by short beams that jut out from put-holes in the surface of the wall. The scaffold at the top of the tower is also supported this way. Climbing up the ladder between the levels of scaffolds is a hod-carrier. This worker has his hod, a shallow tray filled with mortar, on his shoulders. His unenviable job is to carry the mortar from the bottom of the tower up to the top where the mortar is needed to cement the stones in place. At the top is a man-powered crane. To lift stones and other building materials, a man would enter the large wheel on the right side of the crane and begin walking, like a hamster in an exercise wheel. The crane's rope wound around the axle of the huge wheel as it turned, lifting the crane's load (in this case, a block of stone) to the waiting masons (courtesy of the Walters Art Gallery, Baltimore).**

of the building site. Certain types of stone were recognized as being particularly suitable and desirable for building and were sometimes shipped in from great distances for especially fine buildings such as the high quality limestone used in many great English buildings from the time of the Norman conquest onward. This limestone was shipped across the English Channel from the quarries in Caen, France. Limestone, including marble, and other good quality stones were especially desired for the finely cut and joined stones that formed the facing of the wall as well as arches, pillars, and other important features that required careful finishing. Besides limestone, the preferred stones for construction were granite and the harder types of sandstone. While some types of stone were preferred, virtually all types, ranging from large chunks of flint down to gravel and the waste from cutting the major building stones, were used in one place or another over the course of the Middle Ages. Most often, the less suitable stones were used as rubble to fill in the cores of the walls or for leveling the construction site but even stones usually shunned as primary building materials were sometimes used when there was no other reasonable alternative, such as in the northwest of England and southwest of Scotland where castles were built of relatively soft sandstone because it was the only stone available in sufficient quantities near the building sites. In some instances, the builders appear to have made the walls extra thick to compensate for lower durability of the erosion-prone sandstone.

OTHER MATERIALS

In addition to the primary building materials of wood, clay, and stone, several other materials were needed to construct buildings. While they were used in rela-

tively small quantities, these materials were essential in making the completed building fit for habitation.

Metal

Many large construction projects had temporary iron forges opened on site to make and repair tools as well as fasteners and other metal objects, such as hinges, that became part of the building. In some areas, most notably Italy, France, and the Byzantine Empire, smiths were already making iron rods for reinforcing stone buildings as early as the 12th century. These rods were typically secured at the bases of arches, connecting across the span of the arches to provide additional stability by tying the bases of the arches together. A few surviving examples (fig. 7) and many empty sockets also show that wooden beams were sometimes used in this role as well. While some of these tie-rods and tie-beams may have been intended only as temporary measures to provide added stability until the mortar thoroughly set and the building had settled, the long-term effectiveness of such reinforcement was graphically proven earlier this century in France. A church at St. Quentin had many of the iron tie-rods removed from its arches during restoration in the 19th century. After the church was shelled during World War I, only those arches that still had their centuries-old tie-rods were still standing. Similar results have been seen in Italy and in the areas of Greece and Turkey formerly ruled by the Byzantines where medieval buildings with timber or iron reinforced arches have proven more resistant than unreinforced arches to the stresses caused by earthquakes.

Besides iron, lead was a metal commonly found at construction sites in the Middle Ages. As described in the Chapter IV on cleaning, lead was used for pipes to carry water into buildings and to carry

Figure 7. Interior of the Church of Santa Maria dei Frari, Venice. Begun in the 1330s, this church is one of the few medieval buildings which has retained its wooden tie beams. These beams span the bases of each of the principal arches in the church to provide increased lateral stability. This church was built on pilings driven into the mud of the lagoon and thus needed additional strengthening to compensate for the relative instability of its foundation. However, many stone buildings throughout medieval Europe were also constructed with similar tie beams or rods even when they were built on firm ground (photograph courtesy of Robert G. Calkins).

wastes away, but its resistance to corrosion by water also made it a suitable material for covering roofs. Further, unlike wooden shingles or thatching, it was also non-flammable, reducing the risk of fire. To make lead roofing material, molten lead was poured out into shallow molds to form thin, flat pieces and then, if needed, further flattened by hammering to produce rectangular or square sheets that weighed approximately one pound per square foot. These sheets were nailed to the wooden slats that covered the roofing beams, much like modern shingles but obviously much heavier. Lead, though not as expensive or rare as many other metals, was relatively costly and so was used primarily on cathedrals, palaces, and other lavish structures. While it may be odd to think of lead as being valuable, theft of lead from church roofs continued to be a rather common petty crime in Europe well after the end of the Middle Ages and the lead from the roofs of monasteries and abbeys were among the first materials confiscated after Henry VIII dissolved the monastic orders in England.

Lead was also used to make window frames, most notably for the stained glass windows of churches. Glaziers cast molten lead into molds that produced thin strips or bars about half an inch square in cross section. The molds also formed grooves or channels into two opposite sides of each bar along their full length. When assembling the windows, glaziers warmed the lead bar slightly to make it more flexible and then bent it into the desired shape to securely hold the piece of glass. The glazier then slotted the glass into the channels in the bar and soldered the lead frame shut.

Finally, bronze and other alloys were used to make hinges, faucets, and other fittings for especially fine buildings. Cathedrals were likely the largest consumers of bronze, brass, and other alloys since their bells and, in a few stunning examples, even

some of their doors were cast from these metals.

Slate

While a type of stone, slate deserves a separate mention since its physical properties are uniquely suited for use as a roofing material. Slate is a fine grained, hard stone that can be easily split apart to form thin sheets that, like lead sheets, were used to make heavy but durable, water- and fire-proof roofs. Also like lead, slate was often a relatively expensive roofing material, at least in those areas away from the slate mines, because of the costs of transporting stone. The sheets of slate were cut into uniform pieces, rectangles usually about eight by ten inches in size, with a few holes drilled along the top edge of each slate shingle. Wooden pegs were then fitted into these holes. Suspended by the pegs, the slate shingles were then hung over slats that formed the roof. (Long after the Middle Ages, this practice waned and slate shingles were often nailed directly to the slats instead.) Again, because of transportation costs, slate roofing was most frequently used on buildings in areas at or near slate quarries. Thus, England (especially the south and west, near the slate deposits centered in Wales) and northern France were the areas where slate-roofed buildings were most common.

Thatch

One of the most common roofing materials, especially in northern half of Europe, was thatch. Thatch was most commonly made of sheaves of straw though it was sometimes made from reeds and even heather if these materials were more readily available than straw. The advantages of thatch were obvious: it was cheap, far cheaper than lead or slate, and, since it was typically made from a by-product of grain farming, it could be easily obtained throughout large parts of Europe. Further, unlike lead and slate, thatch provided a roof with some insulation value. However, the drawbacks of thatch were just as obvious: it was a tremendous fire hazard, particularly in cities and large towns where having numerous thatched roofed buildings close together ensured the rapid spread of any building fires that broke out. Thus, building ordinances in London and many other cities, from as early as 1212, discouraged or banned the use of the thatch, recommending or requiring that tiles or other nonflammable materials be used instead to lessen the risk and spread of fire. Still, because of its low cost, thatch continued to be popular, though its use was gradually relegated to small towns and rural buildings over the centuries.

Plaster

Plaster was as essential to most medieval buildings as it is for buildings today for finishing walls, making them smooth, covering over less attractive structural materials, and providing a uniform surface that could be painted and decorated. The composition of plaster varied from region to region. Some plaster appears to have been simply a watered down version of mortar, containing the same burnt and crushed limestone or seashells, sand, and water. However, powdered chalk was also sometimes used to make finer plaster and, as early as the mid–13th century, Paris was already noted for its fine, white plaster made from burning gypsum (a type of rock rich in calcium), grinding it, and mixing it with water to form a smooth, spreadable paste. This is the origin of "plaster of Paris" which still denotes white plaster made from powdered gypsum.

Besides covering walls, plaster was also used to cover floors. Plaster floors appear to have been most commonly placed over the top of wooden floors, often in the upper floors of buildings. Plaster for floors had to be more durable than plaster

for walls so it was likely a rather coarse mixture, more like thin concrete than fine, smooth white plaster.

Glass and Other Window Materials

Glass windows were relatively rare in the Middle Ages. Though the availability of window glass increased and the price gradually decreased, glass windows were still rather expensive throughout the period and so their use was commonly limited to churches and cathedrals and the residences of the wealthy. Glass windows were so expensive and prized, in fact, that accounts for some noble households' records that these families took down their glass windows, wooden frames and all, and had them packed and moved with their furniture when moving house from one of their estates to another. A less costly substitute for glass was horn. Horn windowpanes were made by taking the horns of cattle, boiling them until flexible, and then cutting, splitting, and pressing them into thin sheets. These sheets were then mounted in wooden frames like glass. While horn lacked the transparency of glass, it did form a solid, translucent window. A still cheaper substitute was sheets of thin cloth stretched taut in wooden frames. The cloth was usually waxed or oiled to make the fabric more translucent.

Stained Glass

As early as the 5th century, contemporary writers recorded that colored glass was being used to form decorative designs in the windows of some churches in France as well as in the Byzantine Empire. Over the course of the Middle Ages, stained glass, with its unique ability to transform ordinary sunlight into brilliant, heavenly hues, became a fixture in churches throughout Europe. These windows, depicting events from the Bible and the lives of the saints, also served to dazzlingly illustrate sermons and readings from the Bible for the mostly illiterate parishioners.

To produce the colored glass, glass-makers added metal oxides to the silica (sand) and soda or potash (from the ashes of burnt seaweed or wood, respectively) used to make plain, clear glass. For example, mixing in iron oxide (rust) created red glass while manganese oxide yielded green and cobalt oxide produced blue. The glass-maker then turned the pieces of glass over to other artisans, the glass-cutter and the glass-painter. They worked together at a workbench or table with a whitewashed top onto which the glass-painter had drawn the outline of the window. Only one example, in Gerona Cathedral in Spain, of such a tabletop has survived. By the late 14th century, the window designs were sometimes drawn on sheets of paper instead. The glass-cutter trimmed the pieces of colored glass into the shapes needed, then the glass-painter painted designs onto the pieces. These designs ranged from simple geometric patterns on pieces for borders and backgrounds to facial features and other details on the figures and other elements of the scenes that the windows depicted. The paint itself was a dark, thick mixture of iron or copper oxide, ground glass, gum arabic (an adhesive obtained from certain varieties of trees in Africa), and a fluid, such as water, wine, vinegar, or even urine to mix and bind the other ingredients together. Besides painting the lines that defined the images and designs, the glass-painter also used thinner solutions of paint to shade areas of the glass. Just as it does in other paintings, this shading enhanced the quality of the pictures by creating the illusions of depth and texture but in glass painting the shading also filters the amount of light that can pass through the glass. By varying the darkness of the shading, the glass-painter transformed panes of uniformly colored glass into subtly varicolored pieces that gave the finished windows an astonishing range of dazzling colors. Once the painter was finished, the pieces of glass were returned to the glassmaker for a second firing to fuse the paint to the glass. This must have been the most nerve-racking stage in the process since, without a thermometer, the glassmaker had to reheat the pieces to a temperature high enough to fuse the paint to the surface of the glass but not so high as to cause the pieces themselves to melt or crack from the heat. After cooling, the pieces were brought back to the workbench and put back into their spots on the pattern outlined for the window. The glazier (who was also likely the glass-painter) carefully bent strips of lead to hold the individual pieces of glass and soldered them shut, adding strips until the complete pattern of the window was filled in. The windows were then coated on both sides with a clear, thick glue that further secured the pieces to the lead frame and made the windows more weatherproof as well. After this, the window was placed into an iron frame and installed.

Providing the Basic Necessities (and More)

Now that we've seen the materials and some of the techniques employed by medieval builders, let's seen how the builders used them to meet the basic needs of the people who worked and lived in these buildings

PLUMBING

As is explained in Chapter IV on cleaning, some medieval buildings such as palaces, monasteries, and some houses in the cities did have plumbing systems with leaden pipes and bronze taps that provided running water. A few even had boilers to provide flowing hot water. These buildings also usually had sanitation systems, including indoor latrines. However, many buildings, including most private residences, did not have these features and their occupants had to draw and carry their water from wells and rivers. If they needed hot water, they had to heat it up in a cauldron or other large cooking pot. As for waste removal, they had to use outhouses or, in towns and cities, communal latrines rather than *en suite* facilities. Thus, in those buildings in which plumbing was minimal or nonexistent, the residents relied on pitchers, pans, wooden tubs, and buckets rather than on permanent fixtures such as water faucets, sinks, and bathtubs for conveying and containing the water needed for cooking and cleaning.

HEATING

Heating buildings was a chronic problem in the Middle Ages. The Roman technique of constructing raised flooring and using the space underneath the floor (called a *hypocaust*) as a conduit for warm air from furnaces disappeared with the collapse of the empire. In most of Europe, people resorted to using braziers (small charcoal or wood-burning grills made of metal or pottery) or open hearths or firepits constructed in the middle of the ground floor. Drafts through the buildings appear to have prevented dangerous accumulations of carbon monoxide, and smoke from the fires filtered out of the building through a hole in the ridge of the roof. These vents were often fitted with louvered caps on the outside of the roof to keep the rain and wind out. Some of these caps were wooden but others were made of pottery

and at least a few English pottery smoke vent caps that have survived from the 13th century are in the form of human heads with holes in the mouth, eyes, and ears to allow the smoke to escape. Still, regardless of their form, such vents were of limited use in clearing the smoke out of the building since they lacked a chimney to contain and guide the smoke from the fire to the outside. To remedy this problem, medieval builders developed smoke hoods to catch the smoke and direct it out of the building. These hoods functioned and looked something like the vent hoods currently found in most kitchens over the range-top except, instead of being made of metal, they were made of wood or wattle and covered in plaster to make them less flammable. In wooden buildings, where the hearths were still typically located in the center of floor to reduce the risk of fire igniting the wooden walls, the smoke hoods were either suspended down from the ceiling rafters or supported by stone or brick pillars built up at the corners of the hearth. In stone buildings, similar hoods were also used for central hearths but, because the risk of the stone walls catching fire was virtually nil, the hearths were often moved to positions along the walls and placed under hoods attached to the walls. These hoods were connected to flues built inside the walls' thickness. These flues appeared before the end of the 12th century and, by the late 13th century, gradually evolved into what we commonly picture as a chimney: a roughly cylindrical smokestack running up the outside of a wall. Despite the risks involved, hearths in wooden buildings gradually followed this same pattern of development but with chimneys constructed of wood, coated on the inside with plaster or clay, and hearths made of stone, tile, or brick. The danger of wooden chimneys led civic authorities in London to ban their construction in the 14th century and mandate the use of stone or tile chimneys instead. Accompanying the development of chimneys, fireplaces developed as the hearths migrated from their traditional position in the center of the ground floor to the edge of the room. At first, they remained open hearths, adjacent to the wall and vented by the smoke hood connected to flue or chimney, but the hearths were gradually further and further recessed into the wall until they looked much like modern fireplaces. While such placement improved venting of the smoke, moving the hearth out of the center of the room reduced the hearth's ability to heat the entire room. However, the improved ventilation and increasing use of fireproof materials meant that buildings could be built with several fireplaces instead of a single central open hearth, thus compensating for lost heating. Still, despite these improvements over the course of the Middle Ages, Europe would have to wait until the 19th century for the development of central heating systems that finally surpassed those of the Romans.

NATURAL LIGHTING

As with heating, providing adequate lighting was a challenge to medieval builders. As mentioned above, glass, horn, and cloth were all used to make windowpanes but evidence suggests that, despite the availability of these materials, many windows, particularly in the early Middle Ages, were simply openings in the wall that admitted wind and weather along with sunlight. Even glazed windows were poorly insulated and their frames were not as well sealed as their modern counterparts. Thus builders often made windows rather small to minimize drafts and loss of heat. In stone structures, the builders also frequently made the windows small or narrow to avoid weakening the load-bearing walls with too many large openings (fig. 5).

The expense of the better glazing materials may have been another reason that the sizes of windows were limited. Yet another factor that required windows to be small or at least required them to be made of many small panes was that glass and horn could not be produced in large sheets. After all, cow horns only get so big and the technology and skills required to produce large panes of durable glass weren't developed until several centuries after the Middle Ages.

Windows, regardless of whether they had oiled cloth "windowpanes," glass, horn, or nothing at all in them, usually had wooden shutters that could be closed in bad weather or at night (figs. 5 and 8). These shutters, which could be barred shut from the inside, also provided a measure of security.

In castles and other structures where security was a serious concern, builders frequently took additional steps to prevent people from sneaking in through windows or from throwing projectiles through them. In these buildings, the windows, especially those on the lower floors of the building where the windows were easier to reach from the ground, were often quite narrow, too narrow for a person to squeeze through. While the external openings in the walls for these windows were narrow, the windows were constructed so that the openings grew wider towards the inside face of the wall, as shown at Chillon Castle, Switzerland, in figure 8. Since these walls were several feet thick, often between eight to fifteen feet thick, there was plenty of space for the windows to gradually widen from slits just eight to ten inches wide on the outside to broad openings three or more feet in width. This feature allowed more diffusion of light and air through the window without reducing security. Additionally, some windows were constructed in this fashion so that they could be used as arrowslits since the widening of the

Figure 8. Interior of Chillon Castle, Switzerland. Though much restored and renovated in the centuries since its construction, this room retains many medieval features. The patterns painted on the walls and window shutters and the fabric hangings provide a sense of how this room was originally decorated: a far cry from the stark and empty shells to which so many castles have been reduced. The window seat is little more than three feet in depth and reveals the thickness of the wall. This part of the wall is on the second floor and faces an interior courtyard. The outer walls which were more exposed to attack were typically much thicker. To maximize the flow of light into the room, the window opening gradually widens from the exterior to the interior (photograph by author).

window allowed archers defending the building a wide field of fire with little exposure to enemy fire. Finally, besides shutters and narrow openings, windows were sometimes fitted with iron grillwork as an added precaution to bar entry.

In addition to windows, another building feature used to maximize natural lighting was the central courtyard. The best examples of these courtyards are the cloisters found in many monasteries. The cloister was a square garden enclosed on all sides by monastery buildings. The rooms directly abutting and looking out on to the open space of the cloister were frequently built with large windows since the sheltered cloister was less exposed to the weather and other threats from the outside world. These well-lit rooms surrounding the cloister were typically the site of the *scriptorium*, the studios and workshops in which the monks copied and illuminated manuscripts, since such precise work required the best light available.

ARTIFICIAL LIGHTING

Once the sun had set, fire, in various forms, was the only means of lighting available. Candles, the finest of which were made from beeswax, were the best form of lighting available since they provided a reliable light with little smoke. Good wax was expensive and so their use was often limited to churches and cathedrals and in wealthy households. Candles were made of congealed animal fats (better known as tallow) and, though cheaper and more available than beeswax candles, produced more smoke and likely smelled of rancid fat. Whatever their content, candles were a relatively common form of lighting and candlesticks frequently appeared in inventories of household items. By the 13th century, there were even some cleverly made small, folding metal candlesticks for use

while traveling. Oil lamps were likely the next most preferred form of lighting. These were often in the form of a small, flattened clay or metal pot with a spout, a design which had been in use since at least biblical times. A wick was placed in the spout and lit. The quality of lamp light and amount of smoke depended upon the quality of oil used: whale oil and other fine oils, such as olive oil, burned bright and clear while oil rendered from the fat of livestock produced as much smoke as light and smelled bad as well. Still, animal fat was more readily available than the other fuels and so was quite common. Besides being used for poor grade candles and lamp oil, animal fat was also used to saturate other materials, such as rushes, to make them more combustible. As mentioned in Chapter I on food, rushes were cheap and readily available since they grew as weeds along the edges of the many marshy areas that were common throughout Europe before organized programs of drainage turned the marshes into land for farming and building. Rushlights were made by taking the pith or core of a single rush and coating it with grease. The fibrous rush pith acted as the wick for this simple and cheap "candle." Whether saturated with fat or not, rushes, dried grasses, and other easily flammable materials were used to make torches, the cheapest form of artificial lighting then available. However, given the relatively large and high flame produced by such lights coupled with the hot ash and sparks they throw off, it seems unlikely that torches were used much for illumination inside buildings because of the high fire risk they presented. They were more suitable for outdoor lighting.

To accommodate artificial lighting, builders often constructed niches or small shelves on the walls where candlesticks or lamps could be placed. Some of the niches were fitted with spikes to hold candles.

While the flat-bottomed oil lamps could be placed in niches or any other horizontal surface, they were frequently depicted suspended by chains from stands on tabletops, attached to walls, or freestanding like modern floor lamps. The stands probably served two purposes: to hold the lamp in a way that maximized the area it illuminated and to keep the lamp and its flame away from direct contact with flammable surfaces such as wooden walls or pieces of furniture. For large spaces with high ceilings, such as in cathedrals, large versions of hanging lamps were used. These were chandeliers in the form of metal frames that held several candles or oil lamps and were suspended from the ceiling by ropes. The ropes were also used to lower the chandelier to the floor so that the lights could be put out, lit, or refilled as needed.

All these forms of lighting involved open flames and the risk of catastrophic accidental fires from domestic fires used for either lighting or heating was a constant problem. Hence, many towns and cities had regulations that required citizens to dowse their lights and carefully bank and cover the fires in their hearths at night. The time for this safety measure was usually marked by the tolling of bells. The Old French term for this practice was *covre feu*, meaning "cover the fire," and was the origin of the modern word "curfew." Even during the Middle Ages, curfew also had the connotation of being a time to halt activities and retire to the safety of one's home. Outdoor lighting was ordinarily limited to the lanterns or fires kept by citizens serving on the nightwatch or by guards employed by the city or its ruler. Thus, most (legitimate) activities halted at sunset or soon after. Many guilds prohibited their members from working after sunset because of difficulty of clearly seeing the work at hand and the consequent risk of producing inferior goods (though these regulations were also likely part of

efforts to limit production to keep up prices and to prevent more industrious craftsmen from gaining too much of an advantage over the other guild members). Public health regulations routinely forbade the sale of foodstuffs at markets after sunset because of risk of spoiled foods being passed off as fit to eat under the cover of the growing darkness.

Interior Decorating

While the survival rate for medieval buildings is low, the interior decoration (furniture, wall paintings, etc.) of these buildings have suffered an even higher casualty rate, leaving us with relatively few pieces from which to reconstruct the color and details of the lives played out within these structures. Bear in mind that most ruins of castles and palaces look so stark and washed out only because they have been stripped and left exposed to the elements and vandals for so long. Just think of what your home or even a mansion of one of today's "rich and famous" would look like if you took the doors, windows, and roof off and let it set for a few centuries. Assuming the home was even still standing after all that time, a person visiting it would have a very difficult time accurately imagining just how warm and comfortable it had once been. Still, the pieces of interior decoration such as those at Chillon in Switzerland (fig. 8) and elsewhere that have survived from the Middle Ages provide a tantalizing glimpse of a world which was neither so drab nor so barbaric as it is often imagined.

PAINTING

Walls inside palaces, castles, cathedrals, churches, and, later, guildhalls and city halls were frequently decorated in some fashion. Even the external walls of buildings were sometimes whitewashed with a mixture of powdered chalk or painted. Records of expenditures for the castles built by Edward I in England during the 13th century include mention of amounts spent on whitewashing the castles after their completion. After whitewashing, castles, already imposing structures, must have seemed even more impressive, gleaming in the sun and perhaps seeming like they had been carved out of some massive, single block of white stone. Internally, the walls may have been whitewashed or painted as well. Again based on records of building expenses, such whitewashing or painting was often over a layer of plaster that smoothed out the wall's surface.

Painting of internal walls frequently involved more than just covering the wall with a single color of paint. Italy is noted for its marvelous frescoes produced during the Middle Ages and early Renaissance but it was not the only country to produce impressive murals. In the 13th century, Henry III and Edward I of England had the walls of rooms in the Palace of Westminster in England decorated with large murals of biblical and historical scenes while some of the wealthy burghers in Zurich, Switzerland, had the walls of their homes painted with floral motifs or scenes depicting seasonal activities traditionally associated with each month of the year. In the 14th century, the walls of the residential chambers in the palace built for the popes in Avignon in the south of France were painted not with inspirational or instructional bible scenes but with scenes of hunting. In contrast, a secular noble in 14th century England had the walls of rooms in his fortified residence decorated with various moral allegories as well as biblical images. And chambers in secular buildings weren't the only places embell-

ished with paintings and murals. Vestiges of painting from the 11th or 12th century in England's York Minster indicate that at least some interior walls had once been plastered, painted, and then further painted over with a network of lines to create the illusion that the wall was made of finely joined blocks of white stone of uniform sizes. Other wall paintings were more ambitious. Churches from the greatest to the smallest, from Italy to Scandinavia and from Spain to England frequently had their walls covered with paintings of scenes from the bible and the lives of the saints (fig. 9). These murals, along with the stained glass windows, sculptures and other decorations inside and outside the churches, were all used as visual aids to help priests illustrate their sermons and better get their points across to their predominantly illiterate parishioners.

Painting wasn't limited to the walls; ceilings and beams were also often painted (fig. 10). In churches or cathedrals, ceilings were sometimes painted a dark blue with large golden stars to make the ceiling look like the heavenly sky. Starry skies were also painted on the ceilings of some secular buildings as well, most notably in the "Star Chamber," a room in which the councilors of the king of England held legal proceedings and which later became a byword for secretive decision-making. In many other instances, the ceilings and ceiling-beams of secular buildings, such as guildhalls, castles, and city halls, were painted with geometric patterns and, when and where appropriate, coats of arms of nobles families associated with the building.

All this painting, especially when it had gold or silver coloring to catch and reflect the light, must have delighted the eyes of the medieval occupants of these buildings and made the structures far more visually interesting and colorful than many of them now seem. Unfortunately, unless the walls and ceilings were periodically

Figure 9. Interior of the Church of St. Peter and St. Paul, Pickering, North Yorkshire, England. Scenes depicting events from the lives of the saints (as shown here) and from the Bible were common in churches throughout medieval Europe. These paintings covered the walls from floor to ceiling and served as visual aids for priests addressing their largely illiterate parishioners (photograph by author).

Figure 10. The Lower Chapel of Sainte-Chapelle, Paris. Built in the mid–13th century, this ornate chapel shows just how dazzling some interior decoration was during the Middle Ages. Especially noteworthy are the ceiling vaults which are painted a dark blue and bedecked with hundreds of small *fleur de lis*, a symbol of the kings of France, painted in gold. More commonly, golden stars were painted on such ceilings to evoke the image of the vaults of heaven (courtesy of Robert G. Calkins).

repainted, the paint gradually flaked away leaving behind only traces. As paintings decayed and faded, later owners or caretakers often simply painted or plastered over them since, as anyone whose tackled a home remodeling job knows, scraping all the old paint off is usually a more time consuming and difficult job than just painting over it. But, thanks to this natural inclination to do things the easy way, the layers of later paint and plaster actually protected some medieval murals from further damaging exposure to light and air and thus inadvertently preserved them for later generations to rediscover. Ironically, this sort of preservation also occurred in some churches where, in the course of the Protestant Reformation, murals were painted over as part of general efforts to purge churches of extraneous decoration. Little did the zealots who obliterated the murals know that they were actually helping to protect these paintings so that they could eventually be appreciated and enjoyed again.

TAPESTRIES AND OTHER FABRIC DECORATIONS

During the Middle Ages, wealthy people used several different types of fabric items to decorate their walls, including tapestries, embroidered work, and painted or plain cloths (fig. 8). These fabric wall coverings brightened and added texture to the walls of large rooms and also likely helped to cut down on drafts in at least some instances. Tapestries are the form of fabric decoration that most commonly comes to mind when envisioning the chambers of a medieval palace or castle. Tapestries were meticulously woven so that their various colored threads formed elaborate and detailed pictures, typically of hunts and other courtly activities or of legendary events or creatures such as unicorns. They were certainly among the greatest achievement of medieval cloth weavers. As with many other specialty goods, tapestries were manufactured in only a few locations, primarily in a handful of workshops in the Loire Valley of France and in Flanders (modern day Belgium) around Brussels. Of the tapestries that have survived, most can be dated back only as far as the 15th century, near the end of the Middle Ages. Only a few appear to be from the 14th century or earlier. While this lack of early tapestries can be attributed to their perishable nature, it also suggests that tapestries may have been exceptionally rare before the 15th century.

One of the most famous fabric wall decorations from the Middle Ages is the Bayeux Tapestry (Bayeux, France). Produced in the late 11th century to commemorate William the Conqueror's victory in England in 1066, the Bayeux Tapestry lays out the story of William's conquest and the events leading up to it scene by scene with captions in Latin, rather like a history lesson done in the style of a comic strip. But the Bayeux Tapestry is not a tapestry. It's actually a huge piece of embroidery work over 200 feet long, entirely stitched by hand on pieces of linen 22 inches wide. This may seem a rather impractical size but it was probably designed to fit the inside of a church, forming sort of a continuous cloth mural or frieze around the top edge of a wall. While the Bayeux Tapestry is a unique survival of embroidered wall hanging, it is very possible that other embroidered wall hangings of vari-

ous shapes and sizes were made in medieval Europe and graced the walls of churches and palaces, especially before the development of the technologies and skills required to produce the magnificent tapestries seen in the 15th century and later.

Painted cloths were large sheets of fabric with scenes painted on them. They were much cheaper to produce and appear more commonly in household inventories of moderately well-off nobility than in those of royal families. As for subject matter, the painted cloths usually included depictions of the same range of activities used in tapestries and wall paintings. In contemporary illustrations of feasting halls, court chambers, and other settings with decorated walls, it is often difficult to tell whether a wall was covered with a mural or a painted cloth because the painted cloths were often shown covering the entire wall from floor to ceiling. However, the cloths were usually shown with a slight scalloping along the top edge where the fabric hung down and draped slightly from the points where it was attached to the wall. Plain cloths, perhaps with a simple repeating design painted on or woven into it, were also used to cover walls.

Regardless of their exact composition, all these wall coverings served to add color to their settings and please the eyes of the residents. These coverings, especially those made of thick wool, also served a practical function in helping to reduce cold drafts from along the walls.

INTERIOR WALLS AND PANELING

Most medieval buildings had internal walls made of wood. Even castles, which had load bearing internal stone walls, had wooden walls to create rooms of various sizes within their stone shells. Churches and cathedrals, whether of stone or of wood, had internal wooden walls in the form of rood screens, large wooden walls that divided the space within the church between those areas to which the public was admitted and those to which only the clergy could enter. Besides serving as a ritual demarcation, the rood screens also served the practical function of breaking up the space within the church, making them less cavernous and drafty. Choir stalls, wooden screens in front of the small chapels that radiated from the outside aisles of cathedrals and larger churches, and other large wooden fixtures served to further break up the space within churches, creating usable spaces on a more human scale. It is the loss of these internal walls, especially in castles, which has probably contributed most to the misperception that many of the rooms in major buildings of the Middle Ages were vast, inhospitable empty spaces, invariably cold and drafty. But this is like looking at a modern office or apartment building before completion when none of the interior walls, room dividers, or cubicles have been installed yet and then concluding that the future occupants will have a huge, airy open space in which to live or work. Instead, we must try to envision medieval buildings in their heyday when all their walls and other fixtures were in place. Then a different image emerges, one in which these buildings were likely quite inviting with all the myriad rooms needed for human activity, from bed chambers, chapels, and reception rooms to storerooms, toilets, and workshops.

Besides being used to create internal walls, wood was also used to panel walls. As with tapestries and other wall coverings, such paneling was used to cover over stone walls to make the rooms more pleasant by making them seem less stark and, by adding an additional layer to the wall, reducing drafts. Accounts of royal expenditures in 13th century England record outlays for importing fir planks from Nor-

way to panel rooms in several of the king's castles. Rather than being left with a natural finish, as we would typically do with wood paneling today, paneling was often painted to create a more luxurious, finished look that was more fitting for the royal bedrooms, great halls, and other important chambers where paneling was typically installed.

FLOOR COVERINGS

Not surprisingly, there was no linoleum or wall-to-wall carpeting in medieval Europe. As mentioned under "Clay" above, the floors on the ground levels of many buildings were just that: ground, pounded earth or clay. Even as late as the 15th century, floors of packed earth and clay were found in at least some rooms in the residences of English nobility, including those of the royal family. In other instances, though, buildings' owners did lay wooden floors over the bare ground floor but routinely left an open space of earth for the hearth. A better but more expensive option was to have the floor paved with stone. Over the top of stone or hard packed clay floors, the wealthy sometimes added a decorative yet functional covering of fired and decorated clay tiles. Moving up from ground level, in upper stories of wooden buildings, carpenters laid planks over the beams to form both the floor of the upper story and the ceiling of the story below. Wooden floors were also commonly used in stone buildings, as well, though many such buildings did have stone floors in at least part of their upper levels supported by sturdy vaulting on the levels below. Those who could afford it sometimes added a layer of tough plaster over their wooden floors.

To make all these hard floors a little more comfortable, as mentioned in Chapter I on food, floors — especially in the dining areas of palaces — were sometimes covered with absorbent mats of woven rushes. These were occasionally sprinkled with pleasant smelling herbs or water scented with flowers and were periodically replaced with fresh mats. Carpets and rugs seem to have been a rarity in northern Europe until at least the late 13th century. An English chronicler recorded that in 1255, Eleanor of Castile, wife of Edward I, caused a stir in London by having carpets placed on some of the floors in the Palace of Westminster. The sober Londoners were stunned to see such expensive cloth placed on the floor to be trod upon. But instead of putting on an ostentatious display of wealth, Queen Eleanor was probably just trying to make the palace seem more like home and so did some redecorating reminiscent of her native Spain, where the nobility, both Christian and Muslim, covered their floors with rugs that likely looked similar to the traditional hand-woven ones often called "Persian" or "Oriental" today.

FURNITURE

Unfortunately, much of the furniture that has survived from the Middle Ages and is now exhibited in museums and cathedral treasuries poorly represents the variety and number of pieces of furniture produced and used during those centuries. While these items — which include chests for storing vestments, bishops' thrones, other pieces of furniture for churches, as well as pieces from noble households, such as thrones and sideboards for holding and displaying silverplate and other tableware — are indisputably fine pieces of craftsmanship, they give us little insight into what furniture was used on a day to day basis in the workshops and homes of medieval people. Those everyday furnishings didn't receive the careful treatment bestowed on what are now museum pieces.

Rather, they were used continuously until they were worn out and beyond repair. Luckily, the illustrated manuscripts of the Middle Ages contain many pictures of domestic life (often in the context of illustrating events in the life of Christ or the lives of the saints) as well as depictions of various trades and daily and seasonal activities in settings ranging from the humble and rustic to the great and sophisticated. Thus, thanks to these marvelous little paintings, we can get a pretty good idea of what furniture was commonly found in rooms of medieval buildings.

Judging from these pictures and the few surviving pieces, medieval furniture such as that seen in figure 11 was rather thick and heavy, built using the same sort of wood-on-wood joinery employed in the construction of wooden buildings, as described above. Still, despite its massiveness and blocky outlines, the joints and decorative carvings found or depicted on many pieces are evidence of careful craftsmanship along with artistic flair.

Beds

Beds in the households of the middle class and wealthy appear to have most often been canopy beds with heavy wooden frames. These bedframes sometimes had large posts at each corner or had solid head- and footboards that reached from the floor to near the ceiling like small walls. In some instances, the frames supporting the canopies appear to have been attached directly to the ceiling and were structurally independent of the bed itself. Some canopy beds of this type were made with headboards but without footboards. Canopies on these beds could cover the entire bed but often only covered the upper half of the bed in a style sometimes called a half-tester (fig. 11). The drapes of the canopies served two functions: In cold weather, they created sort of a cozy "room within a room," protecting the bed's occu-

Figure 11. The Birth of the Virgin Mary. Manuscript illumination from the 15th century. While depicting a biblical event, this illumination sets the birth of the Virgin in the house of a prosperous family in 15th century Europe. While servants prepare a bathtub, St. Anne rests in a well appointed half-tester bed and hands the swaddled infant Mary to a nurse. The floor of the bedchamber appears to be tiled and one wall is painted or tiled as well. The chair and table, though distorted by the artist's attempt at perspective, are finely made pieces. An interior like this one would have been quite familiar to the people who were wealthy enough to afford books such as the one containing this illumination (courtesy of the Walters Art Gallery, Baltimore).

pants from drafts. Year round, the drapes provided privacy. Needing privacy in one's own bedroom may sound odd but bedrooms in the Middle Ages often had many occupants. These other occupants rou-

tinely included the children of the occupants of the bed as well as a servant or two sleeping in smaller beds or pallets on the floor though, unless the occupants of the bed were engaging in intimate activities that required seclusion, small children often slept in the same bed as their parents. This practice appears to have been especially common in middle and lower class households in which there was typically only one bed for the entire family. In these families, as the children grew older, they likely moved to pallets on the floor.

Smaller beds without canopies were probably quite common and were the standard in less well-off households. Regardless of whether a bed was a great canopied one or a smaller open one, there were no box springs back then so the frames were strung with a gridwork of ropes to support the mattress, a design feature that continued in use well into the 19th century. As for the mattresses, the best were stuffed with feathers, which were likely fairly common given that the feathers were a readily obtainable by-product of that widely consumed food: poultry. Mattresses were also stuffed with wool or, for cheapest grades of bedding, with vegetable matter such as straw or tow, which was hemp or flax that had been partially processed but which was still quite rough and fibrous. In the poorer households, these mattresses were used without any frames and placed directly on the floor. Some accounts indicate that sweet smelling herbs were sometimes added to mattress stuffing.

Chairs, Stools, and Benches

Chairs, with arms and backs, appear to have been rare in the Middle Ages. They were seldom depicted except for the thrones of kings, queens, and other rulers but a few also appear in some late medieval illuminations of prosperous bourgeois households. Far more common were stools and benches. Stools were made in a variety of forms, from finely crafted folding ones used as thrones by rulers on the move to simple, three-legged ones that anyone might own. Where seating was needed for more than just one or two people, benches were the most common form of furniture used. Even in depictions of noble feasts, while the most important personage in attendance was usually shown seated on a chair, the diners, regardless of rank were most often shown seated upon long benches. A variation on the bench was the *settle*. This was a bench with a back and sides, sort of a cross between a church pew and a sofa or couch. Illuminations depict settles being used as daybeds but they were also shown as simply a good place to sit and read, do embroidery, or just enjoy the warmth of a fire. For all these pieces, chairs, stools, benches and settles alike, cushions were a common adjunct but they appear to have been separate, removable pillows rather than upholstery affixed to the furniture

Tables

Much as today, tables were used for many different purposes, from food preparation and dining to writing and working on wood and other materials, and so were made in many different shapes and styles. Some were massive, with thick legs and tops; others were made out of a few planks, cut so they locked securely together but could also be disassembled easily for moving; and others were even simpler, made from planks on trestles or sawhorses as described in the section on feasting, so that they could be completely taken apart and stowed out of the way when not needed. More specialized forms of tables also existed. These included writing tables and desks, pieces frequently found in illustrations of scholarly and monastic activities as well as in pictures of the apostles writing the Gospels. These desks and tables had compartments for holding an inkwell (often a small horn filled with ink) and writing implements close at hand. Some were also shown with angled tops that were adjustable to hold the parchment at a comfortable level for the writer.

Sideboards

In wealthier households, most inventories of furniture include one or more sideboards which were also referred to as an *aumbry, dresser,* and *buffet.* Regardless of their exact names, these pieces were typically found in the great hall or other rooms nearby in which guests were formally received. The aumbry, previously mentioned in the section on feasts in Chapter I on food, was a form of sideboard used to store and display cups and other fine serving pieces, usually made of silver. During feasts, the butler or cellarer used the aumbry as a staging area where they mixed flavored wines and refilled wine jugs. The buffet or dresser was originally simply a table in the great hall that was used by servants to hold dishes until they were ready to be served. However, before the end of the Middle Ages, it had become a specialized piece of furniture with display space as well as enclosed storage for tablecloths and other items.

Armoires

Along with the sideboard, another piece of furniture that frequently appears in the inventories of wealthier households was the armoire or wardrobe. Armoires were made in various forms and sizes but they all had one common purpose: to provide an enclosed space for storage. Some armoires were built into rooms like modern closets or cupboards. In stone buildings, these armoires took the form of small niches built into the thick stone walls and then fitted with metal hinges and wooden doors. In wooden structures, built-in armoires were not part of the load-bearing frame of the building but were securely affixed to the building. These built-in wooden armoires resembled the freestanding ones: large rectangular wooden lockers or boxes, fairly tall, with one or more doors. The doors were often fitted with locks which suggests that the items kept within were considered valuable.

The armoire was used in a variety of rooms and often had specialized features, depending upon the items to be stored. For example, armoires for storing clothing sometimes had holes or grills in their doors or sides to allow ventilation while ones for storing food typically did not. Inside, armoires for storing small objects often had pigeonholes while ones for holding larger things just had shelves. Before the end of the Middle Ages, some were made with drawers, perhaps for storing important documents.

Chests

While enclosed beds, chairs, sideboards, and armoires were found only in the residences of the wealthy, chests were a common piece of furniture for the simple reason that everybody needs a place to put their stuff, from everyday clothes and linens to rare and precious treasures. Chests came in all shapes and sizes, from small coffers that a person could cradle in one's arms to huge trunks about nine feet long. Some chests were made from rough boards and looked as much like a hollowed out log as a finished piece of furniture while others were carefully crafted, their panels decorated with fine carvings and painted details. Iron hinges were fairly common and some chests, such as those made for royal treasuries and mints, were made entirely of iron in the form of bands of metal interwoven to form a very heavy and solid strongbox, often with built-in locks, creating an early form of a safe. But wooden chests were far more common and were used in a wide variety of settings to store all sorts of items.

The Buildings of the Middle Ages

Now that we've reviewed the materials, techniques, and items that medieval people used in constructing and furnishing their buildings, let's look at the variety of structures raised during the Middle Ages. While it should be apparent that medieval European society, like any other complex civilization, had to have a large number of different types of buildings to meet its needs, it's all too easy to focus on the castles and cathedrals that have become the most enduring symbols of that age and overlook the commercial, industrial, agricultural, and domestic buildings which were essential to medieval society. Below, we will discuss some of the principal types of buildings, some famous such as castles and others more obscure such as mills and workshops. Since these discussions will be brief, anyone interested in more in-depth and detailed treatments of these buildings should consult the books cited in the bibliography for this chapter.

First, some general comments about medieval buildings. Of all the thousands of structures built in medieval Europe, only a small percentage have been preserved. Wars, fires, and simply the passage of the centuries have all taken their toll. Houses, for example, are among the most under-represented buildings in terms of numbers of survivals from the Middle Ages. But the subsequent destruction and disappearance of most houses and other buildings should not be taken as proof that the quality of the medieval construction was poor. Rather, many houses and other structures have disappeared because:

• If they occupied good locations in towns and cities or even on prosperous farmsteads, they were typically either completely rebuilt after being destroyed (either intentionally as part of urban renewal programs or accidentally by disasters such as fires, bombardment during any one of the numerous wars since the Middle Ages, etc.) or substantially modified and incorporated into later structures. Both complete rebuilding and drastic remodeling were logical options given that, as the centuries passed and the buildings aged and decayed, they gradually needed more and more repair and replacement, until the only sensible decision was just to level the building and start over. Further, changes in the tastes of their occupants and the development of amenities (such as better indoor plumbing, central heating, etc.) also spurred radical or complete reconstruction; or

• If the buildings were abandoned, as was the case in some villages after the Black Death, people scavenging for building materials or simply the lack of proper maintenance soon ensured that the roof and other key elements of the buildings disappeared, leaving them open to the elements and thus subject to rapid decay.

Second, while the discussion below recaps some of major features of the various types of buildings, please bear in mind that there were considerable variations between buildings, even between those of same general type. These differences can be attributed, in part, to the fact that the Middle Ages spanned a thousand years and people's needs and tastes as well as building techniques and technologies changed over this long time span. Further, there were myriad regional differences in building styles across the breadth of Europe. Oftentimes, even within areas that form a single country today, there were distinct architectural differences between towns separated by perhaps only thirty miles.

Some of the reasons for these differences were:

- Local availability of building materials. In some areas, relatively humble buildings such as farmhouses were made of stone rather than wood because good, easy to work stone was locally abundant.

- Differences in climate. For example, steeply pitched roofs were common in northern Europe and in higher altitudes where the accumulation of snow was a potentially dangerous problem whereas gently sloping roofs and even nearly flat roofs were often built in the milder climes of Italy and Spain.

- Different building traditions and influences. Countries bordering the Mediterranean carried on many of the building traditions which they inherited from Greco-Roman civilization but they also often incorporated elements of Middle Eastern and North African styles introduced both by Islamic invaders as well as through commercial contacts with those regions. While many parts of northern Europe had been part of the Roman Empire, these regions had fewer Roman buildings to serve as example and were generally less bound to Roman traditions. Northern Europe's contact with the East was also more attenuated. Thus, while architects and others traveled and brought back ideas about buildings from across Europe and even from the East, Europeans north of the Alps and the Pyrenees developed styles quite different from their southern neighbors.

All of these factors and others, such as personal preferences of persons who paid for the building as well as those of the persons who drew the plans and oversaw the construction, affected what precise forms buildings took and how they were built.

And this was true not just for houses. Churches, castles, shops, each building of a particular type served the same basic function and had the same basic features as any other building of that type but no two were identical. Each had unique features, some major, some minor. This is quite unlike today, when a housing development will have over a hundred homes and each one is built according to one of only four or five basic designs, or when every fast-food restaurant or store that's part of a national or international chain is identical (or nearly so) with every other one within that chain. There was nothing approaching this level of standardization in building during the Middle Ages.

HOUSES

As discussed above, there were many different factors that guided the design and construction of buildings during the Middle Ages and houses, the most common of buildings, assumed a wide variety of forms as local tastes, needs, and availability of building materials dictated. Because of all these variables, it is impossible to accurately summarize all the different forms of houses constructed throughout Europe over the course of the Middle Ages. With that in mind, the following summary attempts only to capture the major common features of medieval houses and some of the more significant developments in domestic architecture.

In the 11th century, a freestanding house, such as a farmhouse or a house in a village, in many parts of Europe was a wooden building with posts sunk directly in the ground or resting on stone pads or a low stone wall. The house was one-story but with a high roof with lofts for sleeping and storage built up in the rafters. Roofs were typically covered in thatch though tiles, slate, or wooden shingles were used if available. The house had a firepit located in the center of the ground floor for heating and cooking with an opening in the ridge of the roof to allow the smoke to escape. The ground level, with a floor of beaten earth or clay, may have been a single room, an open hall; or have been divided into two or three rooms, one of which was sometimes used as a pen for animals. The interior walls of these rooms were made of timber frames filled in with wattle and daub or boards. The exterior walls were made of planks attached vertically to the wooden frame of the house instead of horizontally as in more modern clapboard siding (the type simulated by aluminum and vinyl siding). Such houses had few windows. Any windows they had were open slits in the walls; sometimes covered with waxed or oiled cloth.

Over the centuries, house designs changed gradually. In most of Europe, one of the early changes in farmhouses was to move the animals out into separate buildings rather than housing them under the same roof as their owners, though farmhouses with a room for livestock were still being built and used through the 18th century in some areas. The number of rooms generally remained low. Most families continued to make do with two or three rooms that served all their basic needs: cooking, sleeping, and performing miscellaneous indoor work (commercial or domestic). More prosperous families added additional rooms. Using this additional space, they created separate rooms for workshops and merchandise storage needed for the family trade. Those with social aspirations added a second hall to provide a suitable setting for receiving and entertaining important guests while the original hall was retained, though perhaps in a reduced size, as a more private space for the household's routine domestic use.

As for their appearance, by the 15th century, houses were still usually made of wood but brick and stone were not uncommon, especially where clay or stone suitable for building was in ready supply. The 15th century house was frequently two stories high with several rooms on each floor. Instead of a firepit, it had one or more hearths with chimneys located in various rooms. Walls were still formed by timber frames but with infilling brick as well as wattle and daub or wooden lath. As for windows, from slits they had grown larger and more square and, while less prosperous people continued to make do with cloth, many could afford glass windowpanes.

Townhouses, that is, houses built with their walls adjoining their neighboring houses, were common in medieval towns and cities and became even more common as urban population rates rose over the course of the Middle Ages. Townhouses were built using the same materials as the detached houses described above but, unlike them, townhouses were often multi-storied from the start since the restricted size of their lots required owners to build upwards to provide sufficient square footage for living space. While a few town or city dwellers engaged in farming land nearby, most citizens were involved in some form of trade and so their houses had to provide space for their workshops and sales counters as well as living accommodations. Bedrooms, sitting rooms, and offices were located in the upper stories while the ground floor was used for commercial purposes. In some of these houses, the main ground floor window on the front of the building was constructed with a shutter that swung down to form a sales counter, allowing goods to be sold directly to passers-by. Many of these houses were constructed with sturdy stone cellars that provided additional secure storage space. The kitchen was typically built on the ground floor off the back of the townhouse. Most townhouses had at least small back gardens where chickens and pigs were raised along with kitchen gardens of herbs and vegetables. As mentioned in Chapter IV on cleaning, the back garden was also usually the site of the latrine or outhouse and the cesspit.

CASTLES

Moving on from ordinary houses, let's now look at that uniquely medieval residence at the other end of the social scale, the castle.

Their Purpose

No medieval landscape is imagined as complete without a castle, a massive stone structure with many high towers, a drawbridge or two, a moat, and thick walls topped with battlements. And, certainly, there are many that had all these features and more. Still, most castles built in the Middle Ages were far humbler buildings, with quite a few made entirely of wood, especially during the first half of the Middle Ages. But, regardless of the materials used, all castles served the dual functions of providing a residence for a noble household while also serving as a military stronghold for both defensive and offensive purposes.

As residences, castles typically had one or more suites of comfortable rooms for the use of the noble family who owned the castle and any visiting nobility they were entertaining. These accommodations were essential even though the lord and his household may have resided at any one castle for only a few days or weeks at a time in any given year. While most nobles appear to have had one or more favorite residences, those who were wealthy and powerful enough to own a castle com-

monly had several castles scattered across the land on their various estates and so many lords, ladies and their families led itinerant lives, moving from one castle to another as circumstances required. Thus, while the finest suites at many castles went unoccupied for prolonged periods, maintenance staff had to keep these rooms ready at all of a lord's castles since the staff never knew when politics, war, or some other matter would draw their noble master back to a particular castle.

As a military building, the castle had to be able to withstand any reasonably foreseeable attacks and serve as a base for aggressive military operations. The defensive function of castles is readily apparent in the thick walls, moats, and other features that made a castle difficult to conquer. The offensive capability of the castle rested primarily in the garrison it housed. From the security of the castle, these warriors controlled all the territory within a day's ride of the castle. During war, an invading army might occupy the lands around castles but the campaign was not a success unless the castles were taken as well since they were critical to effective domination of an area. Unconquered castles and their garrisons posed a constant threat to supply and communications lines, especially since castles were usually sited at key geographic locations such as river crossings.

Besides the basic functions of noble residence and fortress, castles also often served as administrative centers. For example, the lord, as a political ruler, dispensed justice to his subjects from the court held at his castle, either personally when he happened to be in the area or through his agents such as his stewards or seneschals. Castles also served as collection points for taxes and other income owed to the lord. These taxes and income were most often paid in kind; that is, in the form of agricultural products grown by the lord's subjects. Some castles did serve as prisons during the Middle Ages, but most often for nobles who had been captured in battle and were awaiting ransom. Such captives were treated as honored guests and lived in suites of rooms appropriate for their rank in society rather than imprisoned and shackled like criminals. For convicted criminals in the Middle Ages, penalties usually included fines, corporal punishment, or death. Imprisonment was not a common punishment. Thus, most criminals were held in castles or other buildings only while awaiting trial and sentencing. So where did the image of castles as places of horror, torture, and other unspeakable acts come from? These images are based in part on the activities of the Inquisition, the Church's crusade against heretics within Christian Europe. Starting in the 13th century, a few castles were used by the agents of the Inquisition as administrative centers and as places to interrogate and to torture confessions out of persons suspected of heresy. Some heretics were even sentenced to life imprisonment in some of these castles. However, it was primarily after the Middle Ages that castles, made obsolete by gunpowder artillery, were turned into prisons on a large scale with their massive stone walls then serving to keep people in rather than out. The religious persecutions, wars, and other disturbances of the 16th and later centuries created a need for such prisons and filled castles across Europe with political and religious dissidents. From Switzerland to Scotland, many unfortunate people came to experience forms of "hospitality" never envisaged by the original builders and inhabitants of these castles. Even the notorious Bastille in Paris wasn't turned into a prison until the 17th century. While the instruments of torture are long gone and modern amenities have been brought in, some medieval castles are still used as prisons, such as in Switzerland where one beautiful hilltop castle serves as the local detention center for juvenile offenders, a far cry from the building's original purpose.

Their Construction

Most castles are thought of as massive stone structures but throughout the Middle Ages castles were often constructed, in whole or in large part, of wood as well. This was especially true during the early Middle Ages, such as in England after the conquest in 1066 when the forces of William the Conqueror quickly built numerous castles throughout the country to secure their positions in a hostile land. Remains of other wooden castles have been found in France and Germany. As mentioned in the section on wood above, these fortifications bore some resemblance to the stockade forts built along the American western frontier in 18th and 19th centuries. But unlike those forts, wooden castles were often part of a larger defensive plan that included earthworks. These earthworks typically included a *motte*, an artificial mound atop which the castle was built, as well as ditches or even moats encircling the entire site to be protected. Many wooden castles were later rebuilt and replaced with stone works but many others were maintained as wooden structures for their entire useful lives and remained in service for generations, sometimes even for several centuries, but were later abandoned and disappeared, leaving only post holes and earthworks behind.

Wood was not a wholly satisfactory material for castles because of its flammability. Stone, besides being fireproof, also had the advantage of being more resistant to battering by projectiles and other weapons. Still, even when castles were built of stone, wooden elements were vital in a fully functioning castle. These features, virtually all of which have long since vanished, included mundane items such as

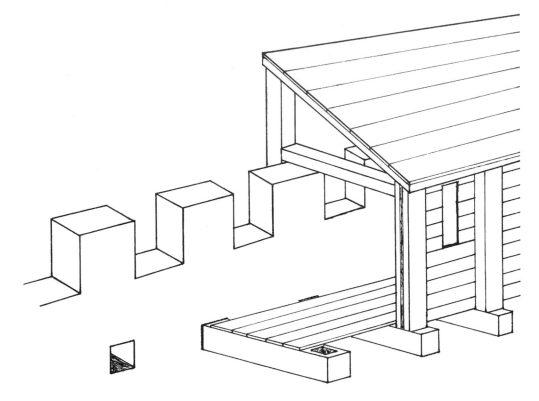

Figure 12. Simplified reconstruction of a section along the top of a castle wall. To enhance their effectiveness, the walls of castles were typically fitted with hoardings. These wooden galleries projected out in front of the wall and were supported by beams that fit through holes in the stone walls. Planks in the floor of the hoardings could be lifted up, allowing the castle's defenders to drop rocks and other missiles on any attackers below. Archers stationed in the hoardings had a broad field of fire for harassing attackers as well. While hoardings provided a means for an active and aggressive defense of a castle, they were vulnerable to bombardment by catapults and other siege engines and they were flammable. Thus, their roofs were sometimes made of slate or tile or were covered with damp animal hides or other nonflammable materials (drawing by author).

doors, internal walls, floors, and roof beams but also important defensive features such as:

- Hoardings (fig. 12), the covered wooden galleries that projected out from the top of the walls and allowed defenders to drop projectiles down on attackers;

- Thick, solid shutters that were suspended between the merlons (the large stone uprights placed at close intervals along the top of the wall) and hinged so that the bottom edge of the shutter could be swung out, creating a narrow, sheltered opening through which castle's defenders could drop things or fire on attackers below;

- Gates, drawbridges, and portculli. The portcullis was a thick and heavy but movable grating that was lowered to block an entrance. They were used in combination with gates and drawbridges to hinder direct assaults against the castle's main entrances;

- All the winches and other machinery required to raise and lower or open and close the gates, drawbridges, and portculli.

Thus, while stone castles become more common over time, wooden elements always remained important.

Early stone castles were little more than fortified houses but soon developed into squarish structures three to four stories high. Often called *keeps* today, these buildings were typically called *donjons* in medieval France and England. Gradually, the term donjon came to mean only part of such a building, specifically the large, vaulted cellars at the lowest level beneath the building. These cellars were originally used for storerooms because of their very secure position within the castle. These storerooms often held supplies of food that were vital to sustaining the castle during a siege. More rarely, as in the case of S'Gravesteen Castle in Belgium and possibly Chillon Castle in Switzerland, the cellar chambers served as underground stables. While an underground stable may not seem practical, space within castle walls was very limited and so castle-builders sometimes constructed such extraordinary features to ensure that all the castle's needs were met within the space allowed. Only much later did the word *donjon* evolve into *dungeon* and take on its modern meaning as a subterranean prison.

Initially, the stone donjon or keep was often incorporated into existing defenses of earthworks and wooden palisades, but the keep frequently became the centerpiece of complex and massive stone fortifications. The rich and powerful gradually replaced their wooden palisades with curtain walls, so-called by later historians because they seemed to stretch like curtains between series of towers. Stone towers placed at intervals along the curtain walls provided strong points in which defenders could rally if the walls were breached. These towers, because they projected out in front of the walls, also provided defenders armed with bows and other missile weapons a clear field of fire at any attackers along the base of the wall. At the height of the Middle Ages, great castles were built with deep, defensive ditches or moats and several concentric rings of stone walls reinforced with towers that required attackers to fight their way through several layers of defense to achieve victory.

The time required for raising castles varied tremendously. Some castles, such as those that occupied locations inhabited since at least Roman times, evolved gradually over the centuries, with intermittent building or remodeling campaigns that lasted decades. In other instances, such as at Château-Galliard in France built at the direction of Richard I (the Lion-hearted) of England in the 1190s, massive castles were raised on virgin sites in only three years. Even in an age when construction was done by hand and the power for any machinery came from men or animals, the urgency of the project and, most importantly, the amount of funds readily available to pay for labor and materials were critical factors in setting the pace of completion.

CASTLES AND CATHEDRALS: SOME COMMON ELEMENTS

Despite their very different forms and purposes, medieval castles and cathedrals shared some common ground. Both were the result of massive building programs that required careful planning and great expenditures of capital and labor. Thus, there were some similarities in how they were built.

Funding and the Pace of Construction

Castles and cathedrals shared a common problem, one which plagues major

building projects even today: funding (or the lack of it) and its direct relation to the rate of construction. Then as now, an adequate and steady flow of money to pay for materials and workers' wages was essential. If the money stopped coming in, construction stopped. Funding problems delayed the completion of some castles but, in several notable instances, such as Château-Galliard, the urgent need for defenses combined with the power wielded by the ruler who ordered the construction guaranteed a completed castle in a reasonable amount of time, though the result was sometimes a castle that was scaled down considerably from the original plans in order to meet fiscal and time constraints. For ensuring completion of their projects, the two most important powers that nobles possessed were the powers to raise funds through taxation and to compel the unskilled and skilled laborers (sometimes numbering in thousands, as in the 13th century castle building campaigns of Edward I of England) to leave their homes and go work on the project. But such intensive castle-building campaigns were exceptional. Most proceeded at the far more leisurely pace that lower funding levels permitted.

The need for cathedrals never had quite the same degree of urgency, even in cases where cathedrals were being rebuilt to replace earlier edifices destroyed by fires or other disasters. And most religious authorities, though their powers and influence were often substantial, seldom had powers as great as a king for raising money or for forcing workers to appear at the job site. Thus, construction of a cathedral was usually preceded by an intensive and sometimes lengthy fundraising campaign headed by the local bishop in which prominent citizens were encouraged to outdo each other in generously giving to a project that would create one of the ultimate symbols of medieval civic pride: a huge cathedral. (Interestingly, modern U.S. cities seem to have continued this tradition in a secular vein in their ceaseless rounds of building larger, more expensive sports venues.) Typically, the initial campaigns raised sufficient funds to make a good start but nowhere near enough to complete the building so construction often dragged on for several decades, marked by long stops and then flurries of intense activity as new building funds were raised and then quickly expended.

Architects

Another aspect of construction in which castles and cathedrals shared more common ground was in the employment of internationally renowned architects. One example was Master James of St. George. He was from Savoy, a country whose lands now lie in modern Switzerland, France, and Italy. In the 13th century, Master James designed and supervised the construction of castles for the count of Savoy until he was hired away by Edward I of England to oversee Edward's ambitious castle building program in recently conquered Wales. Similarly, architects were brought in all the way from Italy to design and supervise the building of the great churches of 15th century Moscow.

Opposite: Figure 13. Interior of the Church of La Madeleine, Vézelay, France. Built in the first half of the 12th century, this church displays many of the elements of Romanesque architecture, including the thick, heavy columns and the round-headed arches. This church was once fitted with tie beams like those shown in figure 7. When these beams were removed, external buttresses had to be added to maintain the structural integrity of the building (courtesy of Robert G. Calkins).

These well-traveled architects, while incorporating some local stylistic elements in the buildings under their supervision, fostered an international exchange of styles and ideas for buildings. The local craftsmen supervised by these international masters learned some of these styles and ideas over the course of the project while the completed building itself provided an enduring example which later architects came from near and far to study. Of course, the transfer of information was always a two-way street. The architects also learned something of the various local styles and techniques during their stays and took that knowledge on with them to their next job. Thus, because of these itinerant professionals, common influences can be seen in many medieval buildings, whether in France, Austria, or England.

Demand for these experts was great, so great that as early as the 13th century, authorities contracting for the construction sometimes included clauses that restricted the architect from accepting other work or traveling out of the area before the building was completed. Some contracts even required the architect to hand over the templates for the stone work when the job was completed (presumably to keep the designs from being replicated for some other building). However, by the 15th century, architects were also obtaining clauses that guaranteed them the right to exercise their own artistic judgment, free of interference from the building's patron, in designing and executing plans.

CATHEDRALS AND CHURCHES

What's the difference between a cathedral and a church? Both are places of Christian worship, so what is that sets them apart from each other? A cathedral is usually much larger than an ordinary church but that isn't the real difference. A cathedral is the site of a *cathedra*, the official chair or throne of a bishop in the Christian Church. Just as is still true in the Roman Catholic and Episcopalian Churches, the medieval Christian bishop was a high ranking Church official in charge of a diocese, which is a geographical area composed of several parishes. Since each parish had its own church, there were many churches within a diocese but there was only one cathedral since there was only one bishop for each diocese.

Besides being a place of worship, a cathedral was part of a complex of buildings that formed an administrative center for the diocese. In addition to the cathedral, this complex included residences for the bishop and the members of his staff or court and buildings for their offices, depositories for their documents, treasuries, and other facilities needed for transacting and recording Church business. Monasteries were a common adjunct to cathedrals as well, though there were many instances in which friction developed between bishops and the monks since, under the Church hierarchy, the monks and their abbot answered to officials within their monastic orders and not to the local bishops. Another feature found at many cathedrals was the cathedral school. These schools were founded

Opposite: Figure 14. **Interior of the Minster of St. John, Beverley, Humberside, England. This view down the north aisle of Beverley Minster reveals three characteristics of the Gothic style of architecture: pointed arches, vaulting created by the intersection of these arches, and the tall and slender columns supporting the arches and vaulting. This part of the minster was built in the first half of the 14th century (photograph by author).**

to train young men in the basic skills needed for a career in the Church, such as reading and writing Latin, the international language used by the Church and by scholars in the Middle Ages. However, almost from their inception, many of these schools also admitted the sons of those families who could afford to pay tuition.

Cathedrals were usually located in major cities which well suited their role as "capital" of their dioceses. In part because of their location in key cities, cathedrals were often the setting for important secular political events such as coronations, state funerals, and other ceremonies. These occasions gave the nobility an opportunity to remind their subjects of the source of their divine right to rule by displaying their close connections with the Church. But these events also gave the bishop, as the representative of God and the Pope, an opportunity to remind the nobility of the obligations which they owed the Church in exchange for legitimizing their rule.

While the Church relied on the donations of the faithful to build and maintain cathedrals and churches and support their staffs, most cathedrals and some churches also helped to generate revenue for their communities by obtaining the relics of saints and incorporating chapels or shrines dedicated to these saints into their buildings. If a saint was popular and had many miracles attributed to his or her relics, a shrine to that saint often attracted hundreds, if not thousands, of pilgrims every year. These pilgrims usually made donations to the church or cathedral that housed the shrine and they also pumped money into the local economy in the form of payments for lodging, meals, and other necessities as well as for souvenirs, which typically took the form of small metal pins or badges depicting the saint or a symbol closely associated with the saint, to show that they had actually been there.

Cathedrals and churches also served as a meeting place for the local community. Town meetings and other gatherings such as guild meetings were sometimes held in cathedrals and churches because these buildings had the largest enclosed and covered spaces available. While using church spaces for secular meetings might seem inappropriate, the meetings were held only in the large open space in which the congregation stood during services. This space was separated from the rest of the church by the rood screen which, as mentioned in the section on interior walls above, was the large wooden wall that separated the public area of the cathedral or church from areas accessible only to the clergy, such as the sanctuary where the sacraments were stored. Besides, given that these churches and cathedrals would have never been built without the contributions made by the guild members and other citizens, it seems only fair that they were able

Opposite: Figure 15. York Minster, York, North Yorkshire, England. The other important characteristic of the Gothic style was the use of flying buttresses. The Romanesque style relied on heavy arches and thick walls to safely carry the weight of the building, but walls in Gothic buildings were much thinner and were frequently pierced with wide openings for windows, as can be seen here. To compensate for these weaker walls, builders invented flying buttresses, the large, arched stone spans shown here. Located below the upper roof-line, these buttresses carried much of the weight of the uppermost level of the minster's stone work along with the tremendous weight of its roof timbers and the wood and lead that sheathed its roof. The flying buttresses transferred the force of the bulk of this weight off the walls immediately below and out onto large, reinforced columns located at intervals along the outer wall below (photograph by author).

to use the space, too. Further, this usage also shows that the people truly thought of the cathedrals and churches as integral part of their community.

Styles of Cathedrals and Churches — Romanesque and Gothic

In the first half of the Middle Ages, the predominant building style for all stone buildings, including churches and cathedrals, was Romanesque. While there were regional variations, this style was characterized by very rounded arches and vaults as well as thick walls and pillars (fig. 13). Many Romanesque buildings appear rather squat and heavy, unlike the more airy, classical Roman architecture which the builders sought to imitate, though the fine decorative work on many surviving Romanesque buildings as well as the solidity of their overall construction show the excellent craftsmanship of early medieval builders. And further, a few builders did achieve a beauty and lightness in construction that met or exceeded their Roman predecessors, such at the church of La Madeleine at Vézelay, France. Another notable example of such an achievement is the *campanile* or bell tower of the great church in Pisa. This building, more commonly known as the "Leaning Tower of Pisa," looks like a building from the Renaissance but it was actually designed and its construction begun in the 1170s.

In the late 12th century, a new architectural style appeared in France and England. This style, called *Gothic*, spread throughout Europe and continued in use in various forms through the 15th century into the early 16th. It was so popular that most of the cathedrals now standing in northern Europe are, either all or in large part, Gothic in style. The Gothic style was characterized by tall and slender pillars, pointed arches, flying buttresses, and graceful vaulting as shown in figures 14 and 15. But why was it called "Gothic"? The Goths were one of the barbarian peoples who swept across western Europe during the centuries that culminated in and followed the final collapse of the Roman Empire and they had absolutely nothing to do with an architectural style that began to appear in Europe some five centuries or more after their heyday. Rather, the term "Gothic" was coined by an Italian architect in the 16th century. Italians and many others during the Renaissance viewed the classical Greco-Roman style as the epitome of architecture and held this other architectural style, which had originated and flourished in northern Europe, in such disdain that they disparaged it as being so barbaric as to be "Gothic." The term stuck and, while there was some Gothic architecture in Italy, the Italians during both the Middle Ages and Renaissance devoted themselves primarily to the classical ideals of architecture.

SYNAGOGUES

Unlike Christian places of worship, few medieval synagogues have survived to the present. During the Middle Ages, there were far fewer synagogues than churches built in Europe though synagogues could be found in most major cities. However, the persecution suffered by the Jewish people throughout Europe at various times over the course of the Middle Ages resulted in the destruction of these synagogues or their conversion for use as churches or other purposes after the local Jewish population had been expelled. In some instances, synagogues appear to have been built in private homes, like chapels, perhaps to help keep a lower profile and draw less attention to their religious observances. Such hidden synagogues were essential in many parts of Europe where, when forced to choose between conversion to Christianity, expulsion, or execution, some Jewish people who did not flee the country feigned conversion and continued practicing their faith in secret.

MONASTERIES

Monasteries, also called abbeys, were places for Christians who wanted to leave the material world and devote themselves to serving God through a life of contemplation and service. Churches were an integral part of every abbey and the monks ordinarily attended seven services over the course of each day, including one service at midnight and another a few hours later. However, monastic communities needed more than a church to exist. There were dormitories to house the monks; storehouses, kitchens, bakeries, and breweries to provide them food and drink; infirmaries to treat their illnesses; libraries for their books; scriptoriums in which they copied books to create additional texts; chapter houses for their administrative meetings; schools to train the novices; guesthouses for important visitors; water supplies, latrines and baths for their sanitation needs; and enclosed walkways connecting many of these facilities. Thus, rather than being a single building, a monastery or abbey was actually a complex of buildings that formed a largely self-contained community.

Besides the core complex, monasteries also often possessed fields, pastures, and other resources which had been donated to them. These resources, usually referred to as granges, were donated to the monastery so that the monks could work the land and generate the goods and income needed for their survival. However, the actual working of the granges was often carried out by rent-paying tenants or by lay brothers who were servants of the monastery and subject to monastic rules but who were uneducated. Houses for the lay brothers as well as mills were constructed on the granges. Some monasteries possessed such vast estates that they also built enormous barns to store the grain and hay they grew, plus that collected as tithes from their tenants. These tithe barns were huge. Surviving specimens measure more than 130 feet in length, and unlike common barns, they were built with high, buttressed walls made of stone instead of wood.

Public Works

Medieval societies needed many of the same public works which societies still need today: water and sanitation systems, health care facilities, and transportation infrastructure, including roads, bridges, and harbors. They also needed a few works that haven't been considered necessary for centuries, such as city walls. Since public water and sanitation systems and facilities are covered in the Chapter IV on cleaning and health care facilities are addressed under healing in Chapter VII, let's look at the transportation infrastructure of the Middle Ages next and then that mainstay of medieval civil defense: the city wall.

ROADS

There is little information available on the construction and maintenance of roads in the Middle Ages. These activities were rarely depicted in illuminations or other pictures made at that time nor was it a topic much mentioned in literature of the day. Most of the information we have is derived from the physical evidence of roads and trails known to have been used in the Middle Ages and from sparse documentary evidence found in accounts of expenditures for public works.

Road building generally stopped with the collapse of the Roman Empire since there was no longer a powerful central authority to plan and direct such projects and raise the taxes to pay for them. Fortunately, the Roman roads were well built and some of them continued to be used through the Middle Ages. In fact, some are still in use today but they now form the foundation layers of later roads and highways that were built directly over them. However, most of Europe's roads in the Middle Ages were unpaved tracks that became virtually impassable whenever heavy rains turned them to mud, especially after the mud was churned up by the wheels of wagons and carts and the hooves of the animals that pulled them. Cobbling roads with stone lessened this problem but, because of all the work involved, it was usually done only for major streets within towns and cities. In some instances, where trees were close at hand, roads were paved with logs to make them more level and mud-free.

In some areas, the work of maintaining roads was part of feudal obligations owed by subjects to their local lord. As the Middle Ages progressed, this service was usually commuted to cash payments which the lord and other local authorities used to pay workers to perform these tasks. Funding for road maintenance and other public works was obtained through taxes on trade, particularly on goods imported into the area. In a way, this tax was a form of users' fee since the goods had been transported over the roads which the taxes maintained. However, some of this money went to the local lord or civic authorities to defray the expense they incurred in policing the roads and keeping them safe for travelers, especially merchants. Failure to keep roads safe had potentially dire con-

sequences. In some instances, merchants boycotted trade fairs held in towns and cities that had failed to provide adequate security on the roads within their jurisdictions. Merchants were especially likely to impose such boycotts if they suspected the local authorities of collaborating with the robbers. These boycotts, which could cripple a town's or city's economy, were often lifted only after the authorities had reimbursed the merchants for their stolen goods.

HARBORS

Harbors were vital to trade in the Middle Ages. Shipping by river or sea was the preferred means of transport since travel by road was so often arduous and risky. Water travel was certainly not without its dangers too but when shipping heavy or bulky items or large quantities of any merchandise, the costs of hiring a wagon, draft animals, and drivers was frequently prohibitive when compared to the cheaper transportation available by ship or river barge. Thus, despite the risks of traveling by water, shipping by boat was the primary means used to transport many goods over long distances. Towns and cities located on navigable rivers and large lakes, as well as those that bordered directly on seas and oceans, depended upon their harbors for their prosperity. Wealth from shipping came in many forms, from hiring out boats and reselling the goods they brought in to collecting customs duties and other taxes on the imported merchandise. But obtaining this wealth was not without costs. As excavations in London and other European port cities have revealed, the medieval residents of these cities often went to great expense to build and maintain the infrastructure needed for a successful port. Besides docks and piers, medieval port facilities routinely included

Figure 16. Ponte Vecchio, Florence. This bridge lined with buildings is one of the last surviving examples of a once common feature of several major European towns and cities. Bridges were a desirable location for houses because waste could easily be disposed of in the river below. By providing a steady flow of potential customers, the high volume of traffic passing over such bridges also made them a good location for shops (courtesy of Robert G. Calkins).

pilings and embankments of wood and stone that stabilized the shoreside and permitted the construction of buildings such as wharves, customhouses, and warehouses right up to the water's edge. While this construction was usually spread out over several generations, it is still an impressive achievement considering that the only tools used were powered entirely by the muscles of men and draft animals.

BRIDGES

Bridge building did not halt with the fall of Rome. While the pace of bridge construction was likely much slower than in the days of the Roman Empire and many of the Roman bridges did fall into disrepair, the thriving regional and international commerce of the Middle Ages required bridges to span rivers that otherwise would have slowed or blocked the flow of trade. Besides commerce, bridges were also needed for defense, not just to allow armies easy passage but also to block navigation on some rivers. For example, the Viking raids on France in the 9th and 10th centuries led the French kings to build bridges across the Seine and other major rivers to prevent the Vikings from continually using these rivers as highways for inland raiding, raiding which had often reached Paris and other cities and towns in northern and central France. Bridges appear to have been used to similar effect in England, where the children's song "London Bridge Is Falling Down" may have originated from an account of one attempt by Vikings to tear down a bridge blocking their passage up the Thames during an assault on the city of London. Bridges were also occasionally fortified like miniature castles to guard important river crossings.

Most of the early medieval bridges were made of wood as were many of the Roman bridges before them. However, construction of bridges out of stone never completely disappeared and was certainly becoming common again as early as the 12th century. At Avignon, France, a stone bridge was built across the Rhone River. With twenty-two arches, the bridge spanned a total distance of well over half a mile. This bridge has another interesting feature: a chapel built on one of the bridge's massive piers. But this feature is not unique. Other bridges in France, England, and elsewhere in Europe also had chapels, some dedicated, appropriately, to St. Christopher, patron saint of travelers.

Chapels weren't the only structure built on bridges. In cities, bridges were often the sites of shops and houses. The Ponte Vecchio in Florence, Italy (fig. 16), is a rare surviving example of such a bridge. This may seem odd, but space inside city walls was often quite limited and bridges provided level building lots with the added benefit of a built-in sewer system (i.e. the river flowing below). As discussed in the chapter on cleaning, public toilets were also occasionally built on bridges in cities for this same reason.

Another interesting aspect of medieval bridge building was that their construction was sometimes underwritten by independent groups of citizens rather than by local governments. These groups appeared in the form of guilds, fraternities, and even religious societies and were found most commonly in France and England. Though the membership usually included businessmen whose trade likely profited from the improved transportation infrastructure, these groups appear to have

been motivated by a genuine desire to improve their society.

City Walls

Walled cities are sometimes confused with castles. While cities enclosed with walls often had castles as well, the walls were a civil defense system for the city rather than a fortified residence for just one household. Most early medieval city walls were composed of wooden palisades built along the top of earthworks that surrounded the city with a protective ditch and high bank of earth. However, in Arles, France, the residents reused the old Roman amphitheater and built homes inside it, turning it into a miniature city with high stone walls. Apart from this extraordinary example, most stone city walls were first constructed in the 13th century, beginning a tradition that lasted well into the 17th century. The walls and their gates helped restrict traffic in and out of the city and the gates were shut at night to defend the city from attack but also in an attempt to prevent thieves and other criminals from freely coming and going under cover of darkness. The walls also helped create and reinforce divisions between the citizens that resided within the walled centers of cities and those later arrivals who built outside the walls as the cities grew and overflowed their original limits. Ultimately, most city walls were demolished in the 19th century to allow for expansion and urban renewal.

Agricultural Buildings

Agriculture was every bit as vital in the lives of medieval people as it is to people today: without it, people starve. But unlike today, a far greater proportion of medieval society was directly involved in raising and producing foodstuffs, from grains and fruits to cheese and meats. Yet despite the widespread and varied agriculture practiced in the Middle Ages, few agricultural buildings have survived. Thus, much of the following discussion is drawn from the many illuminations that include pastoral scenes.

BARNS

While some farmhouses did have accommodations for livestock under the same roof as their owners, medieval farmers built barns for sheltering livestock and for storing produce and plows and other farm equipment. They also built the barns as a place to winnow grain. By thoughtful placement of the barn's doors, the farmers created controlled drafts through the barn that helped blow away the chaff, aiding the winnowing process.

Many barns were wooden buildings that were constructed using the same timber-frame techniques used for houses, but others, mostly those built on great monastic farms, were built of stone. Most barns were large structures, quite long and much bigger than average houses though some specialized ones were built for storing hay. These barns were constructed with open sides with just the roof to keep the hay from being soaked by rain or snow. When needed, these structures were also used to shelter farm equipment and animals. Barns constructed in this manner for these same purposes are still being used today in many countries around the world.

DOVECOTES AND PIGEONHOLES

Dovecotes were a common feature on many noble manors and monastic estates.

They were usually built in the form of a small tower, up to twenty feet in height. The pigeons entered the dovecote through openings located in gables or cupolas on the tower's roof or under its eaves. The tower was hollow with hundreds of little compartments built into the inside face of its walls. These nesting compartments were all placed high enough off the ground to be safe from rodents and other predators but still within easy reach of a man on a ladder. Each nesting compartment housed a pair of pigeons. The birds raised in the dovecotes provided a steady supply of tender young pigeon (squab) for the table. Interestingly, some castles were constructed with built-in dovecotes in the form of rows of little niches, or pigeonholes, on the inside surface of a curtain wall, high up near the top of the wall. The high position again insured that these nesting boxes were undisturbed except when being raided to supply the kitchen.

Industrial Facilities

Medieval Europe was predominantly an agricultural society but the manufacturing and processing of goods were vital to the survival and advancement of medieval society. Although these industries operated on a very small scale when judged by modern standards, they produced an amazing variety of items, from flour and cloth to bricks and metal tools. While the Industrial Revolution that began in the 18th century led to an increase in mechanization and, in turn, productivity which was unimaginable in previous centuries, many basic manufacturing processes were quite well developed before the end of the Middle Ages. Let's examine some of these early industrial sites.

MILLS

Just as today, when a steel "mill" and a flour "mill" are two very different complexes that house equipment for performing two completely different processes, the term "mill" encompassed a broad range of industrial structures in the Middle Ages.

Grain Mills

Mills for grinding grains into flour were the most common type of mills but there were several different forms, including animal- or man-powered mills, windmills, and watermills. The simplest mills were round stone dishes topped with a small millstone turned by hand with a crank, but this was suitable only for very small-scale production of flour. Larger scale man- and animal-powered mills had pairs of ring-shaped millstones, three feet or more in diameter. The lower stone was stationary while the upper stone rotated around a shaft that pivoted on a post mounted in the center of the lower stone. Grain was crushed between the two stones by harnessing a man or draft animal to the shaft and having him or it walk continuously around the mill stones, pushing or pulling the shaft, causing the upper stone to turn and roll along the endless circuit of the lower millstone.

With the development of windmills in the 12th century, medieval millers were able to substitute wind-power for muscle-power. These early windmills were constructed with the entire building mounted on a single massive pivot or post; thus these mills are sometimes called "post mills." Such a mill can be seen in the background of figure 26. When the mill was working, the entire building was turned to keep the blades of the windmill pointed into the wind. It wasn't until the 15th century that Europeans developed windmills in which only the top part of the mill, the part that held just the blade assembly, rotated to keep the blade in the wind.

Unlike windmills, watermills had been developed and used by the Romans and, wherever there were suitable locations on rivers, medieval Europeans continued and expanded the use of watermills for grinding grain. Watermills took a variety of shapes. Some were in the familiar form of a building built alongside a swiftly running river or a specially constructed millrace whose fast flowing water turned a large waterwheel on one side of the building. But some medieval watermills were built as part of bridges with the mill building forming part of a bridge pier while others were built as boats or barges and moored out in the main channels of rivers. These floating mills looked something like the paddle-wheeled riverboats of the 19th century. In manuscript illustrations, they are shown both as single units and as large rafts with several mills lashed side by side. Grain was ferried out to these mills in small boats or carried out on gangplanks to those mills moored close to shore. Regardless of their form, all these watermills harnessed the force of the flowing water and converted it into a rotary motion which, through the use of systems of gears, powered the millstones.

In some areas, wind- or watermills were owned by the local lord. The lord's tenants were required to use his mill and pay him for that privilege. However, commercial mills did exist in many areas and became more common over the course of time. For example, by as early as the 12th century, watermills in the Garonne Valley in France were built and owned by groups of investors, not by the local nobility. These investors were typically wealthy townspeople who had accumulated capital through other trades and then invested the money by buying partial ownership of one or more mills as part a larger group of investors. These groups issued shares that were bought and sold within the region in an early form of stock market. The Garonne mills and their stock outlasted the Middle Ages. The mills were repeatedly rebuilt and modernized until they were finally absorbed into the French national electric company in this century. The evolution of these mills also raises another point: the force harnessed and channeled by watermills could be used for purposes other than grinding grain, as we will now see.

Other Mills

Besides turning millstones, medieval people discovered that watermills could be used in a number of other industrial applications by changing the gearing driven by the spinning waterwheel. With these improvements, medieval millwrights were able to convert the purely rotary motion of the wheel into an elliptical or oval-shaped motion which, in turn, was used to create a reciprocating, up and down motion for powering woodcutting saws. The millwrights also used these modified watermills to drive triphammers. Triphammers were massive hammers which the elliptical gears steadily and rhythmically raised and dropped with great force. Triphammers proved to be great laborsaving devices and found many applications. As mentioned in the chapter on armor, triphammers were used in iron forges for beating large, heated chunks of metal into thinner plates and sheets.

In cloth production, triphammers were used to pound the stiff, raw fibers of flax and soften them so that they could be spun into pliable thread for weaving into linen. Triphammer mills were used in the production of woolen fabrics as well, though for a different purpose. After weaving, woolen cloth was subjected to "fulling," a process that made the cloth thicker or "fuller" by causing the wool fibers to stick or "felt" together. An important part of this process was subjecting the woolen cloth to pressure, pressure which was laboriously provided by the might of human muscle until the introduction of triphammers made such pounding easy. While waterpower replaced manpower in some stages of cloth production, the weaving of the cloth remained a manual task, though the looms themselves grew increasingly more mechanized and complex. Still, commercial weaving continued to be performed primarily in private homes rather than in large, organized workshops.

Finally, as early as the mid–12th century, water-powered triphammers were used in Italy and Spain to tightly compress and bond fabric and other organic fibers together to make paper, a process which gradually spread northward, reaching France in the 13th century and England and the Low Countries in the 14th. Thus, well before the Industrial Revolution and even before the Renaissance, Europeans had already developed many pieces of powerful and complex machinery for manufacturing. While these medieval machines may not have been as revolutionary as the steam engine or electric light bulb, they do show the falsity of the common depiction of the Middle Ages as an age of technological stagnation.

MINES

Long before the Middle Ages, people in Europe had learned to excavate minerals from the earth and process them in forges and kilns to turn them into useful items. This tradition continued through the Middle Ages. Lead, clay, copper, iron, silver, tin, salt, and many other valuable minerals were extracted by medieval miners using a variety of techniques. One of the most basic methods was simply small scale open pit mining in which miners located veins of ore at or just barely below the earth's surface and then just dug shallow pits or trenches that followed the vein. Another method which had been used as far back as the Stone Age was to locate a vein of ore and sink a mine shaft straight down into it, casting the spoil (the earth and rocks removed from the shaft) up and out around the mouth of the shaft. The circular mounds resulting from this method looked somewhat like giant ant mounds. Also with this method, the shaft was often flared out below ground, creating a bell shaped chamber as the miners sought to reach all the ore they could within the immediate area of the shaft. Since the sides of many of these mine shafts were poorly shored up at best, the miners limited the radius of their digging as they increased their risk of cave-in the further they dug away from the central shaft. Lastly, medieval miners did construct mine shafts as we commonly envision them to today: tunnels dug into the ground with timbers shoring the sides and roof of the tunnels. But the costs of excavating such large mines and shoring them up were quite high so this technique was used only for mining when the value and amount of the yield offset the costs. Thus, it was used primarily for obtaining precious metals and salt. However, even when deep mining operations were profitable, there was another obstacle: water seeping into the mine and flooding it, though this problem was somewhat abated before the end of the Middle Ages with the development of more powerful and efficient pumps which permitted deeper mining and the reopening of old mines that had flooded.

FORGES

The centerpiece of any forge or smithy was the hearth where metals were melted and shaped but a fully functioning forge had several different work areas, sometimes located in several different buildings, for carrying out all the steps required to transform raw ore into a usable material. Watermills were a common feature of many large-scale forges because, after the miners had extracted the raw ore, most mineral-bearing ores came out of the mines as large chunks of rock which had to be crushed to further expose the desired minerals inside. While this backbreaking task was initially performed by muscular men with sledgehammers, water-powered triphammers like those described in the section on "Other Mills" above were ideally suited to such work and eventually freed men from this chore. After crushing, the metal-bearing ores were heated in a furnace or hearth to release the metal from the surrounding rock. Generating and sustaining the high temperatures needed for this process was difficult but by the early 14th century the furnaces were aided by watermill-driven bellows that provided strong, steady jets of air to feed oxygen to the fires. The molten metal was collected from the furnaces and usually cast into ingots, ready for further processing. Or, in the case of iron, this process produced *blooms*, masses of iron mixed with impurities. (The high melting point of iron precluded the production of molten iron until late in the Middle Ages. This point is addressed further in Chapter VI in the sections on producing plate armor.) The processing of raw ore into ingots or blooms was typically performed at furnaces and forges located at or near the mines. One motive for locating the furnaces and forges as close to the mines as possible was to minimize the expense and difficulty of transporting the heavy, bulky ore. In an age before locomotives, these were no small concerns.

Once the metal was formed into an ingot or bloom, it was sold to the craftsmen: the ironsmiths, armorers, silversmiths, leadsmiths, or coppersmiths, who would work it into finished consumer products in their forges and workshops. Their forges were typically not as large as the ore processing forges but still contained many of the same elements (hearths, triphammers, etc.) for reheating the blooms or ingots and forging or casting the metal. While some metal products such as nails were finished at the forge, many others, from hinges and armor to fine jewelry, required additional forming and processing to produce a finished product. This processing took place in workshops which were sometimes a part of the forge facilities or in separate mills and workshops.

BRICKYARDS, TILEYARDS, AND POTTERY WORKS

The fate of the workshops that provided the cookware for countless households and the brick and tiles for so many medieval buildings provides an interesting contrast between modern and medieval manufacturing. Modern industrial buildings for processing raw materials are typically large, fixed structures, such as massive factories, refineries, and mills, but many medieval industries were far more mobile and ephemeral. Many of these workshops were temporary structures, built for a particular construction job or at the site of a good deposit of clay and then abandoned later when the job was over or the deposit petered out. Another more obvious contrast with modern industries was the size of manufacturing facilities. For example, vast numbers of pottery jugs, cookware, roof and flooring tiles, and bricks were produced during the Middle Ages but rather than being made in a few large production centers, as they would be today, these products were made in hundreds, possibly thousands, of pottery works, tile-

yards, and brickyards scattered across Europe. These workshops were composed of an open area or "yard" in which the fuel and raw clay were stored and in which partially completed products were placed to dry before the final baking; workshops or sheds in which the clay was worked, molded, and formed into shape; and the kilns in which the products were baked. Using techniques that date back to antiquity, the artisans in these workshops created items from plain but useful bricks and roofing tiles to decorative flooring tiles and functional yet graceful pots and pitchers.

Monuments

Unlike the Romans who frequently erected pillars, arches, and other memorials to commemorate great events, medieval Europeans seldom built monuments per se. Important victories and other achievements were more often celebrated by a donation to the Church and having a window, a chapel, or even an entire monastery built and dedicated as a memorial. However, there were a few instances in which monuments were built. For example, in the 1290s, Edward I of England (the king so wrongly vilified in the movie *Braveheart*) had twelve ornate markers built, one at each of the sites that the funeral procession for his wife, Eleanor of Castile, stopped on its progress from Lincolnshire in central England down to London. These markers, known as "Eleanor Crosses," were delicate, beautiful pieces of architecture and sculpture and the few that survive still bear witness to Edward's love and devotion to his wife of some 35 years. One of these crosses, long called "Charing Cross," has since become a London landmark and given its name to a train station, a subway station, and a major street.

CLOTHING AND DRESSING

Introduction

Despite their frequent depictions in the movies, medieval peasants did not wear burlap rags accented with shreds of gauzy material nor did the nobility constantly wear shimmering silks. Much of the modern image of the clothing worn by the working classes of medieval society is based on the assumption that the Church, the nobility, and a few merchants held all the wealth of medieval society and that everyone else was poor and therefore could afford only rags to wear. This assumption is false. While the Church and the nobility controlled large amounts of the wealth of medieval society, they certainly did not possess all of it. Though there was a broad gulf between the wealth owned by a common person and that owned by a bishop or a duke, most common people were far from destitute by contemporary standards. Except in times of crisis, such as famine or war, they could afford adequate housing and food and they could afford to clothe themselves as well. Admittedly, these clothes were made from much cheaper grades of cloth than those used in the clothing of the nobility but they were still good clothes. As for the clothing of the nobility, some nobles certainly could afford and did wear the latest fashions made from the finest materials but not all were wealthy enough to do so. Further, even for the wealthiest, the very fine silk brocades and furs which they were shown wearing for important occasions were not for everyday use when plainer clothes sufficed. Thus, the peasants wore coarse but sturdy linen and woolen fabrics, merchants and craftsmen wore clothing made of better grades of wool and linen, and the nobility, though they did wear silken clothes if they could afford it, more commonly wore clothing made from the finer, softer grades of linen and wool.

Sources of Information About Medieval Clothing

How people dressed is a fascinating subject but it is also one of the most

93

difficult areas of medieval living to accurately and fully reconstruct. Before the advent of nearly indestructible, non-biodegradable, man-made fibers, cloth was very perishable. Wool, cotton, silk, linen; all are very vulnerable to destruction by rot or by insect pests. Further, clothing was made to be worn and was often worn until the garment could no longer be mended and fell apart. Thus, the number of pieces of clothing that have survived from the Middle Ages are extremely few and are mainly limited to religious ceremonial clothing and a handful of other items which were carefully stored and cared for. While they provide some direct evidence of the materials and techniques used in making clothes in the Middle Ages, these surviving pieces of clothing are usually specialized garments that provide little insight into the form and construction of everyday clothing. So, to recreate the clothes and other items of dress used over the course of the Middle Ages, we are left to rely on the few fragments of common clothing and footwear found in excavations of medieval dumping grounds and other sites and the depictions of clothing found in book illustrations, sculptures, wall paintings, and other sources.

One additional point must be noted about the artistic depictions of medieval clothing: while they are a good source of information about medieval clothing, some of them cannot be taken entirely at face value. For example, there are illuminations in which all people, whether they were farmers or courtiers, were depicted as all wearing clothing of similar or nearly identical fashion and quality, typically high quality clothing in the latest fashions. The illustrators were aware that it was inaccurate to portray a farmer tending his fields while wearing the same expensive and sometimes very impractical clothes worn by the nobility but the illustrators likely chose to clothe their subjects in this manner because the customers for their drawings and paintings were the nobility and they presumably wanted to see colorful illustrations of well-dressed people like themselves (or like they wanted to be) and not drab pictures of ordinary people. Thus, such depictions do not provide good information about what common people wore but they do provide excellent evidence about the clothing of the elite. However, there were also illustrators who strove for more accuracy and, in their illuminations, included images of common people going about their everyday activities clad in plain clothing suitable to their rank and occupations.

Fabrics

As mentioned above, common people did not wear rags. The first step in understanding what they and the rest of medieval society actually wore is to see what fabrics were available for them to make their clothing.

WOOL

Sheep were very common farm animals throughout medieval Europe and their wool was one of the most common fibers for cloth in the Middle Ages. Though wool was produced everywhere, some areas, such as England, were more successful in cultivating large numbers of sheep and became noted for the quality and volume of wool they produced and exported. Sheep were common since they can graze and thrive on lands which are ill-suited for other agricultural uses, such as land that is too barren to support cows or too rocky or hilly for cultivation. Further, they are a multipurpose animal. Besides producing new coats or fleeces of wool every year, sheep also provide milk which can be used to make yogurt and cheese. Sheep can also be slaughtered for their meat if they are no longer needed for wool production.

Wool is usually thought of today as a luxury fabric since it is typically more expensive than the synthetic materials which are used to imitate it. Even in the Middle Ages, woolen cloth was often quite expensive but medieval spinners and weavers did not produce just one type of woolen cloth. Just like fabric manufacturers today, by using different grades of wool or by lengthening or shortening various steps in manufacturing process, they produced many different types of cloth from raw wool, ranging from cheap, poorly finished fabrics to thick, luxurious cloths.

The Production of Wool Cloth

After the fleece was sheared off the sheep, the raw wool was washed, combed, and carded to separate the softer, finer fibers from the stiffer, coarser ones and to align the fibers to prepare them for spinning. The separated fibers were then spun, turning the soft, fine fibers into fine, pliable yarns while the coarser fibers yielded yarns that were rougher and stiffer. (Though "yarn" is commonly thought of only as the thick strands used in knitting, "yarn" actually means any strand of spun fiber, from fine thread up to heavy knitting yarn.) Weavers then wove the yarn into cloth and the finer yarns produced softer cloths while the rougher yarns became scratchy, coarse cloth.

Both spinning and weaving evolved over the course of the Middle Ages. For much of the period, women spun loose fibers into yarn by gradually adding and twisting the fibers into an ever-growing strand of yarn. Women usually stood when spinning and the yarn was attached to a weighted spindle called a drop spindle. In addition to keeping tension on the yarn, the spindle was spun (hence its name) to help twist the fibers together to produce sturdy yarn. By the early 14th century, spinning wheels had begun to replace drop spindles but it would take several more centuries for them to develop into the foot-treadle powered models which we commonly think of as "spinning wheels."

Weaving also became increasingly mechanized. Early looms were simply large, square wooden frames. These frames were mounted vertically and the yarns that formed the warp of the cloth were hung straight down from the top of the loom. The warp yarns were kept taut by tying weights to their bottom ends and later by attaching them to a roller or bar mounted across the bottom of the loom. The weaver stood or sat in front of the loom and wove the yarns that formed the weft of the fabric back and forth and in and out through the warp yarns. By the 14th century, more complex looms were developed. These looms were still wooden frames but, instead of being simple vertical squares, they were now massive machines in which the cloth was suspended horizontally. Weavers seated at these machines used a combination of hand and foot controls to weave the yarns into cloth.

Processing didn't stop at this point. After weaving, all woolen cloth was fulled. Fulling involved both chemical and mechanical processes that changed the texture and finish of the cloth. First, to remove dirt and grease, the cloth was soaked in a solution containing either human urine or a type of clay called fuller's earth. It may seem odd that the fabric was so greasy but wool is rich in lanolin, a thick, fatty substance which is still used today in lotions for softening and moisturizing skin. When available, soaps, most notably those produced in Italy and Spain, were also used in this cleaning process. After soaking, the cloth was rinsed and, while still damp, beaten either by hand or by massive wooden hammers powered by watermills, a method which became increasingly more common over the course of the Middle Ages. The beating caused the wool fibers to stick together, or *felt*. Though this process shrank the wool fabric, it made the cloth denser and stronger. The beating also softened the cloth.

After fulling, the damp cloth was stretched over wooden frames and held in place with iron hooks. Besides providing a place for the cloth to air out and dry, these sturdy frames and stout hooks also helped prevent the fabric shrinking too much as it dried. The frames and hooks were called tenterframes and tenterhooks and provided the English language with the expression of "being on tenterhooks," meaning to be kept in a state of suspense like fabric tautly stretched out on a tenterframe. Controlling the amount of shrinkage was critical to the final quality of the cloth. If the cloth was stretched too tightly during the drying process, it yielded greater square footage of material than cloth which had been stretched less, but it was also thinner, weaker, and less durable than cloth which been dried under the correct degree of tension. The temptation to maximize profits by over-stretching wool fabric was sufficiently common that many cloth-producing towns and cities enacted regulations requiring that all stretching and drying had to be done in public and was subject to inspection. While these quality control measures protected consumers from unscrupulous cloth manufacturers, they also protected the good reputations of the towns and cities involved in the cloth trade. This was more than just a matter of civic pride. Maintaining or failing to maintain a reputation for producing only good quality cloth had significant economic consequences: a city that failed to take action against makers of shoddy cloth could expect consumers to become suspicious of the quality of all

cloth from that city and begin buying cloth from other cities with better reputations.

After drying, the cloth was then groomed with the spiny head of a plant called a teasel. This grooming raised the nap of the fabric and created a soft finish on the cloth's surface.

The thoroughness and care taken during each step of the process determined the final quality of the wool fabric. Generally, thicker cloth was more expensive than thinner cloth and cloth with a fine, soft finish was more expensive than stiff or coarse cloth. Color was also an important factor in determining the price of wool fabric, a point which is discussed further below.

Besides being woven into cloth, wool was also processed into fabric by felting alone. To make felt cloth, carded wool is subjected to heat, moisture, and pressure to cause the individual fibers to stick and lock together, forming a dense fabric. The resulting wool felt was used primarily to make hats.

LINEN

The flax plant was cultivated throughout much of Europe and its fibrous stems provided the durable fibers for linen cloth. Linen is thought of today as being a fairly soft and pliable fabric but much of the linen produced in the Middle Ages was rather stiff, rough, and very durable. In fact, linen was such a sturdy cloth that it was used to make sails. Linen was often relatively coarse because softening the tough flax fibers required prolonged soaking of the flax stems followed by repeated pounding or beating, sort of like tenderizing a steak. Initially, the pounding was done entirely by hand. Though the development of water-driven hammermills, similar to those used in fulling woolen cloth, relieved people of performing this back-breaking labor, the additional time and expense required to fully soften the flax fibers meant that linen woven from the softest fibers was expensive and available only to those wealthy enough to afford it. Thus, most people had to make do with linen made from flax that had been softened just enough to render it fit to be spun into yarn and woven into cloth. However, the linen did soften with wear and washing so that, like a comfortable old pair of blue jeans, even coarse linen clothing gradually became quite comfortable. Besides being spun into thread, loose flax fibers, called *tow*, were also used for padding in clothing and for stuffing mattresses.

HEMP

Like flax, hemp was also cultivated for its fibrous stems. These stems were processed like those of flax but the toughness and coarseness of the hemp fiber led to it being more often used for making ropes and heavy canvases rather than fabric for clothing. Also like flax, unspun hemp fibers were used for padding and stuffing.

COTTON

For most of the Middle Ages, cotton clothing was scarce outside of the lands of the Mediterranean basin. The areas with the best climatic conditions for growing cotton were in southernmost Spain and Italy, along the north coast of Africa, and in Egypt and the Middle East. Most of these lands were controlled by various Muslim rulers for all or part of the Middle Ages. While trade between predominantly Christian Europe and these Muslim lands generally flourished, the expense of importing cotton kept it from being widely used in medieval Europe outside of those countries in which cotton was grown or which had direct trade links with the Muslim lands. However, by the mid– to late 14th century, cotton supplies had increased and cloth made from cotton and from blends of cotton and wool or linen began appearing in northern Europe.

SILK

Apart from certain furs and cloth containing threads of gold, silks were the most expensive fabrics in medieval Europe. As with cotton, silk was not native to Europe and the expense of transporting it from Asia added greatly to its cost. Silk was imported both as finished cloth and as threads of spun silk which were woven into cloth or made into other items such as scarves and hairnets in European workshops. Some silk came from as far away as China and was shipped over the famous but often perilous "Silk Road" across the breadth of the Asian continent. The Silk Road was an ancient trade route and had supplied the Romans with silk for centuries before the Middle Ages. Silk was also amongst the luxury goods that were shipped by boat from India to the Muslim ports on the Red Sea and Persian Gulf and then taken by caravans to ports on the Mediterranean to sell to the European merchants. But not all silk traveled such great distances. By the start of the Middle Ages, silk worms and the mulberry trees that provided their sustenance were already being cultivated in the Middle East and were successfully introduced in Sicily and southern Spain during the Middle Ages.

Weavers in Europe and the Muslim lands transformed silk into a variety of fabrics. These weavers produced cloth with elaborate, multicolored designs woven into the fabric itself as well as rich brocades with raised patterns of varying textures.

These silk fabrics ranged from very light and sheer to thick and heavy but all were soft, lustrous, and quite expensive. Only the nobility and the wealthiest of merchants and craftsmen could afford to have clothes made from this most comfortable of fabrics.

Leather

As today, leather in the Middle Ages was obtained primarily from cows but leather made from goats and other animals was not uncommon. Processing raw hides into leather required soaking the hides in caustic solutions of lime or of stale urine to soften the leather and remove any hair that remained on the hide after the initial scraping. The next step was soaking the hide in other chemical solutions usually derived from tree bark and then drying it. This step, called tanning, toughened the leather and made it more resistant to decay. The pungency of these processes and the toxicity of the solutions used meant that most towns and cities tried to keep leather works far away from central, highly populated areas.

After processing, leather manufacturers sold the leather to a number of other craftsmen who turned the leather into a variety of consumer goods including shoes, belts, bags, and gloves. Leather was also used in some specialized items of apparel such as fireproof aprons for smiths and, after boiling, treatment with wax or oil, and shaping, as cuir boulli armor for warriors (See Chapter VI on fighting). There is little or no evidence of other items of leather clothing apart from these items. The leather jerkin, which was some sort of vest or sleeveless jacket and is sometimes associated with medieval peasants or farmers, does not appear to have been created until the Renaissance.

Furs

Medieval people in cold or temperate climates desired furs because of their practical value in providing good insulation in cold weather and because they were soft and comfortable to the touch. Yet, even at this time, many types of furs were also status symbols. Among the most desirable furs was ermine, a large member of the weasel family, which has a brown coat of fur in the summer that changes to pure white with a black-tipped tail for winter. It was when the ermine was in this white or winter phase that trappers ranged as far north as the Arctic Circle in areas that are now a part of Russia and Finland to find and catch the ermine. The rarity of white fur coupled with the density and softness of its pelt made ermine a very popular fur with European nobility. Besides ermine, martens (also called sables), Siberian squirrels (whose grey and white fur was called *vair*), and other animals that produced desirable, dense, soft coats of fur were hunted and trapped across the extreme north of the Eurasian land mass and formed an important source of revenue for medieval Russia. The trade network that brought these furs to European and Asian markets was as far-reaching and complex as those which supplied spices and silks.

Since furs were worn for their warmth and softness, they were typically used as a lining, with the hair-side turned out toward the wearer and the hide-side of the fur stitched against the fabric of the garment. Using fur this practically meant that status-conscious nobles, although they were kept comfortable and warm, couldn't impress others with their fine furs since the furs were hidden inside the cloaks or robes they wore. To remedy this problem, tailors edged the outside of the hems, collars, and cuffs of these garments with fur to let everyone know that there was fine fur on the inside as well. Over the centuries since the Middle Ages, as fashions and tastes changed and the quality of heating in buildings improved, fur linings disappeared while coats with fur trim or with furs turned to the outside came into style.

For most of the population, showing off fur was far less a concern. Except for those merchants wealthy enough to afford exotic imported furs, people outside the nobility made do with locally available furs such as rabbit, cat, badger, and the now nearly extinct European beaver. While these furs made warm linings for winter clothing, they were coarser or thinner furs and were not considered status symbols. Besides being used for clothing, these common, cheaper furs also found their way into the beds of medieval Europeans in the form of fur-lined blankets. While this may seem an odd use of fur, quilted blankets and down-filled comforters or duvets did not appear until the 18th century.

Hair

Though the practice was officially banned in many areas, hair from goats and other animals was sometimes added to wool to help stretch it, sort of a "Wool Helper." Animal hair was also collected and woven into yarns used to produce fabric for a very specialized garment called a hair shirt. Hair shirts were worn by people as a form of self-punishment, denying themselves earthly comfort to atone for their sins or to otherwise win favor with God. To try to understand what a hair shirt felt like, think of the last time you got your hair cut and some of those short, bristly hair trimmings fell down into your shirt or blouse collar and onto your neck. Rather itchy, wasn't it? Now imagine that you are wearing a snug, long-sleeved shirt over your bare skin and that the shirt is lined entirely with bristly hair trimmings. That's what a hair shirt felt like, so it should come as no surprise that they were worn as a form of penance or for self-mortification.

Other Materials

In addition to fabrics, other materials were often needed to produce finished items of clothing. Medieval clothing-makers used wood, horn, bone, and ivory for many items which are made of plastic and other man-made materials today. Artisans shaped these materials into buttons and toggles for fastening clothes. Besides producing buttons and toggles, woodcarvers also made wooden soles for shoes and pattens, a wooden-soled sandal that attached to ordinary shoes or boots (fig. 21). Medieval craftsmen also cast metal buttons as well as forging and casting buckles, clasps, and pins. They often used iron but they also made these items from brass, bronze, and tin. If a customer was willing to pay for such luxury, goldsmiths and silversmiths were always willing to fashion fasteners from gold or silver or other more common metals plated with these precious metals. Goldsmiths also made the very fine gold wire used to produce "cloth of gold," a fabric in which fibers, usually silk, were interwoven with gold threads to create the premier luxury fabric of the Middle Ages.

Dyes

Today clothing manufacturers can produce clothing in any color, from subdued earth tones to the brightest of neons, simply and cheaply by using dyes synthesized and compounded from a bewildering number of chemicals. In the Middle Ages, the shades of clothing were far more limited because clothing manufacturers had to rely exclusively on organic dyes derived from various plants, animals, and minerals. Further, the rarity of some of the raw ingredients or the expense involved in obtaining them meant that some colors or particular shades of color were quite costly to produce, thus limiting their availability. Still, despite these limitations, medieval clothiers were able to offer their customers some choice in colors.

Medieval dyers obtained red dye from several different sources. Most commonly, they extracted it from the roots of the madder plant. Madder was cultivated in many parts of Europe and therefore relatively cheap. Depending upon the concentration of the dye and the length of time the cloth was soaked in the dye, the shades of cloth dyed in madder ranged from peach through tan and brick red to brown. A more expensive and less common dye for turning cloth a deep, dark red was made from the heartwood of brazilwood trees grown in Africa. (Brazilwood trees are native to both Africa and South America. The country of Brazil did not give its name to this tree. Rather, European explorers named the country "Brazil" because of the numerous brazilwood trees they found there.) For bright, rich reds, dyers had to turn to the animal kingdom. To produce the vivid scarlets and vermillions worn by the both the secular and religious elite, dyers collected and processed a type of insect. Called kermes, these insects are scale insects, small parasites that attach themselves to the stems of plants and branches of trees and suck their sap. They look like little blisters, bumps, or scales. Kermes live only on one type of oak tree which grows around the Mediterranean. Adult kermes are tan colored but their eggs are the source of the dye. Workers collected the female kermes with their attached eggs just before the eggs hatched

(unlike some other insects, the kermes lays its eggs and then remains on top of them until they hatch). The workers then ran the kermes through a sieve to separate and collect the tiny eggs, rinsing them with vinegar and crushing them to create a paste. This paste was one of the most expensive dye ingredients of the Middle Ages.

For yellow, medieval dyers used the plant weld. Except for golden yellow, yellow was not a very popular color in the Middle Ages, but the yellow dye was important since combining it with other dyes produced many other colors. Adding weld to madder-based red dyes yielded varying shades of orange, including a golden color. Green shades were produced by adding weld to blue dyes or by overdying blue cloth with the yellow dye to tint it green.

Blue dyes were derived from two plants: woad, which was native to Europe and indigo, which originated in India. Woad was cultivated in many parts of Europe but France led in its production. The French called it *pastel* and exported it to cloth manufacturing centers in England and elsewhere in Europe. Besides producing blue and green (when added to yellow dyes) colored cloths, dyers used these blue dyes to color clothing purple or black by adding increasing amounts of madder-based red dye. Purple was also available from other sources. The Greeks and Romans had extracted purple dye from murex, a salt water snail, but this source appears to have largely fallen into disuse during the Middle Ages, at least outside the Byzantine Empire. Instead, medieval Europeans used various types of lichens to produce fine purple dyes. Black was produced by other means as well. The Danes, who were noted in the first half of the Middle Ages for their preference for black clothing, appear to have used iron oxides to dye clothing black, though iron was also used more generally in dyeing as a mordant (a substance that is combined with the dye to make it insoluble and bind the color to the fabric).

Dyers extracted brown dyes from tree bark and nuts. Tanners used similar extracts to tan leather.

So, with these dyes at hand, medieval dyers produced a broad spectrum of colors for clothing. Admittedly, the expense of obtaining some of the ingredients for the dyes meant that not everyone could afford every color but the wide availability of madder and woad and the varying shades which dyers produced from them meant that even common people in the Middle Ages dressed themselves in colors more varied and interesting than just drab browns and greys.

Clothing

As mentioned before, cloth is highly perishable and little clothing has survived from the Middle Ages. Further, any patterns for items of clothing have also long since disappeared. This lack of direct evidence makes it very difficult, if not impossible, to reconstruct individual items of medieval clothing with a high degree of accuracy. However, by examining the few remaining intact examples of medieval clothing as well as the scraps that archeologists have uncovered, we can gain some insights into the techniques used by medieval clothiers. Then, by viewing the pictorial evidence found in manuscripts and other sources and applying these insights, we can arrive at some reasonable, if not 100% accurate, reconstructions of common items of medieval clothing.

Before moving on to various items of clothing, there is one more point that needs to be made about clothing manufacturing and how clothes were acquired in the Middle Ages. Today, clothing is typically mass-produced in factories or, for those that can afford it, custom-made by professional tailors. Clothing factories did not exist in the Middle Ages but professional tailors did. While they were likely employed by a broader range of clientele than their modern counterparts, custom tailors were still too expensive for much of medieval society. Since cheap, mass produced clothing was not available back then, what did most people wear? They often wore clothing which they or someone in their family had made. While making clothes at home for one's own family is seldom practiced today, it was commonplace before the Industrial Revolution and even afterwards, well into the 19th century, on the American frontier and anywhere else "store bought" clothing was scarce. Additionally, there was a thriving trade in used clothing. Buying and wearing second-hand clothing appears to have been commonplace and did not carry the social stigma which it sometimes does today. Part of this trade involved clothing that had been pawned. Items of clothing, especially women's dresses, appear listed in inventories of pawned items and even ostensibly well-off bourgeois and noble ladies are known to have pawned some of their clothing as security for or to pay off other debts.

Besides buying new or used clothes or making one's own clothes, people acquired clothing by other means as well. Some individuals received clothing as part of their pay. Contracts for the employment of architects and other professionals often stipulated that the employer (typically a noble, a high ranking clergyman, or a municipal government) had to provide a suit of clothing or fabric sufficient for producing such a suit as part of that employee's yearly salary. These contracts also frequently specified the exact quality and even the color of the material to be used. Servants in noble households were similarly given new clothing once a year by their employers. In some of these households, this clothing, as well as clothing wore by the noble family themselves, incorporated certain colors and symbols that were usually taken from the family's coat of arms. This practice, called *livery*, clearly identified members of the household and served as an outward sign of their loyalty and affiliation. The nobility also bought themselves new outfits at least once a year or so and, through their almoners, traditionally donated their used items of clothing to the poor. However, in actual practice, there was probably an annual "hand-me-down" cycle in these households in which the servants, starting with the highest ranking or most favored, received their choices of the cast off clothing, a practice that continued in many upper-class European households up through the 19th century. Thus, the almoner distributed the servants' used clothing to the poor instead of worn or threadbare noble finery.

Some clothing was inherited. Clothing in the Middle Ages was so durable and valuable that dying persons routinely passed it down to family members and others under the terms of their wills. The recipients were free to use the clothes themselves or sell them. Clothing was also the subject of another type of legal arrangement which was sort of a combination of a will and an annuity contract. Under such an arrangement, an elderly person or couple agreed to turn over all their property and other assets to another person, such as one of their children, or to a religious institution, such as a monastery, in exchange for shelter and specific rations of food and clothing for the remainder of their lives.

Underwear

Underwear is one of the hardest items of clothing to reconstruct. None has survived and there weren't any equivalents to catalogs from Victoria's Secret or even Sears in the Middle Ages either so all that's left is a few illustrations and some scattered written references to underclothes.

Undershorts

Outer clothing was routinely portrayed in illustrations but people were seldom shown wearing just their underwear. Certainly, people were sometimes shown in the nude such as when bathing or swimming or, in some instances, bathing with just a towel wrapped around the person's head but with no other clothing. People in bed were frequently depicted as being naked except for varying forms of nightcaps. But images of people in states of partial dress remain rare. This lack of evidence combined with a few pictures in which people have their outer garments pulled up to their laps, revealing that that they were wearing "knee-high" hose or stockings and nothing more from the waist down, has led to speculation that medieval Europeans routinely wore little if any underwear similar to modern briefs or panties. For women, there is certainly little evidence that they wore such garments in the Middle Ages. Medieval illustrations show women working in fields and vineyards but their long dresses completely conceal any undergarments they may have worn. Even when shown engaged in hot or messy work, such as harvesting grain or stomping grapes to make wine, women were depicted as being more modest than men. In these settings, the women were shown with the hems of their dresses tucked up into their belts but their dresses were so long and voluminous that they still covered their legs down to the knees (fig. 17). The only underclothing occasionally revealed in these illustrations is the chemise, the long underdress, rather like a full-length slip which appears to have been usually made of bleached linen. While this pictorial evidence is ambiguous at best, some documents from the Middle Ages indicate that women did not wear underpants. For example, in the rules for orders of monks and nuns, every aspect of the cloistered life was covered in painstaking detail, from the big issues, including the vows of chastity and poverty, to mundane matters, such as the number and items of clothing each monk or nun was allotted. While shirts, stockings or hose, and breeches appeared on the lists of clothing for monks, chemises and stockings were the only underclothes routinely included in comparable lists for nuns. Thus, it appears that women did not wear underpants until the late 16th or early 17th century when written references to women wearing "drawers" begin to appear.

As for men, there is some evidence that they wore some form of undershorts. In many illustrations of men performing rigorous manual labor, men were routinely shown with the hems of their tunics tucked up in their belts to keep these flowing garments from interfering with their work. Unlike women's dresses, the hemlines on these tunics were often fairly short so more of the man's leg was exposed when the tunic was

Figure 17. Female agricultural worker. This woman is preparing to harvest grain. She has gathered and tucked some of her tunic's skirt up under her belt so that she can work more easily. Like many other farm workers (see figure 18), she is not wearing any shoes. This was a common practice, especially in the warmer months. She is also not wearing any hose. Her lack of hose can be attributed to a desire to keep cool while performing the hot, strenuous work of cutting grain, but pictorial and documentary evidence also suggests that medieval women wore hose less frequently than men. Despite its practicality for protecting the legs and keeping them warm, hose appears to have been worn mostly by men in the Middle Ages. Breeches were an exclusively male item of clothing. Thus, this woman's only item of underwear is an underdress which is cut along the same lines as her tunic. She wears her hair up and covered with a piece of plain cloth. To keep cooler and to keep the late summer sun out of her eyes, she wears a broad-brimmed straw hat. Tunics or dresses like the one this women is wearing were common women's apparel for most of the Middle Ages (J. Walker).

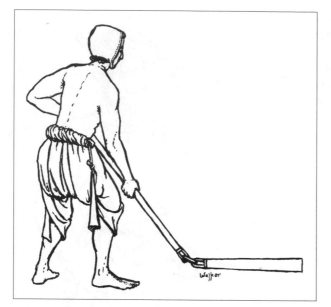

Figure 18. Male agricultural worker in the mid–13th century. This man is using a flail to thresh grain. Beating the grain to separate it from the husks was hard, hot work so he has stripped off his tunic and is working in his breeches. Instead of short breeches, he is wearing breeches with long, loose fitting legs. To stay cooler and to keep the cuffs of his breeches out of the way, he has pulled the legs up and tied them to his waistband. Given that he is performing such strenuous and sweaty work, it may appear odd that he is wearing a snug-fitting coif on his head. However, the threshing kicked up a lot of dust, and it was performed inside a barn with only limited ventilation. Thus, he is likely wearing the coif to keep the dust and chaff out of his hair (J. Walker).

their long undershirts and breeches and, in some cases, just their breeches. Since some undershirts are shown reaching down to the knee, it's also possible that some may have worn only their undershirts without any breeches.

In some of these images, the men's breeches look like strips of cloth swaddled around the man to form a sort of loincloth. More commonly, other breeches appear to have had drawstrings. Up through the early 14th century, these shorts reached down to around the knee or just below it and had fairly loose fitting legs which could be tied up to laces on the waistband to keep them out the way when performing physically demanding work. Having long, loose fitting legs on undershorts may not seem practical but these shorts were intended to be worn exposed when necessary, thus length was required to maintain a suitable degree of modesty. Further, the undershorts were likely made of linen and may have been made so long so that, in cold weather when woolen hose or stockings were worn, the wearer's leg had an additional soft, comfortable layer of insulation under the wool.

By the 15th century, men's breeches had grown much smaller. The hose or stocking worn over the shorts now covered more of the man from the waist down, leaving much less flesh to be covered. More importantly, perhaps, over the course of the 14th century, men's fashions had become much more form fitting (fig. 19). Illustrated editions of Boccaccio's *Decameron* from the 15th century and other contemporary sources show that men's

pulled up. And what was often revealed was a pair of white linen undershorts above the top edge of his stockings. These undershorts were typically referred to as breeches or braies and covered the same part of a man's anatomy as most modern undershorts. Similar brief glimpses of men's underwear are common in scenes of harvesting and threshing grain (fig. 18). Reaping grain and beating it to separate the wheat from the chaff was hard, vigorous work and was performed at the end of summer and beginning of fall during some of the warmest months of the year. Thus, the laborers often stripped down to only

Figure 19: Young aristocrats relaxing. Decorative border of a 15th century French manuscript. These three couples sit in a peaceful garden and are entertaining themselves with games and music. The women are wearing long-sleeved gowns which have long, full trailing skirts. The necks on these gowns are quite wide and open, revealing the upper edges of the women's linen underdresses. Each wears her hair up and completely covered by her *hennin*, a tall conical hat with a diaphanous scarf draped from its peak. The men wear hose and pointed shoes. They also have on *cote-hardies* and doublets. The sleeves of the doublets are visible on the two men who are wearing cote-hardies with split sleeves. Their hats are truncated cones that appear to be almost as tall as their companions' hennins. From left to right, the musical instruments are a rebec, a shawm, a harp, and a lute. The couple in the center is playing tric-trac (backgammon) (courtesy of the Walters Art Gallery, Baltimore).

underwear was also being cut to fit the wearer more closely. This closer fit may have been used to avoid having fabric of the underwear bunch up and spoil the trim lines of the men's new outer clothing (in other words, to prevent embarrassing "visible panty lines"). Instead of reaching the knee, breeches covered to just below the buttocks, similar to modern jockey shorts. These breeches also had a fly in the form of a small flap or pouch that appears to have been secured using the ends of the same drawstring that held the breeches up at waist. Earlier breeches may have had a similar feature but it is not apparent in the illustrations. (Digressing slightly, modern reconstructions of 15th century men's undershorts have proven quite comfortable and practical. Made with plain woven linen rather than stretchy cotton or cotton blends, they provide the comfort of boxer shorts while their closer fit retains the advantages of jockey shorts.)

Undershirts and Chemises

While there was a gender gap in the wearing of undershorts, both men and women wore some form of undershirt. For men in the earlier Middle Ages, the undershirt took the form of a linen undertunic, a T-shaped garment with long sleeves and a long skirt that reached to about the knees. At times, the fashion for men was to wear undertunics which were so long that their lower hems were visible well below the hem of the tunics worn over them. Having such long undershirts might seem impractical but this style was actually well suited to the generously cut tunics favored in most of Europe up through the end of the 13th century. Further, men routinely stripped off their outer tunics when performing physically demanding work and they appear to have often worn undertunics without tunics over them in warmer weather as well as inside in informal settings. This use of the undertunic as sort of a mid- to light-weight casual or work shirt also dictated that its hemline be low enough to maintain the wearer's modesty.

Undertunics had been worn loose, over the breeches and hose, but during the 14th century, men's clothing gradually became more fitted and their outer tunics became shorter. These changes required that undertunics become snugger and more form fitting too. Thus, the undertunic's hemline was raised until the once long and flowing skirt was reduced to a mere shirttail. This shirttail was routinely tucked into the breeches and hose.

As mentioned above, the female equivalent of the undertunic was the chemise and its form does not appear to have changed as much over the course of the Middle Ages. Though women's fashions, like men's, became more closely fitted over the centuries, women's dresses remained long throughout the period and the chemise remained an elongated form of undertunic. Like the undertunic, the chemise was typically a long, loose linen garment, often with long sleeves. Unlike the undertunic which men could wear fully exposed in many settings, it was never considered proper for a woman to appear clad only in a chemise outside the privacy of her own chambers. However, there were some fashions which partially exposed the chemise. These included wearing a dress that was a little shorter than the chemise (a fashion that went out of style before the end of the 11th century), wearing a sleeveless dress that had exaggeratedly large holes cut out for the arms (very stylish in the 14th century but denounced by some contemporary moralists for arousing fleshly desires by providing too tantalizing a view of the wearer's underclothes), and wearing dresses with wide sleeves that allowed glimpses of the long sleeves of the underdress inside them.

Much as the undertunic evolved into the shirt, the chemise also changed over the centuries. It remained a long garment usually made with long sleeves but the fullness of its cut appears to have been decreased over time so that it could be worn under dresses that were increasingly more form fitting. The cloth used to make it was also varied and it was sometimes made of colorful, dyed fabrics instead of plain linen. This appears to have been especially true when the chemise was worn under dresses or other garments that had gaps intended to expose the chemise to view. It also came to be known by other names, such as *kirtle*.

As for support garments, there are a few, isolated references to "corsets" in the wardrobes of noblewomen starting around the middle of the 14th century, but most medieval women relied on the externally visible lacing of their dresses for shaping and support. Besides laces, some of these dresses may have had stays (thin slats of baleen from whales or other firm but flexible materials) to provide shaping like later corsets and girdles. Brassieres were first created around the end of the 19th century and so were unknown in the Middle Ages.

Stockings and Hose

Both men and women wore stockings and hose during the Middle Ages. Throughout the period, women appear to have worn only short stockings that came up to just above the knee. Since there was no elastic or spandex back then, these stockings or short hose were held in place by laces or *garters* around their top edges. This technique of fastening hose lasted through the 18th century. Up through the 13th century, men typically wore longer stockings or hose that reached to the middle or top of the thigh (fig. 20). These stockings were sometimes held up by garters or by bands of cloth wrapped around the outside the stocking. For long stockings that reached the top of the thigh, medieval men commonly used another means of support: tying a lace from the top edge of the stocking to the waistband of their undershorts. However, by the late 14th century, stockings were routinely laced to the lower edge of the man's tunic. (As discussed below, the tunic, or the *gipon* or *doublet* as it was then called, had become

Figure 20: This man wears clothing typical of the 11th century though many of the pieces had existed for centuries before and would remain in use in much the same form for several centuries to follow. He wears a Phrygian cap on his head. His woolen tunic reaches down to his knees with a generously cut skirt. The tunic also has long, fairly close fitting sleeves. Underneath, he wears a linen undertunic cut much like his outer tunic. He also wears linen breeches. His hose are made as two individual legs. Each leg is held up by laces tied to his breeches. His shoes are made with soft leather uppers and slightly thicker and tougher leather for their soles. They are held closed by a lace around the ankle (J. Walker).

much shorter, reaching to just below the waist.) From the late 13th through the early 15th century, men's hose evolved from two independent legs into a single garment with a pair of legs joined together with a codpiece at the front and a gusset filling in the space between the legs at the back. The codpiece was a triangular flap of cloth that covered the crotch and served as the fly.

Laces at its two top corners attached it to the waistband. These fully developed hose completely covered the wearer from the waist down, much like modern pants, and became part of a new style of more closely fitting clothes for men. As part of this style, the hemlines on men's outer clothing rose so that more of the hose was exposed (fig. 19).

There are a couple of other interesting points about the construction of hose or stockings. They were generally of woven rather than knitted fabric. While knitted fabric is usually stretchy and form fitting, two properties which are desirable for stockings, knitting was relatively uncommon in medieval Europe and does not appear to have been used in the manufacture of stockings to any significant degree. Thus, stockings and hose were most often made from woven cloth but with the fabric cut on the bias, that is, with the weave of the cloth running at a 45-degree angle across each piece rather than straight up and down as is normally the case. Cutting the fabric on the bias gave the material a slight elasticity which helped the stocking better fit the leg and its movements. Another interesting feature was the variety of forms that the feet of the hose took. Besides just enclosing the foot like a modern sock, hose were sometimes made with just a strap that ran around under the arch of the foot, leaving the heel and toes exposed. In other examples, hose with complete feet had leather soles stitched on to them as well, somewhat obviating the need to wear shoes, at least indoors.

Fashions

As is true today, the majority of people in the Middle Ages did not wear the most up to date, cutting edge fashions. Most medieval people earned their living by farming or by laboring at a trade. This hard, physical work did not encourage the wearing of fine or impractical clothing any more than it does now. And, much like the present, most people wore practical and relatively plain clothing when performing such work. Many of the items of clothing or their features described below, though very interesting, were worn primarily by members of society's elite. Only the nobility and wealthy merchants and craftsmen had the resources and the motivation to be trendsetters and dress in the latest fashions. Everyone else made do with practical fashions that changed only gradually over the centuries.

Not surprisingly, there were significant differences in fashions and the rate of change of fashion between common workers and the trendsetters in the noble courts. In the smaller towns and out in the countryside, fashions changed at a much slower pace. Partly, this reflects the practicality of the peasants. They didn't need flashy clothes to carry out their jobs nor could they afford such pointless finery. Even in modern times when high fashion designers produce new looks every year, most people content themselves with wearing most of their clothes until they either wear out or become so dated looking as to be unacceptable, like polyester leisure suits in recent times.

Wearing clothes that were basically the same as those worn by your parents, their parents, their grandparents, their great-grandparents, and so on might seem ridiculously archaic now. But, while the fashion conscious will buy in to some of the latest trends, how many people even today can afford and desire to get new wardrobes every time fashions change? Further, when was the last time a truly new piece of clothing was invented? How much has the clothing of the typical working man really changed in the last century and a half? Though the fabrics and some other

superficial matters such as whether the pants have buttons or zippers may have changed, he still wears pants and a shirt made of durable materials which are cut to fit comfortably, not so tight or so loose as to interfere with his movements. And so it was in the Middle Ages as well, but with slightly baggy hose, a comfortable undershirt, and a sensible tunic instead of pants and shirt (fig. 20).

Hose, undershirt, and a practical outer garment was the basic costume shown on laboring men, whether they were carpenters, masons, farmers, or sailors. These men were usually shown wearing other clothing only when performing especially hot or vigorous work such as reaping and threshing grain, crushing grapes for wine, or climbing building scaffolds or ship's rigging. In these situations, they were portrayed as stripping down to their breeches and undertunics or even just to their breeches (fig. 18).

While men's everyday clothes were generally designed to allow the freedom of movement needed for physical labor, women's clothes seem ill-suited for work despite the fact that many women often performed the same back-breaking jobs as men. Yet, for all classes of women, from noble ladies to women who lived and worked on farms, long dresses reaching down to the ankle were the fashion throughout the Middle Ages (fig. 17). Worn over a chemise, the long dresses look like they would have interfered with spinning, tending livestock, and many other of the physically demanding tasks medieval women had to perform. But European women continued to wear similar styles of garments up to the start of the 20th century despite the inconvenience. Still, while this fashion may have been impractical, American pioneer women continued wearing long, fitted dresses even while carrying out all the grueling tasks they had to perform on their homesteads.

One last point before moving on to the individual items of clothing: the rich often distinguished themselves from the less well to do by the quality of their fabrics, finishing details, and accessories. The nobility and other wealthy people did wear certain pieces or styles of clothing that set them apart from the common herd, but these specially distinguishing clothes were usually reserved for important occasions when they felt the need to more visibly display and reinforce their superior status. But for everyday wear for both men and women, the overall cut of the clothing worn by the rich did not differ greatly from those of lower classes. Rather, class distinctions appeared in the types and colors of fabric used and other details. For example, whether a tunic was made of silk or fine, soft linen or wool instead of coarser, cheaper fibers was a status symbol comparable to the modern one of having a shirt or blouse made of silk instead of polyester or a suit made of wool instead of acrylic blend. Even easier to distinguish was the message of wealth conveyed in the coloring of clothes. As mentioned previously, dyes in the Middle Ages were not as uniformly cheap and available as they are today. Thus, wearing a tunic or dress that was a rich, deep scarlet color (a color that could be obtained only from costly dyes) sent a clear signal that the person wearing the tunic was certainly not just some average peasant. Details such as whether buttons were of wood or base metal instead of silver or, up until the mid–14th century, whether there were buttons at all, provided finishing touches that reinforced the status, high or low, of the man or woman inside the clothes. Now let's look more at those clothes.

MEN'S OUTERWEAR

As today, medieval men frequently wore several different outer garments, often in combinations depending upon the weather. These pieces of clothing included tunics (later replaced by doublets), supertunics (which were superseded by *cotehardies*), capes, cloaks, and *houppelandes*.

Tunics and Doublets

The tunic was the basic piece of men's outerwear for most of the Middle Ages. Like the undertunic described above, the tunic was a T-shaped garment. But, unlike the undertunic, tunics were typically made of wool instead of linen. Further, certain features of the tunic changed over time more than those of the undertunic. For example, in late 11th century England, fashionable tunics appear to have commonly had close fitting sleeves that ended a few inches short of the wrist, exposing the cuff of the longer undertunic beneath, and their hemlines were at about the knee with the skirt of the undertunic not usually visible (fig. 20). A few decades later, in the 12th century, tunic sleeves were longer, covering the undertunic's sleeve completely, while the hemline dropped well below the knee, sometimes reaching the ankle. Meanwhile, in 12th century Germany, long tunics were also popular but often with shorter and wider sleeves than their English counterparts. And the length and fit of the tunic's sleeve and the length of its hemline continued to vary over time and from region to region up until the middle of the 14th century when more fitted versions of the tunic started to become popular.

During the 14th century, men's clothing became more fitted. The tunic's sleeves were now long and tightly fitted, often buttoned at the cuff. The tunic was now also more tailored and had buttons, toggles, or laces down its front. This combination of features permitted the garment to be tightly drawn across the upper body down the waist and then flaring over the hips. As a result, these new tunics accentuated (or exaggerated) the massiveness of the wearer's chest and created sort of an hour-glass figure. Meanwhile, tunics' hemlines rose to new heights, just covering the buttocks and tops of the thighs. Reflecting the significance of these changes, the tunic was given a new name: *gypon*, *gipon*, or, more familiarly, doublet. The doublet outlived the Middle Ages and remained a common item of men's clothing through the Renaissance.

The rising hemline of the tunic contributed to another change in fashion. Since the man's waist was now barely covered by his outer garment, he could no longer lace his hose to his breeches without an unseemly display of the waistband of his breeches between the lower edge of his gipon and the top edge of his hose. To avoid this unsightly gap, numerous pairs of eyelets were placed around the lower edge of gipons. Men were then able to ties the laces on their hose directly to their gipons, leaving their breeches completely covered.

Supertunics, Surcoats, and Cote-hardies

Sometimes the combination of undertunic and tunic wasn't sufficient. In cold or wet weather or on ceremonial occasions, medieval men needed additional clothing. Supertunics were a loose fitting garment, usually T-shaped but sleeveless ones were also used. These sleeveless ones were usually called a *surcoat* or a *cyclas* and often had very wide openings for the arms. Their hemlines ranged in length from the mid-thigh (which left the tunic beneath exposed) down to the ankle, such as the one worn by the 13th century physician in figure 36. Supertunics and surcoats with long skirts often had slits from the waist down, either at the front and back or down the left and rights sides, so that the skirt did not interfere with riding horseback or other physical activities.

Some supertunics and surcoats simply served as overcoats, sometimes even being fur-lined for additional warmth. Others were sort of a dress- or suit-coat and were part of the ensembles worn by the nobility. Supertunics and surcoats of this sort appeared in depictions of formal court ceremonies such as holding court, receiving ambassadors, marriages, and other important occasions. For example, in figure 1, the two men on either side of the future St. Cecilia, seated in the center, are wearing supertunics or surcoats with short, split sleeves. These ceremonial supertunics and surcoats were usually far from plain. Some illustrations show wide bands of embroidery around the collars and cuffs while the base material often appears to be a brocade or other patterned fabric.

In the 14th century, supertunics underwent a transformation similar to the evolution of the tunic into the gipon or doublet. Gradually, the supertunics were made with a more tailored fit with buttons and other fasteners. Along with the snugger fit through the chest and sleeves, the supertunic's hemline rose, first to just above the knee and, before the end of the 14th century, to near the top of the thigh. Like the doublet, this new design of supertunic fit closely at the waist and flared over the hips. Thus, this style gave the wearer the appearance of a narrow waist and large chest. This appearance was often further exaggerated by additional padding at the shoulders, much like the effect achieved by shoulder pads in modern fashions. Again, along with all these physical changes, the name of the garment changed as well. No longer a supertunic, it was now the cote-hardie (fig. 19).

From the mid–14th century until they went out of fashion in the late 15th century, the basic lines of the cote-hardie remained unchanged but tailors experimented wildly with the sleeves. One of the first variations was the attachment of tippets, arm bands worn just above the elbow with a long tab or streamer of cloth hanging from it. Flared sleeves soon followed. More flared than the legs of the most extreme bell-bottomed blue jeans, the cuffs of these sleeves sometimes dangled several feet below the wearer's wrist. As the 14th century turned into the 15th century, some fashionable men wore "bagpipe" sleeves. These sleeves had normal, snug fitting cuffs but they bagged out voluminously below the elbow. The effect was something like taking the dangling cuffs of the flared sleeves and gathering them in at the wrist. One other variation was an impracticably long sleeve. Some were so long that they hung down to the wearer's knees. These sleeves were made with a long slit from near the shoulder down to the elbow so that the wearer could thrust his arms out through the sleeve and leave the otherwise impossibly cumbersome sleeve hanging behind him for show. The sleeves on two of the cotehardies in figure 19 are of this type but their cuffs appear to be rolled, diminishing their exaggerated length.

The cote-hardie remained in use

Figure 21. Dressed in the height of the late 14th century fashions, this man wears a *chaperon* atop his head. The chaperon was derived from the *lirapipe*, a hood with a long, dangling tail. Instead of placing the lirapipe over his head so that his head is covered except for his face, this trendsetter has placed the opening for his face on top of his head, rolled its edges up to make a brim, and then artfully arranged the rest of the hood and its tail to create a stylish hat. He wears a houppelande that covers down to mid-calf level. This houppelande has slits in the front and back to allow for easier movement and for riding. Underneath, he wears a *gipon* or doublet. Just as the tunic had evolved into the gipon, his undertunic too was much closer fitting than earlier versions. The undertunic was still long sleeved, but its "tail" was growing shorter, continuing its evolution into the modern shirt. His legs are covered by long hose. Hose were still being made with the legs as two separate pieces but a fashionable man such as this one would more likely wear hose in which the legs were joined together and fitted with a codpiece. Hose were still supported by laces along the top edge, but instead of being tied to his breeches, the laces are tied through eyelets along the lower edge of the gipon. Completing his ensemble, he has shoes with exaggeratedly long toes. To keep their shape, the points of the toes are filled with moss or other light stuffing (J. Walker).

Figure 22. This is a well-dressed man of the 15th century. On his head is a flat-topped, low-crowned hat with a turned up brim, one of the many styles of men's hats that were then popular. He wears a long-sleeved, ankle-length gown with a standing collar. Underneath, he wears a gipon or doublet over a linen shirt and wool hose over linen breeches. His shoes are pointed, but, in keeping with contemporary fashion trends, the points are much less exaggerated than some 14th century examples. The wooden pattens that he wears in addition to his shoes indicate that he is ready to go out in damp weather. The pattens are designed to keep his soft leather shoes (and his feet inside them) dry by raising his shoes a few inches above the wet and muddy streets (J. Walker).

through the end of the Middle Ages after blending with the next item of clothing, the houppelande.

Houppelandes

Like the cote-hardie, the houppelande (fig. 21) was another 14th century variation on the supertunic. However, while the cote-hardie was fairly form fitting and had a high hemline, the houppelande retained more of the qualities of earlier supertunics and was more like a gown, loose fitting with a long skirt reaching the mid-calf or the ankle. And like the supertunic, the houppelande's long skirt often had one or two slits from the waist down to allow freer movement. Another similarity to the supertunic was that the houppelande was sometimes lined with fur to make it warmer. Unlike the supertunic, houppelandes with long sleeves had greatly flared cuffs like those found on some styles of cote-hardies and they had high, close fitting collars that often went up to wearer's chin and followed the line of his jaw up to his ears. Another feature that frequently appeared in houppelandes but not on earlier supertunics were deep, vertical pleats in the garment's upper body. These pleats suggest that the houppelande, at least its upper parts, may have been padded like the cote-hardie.

By the early 15th century, houppelande sleeves were more commonly made with exaggeratedly flared cuffs. Their collars also became less extreme as well with shorter, more open, "standing" collars replacing the high, tight collars. Before the end of the 15th century, the houppelande evolved into or was simply replaced by the gown (fig.

22). The gown was a long sleeved, long skirted garment that, though fitted, was generously cut to comfortably wear over several other layers of clothing, much like modern overcoats.

Capes and Cloaks

While medieval men sometimes wore supertunics as we would wear overcoats or winter coats today, they also wore cloaks or capes in cold or wet weather. However, like supertunics and surcoats, these outer garments, made of suitably rich fabric and decoration, were also often worn for ceremonial occasions as well. Cloaks were usually made in the form of a large semicircle of durable cloth, such as a thick wool. Some cloaks had hoods built in to cover the wearer's head and neck as well. The cloak was secured by a large brooch or pin or with cords and rings permanently attached to the cloak. With the cloak draped completely over and around the left shoulder, the wearer usually attached the fastener over his right breast, thus leaving the gap in the cloak over the right arm and allowing freer use of that arm.

As with other items of clothing, the length of cloaks varied widely. Many early medieval cloaks were shown as short, just reaching to the knees. Short cloaks, despite leaving the wearer's legs exposed to the elements, had the advantage of providing an additional layer of clothing for the upper body without risking entangling the legs when riding horseback or walking. For this reason, perhaps, short cloaks appear throughout the Middle Ages. Short cloaks may have also been favored since they required substantially less material to make and were therefore cheaper. Still, long cloaks were also worn; fine, fur-trimmed ones for the nobility as well as warm, thick ones for use in bad weather. To make them less encumbering, long cloaks were sometimes made with a long

slit down the left and right sides so that the wearer was free to extend his arms through the cloak rather than having to move it aside.

WOMEN'S OUTERWEAR

Wardrobes of medieval women included several different pieces of outerwear. These pieces of clothing included tunics or dresses, surcoats, kirtles, cotehardies, houppelandes, gowns, capes and cloaks. While some of these items bore the same names as items of men's clothing, women's clothing was often significantly different from men's clothing regardless of the names as the descriptions below illustrate. However, as with men's clothing, women's wardrobes changed over time and new pieces of clothing evolved and displaced older fashions. Thus, all the items of apparel listed above were never in use at the same time.

Tunics and Dresses

Women wore tunics that were similar to those worn by men. Women's tunics or dresses during the early part of the Middle Ages appear to have been as loose fitting and shapeless as men's tunics during this same period (fig. 17). Also like men's tunics, the sleeves of these dresses ranged from short to long and from snug to wide and loose. Hemlines always reached to at least a few inches below the knees and were more often lower, reaching down to the ankle or even to the ground. Even when wearing the shorter, knee- or calf-length dresses, medieval women wore chemises that extended down to around their ankles and so did not expose any part of their legs in public.

By the late 11th century, dresses that snugly fitted the arms and upper body (fig. 23) became fashionable and this remained the style, with some adjustments

Figure 23. This woman wears clothing that was fashionable in the 12th and early 13th centuries. Her head and neck are covered with a veil and wimple. From the waist up, her dress fits snugly, a fit achieved by a combination of the cut of the dress and the lacing along the seams that run from under her arms down to her waist. Such lacing was also placed down the center of either the front or back of dresses as well. From the waist down, her dress is quite voluminous and reaches down to the ground, hiding her feet. Around her waist is a belt, fashionably long (J. Walker).

and changes, through the rest of the Middle Ages. To achieve the tighter fit, the dresses were made with long slits. These slits typically started at the neckline and ran down either the front or back of the dress down to the waist. Alternatively, the slits were sometimes placed on the sides of the dress on the seams that ran down under each armpit, as shown in Figure 23. Regardless of their location, these slits provided the room needed to put on the dress. After putting on such a dress, the woman then drew the slit closed by tightening and then tying the long laces that ran back and forth through a series of holes along each edge of the slit. Thus, the dress was drawn snug to the wearer's body. Women used a similar arrangement of slits and laces at the cuff of each sleeve to draw the sleeves tightly over their forearms. Buttons gradually replaced laces in dresses over the course of the later Middle Ages. Using long slits and laces to achieve a good fit appears rather primitive but the merits and necessity of these and other methods of fastening are discussed in the section on fasteners under "Accessories" below.

By the end of the 11th century, fashionable dresses still fit the wearer's body closely, but wide, flaring sleeves replaced the tighter ones seen earlier in the century. The cuffs of these sleeves varied from a foot or so up to several feet in circumference. Evidence of the continued use of long-sleeved chemises can often be seen in illustrations of these dresses since the wide cuff of these dresses routinely exposed several inches of the wearer's arm above her wrist and revealed the cuff of the chemise. This style remained popular through the 12th century and well into the next century. The closing decades of the 13th century witnessed a return fitted sleeves.

Surcoats

During the 13th century, women began wearing sleeveless surcoats similar to those worn by men. In figure 1, St. Cecilia is wearing one of these surcoats. They were worn as outer garments, over the top of the dress and chemise. However, in the 14th century, a new style of surcoat for women appeared. Often referred to as a sideless surcoat, the openings in the sides of these sleeveless dresses were far larger than any found in earlier surcoats, just as the name implies. The oval-shaped side openings usually reached from the top of the shoulder to a few inches below the hip and the openings were often so large that the wearer's body above her hips was covered only by a strip of cloth about a foot wide at most. This strip went from just below the wearer's hips in front, up over

Figure 24. This stylish woman of the 14th century has her hair up in an elaborate headdress. At the top and back of her head, her hair is secured and covered with a hairnet or veil. The rest of her hair has been braided and carefully placed in tubes formed of netting or metal mesh on each side of her head. To simplify hairstyling or if the woman did not have enough hair to achieve the desired look, false hair braids were also used to fill out the tubes. Her dress is a type called a *cote-hardie*. Like the earlier forms of dresses, its sleeves and upper body are snug, though rows of small buttons are used instead of laces to attain the tightness. The sleeves are slightly longer than the earlier dress, having bell-shaped cuffs that cover the hand almost up to the base of the fingers. At the elbows are tippets: long, decorative strips of cloth. As she steps forward, she holds the hem of her skirt up a little and reveals the lower edge of her underdress. This garment was probably long sleeved with a flowing skirt. It was likely very similar to the underdresses worn in the preceding centuries. On her feet, she wears shoes with distinctly pointed toes. This style was popular for both men and women, though the toes on women's shoes never reached the exaggerated lengths found on some men's shoes (J. Walker).

her shoulders, and then down to her buttocks. Below this narrow strip, these surcoats flared out and were as voluminous and long as earlier dresses, reaching down to the ankle or even trailing along the ground. Despite the fact that all that was revealed by the wide openings in these surcoats was the normal, snug fitting outer dress, some preachers and other moralists sermonized against this fashion as being lewd. They appear to have thought that the openings drew attention to and framed the contours of the woman's body, visible through the openings, in a way which was more suggestive than simply wearing just a snug dress by itself. Their criticism may have been based on the idea that this fashion invited onlookers, especially men, to see inside a woman's outer layer of clothing. The moralists feared where men's thoughts would lead them once past that first layer.

Cote-hardies

While sideless surcoats remained fashionable until the end of the 14th century, another style of dress, the cote-hardie, also appeared in the 1300s. Though it was given the same name as the man's jacket-like outer garment that was also then in fashion, the woman's cote-hardie bore few resemblances to the man's and was actually a long gown with long sleeves and a flowing skirt that reached the ground (fig. 24). With a buttoned slit on each sleeve from the wrist to above the elbow, the cote-hardie fitted the wearer's arms very snugly. Another slit fitted with buttons ran from the neckline down the front of the gown to the hips so that the cote-hardie tightly fitted the wearer's upper body and emphasized its curves. As shown in figure 24, two other features often seen on cote-hardies were tippets which, like those worn on men's cote-hardies, were long streamers of cloth attached to arm bands worn above the elbow and flaring,

bell-shaped cuffs that projected a few inches from the end of the sleeves, covering most of the wearer's hand and leaving only her fingers visible. Though rarely visible beneath such a long garment, long-sleeved chemises of plain linen appear to have been worn underneath the cote-hardie. Like the sideless surcoat, the cote-hardie remained in fashion until the end of the 14th century.

Houppelandes and Gowns

Near the end of the 14th century, fashionable women began wearing houppelandes. Unlike cote-hardies, women's houppelandes were largely identical to men's garments of the same name: generously cut gowns with high necks and very wide sleeves. Also like men's, women's houppelandes were sometimes lined with fur for added comfort. However, unlike men's houppelandes, the hemline of the woman's never rose above the floor. Further, while men wore their houppelandes belted around the waist, women usually wore theirs belted just below their breasts, creating a look more often associated with the high "Empire" waists worn by European women in the early 19th century. This look could also make the women appear pregnant since the houppelande billowed out from under belt and made even the trimmest of women look as though they had large bellies. This must not have been considered a drawback since houppelandes with high belts remained at the height of women's fashion from the end of the 14th century until late in the 15th century. Not just houppelandes were worn with belts just below the bust. Gowns were worn belted this way too. Gowns began appearing around the middle of the 15th century (fig. 19). A variation on the houppelande, gowns were long dresses with large, open necklines sometimes edged with broad, flat collars in place of the close fitting, standing collars found on many houppelandes. Initially, the gowns' long sleeves were almost as voluminous as those on houppelandes but, over the course of a few decades, their sleeves became increasingly form fitting until the sleeves on gowns were nearly as snug as those seen on cote-hardies almost a century earlier. Gowns draped closer to their wearers' figures and so seem to have been made from thinner material or with less padding than houppelandes. Both houppelandes and early gowns appear to have been worn with kirtle-style underdresses. The cuffs on the long sleeves of these underdresses were quite visible inside the flaring sleeves of the houppelandes and the wide sleeved gowns. As gowns became snugger, underdresses again disappeared from sight and likely became plainer as well as more closely fitted.

Capes and Cloaks

Like men, women in the Middle Ages routinely wore cloaks or capes for additional protection from cold or wet weather or for ceremonial occasions. One difference, however, was that women were far more often shown wearing longer capes rather than shorter ones. Men, on the other hand, appear to have been less discriminating in their choices of cape lengths. It is possible that women preferred longer cloaks since these garments provided better protection from the elements and, because they were already wearing dresses with long trailing skirts, women didn't share the incentive men had to wear shorter cloaks; that was, to avoid encumbering their legs with large folds of cloth.

Accessories

No outfit, then or now, would be complete without some accessories and the range of accessories really hasn't changed much over the centuries.

HATS AND HEAD COVERINGS

Men

Hoods were a practical and common head covering. Both sexes wore hoods that were made as part of cloaks and other outer garments, much like the hoods worn today that are part of raincoats or winter coats. At least as early as the beginning of the 13th century, men also wore hoods which were separate pieces of clothing. These hoods had wide collars that also covered the tops of the wearer's shoulder as well as a few inches down both his chest and back. Initially, these hoods were plain and practical and covered the head just like the hood on a cloak but, over the course of the 14th century, hoods with long, drooping tails became stylish. Sometimes called a *lirapipe*, the back of this type of hood terminated in a long, thin pouch or tube of fabric that hung down at least a couple of feet and often more. At some point, some fashion trendsetters began wrapping the long, trailing end of the hood around their heads, sort of like a turban. Finally, around the beginning of the 15th century, someone took things a step further. Instead of putting the hood on over his head the normal way, he placed the hood with the opening for the face on top of his head, rolled the fabric up a little to create a band, flopped all the loose fabric of collar across the top, and then wrapped the long end of the hood around the whole pile or just let the end trail down and across his shoulders like a scarf. The result was a massive, somewhat floppy hat that was often jauntily angled to one side of the wearer's head. This style of headgear, shown in figure 21, was called the *chaperon*. By the middle of the 15th century, hat-makers were already producing hats that looked like chaperons made from hoods but which were actually specially designed and fabricated to simulate the original, improvised chaperons.

Besides hoods, the Phrygian cap was another form of hat that was commonly worn by men in early Middle Ages (fig. 20). This cap was given its name by some historians who thought the shape of the cap resembled hats associated with the ancient Phrygians of Asia Minor but most people today are more likely to think of this cap as "the Smurf hat" since it is the same one worn by those little blue cartoon characters from Europe. Made of wool felt, the Phrygian cap covered just the crown of the head and its top ended in a small point or pouch that was usually pointed toward the front of the hat. While this cap may have looked a little odd, it likely provided the same warmth and protection as a modern knit watch cap. The Phrygian cap faded from the medieval men's fashion scene around the end of the 12th century, about the same time that the *coif* appeared.

The coif (figs. 18 and 36) was usually made of white linen and covered most of the top of a man's head, down to and including his ears. The flaps over the ears ended in laces that could be tied under the chin to secure the coif. So, while the Phrygian cap looked like a Smurf's hat, the coif resembled a baby's bonnet, a real step forward in men's fashion. Yet the coif was a very practical hat and was worn by many different classes of society. Scribes and others who worked indoors were often depicted as wearing coifs. In part, they wore coifs because it was the style but presumably they often wore coifs to keep their heads warm, an important consideration in an age without central heating. Construction workers and other laborers in the 13th century were also typically shown wearing coifs. While they too may have worn them for warmth, it is likely that they also wore them to keep dust and dirt out

of their hair when working, a conclusion supported by images in which workers have stripped down to their breeches to perform hot or messy work but have still retained their coifs. Finally, knights wore coifs as well, usually ones with some extra padding, to cushion the insides of their helmets and to shield their hair from abrasive effect of mail armor. (This point is discussed more fully below in Chapter VI on fighting.) Despite its practicality, the coif fell out of favor and largely disappeared by the early 14th century.

Other shapes and types of men's hats appeared, disappeared, and sometimes reappeared over the course of the Middle Ages. These included:

• Wide brimmed hats, often with high crowns, typically made of felt but sometimes of straw or leather. These hats usually appear in illustrations of travelers such as pilgrims, laborers such as fieldworkers and wagon drivers, and others engaged in outdoor activities who needed some protection from the sun, rain, and other elements. While men were most often depicted wearing such hats, women working in the fields or traveling on pilgrimage were sometimes shown wearing these hats (fig. 17).

• Berets. Made of wool felt, these were like modern berets but usually fitted the wearer's head more snugly than is now fashionable, with the result that they looked something like a beanie.

• Hats with very low crowns, either without brims or with narrow brims turned straight up (fig. 22). These hats resembled pillbox hats but with slightly domed tops. These styles of hat were made exclusively of felt until the second half of the 15th century when hat-makers began making some out of beaver fur for their wealthier customers.

And

- Hats with high crowns, frequently made without brims (fig. 19). In illustrations, these hats appear to be ten to twelve inches high. They were nearly cylindrical in form but their tops were usually slightly narrower than their bases. Like the low crowned hats, these hats were made of felt until the introduction of beaver hats. The continued popularity of beaver hats, combined with the widespread draining of marshes to create arable land and the consumption of beaver tails as a "fish-day" food (mentioned above in the cooking and eating chapter), led to the near extinction of the European beaver.

Women

Throughout medieval Europe, fashion and custom dictated that women wore hats or other head coverings that hid some or all of their hair. The only exceptions were for unmarried girls, who were free to wear their hair long and loose, and for prostitutes. Though prostitutes often wore hats like other women, for a woman to go out in public bareheaded was generally considered tantamount to her declaring publicly that she was of loose morals. The equating of a woman's uncovered hair to evidence of her immorality was so ingrained and pervasive in many regions that criminal statutes often included a specific category of assault to address cases in which a man struck or knocked off a woman's headdress in public. In these cases, the assault was deemed to be an accusation that the woman was a prostitute and the issue for the court then became the truth or falsity of that accusation. If the accusation was proven to be true, the assault went unpunished. But, if the woman and her family succeeded in defending her reputation, the man who

struck her was subjected to severe penalties, not so much for the actual assault but for his false accusation. Thus, hats and other head coverings were an essential part of the wardrobe of a medieval woman since she had little choice but to keep her head covered when in public.

Veils were the most common form of head cover for women throughout the Middle Ages. Some veils were made from relatively small pieces of cloth. Usually worn with a headband, these veils covered the top, back, and sides of a woman's head from just above her eyebrows, down over ears, to several inches down the back of her neck. In other words, just enough to keep most of her hair covered. Other veils, made from much longer pieces of fabric, were worn over the head and wrapped around the neck. Sometimes worn with headbands, these larger veils left only the wearer's face and, perhaps, a little bit of her throat visible. Her hair was completely covered. Until near the end of the 14th century, most veils, regardless of their size, were made of an opaque fabric, usually white linen.

Near the end of the 12th century, the veil was supplemented with the barbette and the wimple (fig. 23). The barbette was a band of cloth which the woman wrapped across the top of her head, over her ears, and under her chin. The barbette was several inches wide and so covered and held in a substantial amount of the wearer's hair. Barbettes appear to have initially been worn with the smaller style of veil but were later worn with a variety of other head coverings, the most common one in the 13th century being a style of domed pillbox hat similar to those worn by men. Women wearing barbettes often left a small amount of hair showing in the front as well as a few inches at the back but this modest public display of hair was within the bounds of acceptable behavior.

The wimple was a rectangular cloth

that was pinned either to the wearer's hair just above each of her ears or along the sides of her veil near the veil's top. The woman then draped the wimple down, leaving her face exposed but covering her throat and the sides of her head. The wimple, when worn with a small or moderate sized veil, provided the same coverage as the large veil but was probably easier to put on and correctly arrange than the long piece of fabric that made up the large veil.

One last piece of simple head covering that shouldn't be overlooked was the hairnet. Hairnets were certainly in use at least as early as the beginning of the 13th century. Hairnets were likely in use before that time but they only became noticeable with the advent of the barbette and its exposure of neatly gathered buns at the backs of many women's heads.

While various combinations of the veil, barbette, wimple, and hairnet remained the standard head coverings for most women for the remainder of the Middle Ages, fashion-conscious noblewomen and some of the wealthier women of the merchant class of the 14th century began wearing different styles of headdresses. Besides the domed pillbox hat which had come into fashion in the 13th century, women of the 14th century added rather novel hair accessories to their wardrobes. These accessories included small cylinders and domes made of fine wire mesh, frequently gilded or silvered (fig. 24). Pinned on the sides of the head and often worn with a small veil or pillbox hat, these little cages were filled with coils or mounds of braided hair. As with hairnets, one of the purposes of these devices appears to have been to allow a woman to display and even accentuate her hair while staying within the limits of social restrictions on such conduct. Oddly, sometimes the hair displayed in these headpieces was not actually attached to the woman wearing them.

Records indicate that some well-off medieval women used hair extensions made of cuttings of their own hair or from the hair of other women and that the little hair-cages were sometimes filled with braids made of this "false" hair. Using this shortcut must have been much more convenient and comfortable than having to maintain, braid, and coil the hair needed for this style of headdress. And this was no small problem since the fashion was for larger and larger mounds of caged hair.

In the 15th century, the styles of women's headdresses became even more fanciful. Again, most women continued wearing simple and practical head covers but those fashion-conscious women who could afford such luxury continued to display new and more elaborate hats and headdresses. Made of the finest and most costly materials available, these head coverings came in the most fantastic shapes and the speeds with which some of them appear to have gone in and out of style almost rival the pace of modern clothing fads. In less than a hundred years, medieval Europe witnessed hats for women that included:

• Large, overstuffed tubes of fabric that were shaped into rings or semicircles, placed on the crown of the lady's head (looking like an over-inflated halo), and secured with a scarf tied under her chin.

• Stuffed tubes of cloth shaped into the outline of a heart and perched atop the lady's wide coiffure. These coiffures had evolved from the domed hair-cages of the previous century but which were now cones several inches in height that projected out on each side of the wearer's head. This style of hat was sometimes accented with a scarf draped over the entire hat or attached as a wide fringe. Gradually, as fashions changed, the sides of the "heart" were increasingly folded up to create a more towering, twin-peaked headdress. Accompanying this change, the twin cones of hair that supported such hats grew in height and moved towards the top of the wearer's head. Some headdresses of this style resembled a pair of large horns, which many contemporary moralists seized upon and likened to devil's horns in their sermons against feminine vanity.

And

• Tall cones, some twelve to eighteen inches in height (fig. 19). The tops of some of these conical hats were pointed while others were truncated, ending in a flat top. Both styles were often accented with thin, sheer scarves supported by wire frameworks attached to the hats. The combination of the diaphanous scarf and the fine wire frame made the wearer's head appear as though enshrouded in a fine, colored mist. The truncated cones were popular in several countries while the high, pointed style that is most associated with fairy tale princesses and "damsels in distress" seems to have been popular only in France, where it appears to have been called a *hennin*.

While three basic styles may not seem like that many, variations in length and height as well as in the colors and patterns of fabric and accents such as jewelry, beads, and pearls combined to create a bewildering array of hats in a relatively short span of time.

HAIRSTYLES

Fashion didn't stop with one's clothing and accessories in the Middle Ages any more than it does today. While they changed as slowly as the clothing styles did

back then, hairstyles were also an important part of a person's appearance.

Men

Many illustrations of men's hairstyles in the Middle Ages have survived. Men were not subject to the same restrictions as women concerning the display of their hair and so men appear bareheaded in these pictures far more often than do women. Further, although men generally did wear hats or other head coverings, these were often not as concealing as the headdresses worn by women and so much of the men's hair remained visible even when their heads were covered.

The length of men's hair fluctuated over the course of the Middle Ages as well as from region to region. Other than the tonsure worn by clerics (which is discussed below), the shortest hairstyle was that worn by 11th century Normans, who went forth from northern France to conquer England as well as Sicily. These Norman men had bowl-shaped haircuts so short that the hair in front only covered just the very top of their foreheads and the hair on the back of their heads was shaved off up to a line parallel to the tops of their ears or even an inch or so above that point. This style disappeared by the beginning of the 12th century but a less severe version of the bowl cut became popular again in England and France in the early 15th century. Outside of 11th century Normandy and early 15th century England and France, men wore their hair in a variety of more moderate lengths, including bobs that covered down to the bottom of the ear and longer styles that would be down to or slightly over the back of the collar on a modern man's dress shirt. These styles appear to have been worn either with a center part or with no part at all.

While bobs and collar length styles appear to have been the most popular, long hair that reached down to the shoulders or even lower did occasionally appear during the Middle Ages. Viking men were famed for their long, flowing hair and were quite proud of it. At various times during the Middle Ages, it was fashionable for noblemen to grow their hair. For example, in England during the early 12th century, some noblemen grew their hair so long that it was described as rivaling the length of the tresses of the ladies at court. Reputedly, these men even resorted to using extensions of "false" hair to lengthen their locks. The clergy and other moralists spoke out against long hair for men, calling it a brazen display of vanity. The fashion gradually swung back to shorter hair but very long hair appeared occasionally as a fad at noble courts across medieval Europe.

There is one last style of men's haircut that must be addressed: the tonsure. For a tonsure, the crown of the man's head was shaved, leaving a fringe of hair encircling his head. This style haircut was worn only by priests, monks, and other clerics. They received the tonsure during their training for holy orders and it served as a distinctive mark of their status as clerics.

As for facial hair, its popularity varied as well. Full beards and moustaches appear to have been popular among the Anglo-Saxons conquered by the Normans while the Normans themselves were clean-shaven. Or at least as clean-shaven as they could be. While barbers were found in every city and in many of the larger towns, on a daily basis most men probably shaved themselves. Given the facts that mirrors were scarce, that those mirrors that did exist were made of polished metal rather than silvered glass and so were often murkier reflectors than their modern counterparts, and that most men do not appear to have owned razors and instead shaved using their knives, shaving must have been a somewhat challenging and painful task. Even with a well-honed knife, it could hardly have been as easy or as comfortable as a shave with a modern electric or blade razor. These conditions may explain why men were often depicted with stubble: many men may not have shaved every day because of the inconvenience and discomfort involved and, even if they did shave, it's quite possible that they did not get a very close shave so that they soon had "five o'clock shadow."

Despite the difficulties involved, being clean-shaven appears to have been the style preferred by most men. Perhaps, it was just easier to shave off facial hair than to keep a beard or mustache trimmed and styled. It may have also been more comfortable and practical. Beards and mustaches required additional grooming and cleaning, both for the sake of appearance and for the comfort and health of their wearers, so some men may have shaved to avoid having one more place for sweat and dirt to accumulate. Though we often think of people in the Middle Ages as being heedless of personal hygiene, they likely kept themselves much cleaner than we think they did. This point is addressed more in Chapter IV on cleaning.

Regardless of any advantages shaving may have had over wearing beards and mustaches, beards and mustaches were certainly worn by many men over the course of the Middle Ages and were, in fact, the preferred fashion at certain times, such as in England around the end of the 11th century and again during the middle of the 14th century. And some men grew beards and mustaches regardless of any transitory fads. In the Byzantine Empire and elsewhere along the eastern and southern edges of the Mediterranean, adult men were expected to wear thick beards and mustaches as a sign of their manhood and station in life. In these regions, this attachment to facial hair was so ingrained that the local people sometimes ridiculed crusaders from northern and western Europe for their lack of beards. Those crusaders who stayed and settled in these regions often grew beards and mustaches as part of their adaptation to the local customs. Besides such regional traditions, kings and older men throughout medieval Europe were often shown wearing beards and mustaches regardless of contemporary fashions. Part of the motivation for these men to grow beards may have been the traditional association of beards with wise elders, as seen in many medieval depictions of Old Testament patriarchs.

Women

As mentioned above, women in the Middle Ages generally kept their hair covered, thus it is difficult to discern any trends in women's hairstyles. However, illustrations of domestic life do provide a few glimpses of women with their hair down, literally. These images suggest that many women grew their hair long but wore it up in braids, buns, or coils that could be easily covered when they went out in public. Only in the seclusion of their own homes did these women fully expose their hair. The association of long hair with femininity in the Middle Ages is also demonstrated in accounts of the life of Joan of Arc who, as part of her disguising herself as a man, cut her hair short. These actions were viewed as such unnatural behavior that they were cited in Joan's trial for heresy and witchcraft as evidence of her guilt.

Despite the lack of public display, women did not neglect their hair. Long, flowing, lustrous hair, preferably blond, was a standard feature in poets' descriptions of beautiful women. They kept their hair groomed with combs made of wood, bone, or ivory, a few of which have survived to the present. They also used small mirrors of polished metal, the finest of which had ivory cases decorated with carvings of romantic scenes. Their grooming also included washing, coloring, and con-

ditioning. One 13th century text on women's cosmetics and hair care includes instructions for bleaching and dyeing hair as well as information on using olive oil to keep hair supple and luxurious. It also had advice on controlling dandruff and lice. Though this book was directed toward women, there is little reason to think that women alone were interested in such information. Men, particularly fashion-conscious courtiers, were likely as interested as they are today in keeping their hair looking full and healthy to project an image of youth and vigor.

While much of the hair grooming performed by medieval women was not that different than that practiced today, they did engage in a few practices seldom seen today, such as routinely delousing their hair and the hair of their family members. Starting in the 14th century, noblewomen and other wealthy and fashionable ladies began plucking the hair on their foreheads to raise the front of their hairlines. This practice made these women appear as though they had very high foreheads but the goal was not so much the high forehead itself. Rather, the overall goal was to make the woman's face, when viewed from the front, into an elongated oval shape. This look was considered quite elegant and desirable and was the standard of beauty in much of Europe throughout the 15th century.

POCKETS

Pockets. It's hard to imagine a world without them. What common feature of clothing could be simpler and more convenient than pockets? But what if you had never seen a pocket, how would you know what a great thing it was and how to make one? This was the problem experienced by people during the Middle Ages. Like the Romans and others before them, medieval

Europeans failed to grasp the need for pockets or how to make them. Some surcoats and outer garments were made with slits that resemble pockets but further examination shows that these slits were merely openings that allowed the wearer to reach bags or other items attached to a belt that was worn as part of the layer of clothing beneath the outer garment. Thus, it wasn't until the Renaissance that pockets began appearing as an integral part of men's clothes. Instead of pockets, men and women of the Middle Ages used a great variety of bags, purses, and other devices to carry any small items that they needed to keep handy.

BAGS AND PURSES

Some bags and purses were attached to the wearer's belt (figs. 21 and 22) while others had shoulder straps like many modern women's purses. The simplest purses were made of round pieces of leather with holes punched at intervals around the edge. A drawstring was fitted through the holes and, when pulled tight, created a little bag. This bag could then be hung on a belt by hanging the large loop of the drawstring over the belt and pulling the bag up and through the loop. Such bags appear to have been common in the early Middle Ages but were suitable for carrying only small items such as coins or keys. For larger items, such as a day's ration of bread and other food, pilgrims, soldiers, and farm workers frequently used cloth or leather bags that were fitted with shoulder straps or that hung over their belts like miniature saddle bags. These rectangular or square bags were flat when empty and had large flaps which were sometimes secured with laces, buttons, or toggles. These sorts of bags, along with cloth sacks and woven baskets, also served as the shopping bags of the Middle Ages.

There were many other designs of bags. There were bags that resembled modern "belly bags" or "fanny packs." These bags were made from long, narrow pieces of cloth or from netting. Such bags were shaped like very large croissants and worn like belts. Instead of the zippered opening found on bags today, these bags had a single slit in their tops which was held closed by the tension on the bag and further protected by being turned toward the inside so that it pressed against the wearer's waist. Other small belt bags, commonly made of leather, were hung from the belt by two very short leather straps and had either built-in scabbards or slots to hold scabbards for small knives. (Many people in the Middle Ages of all classes carried small knives. They used them for cutting up food and for other tasks but could also use them for defense if needed.) Other bags that attached to belts were effectively external pockets: small cloth bags, often hung in pairs, with a single vertical slit near the top so that things could be easily placed inside or taken out but still be stored securely.

By the early 15th century, a new type of bag appeared (fig. 22). Using a roughly triangular metal frame, purse makers created a flat bag with a very narrow top and a wide bottom. The bag's opening was at the top and was often secured with a drawstring but some later versions had hinged openings that were held closed with a clasp. These bags had metal rings attached at the top of their frames and were hung on belts either directly with the ring or by a strap through the ring. This style of purse was very popular with the nobility and other wealthy individuals and came to be a symbol of wealth.

Though convenient, the practice of hanging one's purse from one's belt was not without risks. The Middle Ages saw the development of specialized criminals who were skilled at casually approaching a victim, unobtrusively slicing the straps or cords that attached the victim's bag to his or her belt, and then discreetly making off with their ill-gotten gain. These stealthy cutpurses were forerunners of modern pickpockets.

Besides using bags and purses, medieval people used a number of other techniques that allowed them to carry things while keeping their hands free. Knights used belts with scabbards to allow them to keep the tools of their trade at hand but medieval workers and craftsmen, such as farmers and carpenters, simply tucked their sickles, hammers, and other hand tools under their belts to keep them handy. For carrying bulky but relatively light items such as seeds for crops, both men and women routinely pulled up part of the front of their tunics and dresses to form large, waist-high pouches. The edge of this pouch could either be supported with one hand or be pulled up and secured under the belt. This method declined in the late Middle Ages as clothes became more form fitting. Finally, some items, including small scissors and knives and rings of keys, were directly tied or chained to the belt. These collections of small, tethered objects came to be called *chatelaines* from the feminine version of French word *châtelain* (in English, *castellan*), who was the noble official entrusted with maintaining a castle and supervising its workforce. When the castellan was absent, his wife, the chatelaine, often acted as his substitute and wore a belt with the keys to the castle's doors and storage chests attached to it. This practice wasn't limited to the nobility. Ordinary housewives also routinely held the keys for their households and kept them secure but at hand by fastening them to their belts. It also appears that medieval scribes used a similar technique to keep their inkpots and pen cases handy. Inkpots and the small, scabbard-like containers for holding writing quills were often depicted as being connected by a pair of cords. Scribes could loop these cords over their belts with the capped inkpot hanging on one side and the pen case on the other and then have their hands free for carrying books.

GLOVES AND MITTENS

Gloves appear to have been quite common in most of medieval Europe for all classes of people. As early as the 8th century, there were references to gloves in literature as well as depictions of them in art. Further, gloves have been found in Germanic graves dating to this time. In 9th century France, gloves were included among the items of clothing allotted to monks under the rules of some monastic orders. Thus, gloves have a long history.

Of course, not all gloves were of same quality. Members of the nobility and other wealthy individuals had gloves made of the finest, softest leather available, often with designs tooled on the surface. Besides being a minor but visible sign of a person's wealth and status, such gloves were handy for protecting the hands while riding. Fine leather gloves lined with luxurious fur also appear among the winter wardrobe items of the wealthy. Those nobles that practiced the sport of falconry also possessed special gloves, ones with long cuffs and made of tough leather, which protected the sportsman's forearm and wrist from the falcon's talons when carrying the bird. Another specialized form of hand protection associated with the nobility, particularly with knights and other warriors, were gauntlets. These ranged from tough leather gloves, sometimes fortified with small pieces of metal or horn, to mittens of mail or plate armor. For more on these specialized hand-coverings, see Chapter VI on fighting.

Common people needed and wore gloves and other hand coverings as well.

These included gloves and mittens to protect their hands in cold weather. Some of these were made of leather and lined with fur, but instead of ermine or other rich furs, they were lined with cat or rabbit fur. Farm laborers were sometimes depicted wearing gloves or mittens when working, including a specialized form of hand protection that combined some features of a glove with those of a mitten. Likely made of tough leather, these hand coverings were cut so that the thumb, index finger, and sometimes the middle finger were separated like in a pair of gloves but the remaining fingers were grouped and covered together as in a pair of mittens. This hand covering also had a very long cuff that covered the forearm almost as far up as the elbow. All these features combined to create an odd form of mitten that allowed the wearer more manual dexterity than when wearing normal mittens but still provided considerable protection for his hands, wrists, and forearms. These specialized mittens were usually shown worn by workers who needed this combination of protection and dexterity: workers clearing brush and thorny weeds with a variety of tools and men steering plows and other large farm implements.

BROOCHES, BUTTONS, LACES AND OTHER FASTENERS

Many pieces of clothing in the Middle Ages were made in styles that minimized the need for fasteners. Tunics, shirts, and other items were designed to be pulled on over the head rather than opening down the front like many modern coats and shirts. Still, medieval people relied on a number of fasteners to get their clothing to fit and stay on. Some of these fasteners may appear rather cumbersome and inconvenient now in an age when we can easily achieve a good fit using stretchy materials or zippers. However, most elastic fabrics require man-made materials that weren't developed until the 20th century and the zipper wasn't invented until the end of the 19th century. Thus, people during the Middle Ages, just like all other people who lived before these breakthroughs, had to rely on a number of other fasteners, including:

- Brooches. Made of iron or bronze, these fasteners were usually made in the shape of a large ring. Attached to the ring was a long straight pin that had one pointed end and one end that was formed into a loop. This loop attached the pin to the ring but still allowed the pin to move. To use this fastener, part of the garment's fabric was pushed up through the center of the ring and pierced with the pin. The pointed end of the pin was then pushed down and sprung into a catch on the ring's edge. Brooches that used this same technique for fastening were sometimes made in rectangular and disc shapes instead of rings. All these brooches were made in a variety of sizes, from around approximately an inch up to a few inches in diameter or length. Brooches of these types were in use in Europe before the Middle Ages and continued being worn through the period.

- Pins. Besides being used in brooches, straight pins, either plain or with decorative heads, were also used by themselves to fasten head coverings and other clothing.

- Buckles. Buckles in the Middle Ages were made in two different styles. One style consisted of a pair of metal plates, one with one or more hooks and the other with an equal number of holes. The metal plates were attached to opposite ends of a belt or to two opposing edges of a garment and then fastened by locking the hooks in the holes. More commonly, buckles were shaped like many modern belt buckles: an open frame of metal with a single metal "finger" at the frame's center. These buckles functioned just like their modern counterparts. Buckles appeared most often on leather items such as shoes and purses.

- Laces, Drawstrings, Ribbons, and Other Soft Fasteners. These fasteners were probably the most common. The cloth, yarn, or leather needed to make them was relatively cheap and far more likely to be at hand than the processed metal required for the other fasteners mentioned so far. Further, almost anyone could fashion laces, cords, and drawstrings while the metal ones had to be made by craftsmen who possessed the requisite tools. Threaded through holes, slits, or tubes of fabric built into garments ranging from shoes and hose to shirts and outerwear, these fasteners provided a snug yet comfortable fit that was easy to adjust and slightly flexible. Besides using separate laces and cords, some garments were made with permanently attached strips or bands of fabric. Such fasteners appeared on men's shirts in the late Middle Ages in the form of narrow extensions several inches long on each side of the shirt's collar. These strips of fabric were tied together to close the collar. Another style of built-in soft fastener was used in low-topped shoes that had large, slipper-like openings for the foot. To keep these shoes from falling off, shoemakers spanned the openings with leather straps. Sometimes these straps were secured with buckles but another common method was to split the free end of the strap, forming it into two long, thin strips that were then laced through a pair of holes on the opposite side of the opening and knotted together.

And

- Buttons. Though they were occasionally used by the Greeks and Romans of antiquity, buttons were very scarce in Europe up until the end of the 13th century when they began appearing on the clothing of the upper classes. In the 14th century, buttons were an essential part of the form fitting clothing that was popular with both fashion conscious men and women.

Before leaving fasteners, there's a point about buttons that is somewhat puzzling: even though buttons are simple to use, they appear to have been unpopular and seldom used during most of the Middle Ages. One possible explanation is that buttons were viewed as being less practical than other fasteners. For example, brooches and pins were quite common in medieval Europe just as they had been in classical Greek and Roman societies. These fasteners were durable and reliable and could be removed, permitting them to be transferred from one garment to another as needed or to be removed when the garment was being washed. Buttons were typically permanently attached to a single garment, requiring the purchase of multiple sets of buttons and risking loss or damage of the buttons during laundering unless the buttons were first cut off and then sewn back on after washing was completed. Though these concerns might seem trivial or odd to people today, these were real issues for people in the Middle Ages. Buttons were usually cast of metal or carved from materials such as wood or bone and were somewhat costly and difficult to obtain or replace. Brooches and pins also typically had to be bought or bartered for and so were sometimes costly or hard to obtain but a person needed only a few pins or brooches to take care of his or her entire wardrobe instead of a dozen or more buttons. And, as discussed above, soft fasteners such as laces and drawstrings have their advantages too. Thus, besides simply following tradition, medieval people may have continued to rely on brooches, pins, and other fasteners because of their relative advantages over buttons.

JEWELRY

Except, perhaps, for a brooch or two with a design cast or carved into its surface or a leaden pin from a shrine visited on pilgrimage, most people in the Middle Ages did not own jewelry. Rings, necklaces, earrings, and other items were for the rich but there were enough rich people in the Middle Ages to support a large community of silversmiths and goldsmiths. Many of their products were large pieces such as bowls, plates, spoons, and devotional and liturgical pieces including reliquaries (containers for holding and displaying relics of saints), pyx (containers for consecrated communion wafers), and communion chalices. But these smiths also created intricate pieces of jewelry for their customers. In addition to pieces of solid metal, medieval jewelers created pins and other jewelry in which pieces of brightly colored glass and enamel were fused into cavities in metal frames to create sparkling little designs or pictures. Specialized craftsmen also enhanced metalwork by setting precious gemstones such as rubies, emeralds, pearls, and sapphires, semiprecious stones including garnets, lapis lazuli, and rock crystal, and imitation jewels made of glass into settings ranging from rings and crowns to the covers of books owned by kings and queens. Interestingly, unlike modern gems, most gems in the Middle Ages were rounded rather than faceted, that is, cut and finished with numerous flat faces. This difference may reflect the limits of medieval jewelers'

stonecutting skills but it might also have simply been a matter of taste.

SHOES AND OTHER FOOTWEAR

Shoes in the Middle Ages were usually rather insubstantial by modern standards. The upper parts of medieval shoes were made of soft leather from the hides of cows, calves, goats, or deer. The soles were made of thicker leather than that used for the upper parts but the soles were still typically much softer and far more flexible than those found in most shoes today. In addition, medieval shoes also lacked heels as well as any form of arch support (figs. 20–22). In all these aspects, they more closely resembled moccasins than any other form of shoe still currently in use. Medieval shoes provided some cushioning from hard surfaces when walking and some protection from the elements but these advantages may often have been rather minimal since medieval farmers and some other laborers appear to have frequently gone barefoot, at least in warmer weather, when working outside.

Shoemaking appears to have made few advances over the course of the Middle Ages. However, the shapes, styles, and decorations of shoes changed markedly over the centuries. In part, we can see these changes in medieval illustration. Shoes and boots were shown with a fair degree of detail in many medieval illustrations, from illuminations in books to frescos on the walls of palaces. Archaeologists in London have also made some amazing finds of medieval shoes along the banks of the Thames River. Despite numerous ordinances prohibiting such activity, citizens of London used several spots along the Thames as dumps for centuries. Among other household items, archaeologists have found hundreds of worn out shoes and boots that have been dated to between

A.D. 1100 and 1450. After these shoes were dropped in the river, layers of mud settled over the top of them, sealing them off from oxygen and further decay. Centuries later, these shoes and boots were dredged up, and though waterlogged, provide excellent examples of medieval shoes.

The toes of early medieval shoes were usually quite rounded and blunt (fig. 20). The shoes either were low topped like modern men's dress shoes or had standing collars of leather that extended a few inches up the ankle, a form of low topped ankle boot. These standing collars had slits in the front to provide the space needed for putting on and taking off the shoe. In some shoes of this style, the edges of the collar were made long enough to overlap. This overlap served the same function of providing a better, more weatherproof closure that the tongue provided in later shoes. While some were slip-on styles, most appear to have had drawstrings or laces to draw the upper part of the shoe snug and keep it from slipping off. In some cases, the strings or laces passed through pairs of holes like those found in modern shoes but medieval shoemakers also made shoes in which the laces simply wrapped around the top the shoe or passed through just a couple of loops, much like miniature belt loops, placed around the top of the shoe.

Over the centuries, the toes of the shoes became more pointed than rounded (fig. 36). In addition to laces, shoemakers began using other fasteners such as straps secured with buckles or toggles. Additionally, they sometimes moved the slit from the front of the shoe to the side. They also began making low-topped shoes with larger openings. The shoes had wide straps fastened with buckles or with leather laces that were an integral part of the shoe. Despite these changes, the practicality of the low-topped boots and shoes ensured their continued popularity with all classes of society. However, over the course of the 14th century, the nobility and other wealthy individuals began wearing shoes with increasingly pointed toes. By around the middle of the 14th century, low-topped shoes with very long, very pointed toes were the style for the elite (fig. 21). Sometimes called *poulaines*, these shoes had points that extended up to several inches beyond the wearer's toes. Excavated examples have revealed that the toes of these shoes were stuffed with moss or hair that helped the points keep their shape without making them heavy. The impracticality of this style kept it from being imitated by the less wealthy and it gradually disappeared during the early part of the 15th century (fig. 22).

As for decoration, most shoes appear to have been left plain and their color left a natural brown color. However, some surviving shoes and illustrations show that many shoes were sometimes dyed or bleached to color them red, green, black, white, or cream. Shoes were also decorated with embroidery or with designs carved or stamped into the leather. In some cases, the designs were cut all the way through the leather, creating delicate and graceful openwork reminiscent of fine lace. Some illustrations also suggest that some of the very wealthy had their shoes accented with silver or gold foil embossed into the carved designs. Shoes with such delicate and expensive decorations may have been intended primarily for indoor use while plainer shoes were used outdoors.

Despite the fine workmanship that may have gone into medieval shoes, their lack of hard soles meant that they were poor protection against wet weather. As early as the 12th century, medieval shoemakers had developed an additional piece of footwear to try to remedy this problem. These items were called *pattens* and served as detachable hard soles that could be worn with any pair of shoes (fig. 22). Pattens were made of pieces of lightweight wood or of layers of leather sewn together to make a thick stack. These pieces were then cut to about the same shape and size as the bottom of the shoes The top of the pattens, whether of leather or wood, were then carved to provide a recess in the top to fit the wearer's shod foot. The top of the patten was also fitted with one or two wide leather straps that secured over the wearer's shoes. To make wooden pattens lighter without weakening them, patten-makers carved the sole of the patten as well. When viewed from the side, the patten's bottom often formed an arch that touched the ground only at two points: at the heel and across the ball of the foot. A few pattens have been found with double arches that touched the ground at a third point: out at the tip of the toes (fig. 22). Also, at least a few pattens were made with thin, flat wooden soles supported on iron braces instead of wooden arches. Regardless of their exact designs, all these pattens raised the bottom of the wearer's shoe by an inch or more for the purpose of elevating the shoe above the level of any puddles, mud, or other hazards that might otherwise dampen the wearer's shoes and feet. Interestingly, pattens seem to have been the only wooden footwear in the Middle Ages. Clogs with wooden soles and leather uppers and shoes made entirely of wood such as those traditionally associated with Holland do not appear to have come into common use until some time after the Middle Ages.

Two other types of footwear that bear mentioning are sandals and high boots. Despite their simplicity, sandals were not popular in the Middle Ages, even in warm climates. Literary references indicate that people in the Middle Ages strongly associated sandals with Christ and his Apostles. Thus, wearing sandals had significant religious overtones and so it may have been considered inappropriate for routine use.

This conclusion is supported by the fact that records of some pilgrimages document that the pilgrims changed their footwear from ordinary shoes to sandals for the duration of the trip. Also, followers of some religious sects during the Middle Ages wore sandals as an expression of their desire to return the Christian church to the poverty, simplicity, and purity of the early Apostolic church. These sects were condemned as heretical and, in regions where these sects were active; any person caught wearing sandals was subject to persecution.

As for high boots, boots that reached to the knee or above were scarce for most of the Middle Ages. They appeared in significant numbers only in the 15th century, near the end of the Middle Ages. Most commonly, high boots were worn by nobles or soldiers riding horses. These boots were made of soft leather and often had the top few inches or more folded over and seem to have been designed for added comfort and durability for men who spent long hours in the saddle.

One point that's conspicuously absent in the discussion above is the differences between men's and women's shoes. There is little evidence that styles of shoes differed much, if at all, between the sexes during the Middle Ages. In medieval illustrations, women's feet were often obscured by their long dresses but the glimpses we do get show shoes that look very much like their male counterparts. Archaeological evidence as well indicates that there were no significant stylistic or design features that distinguished men's shoes from women's. Shoe size (women typically having smaller feet than men) is the only clue as to whether a particular shoe was worn by a man or a woman. Children's shoes are similarly distinguishable by their size though some shoes for infants do bear a remarkable resemblance to modern baby shoes.

CHILDREN'S CLOTHING

During the first months of their lives, infants in the Middle Ages were often swaddled; that is, wrapped up in pieces of cloth so that only their faces were left exposed. While swaddling may have kept the infant warm, it could also cause sores and abscesses which could become dangerously infected if the swaddling was not kept clean and changed regularly. As the infants grew, diminutive versions of the undertunic or chemise and bonnet-like coifs replaced the swaddling. Some swaddling may have been retained to serve as a diaper but leaving the infant bare-bottomed appears to have been the more common practice. In the looser fitting clothes, the infants could crawl about on their own. When they became toddlers, shoes were added to their ensembles as well as items of outerwear, including tunics, surcoats, dresses, and kirtles, depending upon the era and the child's gender and social status. After the child was toilet trained, hose and underwear such as breeches and stockings were the last items added to complete the child's wardrobe. While no evidence has been found on toilet training in the Middle Ages, modern studies suggest that it likely occurred around the age of two years. Thus, any time after about the age of two years old, a child was dressed like a miniature version of an adult.

The practice of dressing children like adults might appear peculiar now, in an age in which the styles, colors, and fabrics of children's clothes are specially designed for their young wearers. However, in the Middle Ages, choices of fabrics and colors were more limited than today so it is not surprising that clothing for adults and children shared the same materials and colors. As to styling, creating clothing uniquely styled for children is a relatively recent phenomenon. During the Middle Ages and for centuries afterwards, once toilet trained, children wore clothing that was basically identical in styling to adult clothing. This practice of dressing children as adults has sometimes been cited as evidence that children in the Middle Ages were viewed and treated as miniature adults but this is not true. If one was to apply this reasoning to the present, when children and adults are often dressed in clothing that imitates styles created for and worn by teenagers and people in their early twenties, one would be led to the conclusion that children and adults who dress in these fashions are all treated like teenagers and twenty-somethings. Obviously, this is not the case. The fact that children's clothes long mimicked adults' fashions simply shows the dominance that adults enjoyed in setting fashion trends until their recent displacement by teenagers. Further, people likely didn't see any need to differentiate children from the rest of society by their clothing. After all, their height and behavior are usually a dead giveaway.

SUMPTUARY LAWS

In the late Middle Ages, jurisdictions from Italy to England began enacting sumptuary laws. These laws regulated the amounts of money that could be spent to make luxurious, or "sumptuous," clothes. Ostensibly, sumptuary laws were attempts to enforce public morals and thrift by prohibiting citizens from spending excessively on vainglorious clothing. However, there appear to have been other motives as well. In some instances, the laws restricted or prohibited the use of pearls, certain types of furs, and other small but very costly items which had to be imported. It is likely that laws of this type were intended to protect the local economy by preventing excessive amounts of money being exported away as payments for these luxury imports. In other instances, the laws dictated the quality of fabrics and decorations and styles of clothing which the various classes of society were permitted to wear. One surviving example of such a law from the early 15th century divided society into 39 categories, from the reigning ruler and lesser nobility, through doctors, lawyers, common workers, down to the final category: unmarried daughters of laborers. Though the law states that its purpose was to defend public morals against excessive spending on clothing, it appears to be an attempt to reinforce the hierarchical structure of medieval society by making everyone wear clothing which the ruling class deemed appropriate for their station in life. Thus, these laws sought to prevent merchants and craftsmen and women, regardless of how prosperous they might be, from dressing better than the lowest, poorest member of the nobility. These laws also attempted to create uniforms of a sort so that the level of a person's position within society could be accurately determined simply by seeing how they were dressed. Such attempts at "branding" people were found throughout medieval Europe.

CLOTHING TO MARK
SOCIAL OUTCASTS

In 1215, the Christian clergy convened the Fourth Lateran Council. Among the pronouncements made by this body was a recommendation to secular rulers that all Jews and any other non–Christians living within their countries be required to wear clothing with very distinctive colors or markings that identified them as being non–Christians. The council thought that this measure would help stop Christians from inadvertently associating with non–Christians, a practice which the council

believed led to interfaith marriages and other activities which might encourage Christians to forsake their faith. The markings or badges to identify Jews took various forms, including small fabric stars of David and little cloth silhouettes of scrolls representing the Torah. The emblems were usually made of yellow fabric. This discriminatory and humiliating practice was revived in the 20th century by the German Nazis who, as part of their persecution of the Jews, forced Jews to wear yellow stars of David.

Heretics who had renounced their heresy and returned to the Christian church were sometimes required to wear markers or badges, such as large yellow or red crosses, on their clothing to remind themselves and any people who saw them of their past apostasy. These reformed heretics had to maintain these markings at their own expense and were subject to additional penalties if they failed to keep them in good repair. Not surprisingly, reformed heretics suffered discrimination in employment and other areas of social life as a result of this marking.

Religious factors weren't the only basis for forcing people to wear distinctive clothing or other special markings. Regardless of whether their disease was actually contagious, lepers were routinely required to carry a noisemaker such as a rattle or bell to warn people of their presence so that the healthy could avoid coming in contact with these diseased beggars. Prostitutes were another group whose clothing was often regulated to put the public on notice of their presence and occupation. Some municipalities required prostitutes to wear clothing with stripes or only made of certain colors of fabric. Other cities forbade prostitutes from wearing hats or else required them to wear hats or hoods that were striped and so were quite unlike those normally worn. Still others forbade prostitutes from wearing jewelry and fine clothing. This prohibition appears to have been a form of sumptuary law to prevent prostitutes from being mistaken for noble ladies and wealthy bourgeoisie and, perhaps, to prevent respectable women from being mistaken for and being solicited as prostitutes. However, it is also likely that civic leaders did not want the prostitutes' luxurious clothing to remind the other citizens of the profits to be made in catering to carnal appetites.

Religious Garb

Though they were at almost the opposite end of the social spectrum from the social outcasts, members of the clergy also wore specialized clothing that clearly marked their status as men and women of the Church. Besides wearing the distinctive tonsure haircut, monks, friars, priests, bishops, and cardinals all wore very distinctive clothing:

Monks — A monk's habit consisted of a long, loose fitting wool tunic, covered with a *scapular* (long, sleeveless garment similar to the surcoat), and a cowl or hood. Rules for various orders of monks record that linen undershirts or undertunics and undershorts as well as cloaks, stockings, shoes, and gloves were also routinely issued to the monks. While their clothing was not substantively different from those worn by other members of medieval society, the uniformity of style and color of their habits made the monks a very distinctive group. As part of the austerity observed in monasteries, clothing was usually limited to a single color which all the brothers wore. Thus, Benedictine monks became noted for their black clothing while Carthusian and Cistercian monks were distinguished by their white habits.

Friars — These itinerant preachers wore basically the same clothing as the monks though some orders of friars pointedly clad their members in cheaper, rougher fabrics to emphasize the poverty, humility, and simplicity that the friars were to practice. One other difference in the friar's costume was that they often wore sandals instead of shoes. As mentioned above, use of sandals was strongly associated with Christ and his disciples and so this choice of footwear symbolically linked the friars to the founder and original preachers of Christianity. As with monastic orders, orders of friars adopted a single color and style for their habits. For example, Dominican friars were often called "black friars" because of their black habits while Franciscans were known as "grey friars" after the greyish brown color of their clothing.

Priests — Traditionally, priests wore *albs*; plain, long, loose fitting tunics made of white cloth when celebrating mass or otherwise acting in official ceremony. Priests also had a number of different items that they might wear in addition to their albs. Depending upon the wealth of his parish, any personal wealth the priest owned, and the relative importance of the holy day being celebrated, a priest might also wear the *chasuble*, a sleeveless cape with a hole in its center like a poncho; the *dalmatic*, a tunic with long sleeves; the *cope*, another cape like garment; the *maniple*, a band of cloth that was originally held in one hand but was later worn wrapped around one wrist; and the stole, a long scarf worn under the chasuble. There were other items besides these but these were the principal liturgical vestments. And, again depending upon the wealth of the priest and his parish, these items ranged from rather plain pieces to expensively embroidered and decorated ones made of silk and other precious materials.

Bishops — Bishops had the same range of wardrobe as priests with a few differences. First, given their greater status and wealth, bishops usually wore vestments made of very fine materials by skilled craftsmen. Second, since they routinely officiated at important religious observances and other ceremonies, bishops were far more likely than priests to appear in public in full clerical regalia. Third, bishops wore *mitres*. Mitres were originally dome-shaped caps but gradually evolved into a tall hat with a deep fold in its top that created two opposing peaks or ridges. This mitre is the type still in use today but most people are probably more familiar with it from the "bishop" in a traditional chess set. At some monasteries, the abbot, who was the highest-ranking monk and governor of the monastic community, was entitled to wear a mitre.

Cardinals — Cardinals, who ranked above bishops in the Church's hierarchy, had the same basic wardrobe as priests and bishops but, like bishops, their vestments were of the highest quality as befitted their wealth and status. By the middle of the 13th century, cardinals had acquired two unique items of clothing. These were a broad-brimmed hat with a shallow crown that was ringed with silken cords and a large, circular cloak with a fur-lined hood. Both the hat and cloak were dyed a bright yet rich scarlet, a color which could usually be produced only with the very expensive insect-based dye mentioned above under "Dyes."

As for nuns, they were part of the monastic tradition and were usually originally established as offshoots of monastic houses. Like monks, their clothing was not too different from the everyday clothes of the laity and included all the basic pieces of clothing: shoes, stockings, long and loose fitting dresses, veils, gloves, and cloaks. Underdresses or chemises were also frequently issued to nuns but were occasionally objects of contention in debates over whether the nuns were being allowed too comfortable and luxurious a wardrobe.

Though distinctive today, the veils, wimples, and long dresses worn by medieval nuns were indistinguishable from those worn by ordinary women except that the colors and styles of these items were, like monks' habits, austere and uniform.

CLOTHING FOR OTHER OCCUPATIONS

In addition to the basic items of clothing already discussed, persons engaged in some occupations wore specialized clothing while performing their trades. Often this clothing was worn for protection and other practical reasons but some items were worn to display that the wearer belonged to a certain trade, typically a prestigious one.

Protective Clothing

Aprons were one of the most common pieces of protective clothing. Smiths wore leather aprons that covered their chests and the fronts of their legs. These aprons shielded the smiths and their other clothing from damage by the high heat and sparks of their forges. Some smiths were also depicted wearing leather coifs or other close-fitting hats, presumably to protect their hair from stray sparks as well. Along with leather boxes mounted on their belts to hold their selection of knives, butchers wore aprons to protect their clothing. Surprisingly, despite the mess involved in slaughtering and cutting apart an animal, most butchers' aprons were shown as small, white aprons that covered only from the waist to the knees. Though these aprons were usually shown as stained, their relatively small size suggests that medieval butchers were so skilled that little blood or other substances were unnecessarily spilled or wasted during slaughter. After all, edible animal tissue was too valuable to waste and even animal blood was routinely collected and made into a type of sausage called a blood pudding. In addition to smiths and butchers, carpenters, masons, millers, bakers, and cooks were also often shown wearing aprons to keep dust — whether of wood and mortar or of flour and grain — off their other clothes.

Besides aprons, which were useful in a variety of settings, there were other, more specialized protective garments. The heavy duty gloves worn by some laborers and the high leather boots worn by people who spent a lot of time riding on horseback have already been mentioned, and the armor worn by knights is discussed in the chapter on fighting, but there were still other items. By the late Middle Ages, beekeepers routinely wore gloves and hoods to protect themselves. Their cloth hoods sometimes included facemasks of leather. These masks had numerous small holes punched in them around the eyes and mouth, allowing the wearer to see and breath. Miners were also often shown wearing hoods that kept dust and dirt out of their hair and which may have had some cushioning in the top to protect their heads in the cramped quarters in which they worked. Such hoods didn't cover the wearer's face but some miners were shown with scarves around their throats which they likely pulled up across their noses and mouths when working to filter some of the dust out of the air they inhaled.

OTHER OCCUPATIONAL CLOTHING

Persons in some occupations wore clothing with special but non-functional features such as color or styling to identify the wearer as a practitioner of that occupation. We have already seen examples of this practice in the uniform clothing worn by monks, nuns, and members of the clergy. Other than prostitutes, most of the other callings that used this method of distinguishing its members were occupations that required formal schooling. For example, professors at medieval universities and other scholars routinely wore caps and voluminous academic gowns of the sort that are now only seen at graduation ceremonies. Such caps and gowns were worn only by university graduates. Their exact cut and accents — such as colored stripes on the sleeves and tassels on the caps — often indicated which university the wearer had attended, which subject he had received his degree in, and the level of that degree. Practitioners of other occupations that required a university education, such as lawyers and physicians, sometimes wore similar robes. However, the robes of lawyers and doctors were far less standardized than the robes of academics. More often, it was the generous cut and the fine, expensive materials and craftsmanship of their clothing that obviously distinguished these professionals from other people.

CLEANING

"Among the many reproaches made against the Middle Ages one of the most insistent aspersions has been a three-headed slander, barking like Cerberus to this effect. First, that the streets of mediaeval towns were constantly foul-smelling and full of filth, owing to the lack of closed sewers and private or public conveniences, to the custom of throwing refuse into the street, and to the failure of municipal authorities to clean the pavements. Second, that soap and baths were little known in those benighted days. Third, that these dirty and pestilence-breeding living conditions in the crowded towns were accompanied by a complete lack of anything resembling sanitary legislation and administration or care for public health" (Professor Lynn Thorndike writing in *Speculum*, the Journal of the Medieval Academy of America, 1923).

More than seventy years later, Cerberus barks on in the popular imagination of what sanitation and hygiene, both public and personal, were like in the Middle Ages. Movies and other fiction continue to portray all people of the Middle Ages, from royalty on down, as pungently unwashed, living in towns and villages where garbage and sewage were routinely dumped out doors and windows and into the streets. This chapter offers some of the myriad evidence to the contrary. This isn't to say that medieval living was always clean and sweet-smelling but it does show that it wasn't just one long wallow in a pig sty from the fall of Rome until the Renaissance. In fact, there's at least circumstantial evidence that hygiene actually took a downturn during the Renaissance and Reformation and didn't begin to recover until after the Enlightenment of the 18th century.

This chapter may seem to paint an overly rosy picture of sanitation in the Middle Ages, but consider the following information: During the Middle Ages, the population of Europe grew steadily until the appearance of the bubonic plague in the mid–14th century, reaching levels that weren't seen again in many regions until the late 18th century. While the population growth occurred in rural as well as urban areas, the expansion of towns and cities up to the mid–14th century indicates that urban populations exploded. That, for centuries before the arrival of the Black Death, these towns and cities were able to survive and support such growth strongly suggests that medieval people employed effective sanitation techniques. Further, while there were certainly outbreaks of infectious diseases before the Black Death, none of these outbreaks were as rampant and devastating as one would expect had "the streets of mediaeval towns [been] constantly foul-smelling and full of filth, owing to the lack of closed sewers and private or public conveniences." This conclusion is also supported by the fact that epidemics of dysentery and other diseases caused or abetted by inadequate sewage disposal and, consequently, contaminated water supplies were not everyday events but were most often recorded in medieval chronicles as occurring in towns and cities under siege, in military encampments, and other settings where the sanitation infrastructure was either under extreme stress and hampered by external interference or was simply nonexistent. With this in mind, let's look at the surprising world of medieval sanitation.

The Roman Legacy

Among the many technological achievements of the Romans, the creation and construction of public sewers and water supplies in their urban settlements throughout Europe proved one of the most enduring. In some cases, Roman aqueducts, such as the system that includes the Pont du Gard in the south of France, outlasted the empire by centuries and continued to carry water from distant sources to the vast cisterns that fed public foun-

tains in towns and cities well into the early Middle Ages. Part of their durability can be attributed to there being little incentive to destroy them. Made only of massive stone blocks, the aqueducts were extremely difficult to tear down and there was nothing of value to strip from them except the stones themselves. And these became worth taking only later as villages and towns grew up nearby and the people sought easy sources for building materials. Even then, the value of a functioning aqueduct that provided much needed drinking water usually deterred such demolition. Roman sewers proved even more durable. Their placement underground, obviously essential to the performance of their intended purpose, protected them from exposure to weather, vandals, and other damaging forces. Besides their robust and sturdy construction, another factor that contributed significantly to the long useful lives of both the sewers and aqueducts was their fundamental reliance on gravity, the timeless fact that fluids run downhill. Even during the Middle Ages that didn't change, so Roman conduits continued to flow, bringing fresh water in and taking sewage away from those urban areas fortunate enough to have them and wise enough to perform occasional maintenance.

Admittedly, there were areas within Europe with little or no public works from the Romans. These included regions that the Romans did not conquer (such as Scandinavia and the extreme north of Britain), in which they had only scattered settlements (as in central and southern Britain and the rest of the empire's periphery), or where they simply had no motivation or resources for constructing such works (such as rural areas, wastelands and forests, anywhere away from main urban settlements). Still, even in these areas, Rome's influence was felt even after the empire was no more, in part because

Roman facilities and traditions continued in important population centers. In Paris and other major cities, public baths, sewers, and other public works functioned continuously from the Roman era into the Middle Ages while many smaller cities and towns maintained their Roman public waterworks as well. Though the new facilities were not on the large scale of the Roman works, construction of new sanitation and waterworks did continue through the Middle Ages, starting as early as the 8th century when palaces of the Carolingian kings included hot and cold bathing facilities in imitation of those found in Roman villas. Thus, the fall of Rome did not suddenly end all classical public works and traditions of sanitation as though some light switch was turned off. Rather, like a trickle from a faucet, they continued. The trickle kept going through the dark times immediately after the fall, survived, and gradually grew through the Middle Ages.

Institutional and Private Water and Sanitation Systems

MONASTERIES

Monasteries were the great preservers of classical knowledge after the fall of Rome and this knowledge was not limited to philosophy and literature. Even in the earliest centuries of the Middle Ages, monasteries were constructed with both sewer and water systems. Besides their awareness of at least the basics of classical technology, the monks had a driving need for these amenities because they were relatively large communities, numbering from dozens to hundreds of people living in the same quarters year in and year out.

To keep these quarters habitable and disease-free, they had to have reliable water supplies for cleaning themselves and their surroundings and flushing away the waste.

Like most toilet facilities throughout the Middle Ages, monastic sewer systems were often very basic, with latrines that emptied into shafts through which the waste flowed into a cesspit or, more desirably, into the nearest river to be carried downstream. In fact, a good supply of running water for this and other purposes appears to have been a key factor in selecting sites for many monasteries. At least one monastery on a coastline refined this idea further and had the latrines empty out into an area that was flushed out twice a day by the rise and fall of the tides. By the 12th century, if not earlier, some monasteries had advanced to having facilities for regularly flushing the latrines, even without the help of the tides. Large, elevated cisterns provided water under some pressure for this task.

As for cesspits, these were holes dug into the ground, usually in the form of dry wells. Lined with wooden planks or stones pierced with small holes, these pits acted as septic tanks, holding the toilet waste, allowing the liquids in it to leach away out into the ground while the solids gradually accumulated and filled the pit. Though some latrines were located directly over cesspits, most cesspits were covered to contain the odor and as a safety measure to prevent people from falling in. For the covered pits, waste entered through shafts or pipes angling down from the latrine and into the pit.

The latrines themselves consisted of wooden or stone supports topped with long wooden planks forming the seats. There were, of courses, holes of the appropriate size at regular intervals along the length of the planks. Thus, their seats looked and functioned like those found in outhouses and privies. Excavations at some monasteries have yielded evidence that at least some monks used a form of toilet paper consisting of old rags of thin linen, likely torn from worn-out robes or tunics. It has been suggested that monastery latrines had urinals as well, possibly in the form a large basin with a central fountain that flushed away the waste. While they certainly had the technology for such an impressive item, a simple trough in the floor along one wall seems more practical. Chamber pots were little used in monasteries, with the exception of in the infirmaries where those too sick to walk to the latrine were allowed their use.

Monastic water supply systems were more impressive. By the 12th century, some monasteries in England had water piped in from several miles away using gravity-powered systems. Piping was made of two materials: lead or hollowed out tree trunks. Using good, durable hardwoods such as elm, medieval construction workers bored a hole through the length of the tree trunk, making it into a large tube. One end of the tube was flared slightly while the outside edge of the opposite end was tapered down. These wooden pipes were then laid so that the tapered end of one pipe fit securely into the slightly flared opening in the end of the next pipe in line. As for metal pipes, medieval workers continued the Roman tradition of plumbing (from the Latin *plumbum*, meaning lead). Lead was the metal of choice because it was relatively plentiful and easy to work, ductile with a low melting temperature. To make pipes, lead was cast and flattened into long, narrow sheets. The sheets were bent around a long, cylindrical form (such as a log) and the edges overlapped, crimped, and melted together to make a watertight tube. This brings up another characteristic of lead that made it well-suited to plumbing: though it does oxidize, lead better withstands exposure to

water, suffering less corrosion than iron. So, while the dangers of poisoning from lead leached out of leaden water pipes are now well-known and have curtailed the use of such pipes, lead was considered a very useful metal for pipes and other building applications as described in Chapter II.

In addition to the piping, these water supply systems displayed other sophisticated features, including series of up to four or five "settling houses" positioned one below the other on the gradual, downward sloping course of the water system. The settling houses were large holding tanks that slowed the flow of water down, allowing sediment in the water to settle out before the water continued on through the pipes and into the cisterns. Settling sediments and using iron grillwork to screen out large pieces of floating debris, such as logs, aquatic weeds, fish, and the occasional drowned animal, appear to have been the only means of water purification used in medieval water supply systems. From the cisterns, pipes fed the water out to the monastery's kitchen, brewery, latrine, and permanent stone fixtures that held metal basins for washing hands mounted near the infirmary and the dining hall. The ends of many of these pipes were fitted with faucets, often made of bronze, to control the water flow. The sinks in the kitchen, the basins for washing hands, and all the other water receptacles had drains that emptied the used water into pipes to carry it away. Some of these monastic water systems were designed so that the pipes carrying the waste water as well as the pipes that drained rainwater off the buildings emptied into the main drainage system before it reached the latrines. This additional flow helped further ensure that the pipe draining the sewage from the latrine was flushed on a near constant basis.

One additional note about the monks

and their hygiene: besides washing their hands, they washed the rest of their bodies regularly too. Rules for the various monastic orders often recognized that bathing could be a self-indulgent luxury or an occasion for worse sins and so counseled against excessive bathing. But these rules also dictated that regular bathing was necessary for the health and well-being of the monks. Though refusing to bathe was an acknowledged form of self-denial and some medieval saints, such as St. Catherine of Siena, were quite noted for their "pious" lack of bathing, the health problems and discomfort (to others as well as to the practitioner) caused by such abstinence were obvious. Thus, the monastic rules did not endorse or otherwise encourage abstaining from baths for prolonged periods. In fact, records of monastery activities kept by the monks show that cold baths were used as means of quenching fleshly desires of unruly monks while others, especially those in the infirmary, were provided with periodic warm baths. However, there is little, if any, physical evidence that indicates the bathing habits of monks. There are no surviving fixtures, such as bathtubs or shower stalls, at any monasteries that we would recognize as the hallmarks of a bathroom. So how did they bathe without permanent fixtures? A few contemporary plans for monasteries and records for expenditures and other activities provide the answer. They used a practice common throughout the centuries before indoor plumbing — bathing in large, wooden tubs, similar to the one shown in Figure 11. Water was drawn from the taps into buckets (with some of it taken to the kitchen and heated) and then carried to fill the tubs, a very labor intensive process that helps explain why bathing appears to have been only a weekly event in monasteries and elsewhere during the Middle Ages. When needed, the tubs were placed in any suitable room. The tubs could be placed in the dormitory, the laundry, or the refectory (the dining hall) which was conveniently located near the hot water from the kitchen. When not in use, the tubs were stored out of the way. Alternatively, in some monasteries, the large wooden tubs may have been located in rooms adjoining the laundry or the wash tubs in the laundry itself may have doubled as bathtubs. In any event, the perishable nature of the wooden tubs (and the hard use they saw) has meant that no direct, physical traces of this method of bathing have survived.

Palaces and Castles

Though they were centers of military and political administration rather than meditation and prayer, castles and palaces were comparable to monasteries in the numbers and needs of their inhabitants. Thus, there were often similarities in construction.

Not surprisingly, some of the best and most advanced medieval water and sanitation systems were found in the palaces of the nobility. The plumbing of Carolingian palaces has already been mentioned but there are many other examples. In England, 13th century records of expense for the palace at Westminster show that it had a piped water supply with bronze faucets. Fourteenth century financial accounts record expenditure for new bronze faucets for the taps supplying both hot and cold water to the king's bath at the palace and for the renovation of the furnace that heated large earthenware pots filled with water for the king's bath at Windsor castle. Other records and illustrations show that these baths were very large wooden tubs that look much like modern, rustic-style hot tubs. Often they had fabric canopies to shield bathers from drafts as well as fabric liners to cushion them from the tub's hard sides.

As for toilets, the facilities for nobility were about the same as those for monks, except that they were usually called by a different euphemism. While monasteries called their toilets the *necessarium* (a Latin term for the necessary room or place), toilets in the palaces and castles were usually called *garderobes* (a French word for wardrobe or clothes closet, but there is no evidence that clothes or other items of wardrobe were ever stored in these garderobes). Palace garderobes were often communal facilities like those in monasteries but many were more private. For example, the palace of one archbishop had a separate tower for the garderobes connected to the main building by hallways at various levels. On each level of the tower, a central room contained four toilets placed with their backs against a central shaft. All the toilets emptied into that shaft. This circular layout, combined with narrow stone partitions between the toilets, permitted several people to use the facilities simultaneously but out of sight of each other. Still other garderobes were constructed as small rooms with a single toilet and were built within inside the thick walls of the palaces. Palace walls were often six feet or more in thickness so these little rooms could be built inside the walls without significantly reducing their structural integrity. Some of these garderobes adjoined fireplaces. In such locations, they were kept warm and dry by the heat of the fireplace. These garderobes may have also had ventilation systems connected to the chimney that used the draft created by the rising heat of the fire to help draw air up and out of the garderobe, an important feature for a small, closed room. As with monastic toilets, the shafts draining these garderobes were often connected to the rest of the palace's drainage system to provide frequent flushing. Another form of garderobe was fashioned as a small projection from the walls or towers. Rather than emptying into a shaft, the projecting garderobe had seats over holes that emptied directly down and out of the building. Needless to say, medieval architects tried to locate these toilets above the longest, straightest drop away from the palace, preferably into a river or moat or, less desirably, into open ditches below. For the projecting garderobes as well as in cases where the internal toilet shafts deposited the waste into cesspits rather than a river or moat, the financial accounts for many noble households reveal routine payments to *gongfermors*, men who made their living by digging out and carting away the solid waste that accumulated in these pits and ditches. The payments also show that being a gongfermor was a well-paid profession.

Chamber pots and close stools (chairs that discreetly housed chamber pots under their hinged seats) may have been in use at palaces by the late Middle Ages though there is little evidence of this practice. There may have been little incentive for their use. In many noble residences, there were numerous garderobes with many placed near the main sleeping and living quarters and, in several cases, some located *en suite* within the walls of the finest bedchambers (thus sparing their noble residents the difficulties of trying to find the toilet during the middle of the night down unlit corridors and stairways). Despite their bare appearance now, records suggest that the garderobes in the homes of the elite had fine wooden seats while the walls were often covered in wood paneling.

Castles were usually more spartan in their accommodations than royal palaces. Not infrequently, they suffered from inadequate water supplies. Unlike palaces and monasteries which could be located almost anywhere and which were often placed to take the best advantage of water sources, beautiful settings, and other natural features, locations of castles were usually dictated by strategic security concerns. Some castles were located to control vital spots, such as important transportation (and potential invasion) routes, including ports, roads, rivers, and river crossings. Others were located in cities to assert control over the local populace. Regardless of the exact setting, sites for castles were chosen to make them as difficult to attack and as easy to defend as possible, given the natural features available. This principle of defense dictated that castles were usually located on the highest ground nearest the point to be controlled. While occupying the high ground meant that castle garrisons could easily keep watch over wide areas and rain arrows and missiles down on any attackers, it also meant that good water supplies were often hard to find. Medieval water systems relied on gravity to keep the water flowing, so use of springs to supply water was ordinarily out of the question since the castle occupied the highest piece of ground around and was thus at a higher elevation than any neighboring springs. Further, water sources located outside the protective perimeter of the castle could be cut off during sieges. Rainwater was also often collected but it was not a reliable source. This combination of factors meant that castles most often relied on wells inside their walls to provide a reliable water supply that wouldn't be vulnerable during a siege. Drawing water from a well was a laborious process. Further, though castles frequently had cisterns, there was no running fresh water within the castle unless the storage tanks were in the upper levels of the castle's towers. Filling such elevated tanks required even more labor since the water had to be hand carried or hoisted up in buckets or barrels. Thus, water supplies in castles were often limited. Yet, except in times of siege, this limited supply was not a severe problem. When the castle was *not* under attack (which was most if not all the time), its inhabitants were free to have water brought in to fill the castle's cistern

and then use as much water as needed for bathing, cooking, and washing. The water was hauled up to the castle in barrels or waterskins which were waterproof leather bags fitted with resealable openings for filling and emptying. Smaller waterskins were carried by people while larger ones were hung on the backs of horses and mules like immense saddlebags. A few colorful reminders of the practice of hauling water have survived. For example, in Knaresborough, England, a winding lane leading up the steep slope from the river to the castle at the top of the cliff is still called "Waterbag Bank" after the large leather waterbags that mules carried up the lane long ago.

While the elevated location of the castle was a major hindrance for getting water into the castle, it made getting rid of waste water and sewage a much easier task. Though there may not have been pipes to carry flowing fresh water in, there was always some form of plumbing for carrying wastes away, ranging from pipes draining the kitchen sinks and other receptacles of waste water to the shafts or holes that emptied the garderobes. Regardless of the source of the wastes, they all ended up in the same place, the moat or in ditches and pits surrounding the castle, preferably on the side downwind of most buildings. As with palaces, garderobes in castles were located in rooms specially constructed in towers or inside thick outer walls. The garderobes were typically placed along the outside edge of the castle to facilitate the rapid exit of the sewage. Some castles were built with several groups or banks of garderobes in a single tower or within the thickness of one wall, presumably the wall or tower was on the downwind side of castle or was otherwise best suited to this function. The banks of garderobes were built on several different stories, often staggered so that they were not directly below or above one another. The shafts draining the garderobes angled down and joined the main drainage shaft below the lowest bank of garderobes. In some cases, the staggering of the garderobes and the angling of shafts appears to have been designed to lessen drafts of air up from the drainage shaft as well as for structural reasons. All the shafts ran down through the wall and the main shaft emptied out a hole at the bottom of the wall. Having rooms and shafts built inside the walls might appear to undermine the strength of the walls but the spaces created by the shafts and garderobes were so small compared to the overall volume of the massive walls that these few hollow spots did not weaken the walls to any significant degree. After all, castle walls were often eight to fifteen feet or more in thickness and two to three stories in height. Besides being built inside walls, some garderobes were built as small structures that projected out away from the walls with holes that opened directly over the ground or moat below. Usually placed along the top outside edge of the wall, these garderobes functioned like those found in palaces and elsewhere and were designed to help further ensure that the sewage fell as far away from the castle as possible.

Though a few toilets, primarily those adjoining the quarters of the master of the castle, may have been built to be as comfortable as those in palaces, most toilets in castles were intended for the use of the servants and men-at-arms who garrisoned the castle. Thus, the furnishings of these garderobes appear to have been only the bare necessities and less effort was put into assuring adequate ventilation and frequent flushing of the shafts draining these latrines. The scarcity of flowing water in the castle significantly contributed to the lack of adequate flushing. On the inside, most castle garderobes looked like outhouses, wooden planks with a large hole in the center forming the seat. Unlike outhouses, the wooden seat topped a matching larger, circular or rectangular opening in the stones that were integral parts of the castle itself. The wooden seat must have been more comfortable than the bare stones, especially on cold winter mornings. Even with the seat, most garderobes in castles did not encourage long stays. They were drafty and often odorous, depending on how far below the sewage collected and the amount of sewage stuck to the side of the shaft or wall below. Despite the unappealing and unsanitary nature of garderobe shafts, besieging forces on more than one occasion successfully entered castles by having men climb up the shafts. Because of this risk, the outside openings of garderobe shafts were routinely fitted with iron gratings to prevent besiegers from entering.

PRIVATE HOMES

By the 13th century, private houses in the larger, more prosperous cities that had sophisticated municipal water supplies did have running water in the form of a single pipe, often no larger than a modern drinking straw in diameter, capped by a faucet. Not surprisingly, throughout the Middle Ages, homes in towns or on the farm did not have this amenity. As would be the case until the 19th century when "indoor plumbing" became more common, farmers, townsfolk, and many urbanites took buckets, tubs, and waterskins to the nearest spring, river, well, or — if in the city — public fountain, filled them and lugged them home (a wearying task that ensured most consumers used the water sparingly). For sewage disposal, farmhouses and houses in small towns often had outhouses at a discreet distance from them. Houses in cities also frequently had outhouses out in their backyards or had facilities indoors with pipes to drain the waste to the cesspit out back. Public toilets were also a common feature in most cities. Scattered around the city, these toilets were used by people passing through the area as well as by permanent residents whose houses may have lacked private facilities. Supplementing these methods, chamber pots or buckets must have been used in tenements and other places where several households shared a single building which did not have adequate facilities, though pots and buckets were likely used in any of the other settings too, at night, when the weather was bad, or any other time the more permanent toilet facilities seemed too distant.

Public Water and Sanitation Systems

Needless to say, supplying water and removing waste from cities required much more effort than providing these same services to a single castle or even a large monastic community. The responses of medieval cities to the problems of water supply and waste disposal were often less than satisfactory, especially by today's standards, but do reflect careful and creative thought in applying the technology available to solving these problems. Above all, these efforts show that medieval Europeans recognized that wallowing in filth was eminently undesirable and unhealthy and so they strove to secure the cleanest water available and generally kept themselves and their environs clean as best they could.

WATER SUPPLIES

While rivers and streams were the primary sources of water in medieval towns and cities, most cities supplemented these sources by bringing water from nat-

ural springs in to serve urban consumers. As rivers and streams nearest the cities became increasingly contaminated by sewage and other garbage as populations grew and the cities themselves expanded, covering more of the watershed bordering the rivers, supplies of clean water from the springs became vital to the well-being of cities. Even in areas with numerous springs, city and town dwellers, like their rural kin, also dug wells to provide an even greater supply of water. However, in densely populated areas, this well water was often no safer to drink than river water since it was frequently contaminated by sewage seeping into the groundwater from nearby latrines.

Authorities used a variety of methods to bring clean, fresh water into the cities. The choice of methods depended upon the resources available, including finances and transportation as well as the location of the water sources. Often, cities would use a combination of methods. For example, in some cases, immense casks of spring water were shipped in by barge or cart and then emptied into public cisterns which filled pipes that ran to public fountains from which residents could draw water. A more preferable method was to build permanent water mains or re-use earlier Roman ones to connect the city directly to the spring. This method was more economical than shipping and created a more reliable supply but it had several prerequisites. First it required locating springs large enough to meet the city's needs. Second, the springs had to be at a higher elevation than the city (more on this later). Third and last, the springs had to be located within a distance that could be spanned using the technology then available. Authorities fortunate enough to have springs that met these three conditions (and to have cities wealthy enough to afford the construction) built conduits of leaden and wooden pipe to carry the water, just as the monasteries did.

Civic water mains, then as now, were major feats of construction with miles of buried pipes, numerous valves, settling houses, filtering grillwork, storage tanks, and all the other features essential to keep the water flowing. Along with lead pipes, London's conduit in the 13th century had wooden pipes from 10 to 22 feet in length made from trunks of elm trees. The centers of the trunks were drilled out, creating pipes with bores ranging from 2 to 10 inches. The earliest wooden pipes were bored out by hand with large augers but water-powered boring machines were also developed and used during the Middle Ages. Though the materials are alien to modern plumbing, these medieval pipes had Y- and T-shaped joints, venting, and other features common to plumbing today. While the physical layout of the medieval water works generally resembled modern systems, a major difference was the low pressure of the water flow. Medieval water systems relied solely on gravity to keep water flowing through the pipes, hence the importance of having springs at an elevation higher than that of the city. The higher elevation of the spring also significantly lessened the risk that its water was contaminated by harmful runoff from the city's sewage. Pumps, invented by the ancient Greeks, appear to have been constructed and used only on a small scale during the Middle Ages. Large pumps powered by watermills to force water through pipes did not appear until the late 15th century. Thus, though holding tanks and other measures could be used to build up some pressure in the system, the flow of water was usually a trickle at best.

Besides the age-old problem of the capacity of public works being quickly outpaced by a growing public and its demands, low water pressure coupled with the limited amounts of water flowing into the pipes meant that water usage was often a source of contention. Consumers at the upstream end of the system, the end closest to the water source, frequently drained so much water from the system that there was little or no water left for those customers downstream whose taps were lower down in the system and further away from the water source. This problem was worsened by the fact that the conduits served businesses as well as private homes. Householders had to compete with brewers, butchers, and other tradespeople whose businesses required large quantities of water to make or to clean their merchandise. Thus, cities enacted regulations to control water use and appointed officials to safeguard the public water supply. Besides assessing annual fees for water service, the regulations included restrictions on the amount of water businesses, namely brewers, could draw from public fountains. Violating these restrictions typically resulted in the confiscation of the containers in which the water was being carried. Other documents record actions against people who illegally tapped into water mains to divert water for their own use without paying for the privilege. In London, one miscreant was punished for this offense by being made to ride through the streets while water was continuously poured over his head through a small set of pipes symbolizing the water mains.

London also strove to keep its water supplies drinkable by occasionally flushing the conduit as well by prohibiting dumping into its rivers. This latter point may sound odd given how polluted parts of the Thames were even by the early part of the Middle Ages but citizens continued to draw water from the Thames for drinking and cleaning long after the Middle Ages ended. These anti-dumping laws also served to keep river channels open and navigable, an important consideration for any port city. The city-states of northern Italy had comparable legislation to protect their water supplies and Paris imposed similar protections on the Seine. In 1550, Parisian municipal officials successfully opposed a royal plan that would have emptied some of the city's sewers into the river upstream of significant parts of the city, contaminating a water supply used by half the population. Though this event occurred after the end of the period we are examining and the Seine likely suffered from significant pollution before this date, it's indicative of long tradition of trying to keep the river as clean as possible in the face of competing demands on its use.

PUBLIC SANITATION

The mere mention of sanitation in medieval cities conjures up images of gutters and streets serving as open, malodorous sewers, clogged with all kinds of garbage, from kitchen wastes and animal droppings to the contents of toilets emptied directly out the window and onto the street below. Undeniably, such conditions often occurred. However, records of lawsuits, bequests in wills, and civic regulations and expenditures show that these conditions were not viewed as acceptable by citizens during the Middle Ages and that these citizens and their government officials frequently and routinely took action to prevent and abate such unsanitary conditions.

Sewers, Cesspits, and Public Latrines

While a few towns and cities were fortunate and had at least some Roman drainage systems, most urban dwellers, directly or indirectly, used the streams and rivers which flowed through their towns and cities as sewers.

Besides using them as places to throw the contents of chamber pots or to empty pipes leading from toilets, citizens used watercourses for direct disposal of sewage

by placing latrines, both public and private, alongside or even spanning streams and rivers. The practice of building houses and businesses on bridges, something seen today only in a few Italian cities (fig. 16) and in illustrations of long vanished bridges in Paris, London, and elsewhere, was motivated in part by the easy disposal of sewage and other garbage provided by the river flowing below. The unpleasant impact this practice had on persons traveling on the river below was summed up in an adage: Bridges are made for wise men to go over and for fools to go under. But this practice did run into opposition when streams and smaller rivers were choked with sewage from the outfall of too many latrines. For example, in London, there were repeated campaigns to clean up the Walbrook, a stream that ran near the city's wall. In the early 14th century, responding to complaints from citizens in the neighborhood, city officials ordered that latrines emptying into the stream to be torn down and no new ones built. It appears to have worked for a while, but the latrines and the pollution problem returned, as evidenced by the reissuance of the same order some years later in the mid–14th century. Several years later, city officials admitted defeat and agreed that houses adjoining the stream could have toilets emptying into the stream on the condition that residents could not throw any other trash in and that they paid an annual fee to the city to cover the cost of keeping the Walbrook cleaned out and flowing. But this compromise failed and in the mid–15th century, the city finally ordered the Walbrook to be covered over and paved, one of the first of London's streams and rivers to be "lost" underground.

Not all toilets in medieval cities emptied so directly into the water. On streets away from streams or rivers, some residents dumped their sewage out the window or door and into the gutter, a practice that could result in prosecution and a fine. A more sanitary (and legal) method of disposal was to use a cesspit. These pits, ranging from large ones under public latrines to smaller ones located below and behind individual houses, were a common feature in medieval cities. Thus, medieval urban dwellers also indirectly used the rivers (or more precisely, their surrounding ground water) to absorb and carry away some of the contents of these pits. As with the cesspits of castles and palaces, gongfermors were routinely employed to dig out pits that had filled up with sewage. But city regulations added a few refinements. Cesspit cleaning was often limited to the nighttime, presumably to lessen the inconvenience to passers-by and others in the vicinity but this also may have been, at least in the case of public latrines, motivated by the practical consideration of taking the toilets out of service during their hours of least use. Reflecting additional consideration of the need to maintain health and good order in close quarters, regulations of the city of London as early as 1189 specified that cesspits had to be at least five and a half feet inside the property line (though stone-lined pits could be built to within two and a half feet of the property line).

As recorded in a number of lawsuits, some citizens used creative means to avoid the expense of building a proper cesspit. In one case, two men ran the pipe from their toilet down into their neighbor's disused cellar. The neighbor sued the men for the damages. (But the neighbor must have been rather oblivious to his surroundings or else been absent for a long time since he only brought suit after discovering his basement completely filled with so much filth that it was beginning to seep up through the floor and into the rooms above!) In another case, a woman discretely ran a pipe from her toilet into the common gutter out in the street. Unfor-tunately for the woman, the gutter became clogged and officials traced the source of the blockage back to the illegal pipe. She was ordered to dismantle it.

Public toilets were also a common feature in medieval cities. As mentioned before, these were built for the use of both the permanent residents of neighboring homes that lacked private latrines, a condition found in many residences, as well as for anyone else passing through. The public toilets were built to improve the health of the city by providing a convenient and relatively sanitary place for people to defecate and urinate, thus encouraging the people to deposit their bodily wastes in a place where they could be properly disposed of rather than become a noisome health hazard in some street or gutter. However, in cities that processed sheep fleeces into wool cloth, the public toilets served an additional function: the collection of urine for commercial use. These cities continued a Roman tradition of collecting urine from public toilets and selling it to wool processors. The processors used the ammonia-rich urine to remove oils from the wool, an essential step in turning raw wool into good quality cloth. It was also likely that urine was sold to leather tanners and used in the first stages of leather production in the soaking solution that removed hair from the raw animal hides. Animal urine would have worked as well as human urine in these processes but it was far easier to collect human urine, especially in the quantities needed. It is likely that urine was collected in barrels into which drained the fluids from the urinal troughs in the men's latrines.

Maintaining the public toilets was no easy task. In London and other cities, there were repeated complaints by citizens about latrines in dangerous states of disrepair, including at least one instance, similar to an event in Boccaccio's *Decameron*, where a person fell through the weakened floor of a public toilet and drowned in the cesspit below. Thus, in wills of medieval city dwellers, bequests to repair or build new public latrines appear with other charitable donations for the public good.

Another civic sanitation facility common in many continental towns and cities, though scarce in England, was the public bath which will be discussed below as part of personal hygiene. Continuing on with public sanitation, there was more to keeping a city clean and livable than just sewage disposal.

Street Cleaning

Few streets were paved. Most were just hard packed dirt with some gravel. Broader streets typically had gutters formed by shallow ditches running along both sides of the street while narrow streets had only a single gutter down their centers. The gutters had at least a constant trickle running through them from discarded wash water and other liquid waste from houses and businesses lining the streets and were occasionally flushed out by rain water draining off the adjoining buildings and land. But this irregular flow of water was insufficient to keep the gutters clean and did nothing to remove the droppings of draft animals, construction scraps, and other large pieces of garbage that accumulated in the roadway itself.

The cities and towns took several actions to fight the accumulation of garbage in their streets. Most had laws, at first customary but later written down, that required citizens to keep the streets and pathways in front of their properties free from nuisances, including large or especially noxious trash, that impeded traffic. Charters of Italian and French towns and cities from as far back as the

13th century include many examples of such regulations. Records of legal actions to enforce such laws are common and heavy fines were often imposed, especially on repeat offenders. In addition to laws, cities also took direct action to keep streets passable and prevent dangerous health conditions by employing men to clean the streets and gutters. Called "rakers" in London, these street cleaners raked up trash, placed it in their carts, and hauled it away for disposal. Disposal of solid waste hasn't really changed much since the Middle Ages. After being collected, the waste was either carted away to designated dumping areas, usually outside the city limits, or, if the city was located on a navigable river, loaded onto dungboats, the medieval equivalent of garbage scows, taken downstream and dumped into the water.

Some of the waste collected from city streets included horse manure and other organic materials that could have been used as fertilizer, something that was in short supply on most medieval farms. However, waste from the streets also likely contained human waste and other miscellaneous garbage unsuitable for use as fertilizer. (Human waste, in the form of sterilized sludge from sewage treatment plants, is now a safe form of fertilizer but raw human waste, which may contain harmful bacteria and other disease causing organisms, cannot be safely used as fertilizer on crops grown for human consumption. Medieval Europeans were unaware of the existence of these pathogens in human waste, but — in contrast to China and elsewhere in Asia — there is no evidence that they routinely collected and used human waste as fertilizer which suggests that they did understand that such waste was unsafe for use as fertilizer.) Besides the problem of waste from the streets containing garbage unfit for use in fertilizer, the logistical and health problems of moving large amounts of partially liquid waste deterred large scale recycling of the waste. However, some recycling of waste into fertilizer did occur. For example, in records of a prosecution in 14th century London over the nuisance caused by a large dung heap encroaching on a public highway, the defendant stated that this waste was nothing out of the ordinary. It was to be loaded onto her family's boats, taken away, and spread as fertilizer on their estate. She said her family had provided this mutually beneficial removal of waste from London for as long as anyone could recall. On a smaller scale, recycling of animal droppings occurred both inside the city as well as in rural areas. In cities, the population was relatively dense but there were still many kitchen gardens and other areas under cultivation. A householder tending such a garden was unlikely to pass up a lump of good, pure horse manure in the street near his house since it would certainly help boost the garden's output. Similarly, out in rural areas, farmers could help themselves to droppings of horses and other draft animals along highways and town streets. Such manure was unlikely to be contaminated by other garbage and was conveniently located near where the farmer could immediately put it to use.

Other Public Health and Safety Laws and Actions

Sanitary and related public health and safety regulations extended beyond just sewage and street cleaning. There were some forms of environmental protection and anti-pollution laws even in the Middle Ages. For example, by the 12th century, the port of Marseilles employed workers to clean the streets adjoining the harbor to keep garbage from being flushed into the harbor, preventing the trash from con-

tributing to the natural filling in of the harbor by silt in runoff. Further, the crews of all boats entering the harbor had to swear an oath to keep the harbor clean. Anyone who unloaded a boat or began scraping its hull to clean it and remove barnacles before the boat's crew had sworn the oath had to remove or pay for the removal of a boatload of mud from the harbor. Anyone caught dumping garbage in the harbor was subject to the same penalty, at the rate of one boatload of mud per basket of garbage he or she had dumped.

Even more common than these stringent harbor regulations were the actions taken by many towns and cities to control the adverse impact of trades noted for their noxious smells or wastes. These trades included leather tanning and vending of fish, poultry, and the flesh of livestock. Besides the health hazards posed by the caustic solutions used to remove hair and soften the hides, the various compounds used to tan and color the leather also smelled awful. As for butchers, fishmongers, and sellers of poultry, these trades typically involved on the spot killing, gutting, plucking, and or scaling by the vendor of the animal selected by the customer. Consequently, animal viscera, especially those of fish, and feathers were frequently cited both in regulations against littering and dumping as well as in prosecutions against polluters.

Besides requiring that the physical wastes of trades be disposed of properly, that is, placed in the appropriate public dumping ground or otherwise hauled out of the city at the expense of the person producing the waste, medieval cities also enacted zoning laws. These laws dictated that trades which produced especially noxious smells or wastes had to be located to minimize their adverse impact on the rest of the community. The ideal result was to remove all such trades to locations outside the city walls. In reality, the common result was that similar trades were all located together in one part of town, concentrating their pollution but at least minimizing its impact on the rest of the city. To further minimize exposure to odors and other harmful byproducts of these businesses, the city authorities chose locations for these industrial zones that were downstream from where most citizens drew water and that, based on prevailing winds, were downwind from population centers. This practice, along with the custom of grouping practitioners of guild-controlled trades together, left lasting marks on many European cities where streets retain names like "Tanners Court" indicative of the trades conducted in the neighborhood long ago.

Other trade-related sanitation and public health measures taken by most cities included the inspection of foodstuffs and regulations on their sale. Some of these official actions, such as setting prices for breads and other staples and ensuring that items were accurately weighed and measured, were for the protection of the consumer's purse. Others were specifically aimed at keeping spoiled or otherwise tainted foods from sickening customers. These regulations included requiring that meats were sold only in designated markets and were subject to random inspection by city officials. Further, sales times for meats and most other foods were typically limited to certain times of the day well *before* sunset. This ensured that customers could view their prospective purchases under the best light available and not have to make their selection in twilight or by torch-light when defects could be more easily hidden by unscrupulous vendors. Additional regulations forbade bakers of pies with meat, poultry, or fish fillings from using old, stale or spoiled ingredients or discarded by-products from butchers, poultry sellers, and fishmongers. While enforcement of these regulations may not have been as uniform and as stringent as it is today, medieval legal records contain numerous accounts of actions taken against merchants who violated the laws by ripping off consumers or jeopardizing their health or lives. These offenders included bakers who sold underweight loaves and butchers, fishmongers, and piemen who sold spoiled foods. Fines were common but were seldom the only punishment imposed. For example, a baker who sold underweight loaves could be punished by having the loaves confiscated and given to a local prison to feed its inmates or, more commonly, by being paraded through the streets with one of the offending loaves tied around his neck. Butchers and others who sold tainted food had their wares confiscated and burned while the offender had to sit or stand directly in front of the burning pile, inhaling the stench of smoldering spoiled meat, poultry, or fish. Such public punishments may seem to have been mere exercises in taking petty revenge by humiliating wrong-doers, but besides deterring similar bad conduct, they also gave the buying public a good opportunity to look at and identify the offenders so they would know whose products to avoid in the future.

By the latter half of the Middle Ages, beyond these preventative and punitive actions, some cities further attempted to guard the public's health by employing physicians. In most of Europe, these physicians were adjuncts to the city authorities who regulated trade. They acted primarily as licensing officials, verifying the qualifications of persons seeking to practice medicine in the city. Occasionally, they also acted as coroners in cases of suspicious deaths or as advisors to the city government during plagues or other wide spread medical emergencies. However, municipal physicians in Italy, a region noted throughout the Middle Ages for its many centers of medical education, routinely engaged in several more activities to promote public health. These included supervising quarantines for many contagious diseases (not just the plague), conducting health and sanitation inspections, and caring for sick citizens who were too poor to pay for professional medical services, though such secular care of the poor was very rare. Monasteries were the traditional providers of health care to the sick and injured, wealthy or poor, who came to their gates. But there were few other examples of such secular care, the most notable being public hospitals in cities in Italy and France. Though municipal treasuries financed some of their expenses, these hospitals were not secular institutions. They were usually extensions of religious foundations and their staffs typically included monks, nuns, and other members of religious orders.

Building and maintaining water supplies and sewers, cleaning streets, zoning businesses, inspecting food, even employing public health officials: activities more associated with modern cities than medieval ones, yet these were the tools used by many towns and cities during the Middle Ages to keep their streets and homes habitable and their citizens healthy.

PERSONAL HYGIENE OF THE MIDDLE AGES

Like "jumbo shrimp" or "presidential integrity," the phrase "personal hygiene of the Middle Ages" appears so self-contradictory as to be an oxymoron. And certainly medieval Europeans did not bathe or launder their clothes as frequently as we do today. But that does not mean that they preferred being dirty or were oblivious to the benefits of good hygiene. Rather, the generally low level of personal hygiene, especially when compared to modern standards, can be attributed more to the lim-

ited facilities available for washing and the attendant inconvenience of using them than to any cultural bias against cleanliness or any ignorance of its benefits. This conclusion is supported by many surviving medieval tracts on health and numerous illustrations and records of everyday life. These sources provide depictions and descriptions of the washing facilities then existing. Just as important, they provide ample evidence that the pleasures and benefits of bathing and keeping clean were well known and enjoyed throughout medieval Europe.

Bathing

People in the Middle Ages do not appear to have avoided taking baths. Health manuals routinely extolled the benefits of bathing, especially in soothing warm water. This advice wasn't limited to adults. Some medical texts also stated that infants should be bathed at least once a day and some even recommended three.

One of the most striking features of bathing during the Middle Ages was its communal nature. Except when recounting ritual baths before ceremonies of conferring knighthood, even the accounts and illustrations of bathing in palaces and noble residences seldom depict bathing as a solitary activity. While some of these depictions related to amorous encounters, the primary motive for communal bathing within private residences was far more innocent and mundane: conservation of hot water. Drawing a bath was not a minor undertaking. It required carrying enough water to fill the tub, heating some or most of the water in cauldrons over open flames or in earthenware containers in or over furnaces or ovens, draining or bailing the tub after the bath, and carrying away the waste water, unless the tub was located near a drainpipe into which the water could be directly emptied. Bearing in mind that a single gallon of water weighs about eight pounds, one can see that this entire process required major expenditures of labor in addition to the time and fuel needed to prepare the bath and heat the water. Thus, it should come as no surprise that people took maximum advantage of all that effort by having several members of the household bathe together while the water was still hot — or, if the tub was too small, like the one shown in figure 11, bathing one after another. Further, the amount of work involved also makes it more understandable why baths were recorded as occurring only once a week or even less frequently during the Middle Ages. The difficulties of drawing a bath and the practice of weekly bathing are not unique to the Middle Ages. They still exist in much of world today and were common to Western countries well into 20th century, too.

The inconvenience and expense of maintaining private bathing facilities also help explain the popularity of an even more communal form of bathing: using public baths. The most basic public baths were lakes, ponds, or calm stretches of streams or rivers used during the warmer months. Though these were used during the Middle Ages and long after, there were also more sophisticated, man-made facilities in many towns and cities. Illustrations of public baths and bathing are found in many sources, including editions of a popular 14th century medieval health manual and several woodcuts by Albrecht Dürer and other German artists of the 15th century. These illustrations depict public baths as long halls with many large tubs or as shallow pools of varying sizes, either man-made or natural ones, bordered and finished with stone or tile. Sometimes pictured were the large furnaces that heated the water and produced steam for the saunas. As another example of medieval energy conservation, in some cases, public baths worked out arrangements with bakers so that the latter were able to use waste heat from the bath furnaces to bake their products. Illustrations of public baths, along with descriptions of bathing found in stories, confirm that most public bathing was done nude, just as it was done in baths in private homes. However, there were some exceptions. Bathers of either sex, both in private and in public, were sometimes depicted nude except for a towel or cloth wrapped around their hair. Further, a handful of accounts and illustrations depict bathers wearing a light, thin gown or other clothing.

While public baths appear not to have been used in England until returning crusaders brought the concept back with them, many cities on the continent had retained their Roman baths or built new ones. Thus, public baths and saunas were a common fixture in France, Germany, Italy and other regions. Besides the illustrations and the physical remains of the public baths and saunas, the popularity and common use of these facilities is evidenced in many other sources, including official records from 13th century Paris and 14th century London that counted 26 public baths in the former and at least 18 in the latter's metropolitan area; a song from 14th century Italy that mimicked the common cries of vendors advertising their goods and services, including one offering bathing and sweating in hot tub; and a papal emissary's account of bathing while visiting Baden, Switzerland, in 1414.

Though Baden was likely exceptional because of its reputation for its mineral water spas even by this date, the emissary did not seem as surprised by the number or the sizes of the public and private baths as much as he was by the "innocence" of the bathers and the absence of lewd behavior despite the fact that people of all ages and both sexes bathed together nude in the two large public baths and that the sexes were separated only by grills with "numerous windows" in the private baths. The emissary's comments reflect the public morals problem which must have been common for public baths almost since their beginning. However, some public baths likely tried to lessen this problem by setting aside specific days of the week or times of days for the exclusive use of each of the sexes. This means of separating the sexes is still followed in some of the few remaining public baths in Europe.

Besides counting the number of baths, the Parisian and London records cited above also included strict regulations imposed on the baths to curb the conduct of prostitution on their premises. Similar ordinances can be found in cities throughout England, France, and Italy for much of the later Middle Ages. However, authorities in most medieval cities tolerated prostitution. Efforts at prohibiting prostitution at the baths were aimed at keeping the baths a safe place for respectable citizens and ensuring that prostitution, like other trades, was conducted only within the areas allotted to it by the city officials. Ultimately, these efforts failed and public baths became synonymous with prostitution and lascivious activities. This failure led to authorities closing the public baths permanently, depriving many residents of their only means to bathe regularly. Many of the closures were imposed during the late 15th and early to mid–16th century, suggesting that the time of the Reformation and Renaissance may have actually been a lower point in European personal hygiene than the Middle Ages.

Other Forms of Personal Cleaning

While showering would not become common until the 20th century, there were some other forms of cleaning the body that were practiced in Middle Ages (and, in fairness to those ages, probably during the Reformation and Renaissance as well). Though there is little evidence of it except

occasional references to a person "washing one's head," it is likely that medieval Europeans kept somewhat clean during the many days between baths by washing their faces and hair using small basins of water. Washing feet receives slightly more mention than head washing. Like head washing, it required only minimal facilities and was an economical use of water. Though some of the references to foot baths appear to be to ritualistic foot washing done in imitation of biblical practices, the 14th century manual by the bourgeois "Menagier de Paris" and other sources clearly indicate that foot bathing was typically done for cleaning purposes and was especially comforting and soothing in cold weather or after a long day on one's feet in muddy streets or fields. There is also some evidence that they may have taken a form of "sponge bath," using pitchers of water and small towels, moistening and wiping themselves down while standing or crouching in large, shallow pans made of pottery that caught the drippings. Though neither of these methods cleaned the body as thoroughly as a full immersion bath, they would have kept a person cleaner than no bathing at all. Further, these methods used far less water than complete bathing. Minimizing the amounts of water that had to be brought in and later hauled away made these methods quite suitable for use in quarters with no piped-in water supply or drainage system, both of which were common conditions for many people during the Middle Ages.

One last form of cleaning that deserves mention was combing and picking lice off one another. The fact that this form of grooming was commonplace is reflected in a 13th century Italian civic regulation that prohibited citizens from delousing each other under the public arcades. Thus, there were several alternative means for keeping clean that required fewer resources than full baths and which were used in between or lieu of such baths.

Dental Hygiene

Just as in Roman literature, medieval descriptions of personal beauty included mention of perfect white teeth like pearls and pleasant, sweet breath. These descriptions and surviving evidence of dental hygiene indicate that people of the Middle Ages typically viewed good teeth and breath as desirable as we do today. However, many people likely fell short of these ideals, again, just as many do today. Medieval Europeans appear to have commonly practiced dental hygiene in the form of picking food out from between their teeth. The widespread use of this minimal form of dental cleaning is borne out by various written guides on good table manners that criticize conducting such activity in public. More refined people may have also followed the advice of the health manuals and rinsed out their mouths periodically with solutions of wine or vinegar and scrubbed their teeth with towels when bathing. To better clean and whiten their teeth and toughen their gums, they chewed on mallows, reedy plants that grew in marshy areas and from which the substance "marshmallow" was originally derived. At the end of meals, such people were also likely to eat spiced candies, if at a feast, or, more commonly, seeds of anise and fennel, leaves of mint, and other herbs to freshen their breath and stimulate the gums. All these practices helped to maintain oral health, but there is little evidence that most people employed any measures beyond picking their teeth, occasionally wiping them, and rinsing out their mouths with water or some other potable liquid. Further, as is discussed under Chapter VII on healing, the effectiveness of these measures in preventing or curing diseases of the teeth and gums was obviously limited at best, especially given some of dental

problems attributable to nutritional deficiencies which likely plagued much of the population for at least several months each year. For example, deficiencies of vitamin C, caused by lack of fresh fruits and vegetables during the winter and early spring, could have caused scurvy and related illnesses that weakened the gums, leaving them prone to infection and tooth loss. Thus, though people of the Middle Ages recognized the merits and beauty of good teeth and breath, it appears that dental hygiene was in sorry shape at this time and that few people attained these desirable attributes. Yet, despite disease and only rudimentary dental hygiene, it also appears, based on evidence of the foods they consumed and the remains of their bodies, that most people still somehow managed to keep enough of their teeth and kept them in adequate condition for most of their adult lives so that eating solid foods was not a problem.

SOAP AND LAUNDRY

Soap was certainly known and used during the Middle Ages. Throughout the period, it often appeared as an item of commerce in shipping manifests and other records of trade while tales of fiction from as early as the 13th century record the use of soap while bathing. Admittedly, much of the soap recorded in the shipping manifests was soap made in Italy and Spain which was used for cleaning wool as part of the cloth manufacturing process, but less expensive soap was also readily available. Cheaper soap was produced domestically across Europe by combining highly alkaline potash (potassium hydroxide) leached from wood ashes with rendered animal fat (lard) and then allowing the mixture to cool and solidify. This type of soap is commonly called lye soap and it's the same soap that Granny boiled up back by the cement pond on *The Beverly Hill-billies*. Lye soap is rather caustic and harsh but it is an excellent de-greaser. As an alternative to lard-based lye soap, those people who could afford it bought and used milder, olive oil–based soaps, some possibly scented, made in Italy and Spain. In fact, Italian olive oil–based soaps can be traced back at least as far as the early 8th century, when a company of soap manufacturers is recorded as paying rent to the Lombard royal court. Olive oil soaps were also made with lye from wood ashes but were milder than the lard-based soaps because of differences in the chemical compositions of olive oil and lard.

As for laundry detergent, besides lye soap, it is quite likely that householders and professional laundrywomen used the same compounds of naturally available chemicals for spot removal or dry cleaning that cloth producers employed to bleach and to clean oils and other natural impurities from the raw fibers when making them into fabric in the first place.

Dirt was removed from clothing by first soaking the clothes in large wooden tubs or troughs or in tanks made of masonry. In monasteries, hospitals, and other large institutions, these containers were located in specially constructed laundry rooms. If suitable tubs or tanks weren't available, clothes were soaked in calm stretches of water along the edges of streams or rivers. After soaking, to release more dirt from the clothing fibers, the person washing the clothes rubbed and pounded them against the sides of the tub, trough, or tank or on rocks along the shore of the stream or river. Though primitive, this method of cleaning is still used, though updated with corrugated washboards in the 19th century and washing machine agitators in the 20th century. When a tub or other container was used, soap could be added to the wash water and the soap acted as a surfactant to help

loosen and lift soils from the fibers. Thus, adding soap enhanced the cleaning action of the rubbing and pounding.

Having clean clothes and bed linens was appreciated by medieval Europeans. Health manuals recommended sleeping on beds whose linens were changed and cleaned regularly and books on household management stressed that a wife's duties including keeping the bedding and her husband's clothes clean. Along with wives, other female members of the family, serving women, and professional laundresses also washed laundry. "Laundrywoman" was a trade found listed in many employment-related records such as censuses and tax records of towns and cities throughout medieval Europe as well as on the rosters of servants in large households. Laundrywomen also appear listed among the campfollowers of medieval armies from the Crusades through the Hundred Years' War.

As with washing their bodies, it does not appear that medieval people washed their clothes as frequently as we wash ours today. After all, household inventories that indicate that men in prosperous families typically owned just a few sets of linen underwear while owning only one or two pairs of woolen outer hose and a similar number of woolen tunics or, later, "cotes." And in poor and even some middle class households, a person often owned just one complete outfit of clothing. Given this very limited amount clothing, people obviously had to wear the same, or nearly same, outfit day in and day out. When did they have time to wash them? The clothes must have become filthy and just stayed that way. Further, the same difficulties of mustering the resources necessary for bathing also confronted clothes washing, so must certainly have also deterred laundering. However, this cannot be the whole picture. Numbers of professional laundrywomen as well as free-lance laundresses who took in washing from neighbors existed in every city and town, making laundry services readily accessible to most of the populace. The existence of these services also implies that washing laundry was common and that there was a large market for these services. But, while washing bed linens could account for some of the business, how can the seemingly large market for laundry services be reconciled with the small amount of clothing most persons owned?

One possible answer is that people of the Middle Ages regularly washed or sent to the laundry only part of their clothes, the linen garments worn closest to the body (for men, the breeches and shirt or undertunic; for women, the chemise or under tunic; and perhaps stocking or hose for both), while cleaning the outer garments more infrequently. This hypothetical laundry routine would be congruous with both the existence of the professional laundering trade as well as with the patterns of clothing ownership. Under the selective laundering routine proposed, poor people would have washed their underwear at home, needing only minimal facilities like those used for head or foot washing. Sparing members of their own household this onerous task and thereby supporting the professional laundering trade, more prosperous people sent out pieces of their underwear for cleaning while retaining outer garments and at least one set of underclothes to wear. This method would have helped maintain at least a minimum level of hygiene by ensuring frequent cleaning of the clothes most soiled by sweat and other bodily wastes, thus helping reduce odor and deter long term infestations of fleas and other vermin. Additionally, this pattern of laundering would have extended the useful lives of the outer garments which were typically made of wool. Immediately after manufacture, medieval woolen goods may have contained more traces of the natural oils that help prevent shrinkage than are found in modern woolen goods but repeated washing would remove all the remaining oils, leaving such garments as prone to shrinkage as their modern equivalents. Dry cleaning or spot removal, in the form of applying and then blotting up acidic vinegar solutions or ammonia compounds derived from urine, may have also been used but were probably only used sparingly because of the odor such cleaning imparted to the clothing as well as the damage the cleaning fluids could cause to the fabric or its pigmentation.

Still, this proposed solution is only a theory. Other evidence may eventually surface and provide a clearer picture of this and other aspects of hygiene in the Middle Ages.

RELAXING AND PLAYING

People of the Middle Ages enjoyed a surprisingly wide range of leisure activities, from sports that tested physical strength and agility to sophisticated games that tested intellects and reasoning skills. Along with personal preferences and abilities, social and economic factors guided the choice of amusements, much as they still do today. Some of these factors are quite understandable, such as poverty which often deprives people of all but the most basic forms of entertainment, but others are more uniquely "medieval." For example, legally-enforced social and economic distinctions between the nobility and the rest of society ensured that falconry and most other forms of hunting were pastimes reserved exclusively for the enjoyment of the nobility. But there were many games and activities — such as playing backgammon, dancing, and listening to music — that weren't subject to such class restrictions and were popular with all segments of society. In fact, with the exception of some courtly pursuits like hunting, people during the Middle Ages,

from kings down to peasants, enjoyed many of the same entertainments, reflecting a common human need to temporarily forget their cares and relax.

Before examining the specific activities which medieval people found relaxing and amusing, there are a few general points that need to be addressed.

First, many medieval entertainments seem rather simple, with some appearing downright primitive. These perceptions are reinforced by the fact that some of the games and activities enjoyed by medieval adults (like playing blind man's buff, singing musical rounds, and asking riddles) have since been relegated exclusively to childhood. Based on their enjoyment of these activities, medieval adults have been disparagingly characterized by some historians as "childlike," implying that they were emotionally or intellectually underdeveloped. And, certainly, many medieval people were not rocket scientists (or should that be catapult scientists?). However, there is no evidence to suggest that the people of the Middle Ages possessed

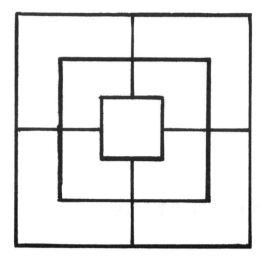

Figure 25. Nine Man Morris Board. In this game for two players, the players took turns placing their pieces at the corners and intersections of the lines. Each time a player formed a line of three pieces, he could remove one of his opponent's pieces.

any less native intelligence than modern people despite the former's general lack of literacy and formal education. Bearing this point in mind, one finds that there is often more to medieval games than first meets the eye. For example, living in an age of video and computer games, it may be difficult to comprehend the attraction of "Nine Man Morris" (fig. 25) to adults five hundred to a thousand years ago. Nine Man Morris was a game somewhat akin to tic-tac-toe, but with a more complex strategic element of play. It was popular throughout Europe from at least as early as the 12th century. Shepherds and other farm laborers played it on diagrams painted onto boards or carved like graffiti into the stone of buildings. But the crudeness of the game boards and the traditional view that, because they were illiterate and unschooled, shepherds and other laborers were "simple folk" are misleading. Nine Man Morris and many other seemingly simple games are intellectually challenging, requiring players to have the abilities

to think rationally and plan ahead as much as many modern games do. Thus, we should not be too hasty in judging all people of Middle Ages as being "simple" or "childlike" based on what they did for fun without more closely examining their games and activities and viewing them within the context of the technological limits of the day.

Second, besides their apparent simplicity, another puzzling and sometimes troubling aspect of medieval recreational activities is the cruel or violent nature of some of the amusements, which raises the question of what did medieval Europeans think was "fun" and how does their concept of "fun" fit with modern standards. As with other areas of social behavior, medieval concepts of which activities constituted acceptable forms of amusement overlap with modern standards on some points, but diverge — sometimes drastically — on others. For example, dancing and listening to musical performances are just a few of the many entertainments which, while the dance steps and music have changed, were as acceptable during the Middle Ages as they are today. Moving away from this area of more or less direct overlap, there are some amusements which were viewed as appropriate by medieval people but which are less acceptable today. An example of these amusements are those mentioned above which were enjoyed by children as well as adults in the Middle Ages but which have long since been deemed appropriate only for children. Finally, there were entertainments which were acceptable to broad segments of medieval society but which are repugnant to most modern sensibilities. These amusements included bear-baiting (watching and betting on the outcome of a fight between a captive bear and a pack of savage dogs), jousting (in which there was always a substantial risk of injury or death), attending executions and other public punishments, and other displays of violence or cruelty. Though violent and cruel activities constituted only a small fraction of entertainment during the Middle Ages, this fraction has often been blown out of proportion to titillate readers and audiences with barbaric spectacles from the "dark ages." But regardless of any exaggeration, these amusements certainly reveal a darker side of medieval people. From sophisticated aristocrats to rustic laborers, most people of the age appear to have had, in varying degrees, a streak of callousness. While recognizing that this callousness stemmed from the harsh conditions these people experienced (high infant mortality rates, wars, famines, plagues, and other disasters) and that such experiences may have numbed them to the suffering of others, it is still sometimes difficult to fathom this brutish aspect of medieval "fun." Yet before assuming that all people during the Middle Ages were unfeeling, nasty louts, the following points should also be considered. While we would prefer to view our own age as an enlightened one in which the misfortunes and injuries of others are always viewed with sympathy and compassion, bloodsports — from legal boxing matches and bullfights to backstreet cock fights and dog fights — are still found today in countries otherwise noted for their sophistication and cultural achievements. Further, people continue to be fascinated and entertained by films depicting extreme violence, tabloid and videotaped accounts of disasters and grisly crimes, and other depictions of human suffering. Thus, while technological developments have freed him from having to seek out and witness such events in person, man's appetite for base entertainments does not appear to have changed much over the centuries since the Middle Ages. Fortunately, however, regardless of the appeal cruel or violent entertainments may have, they are not universally embraced

today. And this was true during the Middle Ages as well. As evidenced by the popularity of the preachings of St. Francis of Assisi and others who opposed cruelty and brutality to animals as well as to their fellow men, there were many people during the Middle Ages who, despite the harsh conditions they may have suffered, were compassionate and found cruel pastimes to be repellent. Thus, when examining the recreational activities of medieval people, one should bear in mind the complex and sometimes conflicting nature of human character and not rush to assume the worst based on a few sensational examples.

With these ideas in mind, let us first look at the sports and games enjoyed by many people throughout all social classes during the Middle Ages. We can then contrast them with those activities, such as hunting and tournaments, that were enjoyed primarily or exclusively by the aristocracy and end with a review of those amusements, other than sports and games, which were widely enjoyed by medieval people without regard to class.

Sports

Life for most people during the Middle Ages was very strenuous. Most of the population was involved in agricultural labor, but even the artisans and the nobility typically led physically demanding lives. Despite the hard physical labor required for survival, or perhaps even because of it, people throughout medieval Europe frequently engaged in sports that required considerable strength and tested the stamina of the players. While some of these sports, such as archery, also served as practice for military service, many others, such as tug-of-war and various rugby-like football games, were done for sheer enjoyment, including the enjoyment of showing off one's physical prowess.

FOOTBALL

There are few depictions of football left from the Middle Ages but from the illustrations and written descriptions that have survived we know that it was played with a leather ball stuffed with straw, rags, or some other wadding; that it was played without any specialized protective clothing; and that points were scored by carrying the ball into a goal area defended the opposing team. It also appears to have been a very popular though very rough sport. One reason that we know it was very rough is from a number of English legal documents that record the injuries and deaths that frequently occurred during the games. These documents also record the civil disturbances that often followed the games when the teams and their respective families and fans sought to settle scores after the game was over. Besides the heated action of the rugby-like games, the violence may also have been fueled by civic pride since games were often staged between neighboring towns and villages. Given the risks of injury to people and property during either the games themselves or the frequent post-game riots, it is not surprising that football was often regulated or even banned outright in some jurisdictions.

SPORTS RESEMBLING GOLF

There are many surviving depictions of medieval people playing games in which they used wooden clubs, often shaped like modern field hockey sticks, to hit balls. While little evidence of the exact rules of these games has endured, it appears that, despite the similarity of the equipment, there were actually several different golf-like games played in Europe from the mid–13th century onwards. One of these games was *pell mell*, the forerunner of modern croquet, which involved hitting the ball back and forth over a short distance and having to drive the ball through a small hoop at either end of the course. In 14th century England, people also played *cambuca* and *chole*. Little is known of their rules (they may have been more like field hockey than golf) but we do know that they were probably popular games. Among the everyday activities recorded in the stained glass of cathedrals, one window at Gloucester Cathedral preserves the image of a cambuca player about to strike his ball. Further, England's Edward III apparently thought that cambuca was too popular because it was among the games he banned in 1363 to encourage his people to return to practicing their skills with the longbow. Another ball-and-club game was *colf*, arguably the most direct, remote ancestor of modern golf. Colf was played in the Low Countries probably by the second half of the 13th century but was not well documented until the 1360s. In colf, players used wooden clubs to hit small balls and propel them from point to point along a circuit defined by well-known landmarks, such as churches or windmills. "Golf," in a form more readily recognizable to modern players, did not appear until the early 15th century in Scotland. Golf was so sufficiently well established and popular in Scotland by 1457 that King James II of Scotland (perhaps inspired by Edward III's example of ninety years earlier) felt compelled to ban commoners from playing it as well as from playing football as part of efforts to encourage them to practice archery and other military skills. It appears that the popularity of golf had risen rapidly in Scotland in the early 15th century for an earlier edict by James II in 1424 to encourage military preparedness and promote civil order had banned only football and had not mentioned golf.

TENNIS

As with golf, tennis appears to have evolved gradually over the Middle Ages and was often played in forms that had more in common with handball and racquetball than modern tennis. However, unlike golf, tennis was a sport usually associated with the nobility. This exclusivity was dictated, in part, by the fact that tennis required a large, level area (a "court") in which to be played. Building and maintaining a tennis court required economic resources which only the nobility possessed. Or, in view of the wealth which some merchants possessed, the nobility possessed both the economic resources needed *and* the inclination to expend them on frivolous pastimes. Still, tennis was sufficiently popular enough with the general public that Parisian authorities in 1397 prohibited working people from playing it (along with bowling, dice, and cards) on work days.

Louis X of France was the first recorded builder of tennis courts. He had attempted to play tennis out of doors but found it unsatisfactory and so had two indoor courts built in Paris around the end of the 13th century. These tennis courts had smooth wooden floors and were completely enclosed to shield them and the players from the elements. While most medieval tennis courts have been swept away, the palace at Hampton Court in England preserves one example. The popularity of tennis with English and French nobility was clearly shown in the alleged exchange between Charles VI of France and Henry V of England in 1415, immortalized by Shakespeare, when Charles sent the younger Henry a chest of tennis balls with the suggestion that it was safer for him (Henry) and more suitable for him to stay in England and play tennis than to dare wage war against France. Given its early ties to French kings, it seems ironic that tennis is also associated with the end of the French monarchy: a Parisian tennis court used by the nobility served as a meeting place for the disaffected Third Estate (the commons) in 1787 and was the site of the "Tennis Court Oath," in which the Third Estate pledged not to disband until a constitution assuring their basic rights was drafted, an action that helped set the stage for the revolution of 1789.

WATER JOUSTING

While football, golf, and tennis outlasted the Middle Ages and became some of the most popular sports in the world, there were other sports that weren't as enduring. One of the more bizarre examples of a sport whose popularity peaked during the Middle Ages is water jousting, sort of a cross between sculling and jousting. Water jousting appears to have enjoyed wide popularity in the Middle Ages. It was included in a description of activities in London written in 1191 and was depicted in French manuscript illuminations well into the 15th century. Now practiced only in a few towns in southern France, water jousting parodied the jousting of knights. Water jousting was run on rivers instead of in castle tilt-yards with a team of oarsmen in a long, narrow rowboat in place of a warhorse. The water jouster, standing up near the bow of the boat, wielded a long pole and attempted to knock his opponent, who was similarly armed and positioned in the prow of an oncoming boat, over and into the water while avoiding being knocked over himself. Further parodying knightly pastimes, as shown in a 15th century illustration, water jousting also included passes at the quintain, a practice dummy that swung around when struck and which was designed to knock over any jouster who didn't get out of the way in time. Unlike real jousting, water jousts were usually held as part of civic festivals in the summer rather than as aristocratic entertainments. The participants in water jousting were young men from the sponsoring towns rather than nobles practicing for war, and the most serious damage inflicted was usually a thorough soaking of the loser rather than any grievous wounds.

SWIMMING

A far more common water sport was swimming. Chronicles from the 8th century record that, among other physical exercises, Charlemagne enjoyed swimming in the Roman-style baths constructed at his palaces. But swimming doesn't appear to have been a pastime reserved for the nobility. Illustrations of pastoral scenes in summer occasionally include depictions of farm laborers "skinny-dipping" in a pond or stream to cool off after a long, hot day of hard work. Pictures of groups of children swimming in streams, complete with some of them shivering from the coldness of the water and others attempting to dunk their playmates, are also found in illustrations of summer activities accompanying calendars in some books. Thus, medieval people appear to have been less averse to immersing themselves in water than is often thought.

BOWLING

Various forms of bowling were found throughout medieval Europe, and some versions have survived to the present with little modification. From the bowling greens of English villages to the town squares of France and Italy, games are still played whose origins can be traced back at least as far as the mid–13th century. Some early bowling games involved trying to knock down an opponent's wooden cone with a ball but other versions were much more like the French boules or pétanque and the Italian bocce in which players toss balls, attempting to land them nearest a target, usually another smaller ball. At least one set of wooden balls for playing such a game have survived from the 13th century and are currently in a museum in Switzerland.

Another form of bowling called *quilles* appears to have originated in France in the 14th century and spread to England and other countries. In quilles, pins approximately the size and shape of modern bowling pins were arranged in a triangular formation and a club or ball was suspended by a chain or rope above the pins. Players sought to knock down as many pins as possible by pushing the tethered club or ball, causing it to swing into the mass of pins. This game survived in its full-size version in Germany until at least the late–19th century but miniature versions, called skittle-ball or skittle-bowling, continues to be played in many countries even today.

QUOITS

A forerunner of the modern game of horseshoes, quoits was a ring toss game in which players threw small wooden hoops at pegs set up some short distance away. It appears to have been played both indoors and out by all levels of society in England and France. It was so popular in England during the 14th century that Edward III thought that it was interfering with archery practice and so banned it.

ARCHERY

During the Middle Ages, the English were famous for their archery. From the late 13th century until the proliferation of hand-held guns made them largely obsolete in the 16th century, skilled archers provided firepower that gave the English victory time and again. Creating and maintaining a large body of men with the physical strength to draw bows that required up to 180 pounds of force and the skill to accurately hit targets a hundred yards away or more required constant practice and drilling. Thus, English kings, right up through Henry VIII, repeatedly issued regulations that required all able-bodied men to practice their archery every week, at least once a week on Sunday after church, and prohibited activities, such as football or gambling, that might divert them from practicing. Villages maintained straw-filled targets or *butts* for archery practice and the stone steps of some village churches bear rounded indentations attributed to archers who, while sitting on the steps awaiting their turn to shoot, honed their arrowheads on the edges of the steps. (However, given that surviving English medieval illustrations depict archery practice being conducted with blunt-headed target arrows, this explanation of these grooves in the steps may be based more on local folklore than on historical fact.) As to be expected, shooting contests, either formally or informally, sprung up around these practices. Skill with the bow also had the unfortunate side effect (unfortunate from the nobility's point of view) of creating a large number of skilled bow hunters such as those legendary figures in the Robin Hood stories.

France and Scotland attempted to duplicate the English and sporadically issued laws requiring archery practice and other incentives to take up the bow, but these measures met with little success.

However, in many cities and towns of Germany and Italy, citizens often used crossbows for both sporting and military purposes and so frequently practiced with them. Sport shooting with the crossbow included both hunting and target shooting. Target shooting in Germany sometimes took the form of shooting at a bird-shaped figure high atop a pole. Such shoots were often staged as part of competitions staged by the civic authorities to encourage crossbow practice. Civic-sponsored competitions also took place in Italy.

WRESTLING

Illustrations in the margins of manuscripts indicate that wrestling, which was a popular sport both with the Romans and with the "barbarian" peoples of Europe, continued to be practiced through the Middle Ages. While written accounts of medieval wrestling are scarce, a few of the references indicate that wrestling matches were held as public entertainments and was likely more of a spectator sport than a participatory one for most people.

ICE SKATING

In northern countries, notably England, Scandinavia, and the Low Countries, ice skating was a popular winter sport. The blades of medieval ice skates were typically made of sections of animal leg-bones. Metal skates did not appear until some time in the 15th century. Along one side, the bone was slightly sharpened for its entire length to form an edge that served the same propulsion and steering functions as the edges of modern steel blades. The opposite side was flattened and possibly attached to a small length of board so that the skater's foot rested firmly on the blade. The blades were then strapped to the boots or shoes of the

Figure 26. Snowball Fight. Manuscript illumination from the late 15th century or early 16th century. Illustrations of labors or other activities associated with the various months of the year were a routine feature in books of hours. Books of hours were religious books for laymen that included common prayers, calendars of feast days, and other useful information for the Christian faithful. In this illumination for the month of December, boys or young men are shown pelting each other with snowballs, an activity which was clearly as much fun back then as it still is today (courtesy of the Walters Art Gallery, Baltimore).

skater. Skaters also often used long poles to push themselves along the ice.

While some may have viewed ice skating as a means of easy, rapid transportation on frozen waterways, skating was done most often just for pleasure. From a brief description written by Thomas à Becket's secretary in 1180 to Dutch and German woodcuts of the 15th century, skating was depicted as an exhilarating, but not infrequently painful, pastime. These depictions of skating are filled with images of experienced skaters gracefully gliding across the glistening ice while novices clatter about and fall, or just as bad, manage to get moving but are unable to stop themselves! Injuries were not uncommon. One surviving 15th century Dutch woodcut illustrates a story from the late 14th century in which a young woman, Lidwina, fell and broke a rib while skating. She was taken to a convent for treatment and later entered a religious order. After her death some years later, she became the patron saint of skaters.

SKIING

Skiing in Scandinavia can be traced back for more than four thousand years. Excavations of neolithic settlements there have yielded wooden skis datable to around 2500 B.C. During the Middle Ages, Norse sagas of the 9th century recorded daredevil skiing competitions between warriors. In Norway, as early as the 13th century, army scouts used skiing as a method of transportation to perform rapid reconnaissance during winter campaigns.

OTHER WINTER SPORTS AND ACTIVITIES

By the end of the 15th century, the Scottish were already playing *curling*. Curl-

ing is sort of a cold weather version of bowling played on ice in which players propel stone disks about a foot in diameter and half a foot thick, trying to place them as close as possible to a target. More common winter pastimes included riding in horse-drawn sleighs, sledding, and snowball fights, an activity which occasionally appears in manuscript illustrations, including a late 15th or early 16th century Dutch illumination which shows rosy-cheeked children gleefully pelting each other with snowballs (fig. 26) and a 15th century French illumination that shows both children and adults throwing snowballs while others roll up a big ball of snow, presumably to make a snowman.

Games

In addition to sports that developed and tested strength and agility, people in the Middle Ages played and enjoyed a wide range of other less physically demanding games of chance and skill. Some of these, such as cards and backgammon, are still familiar to players today while others have disappeared.

KNUCKLEBONES

Played by children as well as adults, knucklebones was a common game throughout medieval Europe. Named after its playing pieces which were made from the toe or "knuckle" bones (about one and a half inches long and three-quarters of an inch wide) of sheep and other livestock, knucklebones was played like the modern game of jacks, with a player having to flip up one bone, scoop up the other bones, and catch the first bone before it hit the ground. However, descriptions of other methods of play also survive. These methods included precision flipping of the bones to hit targets such as other bones or to pass through sort of a goal post formed by the fingers of another player, not unlike, respectively, modern marbles and tabletop football.

CARDS

Playing cards first appeared in Europe around 1370 and rapidly gained popularity. The cards were made of several layers of paper glued together to form thin sheets of cardboard and were slightly larger than modern playing cards. They were usually rectangular but often had rounded corners. In some decks, the corners were so rounded that the cards were ovals instead of rectangles. These early decks were hand-painted and thus were a luxury that only the nobility could afford. To meet the rapidly growing demand for playing cards, medieval cardmakers, using stencils and wood block engraving, mass-produced cards starting around the end of the 14th century. By the 1420s, cardmakers had their own guilds in many German cities and were successfully exporting decks of cards to other countries. The German export business was so successful, in fact, that cardmakers in Venice complained that they were being put out of business by the influx of foreign-made cards and appealed to the Venetian government in 1441 to protect them by limiting such imports. Cardmakers in England made a similar request to their government in 1463.

By the mid–15th century in France, the four suits of cards in use today had already been created. But, throughout Europe, decks were far from uniform. For example, in Germany, decks commonly had suits of stags, hounds, falcons, and ducks instead of clubs, spades, diamonds, and hearts. Even today, playing cards in Germany typically have suits of leaves,

acorns, hearts, and bells instead of the spades, diamonds, hearts, and clubs found in England and France, while in Spain and Italy, cards retain the swords, cups, coins, and clubs or wands found in the tarot. Other hunting items, such as riding crops, bridles or stirrups, and hunting horns also appeared as suits of cards. While the images varied, decks commonly had fifty-two cards divided evenly between the four suits, though decks of thirty-two, forty, forty-eight, or fifty-six cards were also used.

The speed with which cards and card games swept medieval Europe can be gauged by the relatively short lag time between the earliest mention of cards (ca. 1371–1377) and the first ordinances attempting to regulate playing card games in the interest of the common good and public order (ca. 1377–1378). The vices associated with card playing seem to have appeared almost instantaneously with the invention of card games. From the 1370s forward, illustrations of card playing almost invariably show small piles of coins or tokens on the card table. Especially after card playing caught on with the common people and not just the aristocracy, moralists condemned it as a wicked pastime which combined the twin evils of gambling and idleness. In a German illustration of a bonfire of earthly vanities in Nuremberg in 1452, cards (along with backgammon sets, dice, and shoes with long pointy toes) are shown being tossed in the flames. In England, Henry VII forbade servants and apprentices across the country from playing cards or indulging in other forms of gambling except during Christmas holidays. (Apparently King Henry thought the nobility and others exempt from this restriction had sufficient moral fiber to withstand the vices associated with these pastimes.) Cheating at cards also appeared early on. Court records of Paris document that a con game akin to

"Three Card Monte" was already being employed successfully to relieve the gullible and greedy of their cash as early as 1408.

By the mid–15th century, a great variety of card games had been created. Some were played only within certain regions of Europe, such as the game of *Karnoffel*, later called the *Kaiser Game*, in the Germanic countries, but others spread from country to country until they covered all of Europe. These included the Italian games of *Tarot* (a true card game, tarot as a form of divining the future evolved *after* the game) and *Basset* (a game whose odds strongly favored the house), *Poch* (played with aid of a board marked with the various winning hands which were similar to winning hands in poker) from Germany, *Glic* (akin to Poch) which was very popular in 15th century France and England, and *Thirty-One*, the forerunner of Twenty-One or Blackjack (apparently they didn't mind having the hands take slightly longer to play), played throughout much of Europe by the end of 15th century. While Poch was almost certainly the source of the word "poker," modern poker can be traced back only as far as early 19th century America. As with card games today, all these games could be played for money and warnings about the dire consequences of gambling — as well as about the dangers of cardsharps who dealt from the bottom of the deck and practiced other forms of cheating — appeared soon after the games themselves.

GAMBLING AND DICE

Gambling was a common form of entertainment throughout medieval societies and was well established long before the advent of cards. Dice were the most common form of gambling. In the Nuremberg bonfire of 1452 mentioned above,

40,000 dice were reported to have been destroyed as part of an effort to rid the city of vice. Dice games were also depicted in a book of games compiled for Alfonso X of Castile in 1283. Even in this genteel book, dicing was shown as an occasion for fist fights and knife fights among the players. Authorities tried to bar all forms of gambling, including dice, at least among the common people, presumably to maintain good public order by ensuring that unsuspecting players weren't fleeced by conmen and that losers, even in honest games, weren't provoked to violence against the winners. Frequently, as an effort to maintain order and camaraderie, gambling was among the activities (along with drunkenness and other disruptive vices) that were banned by military authorities while on campaign. But gambling was so pervasive that the officials in charge of the religious order of the Knights Templar found it necessary to specifically forbid gambling in the order's regulations. However, even they provided a limited exception that permitted gambling when the stakes were only tent pegs or some other token item, sort of like playing poker for matches.

BOARD GAMES

Board games were also quite popular among all classes during the Middle Ages and dice were used in some of these games as well, such as backgammon (often called *tric-trac* in the Middle Ages, shown in fig. 19) and *tables*, a chase game played on a rectangular board marked out in small squares. Nine Man Morris (fig. 25) and draughts, now often called checkers, were just a few of the other board games played in settings ranging from royal palaces to humble homes and village taverns. Fox and Geese was another popular board game and was recorded in the book of games compiled at the direction of Alfonso

X of Castile in 1283. Based on earlier Roman games, in Fox and Geese two players sought to outmaneuver each other, with the Fox attempting to seize individual Geese without becoming trapped by the rest of the flock. While it appears to have been played by all levels of society, it was especially popular with the nobility.

Though the games were the same, the quality and expense of the playing boards and pieces did vary. Simple wooden disks on painted boards sufficed for most players, but the nobility used intricately carved ivory disks, often depicting mythological heroes, for game pieces while playing on beautifully inlaid tables of precious woods. Even precious metals were used in some extravagant game sets. Household inventories of Edward IV of England document that, in the mid–15th century, he owned not one but two complete sets of pieces made of silver and silver-gilt for playing Fox and Geese. The playing pieces, 14 per set, were small cylinders or marble-sized balls and used on a board similar in appearance to one used for Chinese checkers.

CHESS

Chess, although a board game, was in a class by itself, even as it still is today. Invented in India in the 6th century, chess reached the Islamic countries of the Middle East by the 7th century. From there, after the passing of some four centuries, it began to infiltrate Europe but did not gain wide acceptance until after the First Crusade ended in 1099 and returning Frankish crusaders brought the game back to their courts. Then, it finally broke through and became one of the most sophisticated and popular pastimes of the European nobility. The warlike nature of the game and the hierarchy of pieces on the board

undoubtedly suited the nobility and their outlook on the world well.

Initially, European pieces and boards were identical to the Islamic set because no changes were needed, the Arabic *shah* easily equated to a European king, a *faras* (horse) to a knight, and a *baidaq* (foot soldier) to a *pedes* (Latin for foot soldier, the piece which was later called the *pawn*). The early European sets also used the Arab *rukh* (chariot), *firz* (counselor or advisor), and *al-fil* (elephant) but the Europeans gradually changed these pieces, developing the *rukh* into the rook (usually depicted as a small castle) the *firz* into the queen (to better reflect the actual organization of most European monarchies), and the *al-fil* into the bishop (though some sets had sages, counts, or even fools/jesters for this piece). Over the course of the Middle Ages, additional pieces were sometimes added for special variations of chess played on boards with 10 or even 12 squares per side instead of the usual 8 × 8 configuration. Other specialized boards also existed with elongated grids of 4 × 16 squares. All these variations suggest that some medieval players, however much they may have enjoyed chess, felt a need to take a break from the "normal" game of chess at least once in a while and enjoyed experimenting, trying to create new games rather than just being locked forever within just one set of rules.

OTHER GAMES

Among the many other games played by all classes and ages during the Middle Ages, two more are worthy note. The first is *Hoodman's Blind*, more commonly called *Blindman's Buff* ("buff" was short for "buffet"). This game involved blindfolding one player and having the other players strike him or her without getting caught. The other game was *Prison Base*.

Prison base was played by two teams and was sort of a serial tag game in which the first team sent out a player, then the second team sent out a player to tag the first team's player, followed by the first team sending out a player to tag the second team's player, and so on. The goal was to tag out the other teams' players before they reached their designated "home." As with blindman's buff, this game was popular with adults as well as children. In fact, it was so popular with some citizens of 14th century London that Edward III (that sport and game-banning killjoy we've encountered so many times before) banned it from being played on the grounds of his palace of Westminster because the games were so noisy and rambunctious that they distracted his government ministers at work in the palace.

Sports, Games, and Other Amusements of the Nobility

Because of their social and economic standing, the nobility, both ecclesiastic and secular, had the resources and free time necessary to enjoy the widest range of recreational activities during the Middle Ages, from playing quiet games of chess to staging elaborate pageants with feasts and deadly jousts. Moreover, as the strict laws against poaching game animals or even damaging forests that harbored game attest, they also had the political power to bar the rest of society from interfering with their enjoyment of these activities. So, let's look at the pastimes that appealed to the wealthy and powerful.

READING

It sounds rather dull compared to the other amusements we picture medieval

nobles enjoying, but reading was actually one of the most elite forms of entertainment, a point that wasn't lost on the status conscious aristocrats of the time. To acquire the skill of reading, whether in Latin or in a "vulgar" language such as French or English, one either had to enter a religious order or come from family that had sufficient wealth to hire a tutor or afford tuition at a monastery school. Besides the direct costs of learning, the family also had to be able to afford the additional indirect cost of foregoing any income the child would otherwise have produced by assisting with the family business or in performing other work.

Once a person had learned how to read, he or she still had to acquire reading materials which was neither a cheap nor easy task. There was no running down to the nearest bookstore or lending library to pick up something to read. In an age before printing presses and movable type, books were extremely costly items copied out by hand on to thin sheets of parchment made from the skins of calves, sheep, goats, and, in the case of some small books, even squirrels, and secured between leather or wooden covers typically fitted with metal hinges and hasps. Besides the expense of the materials and labor involved in writing out the words, books were often made even more precious by the inclusion of painstakingly executed miniature paintings, the beautiful illuminations that illustrated the texts. The value and rarity of such books is demonstrated by the common practice in monasteries and universities of attaching chains to the stout wooden covers of books and securing them to the shelves to prevent theft. This was particularly a wise precaution for university libraries since accounts of student life frequently mention scholars selling or pawning books to pay for their drinks and other necessities. Having a private library, even one with only a dozen books, was such a rarity for most of the Middle Ages that palaces and castles housing such collections were often famed far and wide. Further, the inventories of families that possessed these collections indicate that the books were deemed equal to gold, jewelry, and other precious objects among the household treasures. Thus, it is not surprising that books were often especially commissioned and prepared for presentation to kings, queens, and other nobles as gifts to mark royal marriages and other important occasions.

As for content, books ranged from works of poetry and romantic fiction, such as stories about King Arthur's court, to serious studies of law, science, and religion. Needless to say, these latter were enjoyed primarily by scholars, but studies of warfare and agriculture, translated from late Roman texts, were frequently found in noble libraries for the edification of their warlike, land-owning readers. Probably most common were "books of hours." Books of hours contained the prayers to be said at the appropriate hours throughout the day as well as calendars with holy days and saints' days highlighted. They also typically included psalms and other excerpts from the Bible accompanied by vivid illustrations. While reading romances and poetry were obviously leisure activities, reading books of hours and other pious texts may not seem like a recreational activity. Yet the illustrations in such books were sometimes quite fanciful and imaginative and frequently were as enchanting as they were instructive, suggesting that these books were meant to delight and entertain the reader as much as to inspire him or her in meditation.

HUNTING, FALCONRY, AND FISHING

While reading may have been one of the most refined pastimes of the nobility,

hunting was certainly the most popular. Hunting was an activity well suited to medieval aristocrats: It was a vigorous pursuit that provided an outlet for their seemingly boundless energies. It gave the nobility an opportunity to assert their social primacy over the inhabitants within their domains whose lands they ranged across at will during the hunt, a bit of arrogance which is preserved in some European property deeds which, even today, duly record that the local "lord of the manor" retains the right to hunt on the land. It acted as a means of training for combat. It was also a social occasion, an excuse to get together with friends and business associates to impress them with one's hospitality and cement friendly relations. And, relatedly, it usually provided tasty meat for the table afterwards. Small wonder, then, that medieval nobles sought to tightly control the use of their forest lands that provided them with so much enjoyment and thus severely punished anyone who dared to cut down trees without permission or, worst of all, directly deprived a lord of his rightful game by poaching animals.

The Hunt

Staging a hunt was often an elaborate and costly affair. For nobles who were serious about their hunting (which appears to have been most of them), preparing and maintaining the resources needed for hunting was a never-ending process: fences had to be maintained to keep game such as deer from straying and to keep unwanted animals and people out; falcons captured or bought and then trained, housed, fed, and kept in prime condition; huntsmen and forest wardens employed year-round to ensure that the hunting grounds and the game animals were protected; and specialized equipment procured. Boar hunting was one form of hunting noted for the special equipment required, such as spears with crossbars mounted behind the spearheads to hold the impaled boar at a distance to keep it from closing in and attacking the hunter, and armor for the hunting dogs. The most common form of armor for dogs was a large spiked collar that protected the dog's throat from bites and slashes from his cornered prey. In a few illustrations dogs were shown wearing body armor as well in the form of capes of quilted fabric, hardened leather (sometimes studded with small metal plates), or, in the late Middle Ages, plate armor. Regardless of the material used, this armor covered the back, neck and chest of the dog much in the same way that sweaters for dogs do today.

Last, but far from least, dogs, essential for virtually all forms of hunting, had to bought or bred. Good hunting dogs were no less prized in the Middle Ages than they are now. Surviving household accounts reflect payments for building and maintaining kennels, buying bread and other food for dogs, transporting the dogs to the hunt in carts so they would be fresh for the hunt, and, in a few cases, paying a man or boy to sleep out in the kennels with the dogs. (Yes, some medieval nobles were so wealthy that they bought or at least hired boys for their dogs.) Spanish and French medieval poems and books on hunting also record that owners named their favorite dogs, often based on the color or disposition of the dog. The dogs were specially bred for their different roles in the hunt: Pursuit of large game, such as deer or boar, started with the running-hounds, burlier ancestors of modern fox-hounds, that tracked and sought out the prey by smell. Once they caught scent of the prey, the running-hounds "gave voice" (that is, they barked), frightening the prey and alerting hunters of its position, and chased the prey for a while. The running-hounds were relieved by relays of grey-hounds or larger *alaunts*. These speedy, quieter dogs tracked the prey by sight,

relentlessly pursuing and tiring it out. When the quarry was brought to bay, the greyhounds and alaunts often sought to seize and bring down the prey but that task was frequently too dangerous for them, especially if the quarry was a boar or a large hart or buck deer with deadly sharp antlers. Thus, mastiffs, large and powerful dogs with massive jaws, were brought in to finish the hunt.

Not all hunts were so complexly orchestrated. Some were simple events, in which a noble and a few companions went out riding and hunted birds with their favorite falcons, while other hunts were great social occasions. The planning and logistical requirement for great hunts were astounding and varied widely depending upon the quarry sought. For example, hunts for bear, wildcats, chamois (a goat-like deer noted for the soft leather made from its hide), and ibex (a deer-like goat formerly abundant in the high mountain ranges of Europe) required assembling and equipping a group of men, horses, and pack animals for days of camping out in harsh terrain and possibly even climbing mountains while seeking elusive and often dangerous prey. On the other hand, hunting for deer was typically conducted in comfort on lands within an easy ride of the noble's principal residence but it could still demand extensive preparation, including turning out local peasants to help beat the bush to drive the game, placing nets along the hunting route to ensure the game didn't stray away from the hunters, or, a bit more sporting, placing braces of hounds at intervals along the route the deer were expected to follow to drive them towards the hunters. These hunts also often entailed preparing and then transporting sumptuous, picnic-style feasts out to the hunters.

While illustrations in tapestries and illuminations show women in scenes of hunting, they were most often there as spectators. Hunting was usually an all-male event, though noble ladies frequently did hunt with falcons. And images of men and women, either in groups or in solitary pairs, hunting birds with falcons were often included in depictions of courtly romance. Far more rarely, women were shown or described as hunting deer with bows, but this was usually in the context of a staged hunt where the deer were herded past a pavilion where the hunters waited. While the predominantly male nature of hunting probably comes as no surprise, the "maleness" of hunting also related to another aspect of life in the Middle Ages which was less obvious: hunting was a form of military training. In an age when armies were summoned as they were needed rather than being maintained in constant readiness, hunting provided one of the few means for the nobility to acquire and practice many of the skills needed in combat without actually going to war. Hunting weapons were usually the same ones used in war — spears, swords, bows and arrows, crossbows and bolts — and required the same skills and strength whether being used in the hunt or in battle. Much as in warfare, the hunters had to know the terrain and how to use it to their advantage. Also as in war, the nobles leading the hunt had to exercise command over scattered groups of men, both on foot and on horseback, and coordinate their movements to achieve a successful outcome. Chasing through fields, bramble and streams also accustomed the men to some of the hardships of warfare and exposed them to much the same risks of minor and serious injuries. Even incidents of fatalities from "friendly fire" occurred during these exercises, such as when William Rufus, the second Norman king of England, was killed during a hunt by a stray arrow. While rumors of assassination often followed such incidents when the victims were of high rank, the fact that tragic acci-

dents like these still regularly occur every hunting season suggests that they were most often the result of carelessness than intrigue. Thus, as a means of keeping physically fit and skilled in tactics and use of weaponry, hunting had a practical value to medieval nobility beyond just obtaining fresh meat.

While most of the hunts depicted in medieval epics were social hunts in which the nobility directly participated, some hunts were conducted solely by the professional huntsmen retained by the nobles. These huntsmen acted as guides and scouts for noble hunts, locating game, flushing it out, and otherwise assisting as needed to guarantee a successful hunt. However, even the nobility couldn't hunt all the time and the demands for fresh game in most noble households, especially for birds, was such that the professional huntsmen likely had to go out on a daily basis to keep up a steady supply of fresh game meat for their employers' tables.

Falconry

To obtain a sufficient number of birds for the meals of the nobility, huntsmen often netted their feathered prey or, for some small birds, coated branches with bird-lime, a sticky substance that trapped the little birds like flies on flypaper. But such techniques, regardless of their efficacy, were disdained by the nobles themselves. From one end of Europe to the other, from English country manors to the fortified townhouses of the Italian nobility, and beyond, to the courts of Islamic rulers south of the Mediterranean, falconry, hunting with trained birds of prey, was a popular sport for the ruling classes. Peregrines, gyrfalcons, sakers, lanners, merlins, goshawks, sparrowhawks, and hobbies (a breed of small falcons) were kidnapped while still nestlings or were caught in nets soon after they learned to fly. Once caught, the falcons became merchandise in an international network of trade. Accounts survive of big gyrfalcons from as far north as Scandinavia being sold to sultans in the Middle East for use in hunting cranes. For all breeds of falcons, females were preferred over the males, or *tercels*, since the females were commonly larger and thus better able to bring down larger prey. Literature of the age indicates that the nobility savored the powerful, predatory nature of the falcons and identified with their dominance over lesser species. As with chess, the nobility seemed to have recognized and appreciated the symbolism inherent in falconry.

Newly caught falcons were kept in large coops in which they could fly about to strengthen their wings. When deemed ready, a falcon would be taken from the coop at night and fitted with a leather hood or had its eyelids temporarily stitched shut. The temporary blinding of the falcon kept it calm in the same way that putting a cloth over a birdcage quiets songbirds. Next, leather strips called jesses were wrapped and tied around each of the falcon's legs. Each jesse hung down six to ten inches and had a small metal ring at the bottom. To secure the falcon, a leash attached to the bar on which the falcon perched was tied through the rings of the jesses. In many countries, small bells, similar to modern "jingle" bells, were also tied to the falcon's legs to assist the hunter in tracking and locating his falcon later when out hunting.

The blinded falcons were taken to their new quarters, the mews. Mews were anything from small buildings or rooms specially built for housing the hawks to just a spare room or other sheltered space where the hawks could roost in peace. Once there, with the jesses firmly leashed to the perch, the long process of gradually getting the falcons used to being around people and training them to hunt on command began. The trainers gradually opened the eyes of those hawks whose eyes had been stitched shut as they became more accustomed to their new surroundings. This was accomplished by increasing the slack in the stitches. For hooded birds, the trainers took the hoods off for short periods, gradually lengthening the time as the falcons remained calmer longer. Meanwhile, the trainers also periodically carried the falcons around on their arms, protected from the birds' powerful talons by stout leather gloves. This process was repeated in a variety of situations to familiarize the hawks with the noises of everyday living as well as with the sights and motions of being carried by a man riding out to hunt. The hawks were rewarded with bits of food during this process to build up their trust and reliance on their human owners. Then the training for hunting began. While the falcons needed no encouragement or training to hunt other birds, they had to be trained to return to their masters after being released. This required further patient training in which the falcons, at first on long tethers attached to their jesses and later free of any physical restraints, were lured back after release with rewards of food. The training often included making the falcon chase a wooden bird-shaped lure swung on the end of a cord. Later, when the hawk was ready to hunt, the bird-shaped lure provided an additional, visual means of recalling a wayward hawk.

As for hunting with falcons, it resembled modern gamebird hunting in some respects. For example, dogs were often brought along and used to find and flush out birds and to assist in locating and retrieving birds knocked out of the sky but not seized by the falcons. Another similarity was that the objects of the hunt often included birds still hunted today, including ducks, partridges, pheasants, quail. But there were also some major differences with modern hunting. Part of the assistance provided by the hunting dogs also included helping the falcons subdue especially large prey, such as herons or cranes, which the falcons did not naturally hunt but which their masters had trained them to attack. Also, dogs do not appear to have been routinely used as retrievers for birds downed in the water. Accounts of noble hunts more often mention having servants wade or swim out after the downed prey. Finally, the range of prey was much wider than it is today. Besides the cranes already mentioned, hawks brought down herons, larks, bitterns, curlews, and many other species of bird for their masters.

Fishing

Most fishing in the Middle Ages was conducted either as a commercial venture for collecting fish to sell to consumers or as a means to supplement one's own diet. However, some literary evidence suggests that noblemen and others indulged in angling for sport. While they likely ate their catch, these people fished because they enjoyed it, not because they had to. Surviving late medieval tracts on fishing include instructions on making rods, lines, floats, and sinkers as well as lures and flies designed to attract a variety of fish. Sport fishing appears to have been limited to freshwater such as ponds, lakes, streams, and rivers.

Tournaments

One of the most violent and dangerous of sports, tournaments were both a form of recreation and practice for real fighting. In fact, the earliest tournaments held in 12th century France were largely indistinguishable from small wars. Groups of knights on horseback and their retainers, either mounted or on foot, fought one another over large areas of the countryside. The players used the same armor and weapons they used in combat and opponents were captured by any means possible, even by such unsporting tactics as having several "players" gang up against one opponent. The knights that were overcome and captured had to forfeit their horses and armor to buy their freedom, not unlike the ransoming of noble captives in real wars of the age. Gradually, some safety measures were introduced to reduce casualties. (Please see the section on tournament armor and weapons in Chapter VI on fighting for more information on this point.)

Even after it became a more formalized sport, it remained dangerous and volatile, so much so that tournaments were routinely condemned by the Church and suppressed by kings throughout much of the period. The Church condemned tournaments for their needless violence and wasting of money in the ostentatious banquets and other associated festivities that catered to the excessive pride of the participants. In the Church's view, all this wealth and aggression could be put to better use in crusading in the Holy Land. To enforce these policies, participants in tournaments could be excommunicated and those unfortunate enough to die in the games could be denied Christian burial. Royal restrictions on tournaments were based more on practical politics than any moral judgment on their conduct. Permitting lesser nobility to hold tournaments when and where they pleased could present a serious challenge to royal authority because tournaments provided an excuse for large numbers of nobility to assemble fully armed with their supporters. Such assemblies were viewed with suspicion by kings since they provided great opportunities to plan, if not begin, insurrections against royal authority. Thus, throughout most of Middle Ages, kings attempted to regulate the holding of tournaments, prohibiting them unless the sponsors obtained royal permission first.

Figure 27. Jousting. Drawing in a late 14th century manuscript. This is an illustration of a tournament watched by Queen Joan, wife of Charles V of France. The knights are wearing jousting helms. To see out through the narrow eye slit near the top of the helm, a knight must lean forward and look up. When jousting, the knight leaned forward while making his approach and then tipped his head back just before making contact with his opponent (though this illustration does not show this motion). By tipping back, he raised the eye slit to reduce the risk of his opponent's lance slipping in through the slit. Instead, he exposed just the smooth surfaces of the front of helm below the eye slit. The joust shown is a "joust of peace" in which the jousters used coronel-tipped lances designed to catch but not pierce their opponents' shields. As with most jousting, the objective was to knock your opponent out of his saddle, or — as shown by the broken lances in the foreground — to at least shatter your lance against his shield. For protection, their horses have chanfrons on their heads and peytrals over their chests and front legs. The horses are also fitted with an additional piece of armor that covers their riders from waist down. The use of the coronel-tipped lances, the jousting helms, and other details all confirm that these knights are playing a sport (albeit a dangerous one) rather than fighting in earnest. The jousting helm and the additional armor to protect the knight's legs were good protection in the tournament where the forms of combat were limited and governed by established rules. However, the restrictions on vision and movement imposed by these pieces made them impractical for real fighting on the battlefield (courtesy of the Walters Art Gallery, Baltimore).

The tournaments themselves were great social occasions (fig. 27), often staged as part of the celebration of royal weddings, the signing of an alliance, or other significant political or social event. Typically accompanied with feasting and other pageantry, tournaments gave young nobles an opportunity to display their martial skills and, if they were victorious, pick up some riches in the form of captured arms and horses or of jeweled prize items awarded by the host of the tournament. Though the monetary gains were of lesser importance than proving oneself a worthy knight, the financial and political gains could be considerable. For example, in the late 12th century, William Marshall, a knight of modest means, secured a fortune and, indirectly, the good favor of the English monarchy by triumphing on the tournament circuit in northern France.

Tournaments often involved a number of different sports. Jousting, having a pair of mounted knights armed with lances charge at each other and attempt to unseat each other, while the centerpiece of most tournaments, was just one of the sports. Even jousting itself had evolved into several distinct forms before the end of the Middle Ages. Tournament sports included:

• The melee, in which two teams of players fought *en masse* against each other, much as they would in real combat. Though melees were sometimes conducted with lances or, more rarely, wooden clubs, they were most commonly depicted as battles between groups of mounted players armed with swords. Not surprisingly, it was one of the most dangerous events, even with blunted swords or clubs, and was very rarely staged after the early 15th century.
• Combat between two men on foot, either within an enclosure or with the opponents separated by a waist-high

barrier. These forms of sport appear to have first developed during the 14th century, most likely during the course of the Hundred Years' War as a means to enable rival French and English knights during sieges of towns and cities to stage combats with each other without exposing either the besieged or the besieging forces to surprise attack under the guise of sport. Most illustrations of such foot combat show the players using poleaxes, weapons about 5 to 6 feet tall, tipped with steel or iron head typically comprised of a spike topping an axeblade with a back-spike. Some illustrations and a few surviving poleaxes show that the edge of the axeblade was sometimes replaced with a flattened edge, covered in short, closely set spikes, rather like a meat-tenderizing mallet, perhaps to spread out the force of the blow and lessen the risk of inflicting a fatal injury. Poleaxes were ideally suited to fighting at the barriers in which the opponents had to reach over a stout, waist-high wooden fence to hit each other.

• Jousting. A few jousts were depicted as melees in which opposing teams simultaneously charged into one another but most jousts were shown as duels between just two opponents (fig. 27). The scoring and play of jousting evolved over the course of the Middle Ages. The goal in early jousting appears to have been to knock an opponent completely out of his saddle or, failing that, knocking off his helmet or shield to leave him vulnerable to further attack. While unhorsing an opponent remained the goal in most jousts, shattering a lance against his shield also became accepted as a means of "scoring" in itself, particularly after the development of specialized armor and saddles made unhorsing extremely difficult to accomplish.

• Other combat on foot or horseback. Some tournaments were staged as reenactments of famous battles from history or, most often, fiction. These recreations of legendary events frequently took the form of a lone knight or a small, select group of comrades defending a bridge, a pass or, in some very elaborate tournaments, mock castles specially constructed on the tournament field against all comers. Some combats were part of an overall celebration in the true spirit of chivalry and courtly love. Such combats would include costumed pageants and feasts with ostentatious presentations of valuable prizes to the winners.

Despite any whimsical themes their participants played out, tournament sports, especially jousting, remained very dangerous. There were some measures implemented to improve safety: specialized pieces of armor, use of lances that had a ring of several short and relatively blunt points (fig. 27) in place of a single, large sharp point, and, in the early 15th century, the introduction of a wooden fence called a barrier or *tilt* to keep jousters from running directly into each other. Despite these improvements, players still risked serious injury or death in every tournament. Some of the danger was intentionally incurred, as in the case of the jousters who chose to joust with sharp lances instead of blunter ones. This style of jousting was called *scharfrennen* (literally, the sharp course or run) in German, *à outrance* in French, and *jousts of war* in English (after the practice of staging jousts with lethal weapons between selected knights from opposing sides during wars) to distinguish it from the slightly less dangerous jousts run with blunted weapons. Other dangers were simply unavoidable, as exemplified by an accident in 1559 in which King Henri II of France was killed by a fragment of lance that flew through the vision slot in his helmet during a sporting joust held to celebrate his daughter's wedding. While this event took place during the Renaissance rather than during the Middle Ages, the equipment used was comparable or identical to the pieces used in medieval jousts. Still, despite the dangers, or more likely because of them, jousting and other tournament sports were popular among the competitive young noblemen and provided an opportunity for spectacular displays of wealth and martial prowess enjoyed by all who witnessed them.

Besides the tournaments, practicing for the tournament and for real combat were also popular sports for the nobility. These activities included practicing with swords (either sparring with another person or hacking at a target), throwing spears or javelins, and jousting at the quintain. As mentioned in the description of water jousting, the quintain was a practice dummy. Shaped roughly like a man holding out a shield on one arm and fitted with club or some other weapon on the other arm, the quintain was mounted at the same height as the jousting knight on horseback. When its shield was struck, the quintain spun around and would land a blow on the back of any jouster who was too slow in getting clear of the target. This blow served as a gentle reminder of some of the dangers of real combat.

Needlework

Leaving the violent pastimes of the nobility behind, noble ladies were expected to be competent at performing many basic household tasks as well as knowing how to administer a household and conducting other important matters. The household art that many ladies chose to practice was embroidery. While there were also professional embroiderers that produced gorgeous vestments for the clergy, these amateur embroiderers were often no less skilled or productive, as the Bayeux tapestry (actually an embroidery work) and other surviving pieces prove.

Horseback Riding and Horse Racing

Besides providing a means of transportation in peace and war, horseback riding was also enjoyed as a pastime by the nobility and those few others who could afford the expense of buying and maintaining riding horses. Groups of elegantly attired men and women were often depicted going out for a leisurely ride in the country in illustrations of courtly life.

As for races, these were informal events that grew out the natural competitiveness of the nobility and their desire to prove who had the best quality horses, though many races may have been run purely for the exhilarating feeling of speeding along at a gallop. Still, there were at least a few formal races, such as the Palio in Siena, Italy, which dates back to the 13th century. The appeal of horse racing was even reflected in the regulations of the religious military order of the Knights Templar, whose membership was drawn from the ranks of European nobility. In these regulations, racing was prohibited unless specifically authorized by the master of the order and even just riding at a gallop without some good reason was frowned upon. These regulations were intended to avoid unnecessary risk of injury to the order's horses but they were also part of curbing the Templars' enjoyment of many of the worldly activities they had enjoyed before joining the order.

Feasting

The nobility held feasts to mark significant occasions (fig. 1). These included the annual celebrations at Christmas and Easter as well as less frequent events such as funerals, coronations, and marriages. As mentioned above in Chapter I, the dishes served sometimes constituted entertainment in their own right but many other amusements were usually offered to persons attending feasts. Celebrations of very festive and politically significant events, including marriages that cemented alliances and coronations, were sometimes accompanied by tournaments as well as feasts. More commonly, hosts hired professional entertainers to perform during the feasts. These entertainers typically included musicians, singers, dancers, acrobats, and jugglers. Less common but apparently quite popular were mummers who performed silent plays, troubadours and poets who could recite well known verses as well as compose and perform new works, and storytellers.

Entertainers

While modern audiences often have the choice of being entertained by either a live performance, or more frequently, by videotapes, compact discs, television, and other methods of recording and transmission, people during the Middle Ages had to rely exclusively on live entertainers to provide these amusements. Thus, medieval audiences kept many different types of entertainers employed, from tellers of stories to professional singers and musicians. Supplementing these professionals were innumerable amateurs who sought to amuse and entertain their communities as best they could.

STORYTELLERS

One popular form of entertainment was to listen to storytellers who recounted tales drawn from history, classical mythology, the lives of the saints, and many other sources. Since books were scarce and the illiteracy rate was high during the Middle Ages, these oral performances were one of the few means available for most people to enjoy entertaining stories. The storytellers included professionals: bards, poets, and singers who sought to make a living by entertaining paying customers with renditions of popular tales in song or spoken word. But, as Boccaccio's *Decameron* and Chaucer's *Canterbury Tales* show, ordinary people also created or retold stories to amuse themselves and others.

It may be difficult for many modern audiences to understand the broad popularity such entertainment enjoyed. However, one has only to look back as far as the beginning of the 20th century to find a time before the proliferation of electromechanical recording and transmitting when the only means of enjoying such amusements was to seek out and attend a live performance or else rely on the ingenuity of oneself and companions to provide entertainment. Thus, the peoples of the Middle Ages, both the literate and illiterate alike who were fascinated by the tales these entertainers had memorized or created and repeated to their audiences, were not that different than the generations that came after them.

TROUBADOURS AND MINNESINGERS

Troubadours and minnesingers were poets who sometimes recited or sang their poems with musical accompaniment. The troubadours originated in southern France in the 12th century and included nobles as well as talented commoners among their ranks. The minnesingers (*minne* meaning "love" in German) appeared in Germany at about the same time. Their audiences were the courts of princes, counts, and other nobility. These poets helped create and popularize many of the concepts of courtly behavior and love that became an integral part of the code of ideal chivalric conduct.

MINSTRELS AND MUSICIANS

While troubadours and minnesingers usually played some music, there were also minstrels and other professional musicians that filled the more general need for music without poetry, such as for dancing or to accompany feasts or ceremonies (fig. 1). These professionals were exclusively commoners in origin, unlike the troubadours and minnesingers who were frequently of the nobility. Without professional singers and musicians, the people relied on their own musical skills and instruments. This meant that singing was the most common form of music performed during the Middle Ages for the many occasions when professional musicians were not available. Besides human voice, the instrument most commonly used by amateur musicians included bagpipes (an instrument found throughout Europe in the Middle Ages), flutes, drums (often called *tabors* or *knackers*), rattles, bells, tambourines, and small cymbals. However, amateur musicians amongst the nobility were often depicted playing more sophisticated instruments such as the lute, harp, and many others (fig. 19).

To provide a wider variety and (presumably) better quality of entertainment, noble households often engaged professional musicians on both long and short-term bases. Sometimes they were hired to entertain just for one special occasion, a wedding feast or the like, but some great households had musicians as part of their permanent staffs. As part of a noble's staff, they would travel with the nobility, entertaining them — and if they were visiting other nobility — their host's household as well. In some instances, nobles loaned their musicians to other noble households as a favor. Surviving letters also record that they permanently or temporarily traded their musicians with other noble households, suggesting that they tired of hearing the same songs again and again and could only "change the record" by bringing in new performers whom they hoped would know different songs. Towns and individual citizens also hired musicians to play at festivals or weddings, but use of local, amateur talent was also common.

The professional musicians usually played a selection of instruments, including stringed instruments such as the lute, the guitar, the gittern (a small instrument that resembled a violin but which was played by plucking its strings like a guitar), the fiddle, rebec, and other violin-like instruments of various shapes and sizes (the strings of these instruments were typically played with bows but were sometimes plucked instead), the dulcimer, the psaltery (a stringed instrument that looks like a modern dulcimer but was played by plucking rather than striking the strings), the harp, and the symphony. The symphony was a fascinating instrument composed of a rectangular wooden box fitted with wooden buttons or keys along one side and a crank at one end which turned a wheel inside the box. The symphony was played by turning the crank and pressing various combinations of keys to force strings stretched inside the box into contact with the spinning wheel. The results were keening or droning sounds not unlike those produced by a fiddle, but which could be sustained almost indefinitely. The musicians also played wind instruments, including recorders, shawms (an instrument similar to a recorder), flutes, trumpets (long straight ones; ones with recurved tubing, or ones with sliding tubing such as was used later in the *sackbut*, a forerunner of the modern trombone), bagpipes and other horn instruments with air bladders, and the portative organ. The portative organ was a miniature pipe organ that varied in size from laptop models to larger tabletop versions and was often depicted as being played with one hand since the organist had to use the other hand to operate the bellows built in to the back of the organ to provide the flow of forced air required to activate the pipes and produce the music. Last, but not least, they also played the same percussion instruments used by amateur musicians as well.

ACROBATS, ACTORS, AND ANIMAL TRAINERS

More active entertainments were also popular with medieval audiences. Tumbling and somersaulting acrobats, jugglers, actors who performed pantomime plays of popular stories, and animal trainers with dancing bears were also among the ranks of itinerant entertainers who made their living by performing for whoever would pay. Though generally viewed with some hostility, perhaps out of the suspicion that seems to naturally arise towards persons of "no fixed address," these performers and the other wandering players mentioned above were welcomed at fairs and festivals as well as at aristocratic celebrations because the nobility were certainly not alone in enjoying the entertainments provided by these different professionals. Though the settings of the performances weren't as plush as the feasting hall, commoners also enjoyed these same entertainments, forerunners of later circuses and traveling carnivals, whenever and wherever they were offered.

Dancing

Besides watching and listening to paid entertainers, feast-goers and other revelers might engage in their own entertainment and dance to the music provided or to carols (not Christmas carols, but chorale dance music) sung by their companions. Dances performed to carols are usually referred to as *ring dances* since the dancers held hands, formed a ring, and danced in a circle around the room or field where the dance was held. Such dancing, as well as a common variation in which the dancers formed a chain rather than a circle and danced in a freeform style, winding around the dance floor, appears in Italian frescoes and in marginal illustrations in French and English manuscripts in the early 14th century. Similar dancing was also described in the *Decameron* and other literary works. There appear to have been a few other variations on this type of dancing, including having two of the dancers stop and form an arch with the arms under which the rest of the line of dancers passed. Dance music also survives from the 14th century and indicates that dances were performed either with a slow, gliding step in three-eight or three-quarter time or with a faster, more lively, romping step in four-four or twelve-eight time. The slower dance and its music were called the *estampie* while the faster one was the *salterello*.

Simple dances performed as a group appear to have been the most popular, if not sole, form of dancing enjoyed by all classes up to mid–15th century. Then, starting in northern Italy, a more stylized form of dancing appeared. In these dances, couples paired off but still functioned as part of a coordinated group and the dancing was still either slow and gliding, called a *bassadanza*, or somewhat faster, and called a *ballo*. The beauty of the ritualized gestures and the choreographed movements of the couples appealed to late medieval/early renaissance aristocracy and such dancing swept the courts of Europe and the simpler, more spontaneous dances were soon relegated to the lower and more rustic classes of society. But performing these newer dances required formal training to learn the steps. Thus, professional dancing masters appeared simultaneously with the new dances, again appearing first in Italy. The first noted dancing master was Domenico da Ferrara, who was quickly followed by two of his pupils Antonio Cornazzo and Guglielmo Ebreo who have both left us books on dancing. Interestingly, in a predominantly Christian Europe, Guglielmo (whose last name meant "the Hebrew") was Jewish and became one the first of a number of noted Jewish dancing masters who helped develop more elaborate dances and taught them to the Christian nobility, a tradition that continued well into the 18th century.

Regardless of the pace and form, dancing was, as it always has been, part of the courtship process. Ring dances and the later more stylized dances gave members of the opposite sex a chance to see each other, show off, and flirt, in the same way that square dancing and other communal dances continued to do centuries later. Further, even with the generally communal nature of the dancing, there are still many descriptions from throughout medieval Europe of dances in which couples often broke off from the main group or otherwise contrived to achieve more intimacy during group dances.

The amorous nature of dancing explains some of the condemnation heaped on dancing by the Church (or at least by some of its preachers, sort of like in the movie *Footloose*). These condemnations serve a useful historiographic function, for in addition to illustrations and descriptions of dancing becoming more frequent during the 14th century, we can tell from the repeated appearance of dancing among the frivolous activities in religious tracts from throughout the Middle Ages that dancing was probably a very popular recreational activity. However, the focus of some of these tracts indicates that the Church was most concerned with dances that retained strong connections to pagan rituals. These dances included some held at certain symbolic times of the year, such as around the spring equinox (the time of pagan fertility rites), the autumnal equinox (the time of harvest celebrations and sacrifices), and the winter and summer solstices. The continued usage of animal masks and other ritual paraphernalia in some of these dances suggests the Church was likely correct in its assessment that these dances had no place in Christian societies, regardless of whether the participants still understood the original meanings of the dances.

Besides the ritual dances, there were also several odd episodes over the course of the Middle Ages that involved outbreaks of dancing fevers or sicknesses, most often in Germany and France. Sometimes called St. Vitus Dance, the victims "danced" uncontrollably, often writhing on the ground or repetitiously and spastically performing movements as though working at some unseen task. In other incidents of compulsive dancing, entire villages purportedly danced *en masse* to locations sometimes miles away. Many such occurrences have been tied to rainy harvest seasons which promoted the growth of ergot fungus on grain crops. Consumption of foods made from grain tainted with this mold induces ergotism, an illness characterized by hallucinations and delusional behavior. However, at the time, the organic causes of the problem were unknown and the manic behavior of the victims was frequently attributed to supernatural causes, either divine wrath or demonic possession. While these incidents gradually faded into history, they likely were the basis for later fairy tales such as *The Magic Slippers*.

Public Spectacles

Medieval aristocrats weren't the only one who enjoyed pageantry and spectacular displays and staged such celebrations. Most major cities in medieval Europe held public festivals and other entertainments on both a routine and ad hoc basis. On an annual basis, some cities celebrated the feast days associated with regional or civic patron saints, such as the saint to whom the city's cathedral or major church was dedicated and whose relics were contained therein. Besides any such localized events, religious holy days were often an excuse for public holidays. For example, the twelve days of Christmas, from 25 December to 6 January, were a time for feasting and were celebrated in some areas with festivities led by a "Lord of Misrule," a common person selected as part of a symbolic and comic reversal of social order. The days of carnival immediately before Ash Wednesday (the start of Lent, the 40 day period of fasting before Easter) and the week after Easter were also times of indulgence and celebration.

Easter was also often a time for religious plays depicting the Passion of Christ (the events leading up to His crucifixion, the crucifixion itself, and His resurrection). These plays, originally an extension of religious services, took on more of a life of their own over the years and came to be major civic events throughout medieval Europe, as can still be seen in German towns and cities where passion plays are still staged. As far back as the twelfth century, local citizens also acted out events from the lives of saints and martyrs in the form of *miracle* or *mystery plays*. Miracles performed by the saints and the mysteries of the divine reflected in the events gave rise to these two names. However, *mystery* may also derive from the French term *mystère*, another word for craft or trade guild, many of which sponsored these plays. Local clergy supervised the guilds, fraternal organizations, and parish groups that staged the plays and ensured that, while the plays entertained their audiences, they also served as a highly visual form of religious education for the mostly illiterate citizens, much in the same way as the depictions of scenes from the bible in murals and carvings within the church itself did.

Eventually, some mystery plays came to feature complete cycles of performance depicting major events from the bible, from the creation through the life and crucifixion of Christ and on to the Last Judgment. These cycles of plays appear to have been most common in England. After 1264, when the church established the Feast of Corpus Christi, also called Whitsunday, both the passion plays and the cycles of mystery plays appear to have become more common and were usually staged as part of the celebration of the new holy day rather than at Easter. Corpus Christi was a "movable feast" held seven weeks after Easter Sunday, so it took place any time from about the last full week in May up to around the middle of the last week in June. While a few plays were performed within churches, most were performed in market squares within the city or in nearby fields so the timing of Corpus Christi was more suitable for large pageants and outdoor performances than the usually cold and damp Easter weeks in March or April. In England, the mystery plays were usually performed on mobile stages mounted on large wagons that were moved from place to place around the city to reach the widest possible audience. The wagons were sponsored and maintained by different commercial guilds within the city. And, not unlike school groups preparing homecoming floats, there was competition between them to produce the best wagons, loaded with the most colorful costumes and sets, even including special effects such as trapdoors that allowed actors playing devils to vanish from sight or those playing angels or saints to miraculously appear. Staging elsewhere in Europe was often no less elaborate, with fearsome representations of the mouth of Hell, complete with smoldering torches giving off smoke and sparks. By the end of the Middle Ages, stages and performances were so complex that it is likely that professional theater hands and actors had taken over much of the work from the ordinary citizens.

Morality plays evolved as part of the religious plays but, before the end of the Middle Ages, began to diverge slightly from them. While grounded in religious teachings, the morality plays were allegories that illustrated the rewards of virtue and the perils and punishments awaiting the wicked. Unlike the religious plays, they weren't intended to be reenactments of saints' lives or biblical events. Instead, the plays typically featured an "everyman" character facing real problems such as gambling, drunkenness or other common temptations and showed their audiences how the Church's moral guidance should be practically applied. These plays, though burdened with symbolism, were dramatic presentations of fictional events in contemporary settings. Combined with the late medieval and early renaissance rediscovery of the literature and plays of the Greeks and Romans, morality plays set the stage for the rebirth of popular theater.

Besides religious holidays, festivals were also held to celebrate coronations, royal weddings, or formal royal processions through the country. In the many cities that — by the middle of the Middle Ages — held charters granting them special privileges such as exemption from certain taxes and the right to their own city governments and courts, such celebrations and displays were often used for political ends. On the occasion of royal visits, especially those of a newly crowned lord, cities used parades and displays to impress the new ruler with the city's wealth and power. Through banners and pantomimed allegories representing the ideals of good government and important past events, they sought to remind the ruler of the rights and obligations owed to the city in accordance with the customs and traditions of the ruler's ancestors.

In addition to these formal celebrations, the various specialized trade fairs held in various towns and cities, such as the goose fair in Nottingham and the great fairs in Champagne, were also festive occasions. Though the authorities of the towns and cities hosting the fairs did not organize entertainment, performers naturally gravitated to these bustling markets since audiences and money were abundant. Thus, people came, traded their goods, and usually caught a show as well — whether a juggler, an acrobat, a story teller, or whatever else was available.

Travel

We tend to think that peasants, craftsmen, and even nobles traveled very little, except when compelled by a war, famine, or other momentous events. However, many people of all classes did travel for much less drastic reasons. Merchants traveled near and far to fairs and other business destinations. Construction workers, especially skilled masons and archi-

tects, traveled from site to site, such as in Britain during Edward I's castle building campaign in Wales in the 13th century and in France during the age of the construction of the great Gothic cathedrals. Monks and church officials traveled the length and breadth of Europe on missions for their hierarchy, just as diplomats and courtiers did for their secular masters. Though all of this was business travel, surviving accounts of trips indicate that many of these travelers enjoyed the experience of seeing different places, sights and customs, though most record a strong dislike for the actual travel itself, especially travel by boat which was frequently hazardous.

Besides business travel, many people also traveled for pleasure in form of taking a pilgrimage. While some pilgrimages were imposed as a penance for a crime or sin and others were undertaken to obtain divine help with a disease or other serious problem, many pilgrimages seem to have been motivated primarily by a basic desire to take a break from the same old routine and see and do something different for a change. Chaucer's *Canterbury Tales* gives us some sense of the wide variety of people who went on pilgrimages. And there were pilgrimages to suit the pocketbook and disposition of virtually anyone, from grand tours to Rome or the Holy Land, to moderate trips to shrines in neighboring countries within Europe, down to short getaways to see the relics in a cathedral in the next county. To support this travel, there was a support network of hospices, usually located in major churches along the routes to the main centers of devotion, to house and feed pilgrims. Further, even during times of war, rulers often ordered their men to allow safe passage of pilgrims through their territories. Thus, many people during the Middle Ages from widely varied backgrounds and ranks had opportunities to see more of the world than just their own villages, and for reasons more pleasant than fleeing the plague or an invading army.

More Coarse Entertainments

As previously mentioned, the Middle Ages certainly had vulgar and cruel entertainments. Chief among these was animal baiting. Bears were the animals most commonly subjected to the torture of being placed in a pit or other enclosure and attacked by a pack of maddened dogs while a crowd of people looked on and wagered on how many of the dogs the bear would kill before being overcome. The bears were muzzled and chained to a post for the safety of the crowd and to ensure that the dogs eventually won. More rarely, humans with swords and shields fought the hapless bears, as shown in the margin of the Bayeux tapestry which dates from the late 11th century. Bears weren't the only victims of this barbarity. Other animals including badgers, bulls, asses, and even horses were also recorded as having been subjected to such suffering. Unfortunately, the Renaissance brought little relief for the poor beasts and animal baiting continued to be staged well into the second half of the 17th century, most notably in London through the reign of Charles II.

Baiting wasn't the only form of animal abuse arranged for the amusement of human audiences in the Middle Ages. Dog fights and cockfights, all usually fights to the death for one or both of the animals involved, were also held and provided another excuse for wagering. As with animal baiting, these dreadful spectacles also outlasted the Middle Ages and, though their popularity in Europe may have peaked in 16th or 17th century (Henry VIII of England had a private cockfighting pit built in his palace of Whitehall), they can

still be found in many places around the world, from wretched rural villages to the backstreets of the largest, most urbane cities. In fact, in Arizona in the United States, cockfighting was not outlawed until 1998 and it is still legal in three other states.

In addition to animals, people too suffered in public, though usually under the guise of punishment for wrong-doing and providing an edifying example to others. These punishments ranged from public beatings and confinement in the stocks, which inflicted humiliation as well as bodily injury, to executions, either relatively swiftly by beheading or strangulation by hanging or prolonged and painful deaths by mutilation.

Children's Toys and Entertainments

While they played many of the same games and sports as their elders, medieval children also entertained themselves with many of the same activities and objects that children still enjoy today.

Toys

Toys are among the rarest artifacts of medieval living. This scarcity certainly does not mean that they were rare in the Middle Ages but it does reflect the perishable nature of the clay, wood, and fabric used to make most toys and, probably, the hard use they saw at the hands of the children who played with them. Only a few metal toys have survived, likely indicative of the expense of metal during the Middle Ages and the near certainty that any broken metal toys were melted down and recycled. One metal toy that has survived is a splendid pair of mounted lance-wielding

German knights who charged at each other on wheeled steeds. The wheeled horses were drawn towards each other by means of an ingenious set of pulleys operated by having a child behind each knight pull a cord. Pivots built into each of knights allowed them to topple backwards in their saddles when they struck each other (sort of an early version of "Rock'em Sock'em Robots"). A similar pair are also depicted in a German woodcut, dated 1516, and, while children are present, adults are shown playing with the knights on a table-top, showing that even back then adults couldn't resist playing with really neat kids' toys.

Less elaborate and far more common toys included rattles and wheeled pull-toys for the youngest children. Older children played with tops (which were large wooden cones that were kept spinning by lashing them with small whips), balls, marbles made of clay or stone, hobby-horses and rocking horses, blocks, large hoops (which were rolled, usually with the aid of a stick), pinwheels (often called "windmills" and sometimes mounted on long shafts and used by children in mock jousting), wooden cup-and-ball toys (in which the goal is to flip and catch the ball in the cup with one hand), whistles, and figures of people and animals.

These last items were dolls (or action figures, if you prefer) and were part of a long tradition of toys that can be traced back at least as far as 2000 B.C. in Egypt. All cultures appear to have dolls for their children and Europe in the Middle Ages was no exception. Many of these dolls were made of fired clay or brightly painted wood. It is likely that many dolls were made of fabric and other pliable materials but such materials are highly perishable and none have survived. Still other dolls and figures may have been woven out of weeds or grasses, not unlike the cornhusk dolls of American pioneers. A story from the early 12th century suggests the existence of these rudimentary dolls: King Stephen I of England was recorded as playing with a young boy, a hostage son of one his rebel nobles. The two played at knocking down each other's warriors which were made of straw or weeds. But other, more complex dolls were also made during the Middle Ages. These include a pair of toy knights shown in a German manuscript, ca. 1200, that appear to have been articulated and were operated by means of two cords attached to their backs. Some German towns and cities, such as Nuremberg, appear to have become well established producers of dolls before the end of the Middle Ages. Woodcuts depicting various trades in Germany from the 15th century include toy makers, including doll-makers molding and firing clay dolls and others assembling dolls with movable limbs.

Kites

The kite was a very rare toy. While kite-flying was long established as a popular pastime in Asia, kites were scarce in Europe. Kites in the form of windsocks have been attributed to the Romans and were apparently used as military banners around A.D. 105. However, the earliest medieval depiction of a kite, again in the form of a windsock, was in 1326, followed, in the first half of the 15th century, by depictions of dragon-headed kites shaped like long windsocks. The timing and the appearance of these kites strongly suggests that the idea for them had come from the Orient, where Marco Polo had observed Chinese kites and kite competitions in 1282. Flat kites with trailing tails were developed during the late 15th century but the diamond-shaped kite most familiar today did not appear in any European illustrations until 1618. Thus, kite flying appears to have been a pastime unknown for much of the Middle Ages.

IMITATIVE PLAY

Children of the Middle Ages seem to have enjoyed imitating the activities of adults as much as children do today. Chronicles of the lives of saints occasionally mention that, as children, future saints shunned childish games and instead acted out the roles of priests and bishops, imitating religious ceremonies they had seen. On a more mundane level, children were also given toy pots and pans and other miniature models of implements and tools to play with. This practice extended to the nobility who gave toy swords and shields to their sons and, by the end of the Middle Ages, small suits of plate armor as well.

ACTIVE PLAY

As with medieval adults, children of the Middle Ages also enjoyed physical play including leapfrog, tumbling, stiltwalking, hide-and-go-seek, tag, and hopscotch. Hopscotch has quite a long history. Tracings of a hopscotch playing field have been found scratched on the floor of a Roman forum and, while the tracings are not as old as the floor itself, have been dated with some certainty to the days of the Roman Empire. It has been suggested that the Romans, with their construction of paved roads and streets which made ideal playing surfaces, may have spread hopscotch throughout Europe. In any event, various forms of hopscotch were played by children throughout much of Europe during the Middle Ages.

STAGED ENTERTAINMENTS

Traveling entertainers didn't cater exclusively to adults. Children too were among the audiences and were sometimes given special performances of their own in the form of puppet shows. The first illustrations of puppet shows as well as written records of payments for such shows appeared in the 14th century. The illustrations suggest that these early puppet shows used glove puppets and were played out on little stages like those used in later "Punch and Judy" shows.

FIGHTING

By its very nature, combat has always been brutal and dangerous. Even today, when fighting is often accomplished from a distance by dropping bombs and by firing bullets, artillery shells, or missiles, combat remains the most terrible and dangerous of human activities. While technology has extended the range at which combatants can strike each other, the need for close quarters fighting on the ground has not been eliminated and remains an essential part of warfare. Of all the forms of combat, directly engaging an enemy at close range and even fighting hand-to-hand if necessary remains the most demanding and grueling type of combat. And this was the primary mode of fighting in the Middle Ages. Though projectile weapons such as bows were often used in medieval battles, no battles were fought exclusively as duels between opposing archers and crossbowmen. Knights and other warriors armed with swords, spears, polearms, and other weapons always played a vital role in battles during the Middle Ages. Striking a blow with any of

these weapons required the warrior to press in close to the enemy; to be close enough for the combatants to look each other directly in the eyes as they fought, often to the death. To stay alive in these dangerous and horrifying conditions, men sought out the best forms of protection they could afford. This protection took the form of armor for the head and body. Yet, even as armor was being developed and improved, weapons were also being developed to defeat the advantages of armor, revealing that "arms races" existed long before the 20th century.

Armor

Armor could be hot, heavy, and cumbersome, but not as much as it might seem. The image of battles starting with armored knights being hoisted up into their saddles by teams of men using cranes, as immortalized in Laurence Olivier's version of *Henry V*, is inaccurate. Knights were the most physically fit people of their day and their training accustomed them to bear the weight and discomforts of the armor. Just as important, throughout the entire Middle Ages, through the evolution of armor from mail to complete plate, battlefield armor was designed to provide the maximum protection possible while preserving the knight's ability to move and attack. Armor that impaired these abilities, regardless of its defensive value, would have been worse than useless: it would be a death-trap, leaving its wearer a sitting target.

TYPES OF ARMOR

In Europe, armor was made from a variety of materials: cloth, leather, horn, metal plates, and metal rings were among the most common. All of these materials, in varying combinations, were used to make armor at some time in the Middle Ages. However, like other technologies, armor evolved over time so not all types of armor were available during all periods of the Middle Ages. For example, armor made out of large but well articulated pieces of steel (typically called "plate" armor) was clearly a superior form of armor but it was not used until near the end of the 14th and beginning of 15th centuries because the necessary resources (trained armorers with the metallurgical skills needed to produce large pieces of steel and the industrial infrastructure to support them) did not exist. The need for different types of armor was also driven in part by the types of weapons used against them. Weapons were developed to exploit apparent weaknesses in defenses, so the defenses evolved to negate the weapons and so on and so on, a process that has continued to the present day. The changes occurred gradually.

Styles and types of armor overlapped.

Complete plate armor, the latest and most advanced form of armor, would be seen on the same battlefield with much earlier forms of armor such as simple padded armor and mail. This evolution of armor will be discussed in more detail later.

Padded or Cloth Armor

Probably the most common form of body armor from the early Middle Ages to the end of the period was padded armor. Padded armor is simply clothing made of tough material such as linen woven into a canvas fabric, stuffed with wadding of wool or of hemp or flax fibers to pad it, and quilted to hold the wadding and layers of material together. This is, in fact, the origin of the art of quilting. Quilting didn't start out to produce warm, decorative bed-coverings-cum-folk art. Even something as benign and pretty as that old quilt grandmother made can actually be traced back to items originally developed for military purposes.

Padded armor has numerous advantages. It is relatively cheap and easy to make; a skilled tailor with access to fairly basic materials can produce one. Like other clothing, it is flexible and can be made to readily fit all parts of the body, limbs as well as torso. It is also relatively lightweight, weighing from four to eight pounds depending on sleeve-length, hem-length, and other factors of style. It provides good protection against the force of a blow and (especially if treated with wax or oil) can provide a surprising amount of protection against cuts or punctures. It is lighter than metal armor, but like metal, has the drawbacks of trapping body heat and moisture of the wearer. It's much like wearing a quilted winter jacket year-round and then having to engage in a lot of physical activity (like fighting for your life). While it provides significantly more protection than ordinary "street clothes," it cannot protect as well as metal armor, but its other advantages, particularly its low cost, ensured that it remained the most common form of armor for all combatants throughout the Middle Ages.

Leaving Europe and the Middle Ages for a moment, there are stories of fabled Asian "silk armors" made of tightly woven silk so strong that it was impervious to sword cuts and arrow punctures but so light that it did not hamper its wearer's mobility. Credible evidence of such marvelous armor has never been found nor have modern attempts to recreate such a material succeeded. However, there is some measure of truth in the stories. In Asia, silk was woven into a thick fabric which was very tough and durable, comparable to canvas. This fabric was used in padded armor like the European armor described above but it was not significantly stronger or lighter than the linen. This conclusion is borne out by tests performed before and during World War I when countries were desperately searching for some means of protecting their soldiers against shrapnel, bayonets, and bullets. The Americans and British attempted to create body armor from densely woven fabrics, including silk cloth up to a quarter inch thick. Silk was found to be the strongest fiber and some success was achieved but only in protecting against soft, lead bullets at relatively low velocity. Under these conditions, the silk fabric helped dissipate the energy in the flattening lead slug and could actually stop the slug from penetrating. However, the silk provided no significant protection against the sharp steel points of shrapnel, bayonets, and jacketed rifle bullets. Development of more effective "soft armor" would have to wait until the creation of manmade materials like Kevlar. While the World War I tests concluded that natural fiber armor was of little use in modern combat, these tests provide useful insights into the performance of silk and other padded armors in the Middle Ages. Against relatively low velocity impacts from blows of clubs or maces or cuts of swords these armors would provide some protection by absorbing and dissipating the force of the blow. But fabric armors, whether of linen or silk, provided only very limited protection against punctures from thrusts by swords, daggers, lances, or spears or from iron- or steel-headed arrows or crossbow bolts.

Finally, an additional reason that padded armor never went out of favor during the Middle Ages is that it could be readily combined with other types of armor such as mail or plate and provide both a cushioning base layer under these metal skins as well as some minimal protection in any gaps in the metal armor. It could also serve as the foundation and cover for other types of armors such as brigandines, ring armor, and similar body armors as we'll find out below.

Ring Armor, Horn Armor, Scale Armor, and Brigandines

To improve the ability of cloth armor to resist cuts and punctures while retaining a high degree of flexibility, armorers attached pieces of rigid materials such as iron rings or small plates of horn, iron, or steel to sturdy canvas or leather foundation garments. Plates of horn were made by boiling the horns until they were pliable. They were then cut down one side and pressed flat to make a sheet from which the plates were cut. Regardless of whether they were horn or metal, these plates were usually made in the form of small polygons, just a few inches wide. The plates or rings were often attached in an overlapping pattern like shingles on a roof with the lower edge of each plate or ring covering the gap between the two plates or rings directly below it. With shingles, the overlapping ensures that rain flows down and off the roof rather than under the shingling and into the house. Like rain, most blows in medieval combat fell from above. Swords and axes swung overhand carried far more momentum than those thrust or swung underhand (a phenomenon we see even today in tennis). And it is usually easier to swing overhand than to thrust or to swing underhand (again, like tennis). So to better defend against the most common and powerful of blows, armorers attached the rings or plates in a downward overlapping pattern. By using this pattern, the armorers created a surface that the points and edges of weapons would be more likely to slide down rather than to catch and slip into the gaps between the rings or plates and into the person inside the armor. When the rings or plates were simply placed side by side, the gaps between each piece were left exposed, creating dangerous weak spots throughout the armor.

The plates or rings were sewn or riveted to the surface or sandwiched between layers of fabric and held in place with rivets or complex systems of laces. When plates were attached to the surface of a garment, the overlapping pattern resembled the scales on a fish, thus giving rise to the term *scale armor*. There are also manuscript illustrations of helmets apparently made in this manner as well with overlapping plates riveted to some tough base material, probably leather. It is difficult to gather any more precise information from the illustrations since what the helmets depicted really look like small domes of overlapping shingles covering the top of men's heads. When the plates or rings were covered with fabric, the fish scale or shingle pattern was not visible. Instead, all that showed were the rivet heads or networks of eyelets and laces that held the plates or rings in place inside the layers of fabric.

While not as effective as plate armor against heavy blows and cuts or powerful thrusts, these mixed flexible/rigid armors provided most of the advantages of cloth armor and a little of the advantages of mail or plate armor with a relatively small increase in weight. Armor covering the torso weighed ten to twenty pounds depending on the materials used.

Brigandines were a later development of mixed cloth and metal armor that came into use in the late 14th century. Brigandines usually took the form of cloth vests lined with rectangular metal plates a few inches wide and about an inch in height. The plates were riveted in place with the rivet heads showing on the exterior of the vest. Again, the plates were overlapped rather than simply butted edge to edge, significantly lessening the risk of a weapon point or edge finding a gap in the plates. Surviving brigandines weigh around 19 pounds.

Leather Armor

Leather can be used to produce two very different kinds of armor. The first is made by using thick leather to make vests or jackets. As with cloth armors, small metal plates can be attached to reinforce the leather or the leather can be left plain, as in the long, "buff" coats used in the English Civil War and other 17th century conflicts. Such items are resistant to cutting but are less resistant to punctures. The second form of leather armor is made by soaking or boiling the leather in oil or molten wax, then forming the leather into the desired shape and letting it harden. This produces *cuir boulli* which is surprisingly hard, very resistant to cuts and punctures, but lighter than metal. Cuir boulli was used to make gauntlets, breast plates, as well as caps to protect the knees and elbows, but it does not appear to have been used to produce complete suits of armor. Rather, it was used to supplement mail armor during the transition from mail to plate.

Mail Armor

Mail, often referred to as "chain mail," is made by linking small rings of iron wire to form a flexible metal mesh. The word "mail" is derived, via Old French and Middle English, from the Latin word "macula" meaning net or mesh, like a fishing net. It's an apt description for the fine network of rings and openings of mail armor. While our name for it comes from the Romans, mail dates back to at least 400–500 B.C. in Asia Minor/Central Asia.

The long history of mail can be partially attributed to the comparatively low level of technology and relative ease of its production. Though the process was very labor intensive, the individual steps in the process were not complicated, unlike production of metal plate armor. Plate armor required smelting iron and then repeated reheating and hammering to carefully shape it into large pieces while ensuring that the entire piece is properly tempered; that is, it does not cool too rapidly or too slowly, thus becoming too brittle or too soft. Producing plate armor required skilled labor with a good, practical knowledge of metallurgy, access to high quality iron ore, and facilities to carefully work and shape it. Mail production requires the ability and resources to smelt iron as well, but after smelting the iron, the next step is to make wire. This can be done by making small, thin sheets of iron (which are easier to produce than the large, shaped pieces needed for plate armor) and then shearing thin strips off the sides of the sheet to create crude, square wires (fig. 28a). Alternatively, the raw material for wire can be made by repeatedly heating and beating small ingots of iron to shape them into narrow rods. After the basic strips or rods were made, they were then reheated and drawn through conical holes in a block of hardened iron or steel to achieve the desired uniform diameter (fig.

28b). If particularly fine wire was required, the process of reheating and drawing would be repeated through a series of gradually smaller and smaller holes until the wire was thin enough. Once the wire was drawn, it was wrapped around a metal rod to form a coil (fig. 28c). These coils look similar to the long, coiled springs found as closers on old style, self-closing screen doors. The armorer then cut the coil down one side with a pair of shears or with a hammer and cutting chisel, causing the coils to fall apart into separate rings (fig. 28d). The armorer then flattened each ring, probably using a metal forming tool called a die that would simultaneously punch holes through each end of the ring (fig. 28e). Each ring was joined to four others (fig. 28f). The ends of each ring were then overlapped and riveted shut with a small triangular rivet that had been cut with a chisel from a small strip of iron. The process of flattening, punching, joining, and riveting would be repeated thousands of times to produce a single shirt of mail, a *hauberk*.

There are a few surviving examples of a slight variation of mail production in which rows of solid rings that look like modern metal washers alternated with rows of riveted rings produced as described above. The solid rings were made by punching them out of small, thin sheets of metal. Presumably, the solid rings were somewhat stronger than the riveted rings and such mail could be produced more rapidly than mail in which all the rings were riveted. However, mail with all riveted rings was by far the most common.

Obviously, making mail armor was a very labor intensive, time-consuming process. As shown in the Bayeaux tapestry which commemorates William the Conqueror's successful invasion of England in 1066 and other illustrations, hauberks and other armor could be acquired by stripping the dead warriors left on the battle-

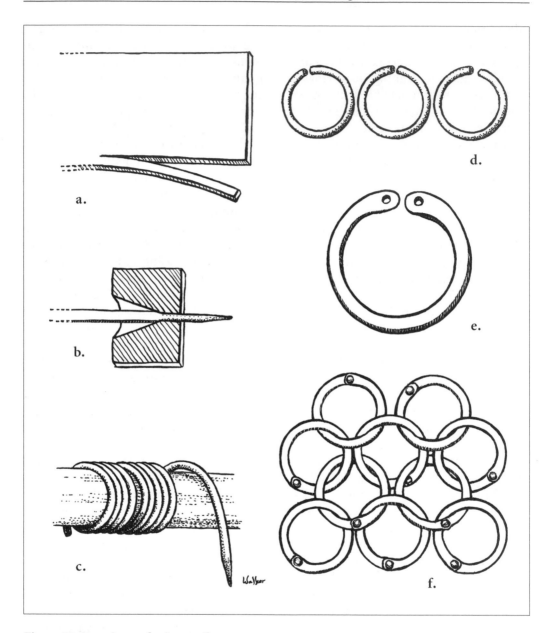

Figure 28. Steps in producing mail.

- a. Strips are trimmed with shears from thin sheets of iron.
- b. The strips are heated and drawn through a conical hole in a metal block to create round wire. If thinner wire is needed, this step could be repeated using a series of progressively narrower holes until the wire is reduced to the desired diameter.
- c. The wire is wound around a rod or *mandrel* to form long, spring-like coils.
- d. A single cut along the length of a coil turns the coil into many individual rings.
- e. Both ends of each ring are flattened and pierced.
- f. The rings are interlaced, each ring linked to four others, while the ends of the rings are overlapped and riveted together (J. Walker).

field, but only the wealthy could afford to purchase such armor, particularly in the early Middle Ages. Thus, a mail-shirt or hauberk was a symbol of rank, of membership of the warrior class, as well as a practical item. And it was a practical, indeed essential, item for a warrior. While heavier than padded armor, mail provided significantly more protection. The flexible rings gave the warrior a metal skin that moved with his body but was nearly impervious to cutting. These properties are still valued today and mail continues to be used in making gloves and arm guards that protect meat-cutters from stray knife cuts as well as in producing entire suits for deep-sea divers that protect them against the raking, sawing cuts inflicted by the close-set teeth of sharks. And, from the mid–10th through the late 13th centuries, when mail was the best armor on the European battlefield, protection against cutting was highly valued for this was the era of swords designed primarily for cutting and slashing rather than thrusting or piercing (figs. 32a and b).

For use in combat, the flexibility of mail was a mixed blessing. Just as it bends to permit the wearer to move, mail also bends beneath the blow from a club or sword. Thus while his flesh might not be torn open or cut by the blow, the wearer's bones could be broken, shattered or crushed despite the armor. Further, while the mail might prevent a sword from cutting into the wearer's flesh, the blow could drive the rings of the mail into the flesh of the wearer, significantly increasing the risk of contracting tetanus or other infections from bacteria on the mail.

While broken bones are serious and debilitating, even relatively primitive medical practitioners can set broken "long" bones in the arms or legs with a high probability of the bones healing correctly and the patient regaining full use of the limb,

assuming adequate time and conditions for recovery. On the other hand, open cuts and tears in the flesh present additional complications, particularly in a time when medical knowledge was very limited. Infection was poorly understood and the means of combating it virtually unknown. Besides cautery and amputation, there appear to have been no other widely known means of halting the development and spread of infection. With this in mind, it is a little easier to understand the willingness for medieval warriors to bear the extra weight of metal armor since their calculations for survival included the equation: lighter, less effective armor = increased risk of cuts and punctures = increased risk of instant death, amputation, and or a slow death from blood poisoning.

So, to enjoy the cut-resistant protection of mail while lessening the likelihood of having the rings of the mail itself inflict or aggravate wounds, medieval warriors wore a layer of padded armor in the form of a padded tunic (called an *aketon*) under the mail. This padding did not need to be as thick as the padded armor worn by itself, but it had to be thick and tough enough to provide cushioning against blows for its wearer and to withstand constant abrasion by the thousands of rings in the mail. Thus, the padded underlayer protected the wearer against his own armor in several ways: It helped prevent the rings from being driven into his flesh by blows in battle. It protected his underclothes and, most importantly, his body from being abraded and chafed into shreds by the mail. As part of this protection, the padded underlayer also prevented premature baldness. Knights frequently wore mail head coverings, called *coifs*, in addition to their hauberks. The mail coif could either be a hood built in to the hauberk, much like the hoods on modern hooded sweatshirts, or it could be a separate piece of armor that covered the head and neck as well as the tops of the shoulders. In either case, the knight typically wore a padded cap, also called a coif, under the mail coif. The arming coif, like the civilian coif described in Chapter II, looked remarkably like a traditional baby's bonnet. It was secured by laces extending from the earpieces which were tied in a knot under the chin. Very cute, but without this covering, the knight's scalp would have suffered constant abrading and snagging by the mail which would eventually have chafed him bald. Second, the padded underlayer also helped protect the wearer against blows. While the mail and padding would still bend under the blow, the combined mass of mail and padded cloth would absorb and dissipate some of the blow's force, significantly lessening the chances that the blows would break the bones beneath while the metal skin of mail would keep its wearer safe from cuts: all very valuable protection in a time of impact combat.

Achieving that energy absorbing mass had a price: mail was heavy. While modern alloys permit the creation of light but very strong mail, medieval mail was made primarily of iron, durable but heavy. The weight of hauberks varied considerably depending on the style. They could be short, reaching to just below the waist, or long, reaching to the knee. Sleeves could be short, ending at the elbow, or long, reaching to the wrist and including built-in mittens. Necks could be simple openings or include a built-in coif. A mail coif alone can weigh from five to seven pounds. Allowing for all these variations, hauberks could weigh from 20 to 35 pounds.

In addition to the hauberk and coif, mail protection was also made for the legs in the form of *chausses*, mail stockings covering either the entire leg or just the front of the leg and gartered to the wearer's waist. These iron "stockings" would never

run, but a pair weighed from seven to ten pounds.

So a knight wearing mail armor from head to toe was burdened with up to 50 pounds of armor, as well as the weight of his padded armor and regular clothing underneath, his helmet, and his sword: approximately 65 pounds of weight in all. While this was a burden most people could not readily carry around, the knight, trained from youth and accustomed to the weight, not only carried it but fought in it as well. Another point to bear in mind is that all this weight did not simply hang on the knight's shoulders. While the helmet and coif would rest only on the shoulders, some of the weight of the hauberk was transferred to the hips by fastening a belt over the hauberk and tucking a little of it over the top of the belt. Chausses and the sword belt would similarly be borne more by the hips and legs than the shoulders and back.

Expecting a man to carry 65 pounds of gear and still fight is not as outrageous as it first seems. Knights were the most physically fit people of their day. Most of the knights in combat were young men in their prime, but there were also more mature veterans, with even a few who remained active on battlefields well into their 60s. They received the best food available and had the time to devote themselves to training, practice, and physical conditioning, not unlike Olympic athletes. Further, the fighting gear of the knight is comparable in weight to that which 20th century soldiers have been expected to carry into combat. From World War I through the Persian Gulf War, 60 to 75 pounds has been the typical range of the complete combat gear for the average soldier. So, despite how much mankind may like to think they've advanced since the Middle Ages, some fundamental human capabilities haven't really changed much in at least a thousand years.

Plate Armor

This is the type of armor most people picture when they hear the word "knight" (fig. 29). Since virtually all fabric-based armors have long ago rotted away and most mail has either rusted away or been recycled into later metalwork, plate armor is also the type of armor best represented in museum collections. The gleaming metal exoskeletons of plate armor capture our imagination and fascinate us. And they should. A well-made suit or harness of plate armor is an exceptional engineering and artistic creation, a sculpture in steel. Even better than ordinary sculpture, it can move! It is fully articulated, permitting the human inside a surprisingly wide range of movement with the freedom to perform physical activities ranging from mounting a horse to swinging a sword to doing cartwheels to scaling a ladder. All these things and more can be done by a trained, physically fit knight in a properly tailored suit of plate armor. And throughout all these activities, it provides good protection against puncturing as well as cutting.

The Production of Plate Armor: One aspect of well-made suits of plate that often puzzles people is that plate armor seems to be too advanced to be the product of such a seemingly primitive time. Some suits look quite "high tech," almost like creations of science fiction. In fact, at the Tower of London, they like to brag that one of their suits, one made for a young and still relatively svelte Henry VIII, was examined in the 1960s by experts from NASA as part of their research in developing spacesuits.

Without doubt, plate armor is the most difficult type of armor to make and embodies many of the highest achievements in late medieval technology. Manufacturing plate armor required natural resources: charcoal, waterpower, and good quality iron ore, as well as skilled workers with the knowledge, tools and machinery to smelt, forge, and shape metal. Given the primitive state of transportation over land, quantities of charcoal and iron ore sufficient to produce armor could be moved only with extreme difficulty and waterpower, created by fast flowing rivers, couldn't be moved at all. Thus, plate armor could only be produced in significant quantities in those few locations where all these resources — powerful rivers, iron mines producing high quality ore, and forests with plenty of trees to burn and turn into charcoal — were within easy reach of each other. In Europe, plate armor production came to be centered in two locations, one in the north of Italy and the other in the region of western Austria and southern Germany. Thus, the cities of Milan and Brescia in Lombardy and the cities of Augsburg, Regensburg, Passau, Innsbruck, and Landshut, among others, in modern day Germany and Austria became the major manufacturing centers for plate armor.

The process started at the iron mines. Ore containing iron was broken up and heated at smelting furnaces at the mines to produce *blooms*, masses of iron mixed with miscellaneous impurities called slag. The blooms were reheated and hammered to force out the pieces of slag. This reheating and hammering was performed at forges located at or near the mines. Once the blooms were sufficiently purged of impurities, they were transported by pack animals to the armorer's forge where their transformation into armor began.

Each plate in a complete harness of plate armor (and a single harness can be composed of hundreds of plates) was individually forged. Forging, particularly forging armor, is not the simple process usually portrayed in old Western movies where a blacksmith just heats up a piece of iron, beats it flat, reheats it, and then bends

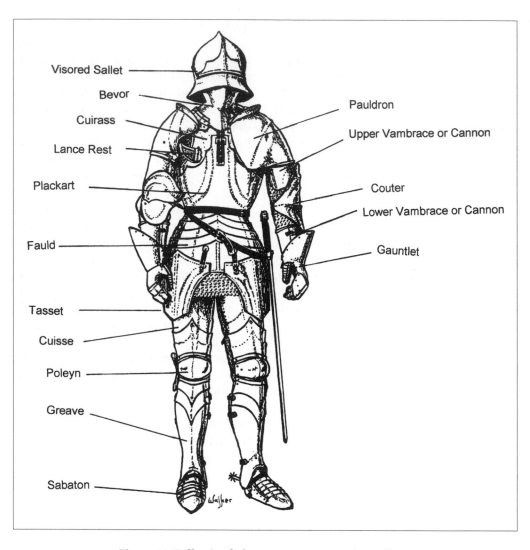

Visored Sallet

Bevor

Cuirass

Lance Rest

Plackart

Fauld

Tasset

Cuisse

Poleyn

Greave

Sabaton

Pauldron

Upper Vambrace or Cannon

Couter

Lower Vambrace or Cannon

Gauntlet

Figure 29. Full suit of plate armor, ca. 1450 (J. Walker).

or shapes it into a horseshoe or a rim for wagon wheel. There is much more to it.

Most modern metal forming typically involves casting metal, machining it into shapes, or, most commonly, pressing and rolling into large sheets of uniform thickness which can then be cut, bent, and welded to shape an item, such as the body of a car or the casings of large appliances, like washers, dryers, or refrigerators. Forming metal by forging is less common than these other techniques and is used primarily to produce tools, cutlery, and

similar items. The techniques of casting, machining, and rolling were all known in the Middle Ages but medieval armorers used forging to produce suits of plate.

Medieval craftsmen knew how to melt and cast metals such as bronze and pewter into forms to produce a great variety of items ranging from great bells down to little buttons. However, to turn iron into liquid for casting requires extremely high heat, approximately 1500 degrees Celsius, about 800 degrees hotter than the temperature required to produce a malleable bloom of iron. While the Chinese had developed the requisite technology for generating such high heat and were producing large quantities of cast iron as early as the 6th century B.C., Europeans do not appear to have started casting iron on a significant scale until almost two millennia later, late in the 14th century. Thus, cast iron was not available in Europe for most of the Middle Ages. Even after it was being produced, cast iron was unsuitable for use in suits of plate armor because it is relatively brittle. When cast into pieces thin enough for a functional, articulated suit of armor, the resulting pieces of iron would likely have been too brittle to have withstood repeated blows in combat.

Machining, taking blocks of metal and cutting, filing, and shaving away pieces to achieve the desired shape, was used on a small scale in the Middle Ages, primarily to make pieces for locks and hinges, including the hinges and catches used in armor. This technique produces hardened pieces of metalwork, but it is not suited for producing the large pieces needed for a suit of plate armor.

So, what about simply flattening the heated metal out into sheets of uniform thickness and then just cutting and bending it to the right shape? This technique was also well known in the Middle Ages and was employed to produce the sheets of lead used to cover roofs as well as to make sheets of fine gold leaf for decorating manuscripts. This is also the technique used by most modern armorers making replica armor today, except they usually just buy their sheets of metal from a steel mill rather than making their own, but this was not the technique used by the medieval armorers. First, medieval armorers lacked the rolling mills needed to produce large, uniform sheets of steel or iron. Second, the armorers did not want uniform sheets because they did not make their armor by simply cutting and bending the metal to shape.

Armorers did not want metal of uniform thickness because, within each single plate, different thicknesses were needed to optimize the plate's strength while minimizing its weight and bulk. Practically, this meant that the armorers designed their suits with an eye to how they would actually be used: Most combat was face to face and involved frontal attacks. Thus, the armorer made the front plates, such as the breast plate and the front of the helmet, thicker than back plates where blows were a little less likely to be directed. Additionally, to allow for smooth articulation of all the joints, most pieces tapered gradually, getting thinner at the edges where they overlapped other plates. How did the armorer accomplish all these fine graduations of thickness while simultaneously crafting pieces that fit and moved with the human body? By starting the shaping of each piece almost with the first strikes of the hammer on the blooms of iron reheated in his forge. This is the importance of skilled metal forging. It can produce finely shaped, very hard pieces of steel from iron. This is how the process worked:

1. The blooms were reheated in charcoal-fired forges. Charcoal burns hotter than wood and heats the metal to the higher temperatures needed to well temper it. Carbon from the burning charcoal also transferred to the iron, starting the gradual transition from plain iron to hardened steel.

2. Men with large hammers would beat the reheated blooms into rough plates under the direction of the armorer, beginning the shaping of each piece. Water powered trip-hammers gradually replaced the men and their hammers with increasing frequency by the end of the Middle Ages.

3. The process of reheating and beating was repeated several times except that the armorer or his skilled journeymen

would take over from the hammermen as the pieces developed and the shaping became more precise and difficult.

4. Through repeated exposure to the carbon in the smoke from the charcoal, the outer layer and sometimes the entire piece of plate was transformed into steel by the bonding of the carbon with the iron. While we know this to be a scientific fact, medieval metallurgy was as much art as science. Surviving records do not indicate that the armorers were aware of the chemical process (applying heat and pressure to iron in the presence of freely available carbon) that resulted in steel but they learned through generations of manufacture and trial and error that following specific sequences and timing for heating and quenching, watching for the metal to turn a particular color while reheating before quenching it, using ore only from certain mines, and many other practices usually yielded the desired results. And the knowledge of these practices and factors were closely guarded trade secrets of the master armorers.

5. When shaping was nearly complete, the pieces of plate would be temporarily assembled into the subcomponents of the complete harness and checked for fit. They would then be disassembled and finished by smoothing and polishing by hand or on water-driven polishing mills. Using grindstones ranging from coarse to very fine, the polishers performed the final thinning of the metal and polished away the last traces of the hammer marks on the armor. These grindstones were also used for sharpening weapons and cutlery. Final polishing of the armor was done by hand with pieces of leather.

6. The plates were then joined together to make the components that made up the complete harness. Again, even this process involved more than it might seem at first glance. It was more than just hammering a few rivets. A variety of fastenings

were needed to join the pieces and still permit them to move as needed. Hinges, often made by locksmiths employed by the armorer, were riveted onto pieces that had to swing open to be fastened onto the knight, such as the pieces for the thighs, calves, and arms. Overlapping pieces that made up the carefully formed joints of the knees and elbows were riveted directly to each other but other pieces for the limbs and especially the fauld (the multi-tiered metal skirt) had rivets fitted into slots that permitted them to slide without coming loose or were joined by leather strips riveted to each piece. Finally, a variety of spring catches as well as buckles riveted to the plates ensured that the armor could be securely sealed around its wearer.

These were just the basic steps in producing plate armors. There were many variations. For example, not all armor was polished to a smooth finish. Some was left rough from the forge, possibly in an attempt to leave it more rust resistant than the highly polished suits. Suits could also be decorated by using acid to etch designs or pictures onto them or by chiseling shallow channels into the surface of the armor and then by applying niello (a black material made of sulfur and a metal such as silver) or hammering thin strips of gold, silver, or brass into the channels. By coating the armor's surface, some of these decorative treatments also served to inhibit rust. Fabric coverings might be glued over the armor and fabric linings were frequently attached to the inside of pieces.

So, unlike the other forms of armor discussed, plate armor could not be readily manufactured just anywhere or by any one. It was a complex manufacturing process that gave rise to some of the first industrial production seen in Europe since the fall of the Roman Empire. By the end of the Middle Ages, armor production had become so specialized that many armorers made only certain parts of the complete harness, making just gauntlets or armor for the arms for example, and the most successful master armorers, while still making some magnificent armors themselves, also often acted as middlemen who contracted with these specialists to fill many of their routine orders.

Plate Armor in Combat: Plate armor was the epitome of medieval armor. On the battlefields of the late 14th and early 15th centuries, plate proved its worth against the weapons of the day. The large, rigid but carefully articulated plates of hardened steel were as resistant to cutting as mail but had the extra advantages of not bending under the force of the below, thus protecting the wearer's bones from being broken, and of being very resistant to punctures from lances, swords, or arrows. It is this last advantage that highlights the unique strengths of well-made plate armor. As discussed above, the armorers shaped the suits very carefully not to interfere with the movements needed by a man for combat but shaping the armor to the contours of human body had another bonus: it created a suit with very curved and rounded surfaces. These rounded surfaces significantly decreased the likelihood that a blow, whether from the cutting edge of a sword or the tip of a crossbow bolt, would hit at or close to perpendicular to the surface. Preventing blows from hitting at a 90-degree angle to the surface decreased the probability that the weapon would penetrate and increased the likelihood that it would instead glance off and slide away, wasting its energy and doing little or no harm to the man inside the armor. This principle has been used in modern warfare as well. The sides of modern tanks and their turrets are sloped down and outwards so that they present steeply angled surfaces to an enemy. These sloped surfaces are designed to deflect incoming shells rather than let them hit the surface squarely just as the rounded and angled

surfaces of a knight's armor were made to deflect the points of incoming weapons. Thus, by making a suit of armor so that it was shaped like the human body, the result was armor which not only moved easily but was also a better defense.

But the medieval armorer did not stop there. The glancing properties of the plate armor's surface were often enhanced by adding fluting or corrugation to the plates, as seen in the suit in figure 29. While usually seen as just being a decorative flourish, fluting and corrugation actually improve the performance of the armor by providing channels designed to catch and carry the points of weapons along the glancing surface and out and away from vital and or thinly armored areas. Additionally, fluting and corrugation strengthen the plates. Modern examples of this use of corrugation can be found on many metal cans for food such as soup or juice as well as in corrugated pipes like those big ones used for drainage. The bends and ridges in these cans and pipes function like those found on the armor plates: they make the finished pieces stronger and more rigid than if they were left plain and flat by distributing pressure through all three dimensional planes rather than just on one spot in a two-dimensional surface. By using corrugation, objects made of thin pieces of metal can be given strength and rigidity that could otherwise be achieved only by using much thicker and heavier metal plates. In modern applications, use of corrugation means that cans and pipes can be made lighter and more economically. In the Middle Ages, its use meant that armorers could make lighter pieces of armor without weakening their defensive value.

The main point to get from all this is that quite a bit of practical experience and a working knowledge of metallurgy and applied physics, combined with a lot of artistic skill, went into production of plate armor.

Some More Things About Plate Armor:
Like mail armor, a complete head to toe
harness of plate armor for battlefield use
weighed from 50 to 65 pounds. The weight
is slightly better distributed than with mail
armor in part because of the specialized
clothing worn under the armor. Plate could
not simply be thrown on over street clothes
nor will a suit stand by itself. As with mail,
padded clothing was worn under plate
armor but, whereas the mail simply rested
over the top of the aketon, coif, and other
padded pieces, the quilted arming doublet,
a snug jacket-like garment, worn under
plate was attached directly to the armor
and served as a foundation to keep the
pieces, particularly the shoulder and arm
armor, held in place. This was accomplished by making eyelets in the appropriate spots on the doublets and threading
braided laces, described as being "as strong
as the strings for crossbows" (indicating
really tough, durable strings), through the
eyelets and through corresponding holes
in the plate armor itself.

Places where a high degree of flexibility was required, such as the armpits,
inside of the elbows, and the tops of the
thighs were still typically protected by
pieces of mail. Gussets of mail or entire
sleeves of mail were attached to the arming doublet to protect the armpit and
inside of the elbow. Skirts or shorts of mail
were worn to protect the tops of thighs,
the buttocks, and other vital parts in that
area. Skirts were more common in France,
England, and Italy while the shorts were
preferred in Germanic countries. However, as the suits of Henry VIII in the
Tower of London and a few other top of
the line plate harnesses prove, it was possible to make a suit with dozens of small,
thin, articulated plates that could protect
the armpits, inside of elbows, and all those
other areas where flexibility was needed
but the extremely high degree of skill
required to produce such suits and the

expense of their production ensured that
few were ever made.

MAINTAINING AND WEARING ARMOR

The image of the lone knight errant,
fully clad in armor, out seeking daring
deeds to do, is hogwash. While it is possible to fully armor up in mail without help,
it's a lot easier with help. And as for plate
armor, while a few of the pieces can be put
on without help, it is impossible to fully
armor up alone. So besides providing a
sort of "on the job training" program for
future knights, squires and other servants
served the vital function of maintaining
the knight's armor and assisting the knight
in putting it on.

Maintenance of Armor

Keeping armor in shape for use was no
small job. Men's lives depended on keeping
their armor in good condition. Mail rings
weakened by rust, hinges or joints on plate
armor damaged by corrosion or wear, worn
or frayed straps: any of these problems
could cause fatal results in a battle.

Mail Armor: Mail is the ideal shape to
maximize rust. The thousands of rings in
a typical piece of mail armor provide
almost the maximum amount of surface
area possible for that volume of metal.
Additionally, the use of iron rather than
steel or any more rust resistant material to
produce the wire for mail further rendered
it highly vulnerable to rust, which is one
reason why so little mail armor has survived from the Middle Ages to the present.
Mail was very difficult to clean. All those
tiny, overlapping surfaces created innumerable "hard to reach" spots. Rust could
be minimized by keeping the mail packed
in oil or grease when not being worn but
the only effective means of cleaning it was
to abrade the rust away. This could be done

by packing the mail into a barrel or heavy cloth sack partially filled with sand and then rolling the barrel or sack around. Vinegar might be added to the sand to enhance the removal of oxidation. This cleans it well but repeated cleaning wears the metal down and weakens it.

Plate armor: While steel holds up better than iron, plate armor rusts too and could be kept oiled or greased to retard oxidation. Oiling and greasing would also help keep all the leather straps in good shape as well as ensuring smooth movement of hinges and riveted joints. Rust could be removed with chamois or other pieces of leather as well as with oiled rags, possibly dipped in sand to add abrasive power, a slightly easier process than having to roll the suit in sand as described above for mail and a process less likely to cause indiscriminate weakening of the metal through excessive polishing. Some of the decorating mentioned above could also prevent rust by covering the steel in a rust-proof or rust-resistant material but probably a very common means of slowing rust (and ornamenting plate armor) was to paint it. Very little painted armor survives, probably because paint naturally wears off over time if it isn't renewed and in part because armor collectors of the 19th century favored shining bare metal pieces so any remaining paint was polished off to make the pieces more salable. Certainly, many suits were never painted but the fact that one of the large mercenary companies of the 14th century was known as the "White Company" because its members wore "white" (i.e. unpainted) armors strongly implies that painting armor must have been a fairly common practice if the use of only unpainted armor was distinctive enough to be noted.

Putting on Armor

For mail armor, the first step is to put on the padded clothing over the "street clothes" so the knight would put on his aketon and arming coif. The aketon could be made either with or without sleeves and could be either a "pullover" style or open down the front with laces or buckles to close it. The arming coif was secured by tying its laces in a bow under the chin. He would then put on his hauberk, either with or without assistance. This involved bending over, grabbing the insides of the shoulders and then lifting the whole hauberk over his head and letting it fall down over him while wriggling into the arms and attached mail coif (if the hauberk had one). Gravity helps the mail drop down snugly over the body but it can be a difficult process, particularly if the knight has gained weight since he was first fitted for the hauberk. At best, it's an awkward process; a modern equivalent might be trying to get into a large, long wet sweater. Some modern Hollywood reconstructions of hauberks often have buckles or laces up the front or back of the mail shirt, presumably to close up an opening designed to make it easier to get in and out of the armor. I am not aware of any contemporary illustrations that support such a reconstruction, at least for the period when mail was the paramount form of armor in Europe (ca. A.D. 1000 to 1300). Further, such openings and fastenings would have created unnecessary vulnerabilities and hauberks can be quite well tailored and fitted even without such adjustable fastenings, so it is likely that most hauberks were constructed without them. In any event, the next step would be to fasten a belt around the hauberk at the waist and pull a little of the mail up over the top of the belt to transfer some of the weight off the shoulders and onto the hips. This frees up the shoulders some, making it easier to use the arms for swinging weapons and in general causing less fatigue of the upper back. Helmets were typically worn over the top of a mail coif and an additional metal skull cap was often worn on top of the arming coif but under the mail coif as an additional bit of protection. Leather gauntlets, often with pieces of metal, horn, or other tough material sewn to the backs of the hand, wrists, and fingers, were worn to protect the hands if the hauberk did not have built-in mittens of mail.

The process of preparing for combat did not stop there. The squire would also buckle on the knight's spurs, if he were to fight on horseback, and his sword belt. But, by the early 12th century, the sword belt would not go on until after the knight had put on his surcoat, a flowing, sleeveless garment worn over the hauberk. The surcoat served several functions which will be discussed later.

Putting on plate armor is a more involved process than putting on mail. Starting almost from his bare skin, the knight had to be specially dressed to wear plate. The knight wore his usual breeches and hose but little else of his ordinary clothing when wearing armor.

On his feet, he wore low-topped boots or shoes with a pair of holes in the toes. An arming point, one of those braided laces "tough as a crossbow string," was fitted through the holes. On his upper body, he wore an arming doublet. The doublet was a long sleeved jacket tailored to fit the knight snugly but not impede his movement. It tapered to the waist and then flared slightly, its lower edge reaching just a few inches down the thigh. It also had a short, standing padded collar to provide some cushioning around the neck. For several reasons, the knight did not wear a shirt under the arming doublet. First, it was usually warm enough inside the armor without an additional layer to trap heat. Second, the additional layer of hot, sweat-sodden cloth provided by the shirt was uncomfortable and, with the intense physical activity of combat, would ride up or

twist and possibly become binding. Thus, arming doublets, while covered in tough, durable canvas, were lined with the softest, most comfortable material the knight could afford. The best doublets had fine silk linings which assured smooth movement of the doublet over the knight's body while in combat. Silk also is a very "breathable" fabric and helped transfer at least some of the damp sweat away from knight's skin. As mentioned before, the arming doublets had eyelets placed for lacing on the armor and usually had pieces of mail sewn or laced on to cover the armpits and the insides of the elbows. A collar of mail was also worn around the arming doublet's collar. Called a *standard*, the mail collar provided the last line of defense for the knight's throat. Finally, depending on the style of helmet being used by the knight, he might also wear some form of padded arming cap on his head.

Once the knight was properly clothed, the squire began attaching the armor to the knight starting at the bottom and working his way up. The squire attending the knight would buckle on the knight's spurs if he were to fight on horseback, otherwise the spurs would be left off to avoid hindering the knight in foot combat.

Next, the squire placed the *sabatons*, articulated metal shoes, over the knight's leather shoes and secured them by lacing the arming point from the leather shoes through corresponding holes in the toe of the sabaton. Buckles and straps further secured the sabaton at the back and the bottom of the foot. A slot in the back of the sabaton allowed the shaft of the spur to pass through while minimizing exposure of the heel area. Such elaborate protection of the feet may seem overly fastidious but it was necessary. When on horseback, the knight's legs from the knees down to his feet were the areas most exposed to attack by soldiers on foot. Much of the advantages the knight gained by fighting from horseback would have been quickly lost if his legs and feet were sliced to ribbons by swords, daggers, and axes anytime he rode down on foot soldiers. However, as with the spurs, sabatons were typically not worn for combat on foot: feet were far less of a target when down on the ground rather than up in the stirrups. Additionally, foot combat required as much mobility and agility as possible, both attributes with which the sabatons could interfere.

The squire next attached the *greaves*, the defenses for the calves. Greaves were composed of a pair of gutter shaped plates attached with hinges along one side. The squire opened the hinges, placed the greave around the calf, closed it, and secured the unhinged side with the attached fasteners. These fasteners could be permanently attached straps and buckles, pivoting hook and eye catches, or spring catches depending up the date and origin of the armor.

In all cases, the hinges would be along the outside part of the leg while the fasteners would be on the inside of the leg. This positioning reflects the armorer's understanding of the potential weaknesses of his product and of the realities of combat: the fasteners are more likely to fail if struck than the hinges so the fasteners were placed along the inside of the leg, the side least exposed and least likely to be struck.

The greaves rested on top of the sabatons and overlapped them. While this is the most natural arrangement for these pieces, it also has additional defensive value and is a feature repeated throughout the rest of the suit of armor. Overlapping the lower edge of the greave over the top edge of sabaton ensures that any weapon striking down along the greave will continue down over the sabaton rather than catching on the sabaton and thus perhaps forcing its way between the two pieces of armor. As mentioned before in the description of ring and scale armors, it's

the same principle used in roofing and siding houses: shingles and siding are always placed with the lower edge of the upper shingle or siding slat overlapping the highest edge of the shingle or slat below to ensure that rain flows over and off the roof or down the siding rather than under the shingling and siding and into the house. Since most blows in medieval combat fell from above (as described in the section on ring and scale armors), armorers overlapped the plates downward instead of upward wherever possible to minimize the risk of the edges or points of weapons catching and sliding under the plates and into the warrior inside the armor.

The next piece attached was the *poleyn*, the articulated cover for the knee. The poleyn was usually permanently riveted to the *cuisse*, the protection for the thigh, so that the poleyn and cuisse went on together. The poleyn was composed of a central "cop," a curved dish-shaped piece that covered the kneecap, and several lames, curved rectangular pieces that provided the articulation. The lames and the cop were riveted together to cover the knee joint, allowing the knight to completely flex and relax his knee as needed. The squire would place a piece of blanket or other sturdy padding on the front of the knight's knee and then secure the poleyn by buckling its straps around the knight's leg. The poleyn usually had at least two straps, one that fastened at or just above the knee and one just below the knee. The lower strap was often secured by a hook at the back of the greave to help ensure a snug fit and no gapping between the greave and poleyn. The poleyn could also be secured to the front of the greave by having a metal pin affixed to top front edge of the greave which would lock into a matching hole in the lowest lame of the poleyn.

The kneecop of the poleyn was typically made with an additional projection along the back, outside edge. Shaped like a broadened, stylized spade (like those depicted on playing cards), this projection helped protect the back of the knee from slashing blows from the side by stopping the incoming blade before it reached the leg. The projection was spade-shaped to help carry the blade back and away from the leg.

Moving up the leg, the next piece of armor was the cuisse, the large defense for the thighs. As mentioned before, cuisses were usually permanently attached to the poleyn by having the highest lame of the poleyn riveted to the lower edge of the cuisse. In this instance, the upper edge of the lower plate overlapped the lower edge of the top plate, contrary to the better defensive overlapping described above and so created a potential vulnerability in the armor. However, the need for articulating the joint to permit the knee to move required this pattern of overlapping.

The cuisse had a large gutter-shaped piece of metal for the front and had one or more slightly curved rectangular pieces attached by hinges along its outside edge to more fully enclose the thigh. Again, to minimize the exposure of the fasteners to blows, the hinges were along the outside and the fasteners were along the inside of the thigh. For cuisses, the fasteners were always straps and buckles rather than hooks or other all-metal closures since more room for adjustment was needed for the thighs than for the calves and since the metal plates did not completely encircle the thigh. For securing the top of the cuisse, a leather tab was permanently riveted to its top and arming points located below the waist on the arming doublet laced through holes on the tab. It is also possible that cuisses could have been fitted with straps and buckle that permitted fastening their top edge to belts rather than directly to the jacket. This would have had the advantage of transferring more of the weight of the leg armor to the hips rather

than having it all hanging from the knight's shoulder (via the doublet).

Next, the squire helped the knight into the first layer of metal armor to protect his buttocks and the tops of his thighs. The knight already had some protection for these areas in the form of the padded armor of the skirt of his arming doublet but better, yet still flexible, armor was obviously needed. Thus, the squire would help the knight into a mini-skirt of mail or, if in a Germanic country, breeches of mail. The squire would draw the leather cord along the top of the skirt or breeches tight and tie it securely, in the same way that any drawstring clothing is put on. While the mail was not as good a protection as plate, it was the best option for providing the high degree of flexibility needed while still providing significantly more protection than just fabric armor.

The next step was to attach the upper body armor. *Breast* and *back plates* were typically divided horizontally a few inches above waist level into two separate pieces. The upper breast plate, often called a *cuirass*, and the upper back plate were usually hinged together along one side and then buckled at the shoulders and along the unhinged side. The lower breast plate, sometimes called a *plackart*, and the lower back plate attached to straps or nuts mounted in the center of the upper back and breast plates. One advantage of having the breast and back plates broken up this way was that it allowed some slight room for adjustment of the fit and some slight additional flexibility. To supplement the fasteners built in to breast and back plates and to further ensure that they stayed together without gapping, some knights wore a belt around the pronounced waist of the harness.

At the bottom of the lower breast and back plates was the *fauld*, a skirt of rectangular plates curved to fit the body and suspended on leather straps to allow the skirt to ride up or hang down to accommodate the knight's leg movement when riding or on foot. Additionally, *tassets*, large pentagonal plates, were often attached to the front and occasionally the sides of the fauld to cover the seam between the upper and lower body defenses. The tassets provided an additional, free-hanging layer of armor over the top of the mail skirt or breeches. The tassets also overlapped the cuisses, again to help downward blows to flow over and down the knight's body without catching and penetrating.

The knight's arms were protected with *couters* and *vambraces* or *cannons*. The couter was the articulated protection for the elbow and was constructed like the poleyn, except slightly smaller. The similarity usually included the presence of an oblong or spade-shaped projection on the outside of the elbow-cop that protected the inside of the elbow the same way that the projection on the poleyn protected the back of the knee. Much like the greaves, vambraces were made of paired gutter shaped pieces of metal, hinged along one side and fitted with fasteners along the other. The lower vambrace enclosed the forearm. The lower vambrace was often laced to the arming doublet but later versions were frequently riveted directly to the lower edge of the couter. Through holes either in its upper edge or in a leather tab attached to that edge, the upper vambrace was laced to arming points at the shoulder and buckled shut. At the lower edge of the upper vambrace, the couter was usually permanently attached by rivets though it could also be attached by lace from the elbow of the arming doublet.

Next the squire would lace on the shoulder armor, either *pauldrons* or *spaudlers*. Pauldrons were large, shell-like pieces that covered the tops of the shoulders in front and back down to about the middle of the upper arm and attached to laces at the top of the shoulder of the arming

doublet. Again, the arming points or laces were threaded either through holes in the top edge of the pauldron itself or through a leather tab riveted to the pauldron. Later versions of pauldrons and spaudlers were attached directly to the upper breast and back plates by locking rivets: specially constructed rivets with spring loaded tabs that held the armor in place. Pauldrons were fitted with additional straps to secure the lower edge around the arm, preventing them from being flipped up to expose the top of the arm. Later pauldrons were fitted with grooves at the lower edge that engaged flanges at the top of the upper vambrace to ensure no gapping. Spaudlers had smaller shell-like pieces at the top to cover the top of shoulders but then had a series of articulated curved plates attached at the lower edge. These plates were contoured to match the shape of the upper arm more closely than the pauldrons and attached directly to the upper edge of the upper vambrace.

Shoulder defenses were usually asymmetrical. Pauldrons and spaudlers for the left side were usually large and covered more of the side and armpit than those for the right side. This reflected the fact that knights fought only right-handed: that is, they used their left-hands to hold the reins and wielded their weapons in their right hands. Gauntlets and vambraces were also often designed with this in mind as well: left gauntlets and vambraces larger and less mobile than those on the right since less movement was required on that side and, since plate armor had rendered shields largely unnecessary for knights in battle by the 15th century, so they could better withstand blows. In some suits of armor, the difference between the left and right sides is so pronounced that the suits are reminiscent of lobsters, with one claw far more developed and oversized than the other. Pauldrons and spaudlers on the right side frequently had semicircular cut outs on the inside front surface. While such a cut out may seem like a needless exposure of the highly vulnerable armpit it was necessary to allow the knight to couch his lance properly under his right arm. Complementing the cut-out in the right spaudler or pauldron, breastplates designed for mounted combat usually had a small detachable bracket on the right side. This bracket was the lance rest which helped support the lance and engaged the back of the *vamplate*, the flared hand guard on the lance, preventing the lance from simply being forced out back under the knight's arm when he struck his opponent. The combination of cut-out, lance rest, and vamplate ensured that a knight's lance would strike with the full force of the combined mass of the knight, his charging horse, and their armor: a great amount of power, all concentrated in the sharp, iron or steel point of the lance.

At this point, the knight could don his gauntlets. Gauntlets were metal gloves or mittens made of articulated plates with flaring cuffs that could reach half way to the elbow. Personal taste as much as anything else appears to have been the determining factor as to whether the gauntlets were made with individual fingers like gloves or with only the thumb separate like mittens. In either case, the gauntlets were fitted with leather gloves permanently riveted or sewn into the gauntlets and these gloves ensured a good, comfortable fit and grip regardless of whether the metal portion of the gauntlet was styled as a glove or a mitten. To provide even more protection, the leather gloves could also be faced with very fine mail.

Besides being a defense, gauntlets were also weapons. In the 14th century, England's Black Prince, the son of Edward III, had the knuckles of his gauntlets fitted with small, metal statuettes of leopards. While the leopards were highly decorative, they would also act as tough points like brass knuckles if the prince struck anyone with armored fist. Even without such enhancement, gauntlets provided sturdy implements for pummeling if the knight had lost his other weapons and still had to fight on.

The next step would be to place armor on the knight's neck and head. Before the helmet was strapped on, the squire would attach the *bevor* or *gorget* to protect the knight's throat and neck. The bevor and gorget were metal collars that buckled or laced to the tops of the upper breast and back plates. Gorgets were formed of a ring of graduated, semi-circular plates that protected the neck and throat. Since gorgets completely encircled the neck, they were usually more articulated than the bevors to allow for some movement of neck and head. Bevors typically were open in back but extended up above the wearer's jaw on the sides and front. Use of a bevor or a gorget depended upon the type of helmet the knight wore and, by 15th century when plate was at its peak, there was quite a varied selection of helmets:

The *armet* was the classic visored helmet (fig. 30f). The armet was a close fitting helmet of rather ingenious construction. It was formed of a crown or skull piece with a tail that went down the back of head. In the middle of each side of the skull piece, roughly over the ears, there were hinges that attached to cheekpieces. These were plates that swung down to enclose the sides of the head, flaring out slightly at the bottom where they neared the shoulders. The cheekpieces overlapped each other at the wearer's chin. In the back, they overlapped the edges of the tail of the skull piece at the back of the neck. The squire would place the helmet on the knight's head, lower the cheekpieces, fasten them together at the chin, and then secure them with a strap that fastened completely around the neck. This strap and its buckle were protected at the back by a *rondel*, a small metal disc centered on a short rod at the tail of the skull piece. The knight could then lower the armet's visor which was attached by pivots in front of each hinge on the side of the helmet. On the right side of the visor, there was a short metal peg or a tough knotted leather lace which the knight used for raising the visor. Armets were worn with gorgets, though a form of bevor called a *wrapper* was sometimes also worn to supplement protection for the lower face and throat.

The *sallet* (figs. 29 and 30e) was another common type of helmet and it was typically worn with a bevor that protected the front and side of the neck as well as the face almost up to the nose. The sallet was a deep, domed helmet with sides reaching down to the line of the jaw and a tail that extended over the back of the neck. The sallet could have a visor or could be formed in a single piece with a solid front with vision slot. The tail came to a point a few inches behind the back of the neck and, when worn with a backplate, provided excellent protection against blows at this vital spot. Some experts have opined that the tail might have actually been a liability, that blows on the tail would have snapped the knight's head back sharply causing neck injuries since the helmet was firmly strapped under his chin, but this fails to take into account that the tail rested on or just above the back plate and thus could not have been "snapped down" to any significant degree.

A third type of helmet was the *barbute* (fig. 30d) which looked much like the helmets of the ancient Greeks. Basically, it was a cylinder with a domed top and sides that came down to just above the shoulders and flared out slightly at the bottom. The barbute had a "T" shaped opening in the front to allow for vision as well as ventilation. Raised edges around the opening provided some protection

against incoming blows but it still rendered the face more vulnerable than the other styles of helmets. However, the target area was still quite small and the better sight and ventilation it provided was considered by some, particularly those in hot climates like Italy, to be worth the risk. Barbutes could be worn with gorgets but are most often shown with knights wearing only mail collars (*standards*) to protect their necks.

One final design point about plate armor which is well illustrated in most of the helmets as well as the breast and back plates of this period is the use of stop ribs to prevent the points of weapons from sliding into vital or weakly armored areas such as the eyes, neck, armpits, or groin. As discussed previously, plate armor, both for body armor and helmets, employed very rounded surfaces that helped deflect weapon points rather than letting them hit perpendicular to surface, thus lessening the likelihood of the point penetrating the plate. However, these deflected points must go somewhere. Properly placed grooves or fluting in the armor increased the probability that the weapon points were carried out and away from the body but there was still a risk that the points could glance off into a vital area. Thus, edges of breast and back plates around the neck and armpit were folded over and raised at ninety-degree angle to the rest of the surface. This created stop ribs: solid strips of metal that would catch points and hold or channel them away rather than let them slide up into the neck or across and off into the more lightly armored armpits. Similarly, the inside edge of the tassets that covered the tops of the thighs would be finished with a stop rib to prevent lance or sword points from sliding into the groin. And helmets were usually made with raised edges around the slits for the eyes, also to prevent weapon points from sliding in.

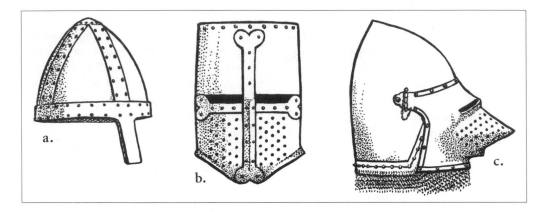

Figure 30. The evolution of helmets.

a. Conical Helmet. This style of helmet is an ancient design which changed little during the Middle Ages except for the addition of the nasal bar to provide some limited protection for the face. Conical or round-topped helmets like this one were used throughout the Middle Ages, but were most common before the 13th century.

b. Barrel Helmet. Flat-topped helmets appeared in the last half of the 12th century. Initially, they were equipped with only face guards, leaving the lower half of the back of the warrior's head and his neck exposed. Still, this was an improvement over the nasal bar. By the early 13th century, additional plates had been added to protect the back as well as the front of the warrior's head. By the mid–13th century, these plates encased the head and neck almost down to the shoulders. The holes on the lower face plates are for ventilation.

c. Bascinet. Developed over the course of the 14th century, the bascinet was produced in a number of styles, but all had the characteristic high, rounded top and deep sides. Early bascinets were made without visors and the face either was left open or was only partially covered with a flap of mail. By the late 14th century, visors were common. Some were rounded but many were pointed as shown here. The visor was equipped with holes for ventilation like the earlier helmets, though there were always fewer holes placed on the left side than on the right side. Armorers did this because they did not want to significantly weaken the left side of the helmet because of the way that knights and other combatants fought. They held their weapons in their right hands and their shields on their left sides. Thus they tended to block blows with their left side instead of with their right. An *aventail* is laced to the lower edge of the bascinet. The aventail was a collar of mail that protected the base of the wearer's neck and then flared out to cover the tops of his shoulder.

The squire completed the arming by girding the knight with his sword belt. If fighting was to be done from horseback, the knight could then mount his horse unassisted, just as he would have to do on the battlefield if he was knocked off his mount. While this sounds like quite a long and involved process, based on modern reenactments, a trained squire can fully arm a knight in less than twenty-five minutes even without the motivation of the threat of imminent attack.

Shields

Shields from the fall of the Roman Empire through to the 11th century appear to have been mainly circular (fig. 31a) or

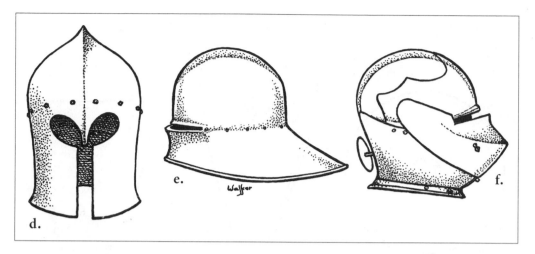

(Figure 30. continued)

d. **Barbute.** In the 15th century, armorers created a number of distinct styles of helmets derived from the bascinet. The barbute closely resembled the late bascinet, but was visor-less. In place of the visor, the barbute enclosed most of the face, leaving only relatively small openings for the eyes, nose, and mouth. Some barbutes, such as the one shown, appear to have been modeled on ancient Greek helmets.

e. **Sallet.** Another 15th century helmet, the sallet was made in several forms including open-faced, visored, and, as shown here, closed-face with only a narrow slit for the eyes. Regardless of how they protected the warrior's face, all sallets had deep crowns and tails that projected out over (and thus protected) the back of the neck. As with both the bascinet and the barbute, the rounded shape and smooth surfaces of the sallet were designed to deflect the points and edges of weapons, increasing the chances that the weapons would glance off rather than strike the helmet solidly. Like the barbute, the sallet had no aventail. Instead, to protect the throat, sallets were often worn with some form of bevor.

f. **Armet.** One of the most elaborate helmets created in the 15th century was the close fitting armet. It remained in use well into the 16th century (J. Walker).

oblong, depending on the region. Archaeological evidence as well as contemporary illustrations show that round shields with central bosses (metal domes that covered the hand-grip) were popular with the people of northern Europe, while large oblong shields were used throughout Europe. These shields were not made of sheets of metal. As stated before, large pieces of metal were too scarce and expensive for such uses and would have been too heavy in any event. Thus, shields were made out of wood. To form a piece of wood wide enough for a shield, the shield-maker joined planks of wood together and then placed a few strips of wood or metal across the back of the shield for reinforcement. At some point during the Middle Ages, shield-makers developed an alternative method for forming the large sheets of wood which they needed. Instead of making just one thick layer of planks, they made multiple layers of thin planks. The planks in each layer were joined together and then placed so that the grain of each layer was at a ninety-degree angle to the grain in each adjoining layer. This pattern of layers is still used in making plywood today because it maximizes the natural strength of the wood grain and produces a

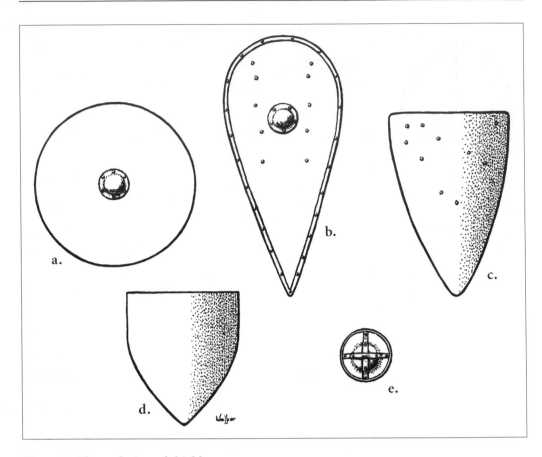

Figure 31. The evolution of shields.

- a. Round, the most common form of shield through the end of the 11th century.
- b. Kite, developed during the 11th century.
- c. Flat-topped Kite, appeared during the 12th century.
- d. Heater, developed from the flat-topped kite shield in the 13th century and used through the end of the 14th century.
- e. Buckler, a later form of round shield used only in combat on foot from the mid–14th century through the 15th century (J. Walker).

much stronger product than placing the grain in all the layers the same direction. Like modern plywood, the layers in medieval plywood were glued together though the gluing was routinely supplemented with large metal staples. Besides these staples and any other fasteners used to hold the planks or layers together, the only other metal fittings used on these shields were for the grip and to attach the straps used to support the shield, and perhaps for edging the shield to strengthen it against cuts. To complete the shield, shield-makers usually attached a cloth cover over the front of the shield.

By the middle of the 11th century, a different shape of shield appeared. Usually associated with the Normans, this shield had a round top but the lower half tapered gradually to a point (fig. 31b). Because of its shape, this type of shield was nicknamed a "kite shield" by historians and scholars. The kite shield was well suited to the Normans' cavalry tactics because it was shaped to cover the left side of the body from the shoulder down to the ankle. Though its length and bulkiness appears to have made it somewhat less practical than a round shield for combat on foot, the kite shield spread throughout Europe and appears to have remained popular through the 12th century. To compensate for the unwieldiness in handling, kite shields were supported by arm straps and a hand grip or strap rather than by just a central grip like the round shield. Also, to facilitate carrying the shield or to keep it in place even if the knight relaxed his left arm, kite shields often had a *guige* strap. This was simply an extra long strap that supported the shield by passing over the knight's shoulder and back, then around under his arm, back to the shield.

During the 12th century, shield-makers began making the top edge of the kite shield flat (fig. 31c) instead of rounded. This change made it easier for the warrior to keep his shield held high without blocking his field of vision. In the late 12th century through the early 13th century, the flat-topped kite shield was superceded by a smaller shield, often called a "heater shield" (figs. 27 and 31d). Again, this is a name created by later historians. They gave it this name because the shield's outline resembled the outline of the bottom of irons, colloquially "heaters," used to press clothing. As with the shields before them, heater shields were made of wood with leather or fabric coverings and metal was used only for edging and to attach the straps. The arrangement of straps on a heater shield was comparable to straps on a kite shield. Besides its outline, another distinguishing feature of the heater shield was that it was curved rather than flat. While some curving is seen in late kite shields, all known examples of heater shield are curved to better enclose the

knight's left side. Heater shields were also shorter than kite shields, usually around three feet, making them easier to use on foot. Based on tomb effigies and illustrations, heater shields were in general use from the end of the 12th century until at least the mid–14th century.

By the end of the 14th century, knights seldom used shields on the battlefield. For them, plate armor made shields obsolete though knights did continue to use shields in tournaments. In real combat, common foot soldiers used small round shields, called bucklers or targets (fig. 31e), from the mid–14th century through the end of the Middle Ages. These shields were about 14 inches in diameter and were used to block blows as well as to deliver punches. Another form of specialized shield that did see service on the battlefield from the late 14th century through the end of the Middle Ages was the *pavise*. This was a large, flat-bottomed shield. Made of thin wood covered in leather, pavises were up to a yard wide and four or more feet tall. They were used by crossbowmen to provide cover while reloading their bows.

The Evolution of Armor

As with many other areas of technology, the medieval Europeans inherited much of their early armor and armor-making skills from the Romans. By A.D. 400, the Romans had established a network of factories and depots throughout western Europe for making, storing, and distributing basic armor to the legions and their auxiliaries, those barbarian tribes that had at least nominally submitted to Rome. Roman armor included helmets and body armor pieced together from plates or sheets of iron (*lorica segmenta*) as well as mail shirts (*lorica hamata*).

After the collapse of the Empire, the

former auxiliaries and invading barbarians reused Roman armor. In this time of "dark ages" and throughout the Middle Ages, processed metal was far too valuable to discard so armor was used until it fell apart and then the parts were reused. For example, a late Roman helmet was typically composed of a frame and four or more plates riveted together to form the crown with additional plates to protect the cheeks and back of the neck. As plates were damaged, smiths would replace them with pieces salvaged from other helmets or parts of their own manufacture if they could. Smiths would also attempt to copy the Roman originals, with varying degrees of success. Gradually, the Roman armor itself disappeared but some of the design elements continued to appear for centuries afterwards as smiths copied old designs.

By the early Middle Ages, ca. A.D. 700, production of the large plates of iron needed for body armor had long vanished but helmets of oblong or slightly triangular plates, either overlapping or supported by a frame, could still be made from smaller pieces of iron (fig. 30a). Other tough materials such as horn or leather boiled in wax were also substituted for metal plates in the helmets. But for body armor, the materials and options were then very limited.

Armor incorporating plates of metal remained in use in the eastern Roman empire of Byzantium but largely disappeared from the empire's former lands of western and central Europe. The sketchy information provided by references in old Norse sagas like *Beowulf*, illustrations in manuscripts, and architectural carvings indicate that mail continued in use — though only for the very wealthy and powerful — and that other forms of armor based on leather or cloth were more common. These armors were typically comprised of metal rings sewn flat onto the exterior of coat-like garments. While less protective than mail, such armor would still provide significant protection against the broad, cutting swords of that time (fig. 32a).

As for shields, round shields about two and half feet in diameter with central grips covered by bosses were the most common (fig. 31a). However, some illustrations from Mediterranean countries such as Italy and Spain show much larger oblong shields being used as well.

From the fall of the Roman Empire in the 5th century to the end of the 10th century, there appears to have been little progress in the development of armor, but this is not surprising given that there were no major developments in weaponry and little change in tactics during this same period. There is much debate over the rise of cavalry warfare from the 8th century onwards. Changes, such as the introduction of stirrups to Europe which allowed the rider a firmer seat on his horse and thus a more stable platform from which to strike, did occur but none of these developments were revolutionary. Certainly, the use and effectiveness of mounted warriors, most noticeably by the Franks and later by the Normans, increased throughout this period but many factors, such as improved social and economic stability at the local and regional level that provided resources and conditions amenable to raising horses on a large scale, contributed to evolutionary, not revolutionary, changes in warfare.

By the early 11th century, the mounted warrior was well established as the most powerful figure on the battlefield. Clad in a short or mid-length mail shirt and conical helmet and slinging a kite shield on his left side, the knight was well protected against the slashing swords, axes, and broad-headed arrows commonly encountered in combat. He was more vulnerable to spear and lance thrusts but these thrusts were only as strong as the men delivering them. The tactic of inflicting devastating lance thrusts by couching the lance under the right the arm and charging into an opponent with the combined mass of horse and rider was just beginning to be developed by the end of the 11th century.

By the end of the 11th and beginning of the 12th century, hauberks were typically long sleeved with mittens and coifs built in. Hauberk hemlines typically reached to just above the knee. Chausses (stockings of mail) appeared, at first just covering the front of the leg and top of the foot and later completely encircling the leg from the mid-thigh down.

Conical helmets (fig. 30a) remained in use but the simple nose-guards were increasingly replaced with face-guards that reached from ear to ear and covered down to the chin. Pierced with slits for the eyes and holes for breathing, these face guards mark the start of the changes in armor design that would eventually lead to the complete encasing of the knight's head in a protective layer of metal.

By the mid–12th century, plate protection for important areas other than the head were developed. Dish shaped cops of either cuir boulli or iron, either made as part of chausses or added on by lacing, protected the knees. Disks of iron were also laced onto the hauberk to protect the elbows and armpits. These pieces were called, respectively, *couters* and *besagews*. The fact that the first body parts after the head to be given the better protection of rigid plates were the principal joints suggests that these areas were often targeted in combat in attempts to disable an opponent before capturing or killing him. The early development of plate protection for the joints may also reflect an awareness that joints seldom if ever fully healed after severe injuries. In the Middle Ages, fractures of the long bones in the arms and legs could be set with a fair degree of success but damage to the cartilage, tendons, and other tissues that make up the joints

remained largely untreatable until the development of advanced surgical techniques and physical therapy in the 20th century. And even today, joint injuries can still be difficult to treat, as shown by the number of athletes whose careers are ended by such injuries.

As for helmets, while conical helmets remained in service at least with the common soldiery, cylindrical, flat-topped helmets were the latest fashion for knights. At first, these helmets had face guards like the conical helmets but by the early 13th century they had neck guards as well (fig. 30b) and so resembled modern metal buckets or waste paper cans with slits for eyes and ventilation holes for speaking and breathing. Specialized head coverings had to be worn under these helmets to hold them in place since the motion of moving the head from side to side (let alone the impact from being struck on the head) causes the helmet to spin, potentially leaving the wearer in the embarrassing if not fatal position of being left blind if his helmet has rotated so much that his vision slots were now facing the side or back of his head. To prevent such a humiliating and disastrous faux pas, the knight would wear an arming coif that had a stuffed oval of fabric, shaped rather like an oversized donut, attached to its top. This could be worn either under or over the knight's mail coif and provided a snug fit between his head and the helmet so that the helmet stayed in the correct position.

While the cylindrical helmets remained in widespread use through the 13th century, they were actually a technological dead-end. Despite the seeming defensive advantages of fully enclosing the knight's head in metal, the shape of the helmet was seriously flawed. The flat top and perpendicular sides allowed blows to land solidly rather than glance off, with the result (as shown in contemporary German and French illuminations) that swords and axes could shear through the helmet with unfortunate consequences for the knight inside. Thus, by the early 14th century, helmets returned to a more rounded, dome shaped top comparable to the earlier conical helmet but with many improvements.

Returning to limb and body armor, by the early 13th century, more rigid pieces began to supplement the mail. In addition to the kneecops, couters, and besagews, gutter shaped defenses for the calves and arms were developed. These early greaves and vambraces buckled around the limbs but were also often laced to the underlying mail armor to better hold them in place. These pieces could either be solid, shaped pieces of iron or steel or be composed of strips of metal riveted to a layer of stout leather. In either case, the knight now had enhanced protection against cutting and piercing. At some point in the late 12th or early 13th century, rigid armor for the torso was also developed but no known examples survive and the practice of wearing a surcoat over the armor makes it virtually impossible to precisely determine from pictorial and sculptural images what layers of armor a knight might have worn. However, during this time, household inventories began to include references to "pairs of plates" among the armor for knight. Additionally, by the mid–13th century, buckles are visible below the armpits of some tomb effigies of knights (in cases where the knight is wearing a sleeveless surcoat with a wide opening for the arms). Combining this meager evidence with known later development of breastplates, the "pairs of plates" are believed to have been a pair of plates of either cuir boulli or metal that covered the top of the knight's chest. These plates were part of a larger defensive garment similar to a brigandine and covered the knight from his shoulders down to his waist or just above it. These garments were worn over the mail, buckling at the shoulders and down each side.

This process of enclosing more and more of the body in rigid but articulated plates continued through the 14th and into the 15th century until the complete head to toe suits described earlier were produced. While progress was steady, it took time and practice to develop smoothly moving joints for the knees and elbows from the simple dishes and disks of the kneecops and couters. Similarly, protection for the body went through an evolution from just protection for the upper chest to the whole torso in a process that included *coats of plate*, heavy fabric vests lined with large plates of iron or steel, and breast plates that covered just the front of the body before developing into the complete armors seen by the 15th century.

While the development of more and better plate armor proceeded steadily, it was not without problems. It took the armorer and his customers some time to realize that if a person wore a good outer layer of plate armor that there was no longer a need to wear mail armor underneath to cover those same body parts. After all, the plate was at least as proof against cutting as the mail and was superior to mail in its protection against punctures and crushing blows. In hindsight, this seems obvious but it was not so apparent to the tradition bound warriors who were loath to needlessly render themselves more vulnerable on the battlefield. Thus, in the mid to late 14th century, the weight of battlefield armor reached a peak of some 95 pounds since the armor included padded underclothes; complete mail armor for head, body, and limbs; and nearly complete plate armor as well. Even the fittest of knights must have found this weight excessively burdensome. Thus, before the end of the 14th century, chausses almost completely disappeared, replaced by plate leg armor with perhaps only a little mail to protect the joints around the knees and ankles. Mailshirts shrank, barely covering to the waist with shorter sleeves as well. All the changes helped reduce armor's total weight back to the range of 60 or so pounds which a knight could reasonably bear and fight in.

During the 14th century, armorers also improved helmet designs to eliminate the problems of the old, cylindrical "bucket" helmet. Rounded helmets, called *bascinets* (fig. 30c) rapidly became popular. Elegantly curved, these helmets provided the same rounded glancing surfaces that the rest of the body was beginning to enjoy. Variations and improvements on the bascinet gave rise to the other helmets (the armet, barbute, and sallet) of the later Middle Ages discussed previously. Additionally, the bascinets were the first helmets with movable visors and so allowed the knight to maintain maximum vision and ventilation until he had to drop the visor for combat. It's often been proposed that the modern salute is derived from the gesture of a knight raising his visor to greet a fellow knight but illustrations from the 14th and 15th centuries indicate that the practice of common soldiers saluting their commanders by raising a hand to their foreheads was already well established by the time that visors came into use. It seems more likely the salute was derived from the traditional removal of the hat and "tug of the forelock" gestures long used by peasants as a gesture of obeisance towards their superiors.

By the early to mid–15th century, plate armor had reached the apex of its development. While there would be some later minor improvements and embellishments, plate was now as perfect as it ever would be. But by the time plate was reaching its peak, it was already becoming obsolete. Gunpowder weapons, which appeared in Europe by the beginning of the 14th century, were proliferating and increasing in power. Other missile weapons such as steel-bow crossbows with draw-weights of

at least 200 to 300 pounds and English long bows with draw-weights of up to 180 pounds were also capable of penetrating armor or, at the very least, causing concussion to the knight inside the armor. It was possible to make armor "proof" against all these projectiles, including bullets, but such armor was so heavy as to be unwearable. For example, a bulletproof breastplate made during the English Civil War weighed 70 pounds! No one could be reasonably expected to wear such armor.

But bullets alone did not end the era of plate armor. Changes in tactics, particularly the rise of large bodies of trained, disciplined foot soldiers were the real death knell for the dominance of the heavily armored knight on the battlefield. While Frankish encounters with the Saracens in the Crusades of the 12th century had shown the weaknesses of heavy cavalry, Europeans did not effectively exploit these weaknesses until late in the following century. Then, by combining archers and gunners with other foot soldiers armed with pikes and other pole weapons, commanders found they could blunt or break the force of the knights' charge and thus deprive them of their greatest advantage. Still, the changes in warfare were gradual and armor still provided protection against swords and other common weapons. So plate armor, in ever diminishing form, remained on the battlefield through the end of the 1600s.

Of course, the story of European and European-derived armor does not end here. French cavalry wore steel helmets and breastplates during the Napoleonic Wars and were called *curaissiers* after their curaisses, the French word for breastplates. In the 1860s, a factory in Connecticut produced steel breastplates that were privately purchased and used, with mixed results, by some Union officers in the American Civil War. The same armor development programs from World War I that experimented with silk armor also led to a reexamination of medieval armor, as well. All the belligerents pressed their art and armor historians into service to help develop armor suited to modern warfare. The British produced a helmet with a shallow dome and broad brim. This was based on the *chapel-de-fer* (iron hat) which was popular with common foot soldiers from the early 13th century onwards because it did not interfere with vision, hearing, or breathing while still protecting from downward blows, a reason it was particularly favored for use by troops besieging fortifications since it would protect the head and shoulders from items dropped or hurled from the battlements above. This protection against overhead bombardment was thought to be valuable again in the trench warfare of World War I. The Germans created a truncated, open-faced sallet for their regular troops as well as visors and bevors for use by snipers, machine-gunners, and others exposed to more risk. As for the Americans, they developed their own version of the truncated, open-faced sallet. This helmet was developed by armor specialists at the Metropolitan Museum of Art in New York but would have to wait until World War II to prove its worth since the Americans simply adopted the British helmet instead of producing their own design.

Weapons

The knight's most important weapon was himself. He was trained and conditioned from an early age for the profession of fighting. While ideal chivalric training for a would-be knight included learning to wait on his lord and other such niceties, far more important was developing the physical strength and skill needed for victory on the battlefield. This training included practice with blunt swords, mock mounted combat (sometimes using wooden horses on wheels pushed by other trainees), and other drills. It also included becoming accustomed to the weight and feel of armor. Since only the extremely wealthy could afford to outfit their growing sons in scaled down suits of armor, many may have used coats with special pockets that could be filled with sand or other weights to simulate the weight and drag of real armor. Besides helping develop overall body strength and toughness, weighted clothing also helped the knight to learn how to move with his armor and to better use the armor's mass and inertia to compliment rather than hinder his movements. For example, the weight of the armor could be used to the knight's advantage in delivering pile-driver blows that had the force not only of his own muscles behind it but the weight of his armor as well. Besides the training, knights also enjoyed the best food available. They were at the top of the food chain, so to speak, and had protein-rich diets to fuel their muscle development. More details on the diet of knight and others are set out in the section on cooking and eating.

Swords

Like metal armor, swords were a very expensive item throughout the Middle Ages and so were highly prized. In the Norse sagas, swords were given names and mentioned again and again as they are passed down as family heirlooms from one generation of warriors to the next. Or, as archaeological finds prove, were buried with great leaders for their use in the afterlife. Many of these swords had decorative inscriptions, perhaps to invoke the favor of the pagan gods. Even after the Christianization of Europe, legendary heroes such as Roland gave their swords names and inscriptions, now invoking the God of the Christians, appeared on blades and pommels. Why were swords such important objects? Turning aside from their symbolism, swords were valuable because of the nature of medieval combat. While long bows, crossbows, and other projectile weapons were employed, most of fighting was done at close quarters, face to face, hand to hand, and the sword was the best close quarter weapon of its day.

Swords were always made of the best steel or iron available since they had to be highly durable to withstand the stresses of impact against solid objects like armor, shields, other swords, and opponents' bodies. While later swords were forged entirely from steel, early swords were mostly made of iron. Steel was especially scarce in the early Middle Ages and so was used sparingly, only where absolutely essential. Thus, early medieval swordsmiths, such as those that made swords for the Vikings, made the core of the sword blade by heating thin iron rods, twisting them together, and then "hammer welding" them together by heating them in a forge and flattening them into the shape of the blade using a hammer and anvil. This process gave the swords sort of a coiled spring for a center, endowing them with amazing flexibility and resiliency. Even today such swords can be bent to a considerable degree and will still spring back to their original straightness. While the iron core was tough and springy, it was relatively soft and could not hold a sharp edge so strips of steel were welded to edges and faces of the core to provide the hard edge necessary for a good cutting sword. And swords of the early Middle Ages were designed primarily for cutting. The blades were long and straight with very little tapering, often ending in a nearly blunt point (fig. 32b). The powerful slashing blows from these weapons were quite effective against the padded and soft leather armors common on the battle-field. Mail armor was developed to counter the cutting force of these swords, but was of only limited use against their impact which could still break bones beneath the flexible armor.

Another feature to note about these early swords and most swords throughout the Middle Ages up to the mid–14th century is the *fuller*. The fuller is the long, shallow groove that ran for most of the length of either side of the blade (figs. 32a–c). It is often misdescribed as a "blood groove" that somehow channeled an opponent's blood, making it easier to pull the blade out after sticking it in. Like most of the fanciful yet gruesome explanations concocted about the Middle Ages, this is completely false. The purpose of the fuller is two-fold and neither involves blood. First, the fuller makes the sword blade lighter and easier to maneuver without weakening it. It's similar to the corrugations in plate armor and actually make the blade stronger, more capable of resisting the stresses of impact, yet lighter. Second, the fuller makes the blade more flexible, able to bend without breaking. Again, a very important feature for cutting swords since a warrior would much rather that his sword bend slightly when he hit a hard target rather than having the sword so rigid that it would break.

A final feature to note about swords designed for slashing combat is the *pommel*. The pommel is a decorative-looking chunk of metal located at the bottom of the grip, the end furthest away from the blade. Pommels were made in many different shapes but the most common shapes were polygonal or disk-shaped. The purpose of the pommel was to make the sword easier to use by acting as a counterbalance for the blade. While cutting swords were designed to be "blade heavy," made so that the top part of the swordblade would naturally strike with great force when swung, a counterweight was needed to balance the sword to make it easier to maneuver and less tiring to wield. Thus, the pommel helped balance out the weight of the blade but it did so without diminishing the advantages of "blade heaviness" and, in fact, added to the blade's striking force. To understand this better, envision the sword as a lever with its pivot point located just above the *crossguard*, that crosspiece above the grip that protects the warrior's hand. It's a very poorly balanced lever because on one side it has a long, relatively heavy blade some 28 to 32 inches longs and on the other side of the pivot it has the grip, just 6 to 8 inches long and much lighter than the blade. However, by adding a steel, iron or brass pommel,

weighing several ounces, to the end of the grip the balance is greatly improved. And, when the sword is swung, the pommel actually helps drive the top of the blade down into the target with greater force. This additional force occurs because, as the blade is being swung down and forward, the pommel on the opposite side of the pivot is being thrown back and upwards, adding its force to the blade's swing.

As plate armor developed through the 14th century, the swords evolved from being primarily cutting and shearing weapons to cut and thrust weapons. One sign of this change was in the outline of the blade. Rather than having nearly parallel edges, swords now tapered markedly

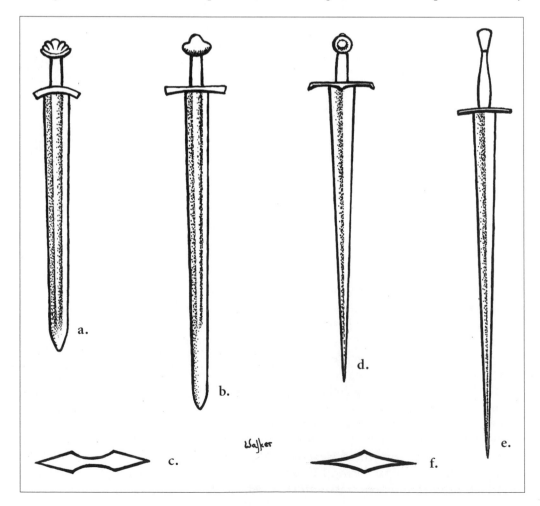

from a width of two to two-and-a-half inches at the hilt down to a very sharp point, but the edges were still sharpened for cutting (fig. 32d). Another part of the blade that was changed to improve its thrusting use was the cross section of the sword. Where cutting swords had a wide, flat section with an indentation for the fuller, blades in the 14th century gradually changed to a flattened diamond-shaped cross section (fig. 32f). Thus, the fuller was eliminated and replaced with a thicker center with a medial rib that made the sword less flexible and more rigid. The combination of tapering of the blade and thickening its center-line produced a sword that concentrated all the force of the knight's thrust in a fine, hard point driven by a tough metal wedge that wouldn't bend under the force of impact. The result was a weapon designed to puncture layers of plate, mail, and padding.

Through the end of the 14th century and through the 15th century, swords continued to be improved for thrusting. Tapered blades with sharp points and ribbed or ridged centers became the norm. Additionally, the swordsmiths made the blades longer, up to 37 inches in length, to improve the weapon's reach (fig. 32e). Swords for use from horseback were made especially long, up to 42 inches in length, allowing the mounted knight considerable reach for striking down at targets from the

Opposite: Figure 32. The evolution of the sword.

a. 10th to early 12th century. This sword was designed primarily for cutting. On both sides of the blade, a groove or *fuller* runs nearly the full length of the blade. The fuller makes the blade lighter and easier to wield while also making it more flexible so that it would bend rather than break under the force of impact. Surviving blades of swords like these still display amazing resilience, capable of bending and then whipping back to their original shape.

b. 13th century. Swords of this type were primarily cutting weapons. The increased length of these swords extended the warrior's reach and made them well suited for use by mounted knights.

c. Cross-section of a sword blade with a fuller.

d. 14th century. During the 14th century, swords were made for both cutting and thrusting. In place of the almost rounded tips found on most earlier swords, swords now had very acute points in addition to sharpened edges. Another change was the gradual elimination of the fuller. When thrusting, a warrior wanted his blade to stay rigid and not bend at the moment of impact. Thus, the fuller was replaced with raised ribs that ran all or most of the length of both sides of the blade. As shown, the ribs give the blade a diamond-shaped cross-section.

e. 15th century. The increased use of plate armor encouraged the development of swords designed for thrusting since plate was largely impervious to sword cuts but could be pierced by a stiff, steel point if that point was driven by enough force. Generating this force required gripping the sword with both hands, another factor that contributed to the increased length of the sword's grip. These swords were also increasingly made with the first several inches of the blade left unsharpened so that the warrior could grasp the blade as well as the grip. The need to use both hands was complemented by the fact that plate armor eliminated the need for shields in combat, freeing the warrior who was fortunate enough to afford such good quality armor to use both hands to wield his sword.

f. The diamond-shaped cross-section of a 14th or 15th century sword.

"portable high ground" provided by his secure seat atop his warhorse. Since the hand-grips of these swords were also longer than earlier swords, some 8 to 10 inches long, such swords were also well suited for using two-handed when fighting on foot. Besides the lengthened grips, another common feature to facilitate two-handed use of these longer swords was the *ricasso*. Ricasso refers to the part of the sword's blade a little over a hand's width long above the sword's crossguard when it was made with a blunt edge instead of sharpening the full length of the blade's edges. Leaving the edges blunt in this part of the blade allowed a warrior to grip the sword solidly both above and below the crossguard, better balancing the blade and allowing the warrior to put more force into the sword, particularly two-handed thrusting. Lastly, even with the changes in swords' use (from cutting to thrusting and cutting) and design (rigid, longer blades and longer grips), pommels were still needed to help balance the sword and make it easier to handle.

Despite the changes in the shape of blades, swords typically weighed around three pounds throughout the Middle Ages, though some of the largest of the late thrusting swords as well as the late Medieval and early Renaissance two-handed swords weighed in at between five to seven pounds. Many people are surprised that the swords were that light, but — as functional hand weapons — swords had to be relatively light so that knights could easily wield them without undue fatigue.

One last observation about swords that demonstrates the direct connection between their designs and the types of armor being used is the change in swords with the decline of plate armor in the late 16th century through the 17th century. As plate armor gradually disappeared, sword development split into two main lines. Many swords continued to be made as thrusting weapons, but — since they no longer had to penetrate metal — the sword blades were made thinner and lighter, eventually developing into rapiers and épées suited for puncturing soft leather and cloth armors and their wearers. The other line of development, also driven by the decline in use of plate and other metal armor on the battlefield, led to a renaissance of cutting and slashing swords. This development produced cutlasses and sabres which would have had little effect on mail or plate armor but which were ideally suited for hacking down combatants wearing no armor or only lighter armor, such as the padded jackets and leather coats common to the battlefields of the 17th century.

SPEARS

One of the most common weapons of the Middle Ages was the spear. With a sharpened iron or steel head with a socket affixed to a stout wooden shaft up to ten feet in length, it was considered a suitable weapon for all classes of society. Early laws of both the Saxons and the Franks specified the spear as the weapon which all common soldiers were to own and to bring, along with their helmets and shields, when called for military duty. Spears were popular for several reasons: they required far less metal to make than swords and were easier and cheaper to make. Spears were, as in classical times, also well suited to infantry tactics. Lines of men with spears leveled were a formidable obstacle to mounted opponents as well as to other infantry units. Alternatively, the spear could be wielded from horseback, delivering devastating thrusts from above the heads of the men on foot.

While with some slight variations in the length of the shafts and the shapes of the heads, spears saw service throughout the Middle Ages. Specialized forms of spears were also developed: lances for mounted combat and pikes for foot soldiers.

Lances were initially indistinguishable from long spears, ten to twelve feet long. To withstand the strains of impact, lance shafts gradually grew thicker and were tapered from three to four inches in diameter just in front of the grip down to an inch or so at the point where they fit into the socket in the lance head. Since a shaft three to four inches in diameter was too wide to be grasped easily, the lance shaft was made thinner where the knight grasped it but then flared out again, giving an hour-glass shape for part of its length. The reason for flaring the shaft back out, and in some cases, fitting it with a piece of metal on the butt-end, was the same reason for the pommel on the sword: to serve as a counter-balance to make an otherwise unwieldy length of metal-shod wood into a manageable weapon. A final accessory common on lances from the late 14th century to the end of the Middle Ages was the *vamplate*. The vamplate was the flared metal collar fitted just before the grip on the lance (fig. 27). It protected the knight's hand, and together with the lance stop on his breastplate, helped ensure that the lance did not simply fly out back under his arm when he hit his target.

For infantry use, spears were gradually made longer and longer as well, reaching some sixteen to twenty feet in length by the end of the Middle Ages. These longer spears, usually called *pikes*, were part of the changing battlefield tactics and strategies. As mentioned before, bodies of infantry with their spears leveled were a daunting target for an enemy to charge, either on horseback or on foot. Trained and disciplined units could keep their foes at a distance with their "hedge" of spears, slowing down or entirely breaking the force of a charge, and with longer spears this tactic was even more effective. Thus,

pikes emerged as an important weapon on the late medieval battlefield and continued in use well into the 17th century.

AXES

Axes were used both as tools and as weapons during the Middle Ages. For domestic and agricultural chores, small axes that were wielded with one hand were commonly used for carpentry work, clearing brush, and similar tasks while larger, two-handed axes were used for chopping down trees. In war, these axes readily served as weapons, but some specialized forms of axes were developed for military use. One of these specialized axes was the *francisca*, a small throwing axe used primarily by the Franks in the early Middle Ages. Another form of military axe is often referred to as the Danish axe. The Danish axe had a shaft of four to five feet in length and a large crescent edged head. To wield such a large axe, a warrior had to use both hands. The Vikings used such axes and similar ones were employed on many battlefields across Europe through the end of the 13th century. These axes could shear off limbs or cut through a man's torso. Even a heavily armored warrior could be knocked down, injured, or killed by such an axe if it were in the hands of a strong and experienced opponent.

In the 14th and 15th centuries, axes continued to be used, but the large, two-handed axe was increasingly replaced by specialized polearms such as the halberd and bill. As discussed below, these weapons combined the powerful cutting edge of the axe with hooks or sharp spikes which increased the number of ways in which a single weapon could be used for attacking an enemy. The late medieval poleaxe is another example of such multifaceted weapons. Poleaxes were typically around five to six feet in length. The poleaxe head had a blade with a curved edged, like a smaller version of the Danish axe, but it also typically had a short spike on the side opposite the blade and a long spike at its top so that it could be used for thrusting as well as hacking.

One last late form of military axe was a long handled axe designed to be used with one hand by a mounted warrior. The handle was approximately three feet long and the head was crescent edged but was much smaller than the head of a Danish axe. Like the poleaxe, these axes were sometimes made with a small spike on the head opposite the blade.

MACES, WARHAMMERS, AND FLAILS

Maces, club-like weapons with an enlarged head on the end of a short shaft, were used in various forms throughout the Middle Ages. Wooden clubs with heads covered with metal studs are depicted in the Bayeux Tapestry. A mace head of solid metal with six vanes or flanges, recovered from the Thames River in London, has been dated to the 13th century. The head was originally fitted to a wooden shaft, long rotted away. By the 15th century, elegantly shaped maces were made entirely of metal, scepter-like objects of great beauty and destructive power (fig. 33b). Refinement and improvement of the mace appears to track the rise of plate armor. As cutting swords were proving less effective and thrusting swords were still being perfected, warriors may have resorted more frequently to the simple smashing power of a mace.

In varying degrees, maces were effective against all types of armors for their ability to inflict concentrated crushing blows. While padding could absorb and cushion against some of the blow's force, a mace could easily break bones,

even through mail armor. Against plate armor, it was less effective but the mace could break through plates that were either too soft or too brittle from inadequate tempering or could dent and deform even well-tempered plates, potentially immobilizing the wearer by bending articulated joints out of shape. To enhance its effectiveness against plate, maces of the 1400s usually had more pointed vanes or flanges. These points better concentrated the force of the blow into smaller areas, increasing the likelihood of penetrating or, at least, more severely damaging the armor plates. The points on maces were usually short with broad bases, a feature that helped them withstand the pressure of impact without breaking.

The warhammer (fig. 33a), a weapon related to the mace, developed in response to the rising use of plate. The earliest surviving examples and depictions of the warhammer are datable to the last half of the 14th century. The warhammer combined several lethal features into a single weapon effective against plate and more flexible armors. The weapon is shaped something like an enlarged version of the modern carpenter's claw-hammer but with some obvious differences. Overall length was usually just under two feet, making it easy to wield with one hand but allowing a long enough grip for two hands when needed. Like a common hammer, it did have a flared face on one side of the head but, instead of being flat, the face had one or more raised knobs to better concentrate the force of the blow for smashing and bending armor plates (possibly breaking through plates that were brittle from poor forging) or shattering bones beneath mail or padded armor. Opposite the face, in place of the "claw" of the normal hammer, the warhammer had a single, short, thick-based spike, again to concentrate the force of the blow to better pierce armor plates, especially those that had any soft spots from poor tempering during forging. Crowning the head was a top spike, again short, and broad based to withstand great pressure. The top spike appears designed for administering the *coup de grace* to a fallen opponent: gripping the warhammer with both hands and reversing it so the top spike pointed down, the knight could plunge the spike through the opponent's armor. This is the reality of medieval combat. While we can admire these objects for their elegance and craftsmanship, we shouldn't lose sight of why they were made and how they were used.

Flails were any weapon composed of a handle linked by a chain to a short piece of wood or ball of metal studded with spikes. The image this usually calls to mind is the *morningstar* common to most Hollywood medieval epics: a wooden shaft about two feet long with a foot of chain on the end connected to a very wicked looking spike covered metal ball. But there are a few inaccuracies in these modern depictions. First, the term *morningstar* (or, *Morgenstern* as it was called in the Germanic countries where it was most common) referred not to a flail but to two other weapons. The term morningstar denoted both a form of mace that was a short club with a spherical spiked head rather than a flanged head and a polearm about six feet long that had a large spike at the top and many more spikes studding the top foot or so of its shaft (fig. 34a). Second, ball-and-chain flails were very rare weapons. Apart from some that date back to the Bronze Age, the few surviving European examples are datable only to the very late 15th or early 16th century at the earliest. Further, unlike all the other weapons discussed here, ball-and-chain flails were not mentioned in literature of the period nor were they frequently depicted in contemporary art. In fact, the only depiction I have been able to find is in one 15th century tapestry in the Victoria and Albert Museum in

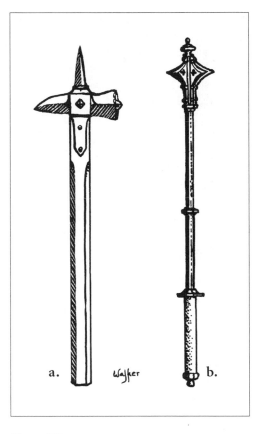

Figure 33.

　a. Warhammer, 15th century.

　b. Mace, 15th century (J. Walker).

London. This dearth of evidence supports the conclusion that, despite the fact that they look cool, ball-and-chain flails were seldom used in medieval combat. Another supporting fact is that such a weapon is not very practical. Attaching a spiked ball to a chain on a short handle extends the reach of the weapon, but no better than simply making the handle itself longer, like a mace with a long handle. Moreover, while a mace handle was rigid and ensured maximum leverage, the chain was flexible and sagged upon impact, lessening the force of the blow. Finally, because of the flexibility of the chain, flails were more difficult to control and aim than maces and other hand weapons. Now this isn't to

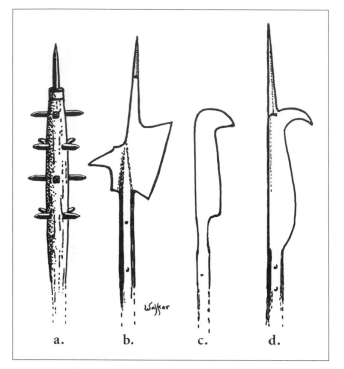

Figure 34. Polearms

    a. Morgenstern

    b. Halberd

    c. Billhook mounted on a pole

    d. Bill developed from the simple billhook (J. Walker).

say that ball-and-chain flails were use-less or harmless. They just weren't very practical or effective compared to other weapons readily available to the medieval warrior.

But ball-and-chain flails were not the only type of flail. A second form used at least as early as the beginning of the 15th century was derived from an agricultural implement, the threshing flail (fig. 18). The threshing flail was made of a stout wooden shaft about five to six feet long with a metal ring at one end. This ring connected to another ring fitted to one end of a thick cylinder of wood about two to two and a half feet long. Swung with both hands, these flails were used in peacetime to beat wheat and other grains out of their husks

as part of processing the grain into flour. During rebellions and wars of religion in the 15th century, common farm labor-ers and other peasants took these same flails into battle to beat the brains out of their foes' skulls, the only modifica-tion was the occasional fitting of metal spikes to the flail's wooden head. These flails were effective weapons for several reasons. First, because of their length, they provided their users with extended reach, allowing them to strike the heads and shoulders of oppo-nents on foot and the torsos of those on horseback. Second, threshing flails were used only by those men who had worked long hours with them and had thus developed the con-siderable strength and control needed to wield them effec-tively. Third, the head was con-nected by just two rings that formed a hinge rather than by a flexible length of chain. This feature made it easier to control than a ball-and-chain flail and, because the hinge allowed the head to flip forward with little loss of force, the head could deliver hard blows as it snapped sharply down as the warrior-peasant swung the flail.

POLEARMS

Several other forms of polearms besides the flail developed from agricul-tural implements. These include the hal-berd, the bill, and their myriad variations. The common feature of most polearms is that they were multipurpose weapons typically incorporating a blade, a point or top spike, and a back spike or hook.

In use by at least the early 14th century, the bill (fig. 34d) had a large iron or steel head around twenty inches long fitted to a sturdy wooden shaft six to eight feet in length. The head was several inches wide and had a sharpened cutting edge and a thrusting point four to eight inches long. On the side of the head opposite the cutting edge, the bill commonly had a short spike or a hook. The hook, useful for pulling down mounted opponents, was a feature of the billhook (fig. 34c) from which the bill evolved. The billhook was an agricultural tool used to cut vines and brush and to lop limbs off trees. This tool, with little or no modification, was found to be equally suited to lopping limbs off men.

The halberd (fig. 34b), also developed during the 14th century, was similar in shape and dimension to the bill except the head was much wider and axe-like and a spike three to six inches long replaced the hook on the back side of the head, opposite the cutting blade. Some historians track the origins of the halberd to Swiss farmers who mounted small plowblades on wooden shafts to create makeshift weapons.

Regardless of their exact form and origin, polearms like the bill and halberd were valuable weapons for warriors on foot. When fighting against mounted opponents, they acted as "equalizers," giving foot soldiers the reach needed to strike at knights atop their warhorses, even enabling foot soldiers to pull knights down out of their saddles with the hooks and back-spikes. Polearms could also be used in massed formations to dissipate and break the force of cavalry charges since even the most reckless of knights could not effectively charge through a tight hedge of blades at the end of long shafts. When fighting against other warriors on foot, bills and halberds could be swung or thrust to inflict horrific wounds. Skulls recovered from one 15th century battlefield in Switzerland provide graphic evidence of the effects of halberds: some skulls have large sections sliced off by halberd blades; others have large, tapered holes punched in them from either thrusting points or back-spikes of these weapons or from the spikes on the polearm version of the morningstar.

Polearms and their use in massed formations by disciplined troops helped change the nature of warfare in the late Middle Ages, paving the way for the ascendancy of infantry over heavily armored mounted warriors. The other form of weapon that was combined with polearms to secure the supremacy of infantry over mounted knights was projectile weaponry.

PROJECTILE WEAPONS

Striking an enemy first from a distance, before he can close in and strike a blow, has always been a preferred form of combat. After all, few people would voluntarily opt for the horror and dangers of hand-to-hand fighting if they had a less unpleasant and slightly less risky alternative. Thus, though knights occasionally denounced such weapons and the people who used them as cowardly and unchivalric, projectile weapons were common on medieval battlefields.

Slings

Slings are an ancient weapon. Mankind discovered long ago that rocks could be thrown with great force by taking a long strip of leather or cloth, placing a small stone in the midpoint of the strip, folding the strip over lengthwise, and then holding both ends of the strip in one hand and swinging it with either an overhand or sidearm motion. With practice, the slinger learned exactly when to release one end of the strip to release the stone to achieve optimal force. With additional practice, the slinger learned to coordinate his swing and release to place his shot with deadly accuracy. The need for all this practice meant that slingers were usually recruited only from among shepherds and other men who herded animals and used slings to kill or drive away predators from their flocks. Most of these men had used slings since childhood and were quite skilled.

Slings had been a relatively common military weapon in the Classical Age. Instead of using stones, Greek and Roman military slingers often used small lead balls that were cast and mass-produced. While slings continued to be used by rural people to protect their animals, slings generally fell out of military use in the early part of the Middle Ages. There were isolated instances in which slingers fought, but these were rare, especially when compared to their use under the Greeks and Romans. Along with the difficulty of recruiting experienced slingers, the increasing availability of other more powerful projectile weapons such as the longbow and crossbow discussed below and the increasing use of tougher armor likely contributed to the decline of the sling. However, one specialized form of the sling was used in military applications up through the 14th century. This weapon was the staff-sling. A staff-sling was composed of a stout pole about five feet long fitted with a sling at one end. The sling had a very wide section at its middle which accommodated larger projectiles than an ordinary sling. Staff-slings were used to throw small clay pots of Greek fire (an incendiary compound) and powdered quicklime (a caustic material). The pots shattered on contact to spread fire or to blind opponents. Staff-slings were usually shown in use in ship-to-ship combat.

Bows and Arrows

One of man's oldest weapons, wooden bows made from a single, shaped wooden stave were used throughout Europe in the Middle Ages for hunting as well as in warfare but their effectiveness varied greatly from one region to another and from one era to the next. They were a very common weapon. Under Frankish and Saxon laws, bows were usually mentioned right along with spears as weapons which every warrior was expected to bring when called to active duty. The raw materials for bows and arrows were all relatively common and plentiful and were easily and quickly turned into finished products by artisans even of modest skill. Bows were made of hazel, ash, elm, or, best of all, yew. The tips of the bows, the *nocks*, were usually fitted with small caps made out of horn to reinforce the bow and firmly hold the bowstring in position. The bowstring itself was braided from the strongest fibers available: linen, hemp, and silk among others. Arrows, with shafts 28 to 36 inches long and about ⅜ inch in diameter, were made of birch, ash, oak and other woods, fletched with trimmed feathers from large birds such as geese, and tipped with hardened iron or steel heads. An interesting fact about the feathers: the feathers on each wing curve in the same the direction, but the ones on the left wing curve in the opposite direction from those on the right. So when fletching arrows, each of the three feathers used to make the vanes on a single arrow were taken from the same wing of the bird and placed so that the curvature of the arrows all pointed the same direction and thus smoothly spun the arrow as it flew, ensuring greater accuracy just as guns are rifled to spin bullets to make them spiral in flight for a longer, truer flight.

As with swords and other weapons, the shapes of arrowheads reflect the arms race of the Middle Ages. Early war arrows were indistinguishable from ordinary hunting arrows: all were fitted with broad, flat metal heads two to three inches long and two inches wide, with barbs on either side. These arrows were designed to cut through hide or clothing and the barbs ensured that the arrow would catch in the flesh and be difficult to remove. This ensured that, even if the arrow failed to kill instantly, the target, human or animal, would be disabled and suffer further injury trying to draw the arrow out. These broad arrows were used throughout the Middle Ages although mail and plate armors usually prevented them from penetrating. They continued to be used because they were still effective against more lightly armored opponents and were useful for opening volleys against mounted warriors since their horses were seldom adequately armored to avoid injury.

While the broad arrow was still used, other specialized arrowheads were developed to counter improved armors. By the early 13th century, arrows were made with the barbs swept back. Narrowing the arrowhead increased the chances of the arrow penetrating the spaces in the rings of mail armor. By the mid– to late 13th century, narrowing increased to produce barb-less arrows. They were also now made with diamond shaped cross section, just like later swords, to further increase their penetrating power by ensuring the point stayed rigid upon impact. Some were made with long points three or more inches long. Often called *bodkin* points after the small daggers of the same name, these were designed to pass right through rings of mail and puncture the warrior beneath.

As plate armor became more common through the 14th century, arrowheads further evolved, shrinking back to two to two-and-a-half inches long but becoming much broader. Some were shaped like three- or four-sided pyramids, with sides about three-quarters or half an inch at the base and tapering to a very sharp point. Others were made with an elongated oval outline, pointed at one end. This type was made with a diamond shaped cross section and was also made thicker in the middle and narrowed at each end. Both these types of arrowheads were made to penetrate plate armor and were used by English longbowmen of the late 14th and early 15th centuries to great effect against the French in the Hundred Years' War. While penetrating hardened steel with a simple wooden bow may seem impossible, it must be remembered that the English bowmen had trained since youth and developed the enormous upper body strength and skill required to use bows with draw-weights of 120 to 180 pounds. Draw-weight refers to the amount of force required to pull the bowstring back to the firing position. For example, a 120-pound draw-weight bow requires an archer who can simultaneously push the bow away from him with one arm while drawing the bowstring back with the other with a force equivalent to 120 pounds of pressure. Even if these arrows did not penetrate, their force on impact was sufficient to break bones through layers of padding and mail as well as cause concussive injuries even through plate armor.

Another form of bow used in the Middle Ages was the crossbow. This weapon was composed of a bow fixed horizontally to one end of a wooden stock called a *tiller* which contained the trigger that held the bowstring in place until it was ready to be fired. The trigger mechanism was composed of a *nut* and trigger lever. The nut was a small wheel mounted on an axle in the center of the tiller. It had a grooved rim, like a pulley, with a notch across the width of the rim to hold the bowstring. The tiller also had a groove running from the bow back to the nut. This groove and the groove in the nut allowed the end of the crossbow's projectile, called a *quarrel* or a *bolt*, to rest firmly and directly against the string. A second notch in the nut fitted the end of the trigger lever and ensured that the nut did not revolve once the bowstring was drawn back. To fire the crossbow, the archer aimed and then squeezed the trigger lever to release the nut, allowing it to spin forward and release the bowstring.

Bolts or quarrels looked much like arrows but with a few differences. Their heads were usually of the last two types described above: pyramidal points and flat ovals with diamond shaped cross sections. Their shafts were much shorter, around 14 to 18 inches, and broader, around ½ to ¾ of an inch. Additionally, they were usually fletched with only two vanes instead of three like arrows since three vanes would have prevented the bolts from resting flat in the crossbow's groove. Bolts also differed from arrows in that they were fletched with leather or, in rare cases, thin copper strips instead of feathers. Since these materials lacked the natural curving of feathers, they were usually attached in a slight spiral around the bolt shaft to provide the spin necessary for accuracy and improved flight. All these features (shorter, more rigid heads; thicker, shorter shafts; and highly durable fletching) reflect the fact that most crossbows were powerful weapons and their projectiles had to be made to withstand tremendous force upon launch and impact.

One of the advantages of the crossbow was that it could be cocked, loaded, and then held ready to fire without further exertion by the archer, unlike the ordinary bow which had to be fired nearly immediately upon drawing. The process of cocking crossbows changed over the years as their bows grew in strength. Early crossbows were fitted with a stirrup, a loop of metal or tough rope attached to the front of the tiller. The archer would place one or both feet in the stirrup and then pull the bowstring up with both hands until the string caught in the groove of the nut. This points out another advantage of the cross-

bow: since an archer could use the strength of his entire body to draw it, he did not need to have the upper body strength of a longbowman. By the mid–12th century, if not earlier, drawing crossbows was made easier by mounting metal hooks on the archers' belt. While he still used the stirrups and his hands, the archer would attach the belt hook to the bowstring when he bent down to draw the string then, as he pulled the bowstring up with his hands, his entire body straightened up, pulling the belt hook up as well, thus allowing him to exert even greater force in drawing the bow. The combination of hands and belt hook remained the most common means of drawing the crossbow until the mid–14th century. By this time, some crossbows were drawn with levers that attached to pins on the sides of the crossbow but this method was quickly superseded by use of mechanisms called racks or windlasses that used gears and cranks to draw back the bowstring. These cranked crossbows were the first form of crossbow that was practical for use while on horseback. Another method of drawing crossbows in use by the mid–15th century was an improved version of the belt hook that incorporated pulleys, enabling archers to further magnify their bodies' strength through mechanical means.

The necessity of mechanical devices to draw the crossbows reflected its greatest flaw: crossbows were much slower to load and fire than a longbow. Modern recreations have shown that a longbowman can draw and fire six to twelve arrows in about a minute, the same time it takes to load and discharge a single crossbow bolt. However, supply records indicate that longbowmen usually carried at most sixty arrows at a time, meaning that at the top rate of fire they would have exhausted their ammunition in just five minutes. Though more arrows were kept in the supply wagons, most medieval armies do not appear to have been organized for efficient resupply in the midst of a battle. Yet it does appear that longbows were used in just such fashion to deliver short but devastating barrages against opponents, particularly opponents formed in tight ranks, preparing to charge. After their arrows were exhausted, the longbowmen resorted to secondary weapons (daggers and polearms) for the rest of the battle. These tactics were used by the English throughout the Hundred Years' War against the French, often to tremendous effect, as at Agincourt. Crossbows were also used in the opening stage of battles but their slower rate of fire meant they delivered fewer missiles before the armies closed to hand to hand combat, at which point projectile weapons could not be used without significant risk of causing "friendly fire" casualties. However, for sieges, crossbows were ideal weapons for both the attackers and the besieged since the style of combat was different from open field combat and they could be deployed from protected positions that allowed reloading in relative safety. There were many examples of their effectiveness in this role, such as the death of Richard the Lionhearted who died after being struck in the neck by a crossbow bolt while he was besieging a castle in France.

Changes in drawing crossbows were driven by improvements in the construction of the bows. Early bows were made of single, shaped staves of wood, like ordinary bows, but by the end of the 12th century, bows for crossbows were being made of composite materials: layers of wood laminated to layers of horn, leather, and sinew. These bows were much stronger than bows made from a single piece of wood. Lamination was continually refined and improved to produce stronger and stronger bows over the next two centuries until, in the 15th century, steel bows were created. Matching the improvements in bow strength, draw weights increased from around a hundred pounds for the simple wooden bow to several hundred or even a thousand pounds for a late medieval steel bow.

The power of the crossbow, its less demanding requirements on the physique of its user, and its ability to store the energy of its drawn bow until needed made it an excellent and devastating weapon, which may explain why its use was formally banned by the Pope in 1139 at the Second Lateran Council. However, it should be noted that the Papal anathema was against the use of both crossbows *and* ordinary bows against fellow Christians, indicating that all forms of bow weapons were viewed as unfairly efficient means of killing people. It seems that most English historians usually ignore the fact ordinary bows were also banned, possibly because of their country's proud heritage of the long bow and the view that the crossbow was a gadget from the Continent designed to compensate for the lack of skill and strength needed for the use of the long bow. In any event, the long bow in England and the crossbow on the Continent proved highly effective in combat when coupled with infantry wielding polearms that could protect them while they drew their bows. The other type of projectile weapon that complimented and furthered the effectiveness of this style of fighting was the handgun.

Handguns

In the Middle Ages, the term "handgun" did not have its current meaning of a pistol or other small firearm capable of being held and fired with a single hand. Rather it was used to distinguish between those firearms that were held in the hands of the gunner and those mounted on carriages or frames. The earliest of Medieval handguns, those from the beginning of the 15th century, were actually small muzzle-loading iron, brass, or bronze cannons up to four or five inches in diameter and about a foot and a half to two feet long. Each gun was strapped down with metal bands onto a stout wooden pole four to six feet long. Powder, wadding, and shot were rammed down the muzzle and the device was fired by lighting the powder through the touchhole at the base of the gun's barrel. Sometimes, firing the handgun was a two-man operation: one held the pole and aimed while the other lit the powder.

By the mid–15th century, handguns were beginning to look more like modern rifles. Their barrels had changed to longer, narrower tubes, about an inch and a half in diameter and three feet long, attached to wooden stocks designed to be fired from the shoulder. Aiming and firing could now be easily performed by a single man.

Despite their primitive construction, handguns were surprisingly effective, though mostly at short range. Besides their value in simply scaring the enemy, their bullets could kill heavily armored knights as easily as unarmored foot soldiers. One reason for their effectiveness against even plate armor was that many of these early ball-shaped bullets were iron rather than lead. Lead balls are relatively soft and tended to flatten out on impact but iron bullets are hard and retain their shape. So, while plate armor could potentially stop or at least significantly dissipate the energy of a primitive soft lead bullet, hard iron balls were able to punch through the plate.

Warhorses, Their Armor and Equipment

While we've discussed other elements of the knight's equipment, we've yet to address one the most important pieces of his equipment: his warhorse. With the notable exception of English which is stuck with an Anglo-Saxon word that originally meant "servant" or "retainer," most European terms for "knight" are derived from either the words for "horse," as in the French *chevalier*, or for "rider," as in the German *ritter*. One of a knight's most important attributes was that he fought from horseback. Thus, without his horse, a knight is not truly a knight. So, what was a "warhorse"?

It is difficult to point to any one breed of modern horse and say, "There, that's what a medieval warhorse was like." Like many other specially bred, domesticated animals of the past, true warhorses are now extinct because they are no longer needed and so are no longer bred. They were working animals and when their work disappeared with the end of heavily armored mounted combat, they gradually disappeared as well. They weren't simply kept around as pets after the real need for them was gone. However, their genetic stock may live on, scattered in succeeding generations of other breeds.

So what was the medieval warhorse really like? Again, thanks to the movies, the popular image of the medieval warhorse is of a great, lumbering plow or draught horse, like Scottish Clydesdales, English Shire horses, or French Percherons. Certainly, late medieval warhorses that were expected to carry a fully armored knight (160 pound man plus 65 pounds of armor and other gear) as well as a war saddle (a leather covered, wooden saddle reinforced to help hold the knight firmly in place, 20 pounds) and horse armor (often referred to as *barding*, another 40 to 50 pounds) were not small. They were referred to as "great" horses and, as a result of careful breeding and care, were larger than the common riding and packhorses of their day. However, while the warhorses were not slight-framed racehorses, they did not need to be ponderous giants to carry their 300-pound loads. To get a better answer, we need to go back to the beginning of the period because warhorses, just like the rest of the knight's arsenal, evolved and changed over the centuries.

In the early Middle Ages up through the 12th century, horse armor was rarely used. Mounted combat included using the lance, but it was more often used as a javelin or spear (thrown or thrust by the rider using only his power) rather than couching it firmly and driving it home with the combined mass of horse and rider. This combat did not require an especially large horse, but it did demand tough, fast horses with stamina. Modern studies as well as contemporary illustrations and accounts praising Arabian horses from Spain indicate that the Arabian horses, originally brought from North Africa by Muslim invaders, were the ideal warhorses of this era.

As the weight of armor and the use of horse armor both increased, larger horses were needed. Incidentally, horse armor went through a similar evolution to that of armor for the knight. Padding and mail were in use by the beginning of the 13th century to make skirts or *trappers* to protect the sides and rump of the horse. During the 14th century, pieces of plate were gradually added. These included:

- the *chanfron*, which, as shown in fig. 27, protected the top and sides of the horse's head,
- the *crinet*, which covered the top and sides of its neck,
- the *peytral*, which shielded its chest and the tops of its front legs (fig. 27),
- the *flanchards*, large plates which covered the horse's flanks, and
- the *crupper*, which covered its rump.

Thus, by the middle of the 15th century, plate armor was available to cover most of a warhorse. However, even more than armor for men, armor for horses was limited to only the most wealthy warriors and so was comparatively rare.

Returning to the horses, from the 13th through the 15th centuries, they were bred for increased size and strength but not to the point of becoming the size of draught horses. Surviving armor, saddles, and other fittings for these horses indicate that their size was comparable to a modern riding horse, though obviously stronger to bear the weight. A number of illustrations, carvings, and other art items from the late Middle Ages also provide evidence of the appearance of the warhorse and clearly show it to be a tall, powerful horse but certainly not as broad or massive as Clydesdales or Shire horses. From appearances (height, powerful build) and significant attributes and traits (strong legs and back, stamina, capable of good rates of speed, intelligent and trainable), some breeds of horses used for cavalry up through the 19th century, such as the Holstein in Germany and the Norman in France, retain significant degrees of the bloodline of the late medieval warhorse but a sub-breed of the Norman called the Norman Cob is probably the closest descendant. These are stout, thick-legged, strong-backed horses but more gracefully proportioned than draft horses and with girths far more suited to riding. A draft horse such as a Clydesdale can have a girth up to eight feet around, something even the most bow-legged of cowboys would have difficulty spanning!

One last word about the Percheron, Clydesdale, and Shire horses — the earliest generations of these ultra-heavy draft horses were starting to appear on the battlefield in the 15th century, the same time as complete plate armor, but they weren't used directly for combat. Rather, they were needed to haul the heavy artillery pieces that were now a regular fixture of every major battle. And for the next five hundred years, these heavy horse breeds would serve as the prime movers of cannons, ammunition, and baggage for European armies.

The Care and Use
of the Warhorse

A knight would own many horses, including ordinary riding and packhorses as well as warhorses. He would use the riding horses for traveling, even for traveling to battles or tournaments. His warhorse would be led or ridden by one of his pages, the lightest and smallest members of his entourage. Though these were horses bred for their strength and stamina, their owners did not want to tire them out unnecessarily or to risk their being injured by hard riding. This may seem like mollycoddling of the warhorse. After all, weren't these horses bred for their toughness and didn't the knight subject it to far greater risks every time he rode it in a battle or tournament? These points are true but it is precisely because the knight relied so much on his warhorse that he had it so carefully tended. The point of the "coddling" was to ensure that, while he received some exercise, the warhorse was kept as fresh and healthy as possible for combat or sport. It's sort of analogous to sports car racing: these cars are given great care and are subjected to punishing treatment in races but, even if they were "street legal," their owners and drivers certainly would not subject them to the routine wear and tear and risk of accidents in everyday driving.

Carrying the auto racing analogy a little further, another reason racing cars aren't used for everyday driving is that they are far too expensive to unnecessarily risk such a mundane activity, particularly given the devastating consequences to the racing team if its prize vehicle is destroyed or seriously damaged. So too, the knight's warhorse was one of his most costly possessions and without it his effectiveness was greatly diminished. Horses were expensive to raise and maintain. For example, while they eat some grass, horses require oats and other grains for a healthy diet. These oats and grains had to be cultivated and prepared, incurring additional expenses not required for oxen, the main draft animal of the time, that could subsist on grass.

As reflected in many contemporary documents, the value of horses, particularly warhorses, was quite obvious to medieval people. For example, the Rule of the Templars, the regulations for the noted warrior–holy order of the Crusades, contains several restrictions against horse racing and against running horses at a gallop without permission from high officials in the order. While this curbed frivolous activities unbecoming warrior-monks, it also limited unnecessary risking of injury to horses. This second goal of the regulations is further born out by separate restrictions that imposed severe punishments, including possible expulsion from the Order, on those Templars who killed, injured, or lost horses or abused them by riding two warriors on a single horse (despite the fact that an early seal of the Templars depicted just such conduct to illustrate their combined ideals of poverty and holy warfare). Such harsh punishment was seen as reasonable in the embattled Crusader states where horses were in chronic short supply.

The scarcity and value of warhorses is also reflected in various official government documents throughout the period and throughout Europe that recorded export controls. Time and again, in the interest of national security, warhorses were listed along with swords and armor as items which could not be exported.

In addition to their breeding, training was critical to produce a useful warhorse. They were trained not to balk at the noise, smoke, and other distractions of battle. Most were also trained to be guided by pressure from the rider's knees rather than just by the reins. Perhaps most difficult of all, they were trained to charge headlong at dangerous targets like lines of infantrymen or just to the side of an oncoming knight. The value and difficulty of this training cannot be overestimated. For example, in modern re-enactments of jousts in Germany, riding horses pressed into service as "warhorses" have often displayed more common sense than their riders and balked at galloping towards another horse and rider separated by only a narrow wooden fence. In many ways, their training was comparable to that of the knights: getting them in condition and accustoming them to functioning on the battlefield.

Surcoats and Heraldry

Metal isn't a material that breathes well like the more common natural fibers of cotton and wool. In the summer, it traps all the heat and sweat of the wearer. This discomfort is worsened by the layers of quilted clothing worn under the armor. Additionally, as with any other metal surface (think of the last time you touched the exterior of a car in August), it readily absorbs the heat from the sun's rays so that a person wearing armor is heated from both the inside and out, an experience best described as being simultaneously poached and grilled. This unpleasant phenomenon explains in part why, even in the mild climates of northern Europe, spring and early fall were the preferred seasons for military campaigns. After all, even today, football, the only outdoor sport which combines intensive physical activity with the wearing of layers of protective armor, is usually limited to the cooler months. But even in winter, metal armor can be quite uncomfortable. In the winter, metal armor has the same insulating value as an overcoat made of aluminum foil or that heatsink material used in computers to conduct heat away from the chips. (Remember the last time you were outdoors when the temperature was near or below freezing and touched any metal object that had been left out in the cold?) While the quilted clothing under the armor does help some, the heat-conducting property of the metal armor continually transfers all the wearer's vital warmth out of him and into the air as rapidly as possible. This chilling outer surface combined with the moisture trapped in the layers of padded clothing seems to be guaranteed to cause exposure. Though there are no records of this happening, it's also easy to imagine knights getting their lips or other parts frozen to the armor in the same way as that legendary gullible child fooled into sticking his tongue to a flagpole or pump-handle in January.

By the early 12th century, fabric coverings for armor, in the form of surcoats, appeared in Europe. The surcoat — a long, flowing, sleeveless gown worn over the mail shirt — certainly possessed some ability to mitigate the impact of extreme temperatures. This does not preclude the possibility that cloaks or robes might have been worn over armor when traveling or at rest but surcoats are the first garment shown over the top of armor on knights while fighting. As with most clothing styles of the Middle Ages, contemporary depictions in art provide most if not all the evidence since the clothing itself has long ago rotted away and vanished. Thus, from the timing of the appearance of illustrations of knights wearing surcoats, it appears that the Europeans began wearing surcoats in the early 12th century after adopting the idea from the Saracens of the Middle East after the First Crusade (A.D. 1095–1099).

Besides the fact that surcoats appear only in illustrations datable to after the First Crusade, this theory is also supported by the concepts that necessity is the mother of invention and the greater the necessity, the more inventive one is likely to be. As discussed above, the Europeans did have a need for some means of compensating for the intensely uncomfortable and potentially disabling effects of wearing metal armor in extreme weather. However, for Saracens, as residents of a notably hot and arid region, the need was far more pressing. Without some means of lessening the heat, armor would be highly impractical if not impossible to wear for much of the year. Covering the armor with light-colored, lightweight fabric reflected away some of the sun's heat before it reached and was absorbed by the armor. Additionally, by making the garment loose, but not so loose as to entangle the wearer, the covering could provide the same cooling air flow that other seemingly bulky but loose fitting clothing of the Middle East and North Africa (like the aba, burnoose, or kaftan) provide. Thus, the surcoat appears to have originated in the Middle East and was quickly embraced by the Europeans soon after their arrival.

Through returning crusaders and others traveling to and from the Holy Lands, the fashion quickly spread and was further adapted to fit local needs and tastes. Since heat was less of a problem in Europe than in the Middle East, surcoats were soon made out of other materials than just light-weight, light-colored fabrics. Colorful designs appeared on surcoats by the mid–12th century, presumably to show off the style and taste of the wearer, but at some point the designs evolved into formal symbols that signified who the wearer of the surcoat was. This was a major step forward for heraldry, the art of representing and identifying persons and families through a system of symbols

whose meaning are widely recognized. It's easy to undervalue heraldry and think of it as just an elaborate, stylized decorative scheme but it served an important role in helping to identify combatants on the field. There were no uniforms at this time and writing names on the surcoat would have been pointless since few if any of the persons fighting would have been literate. Further, helmets which covered all or part of the face also hindered identification. For example, as depicted in the Bayeux Tapestry, William the Conqueror had to raise his conical helmet with nasal guard up so that his troops could clearly see him and see that he was still alive. So some means was needed to mark the identity of the primary combatants and it had to be a means that most people would quickly recognize and understand. Thus, large colorful emblems with symbols associated with particular families came to be embroidered or appliquéd onto surcoats, horse trappers, and banners or painted on shields to identify who was on the field so that their own men, as well as the enemy, would be able to tell who was there and identify ally from foe. Obviously, this worked well since even today team uniforms bear distinctive colors and designs so that in the heat of action the players can quickly tell who is or isn't on their side.

Tournament Armor and Weapons

In the early tournaments held in the 12th century, there were few if any differences between "real" armor and weapons and tournament armor and weapons. Swords might be blunted but that was about it. As the sport developed, specialized armor and weapons were developed to better protect the participants from injury. For example, for a tournament in the 14th century, the list of expenses include payments for swords made of whalebone. ("Whalebone" isn't bone. It is baleen, a flexible, plastic-like material from the mouths of certain species of whale. These whales have baleen instead of teeth and feed by using it to filter plankton out of the seawater. This is the same material later used to make "whalebone" corsets in the 18th and 19th centuries.) Other items from this tournament include cuir boulli armor in place of metal armor and wooden clubs to substitute for metal-shod maces. Another specialized tournament weapon that appeared in the 14th century and was used through the end of the Middle Ages was the coronel tipped lance (fig. 27). It was called "coronel" because the tip had three or four small blunt points forming a ring that looked like a small crown or "coronel." This ring of blunt points spread out the force of the lance thrust rather than concentrating the lance's force like the usual single sharp point of the iron or steel shod combat lance did. Though the coronel tipped lance still packed quite a wallop and could knock a knight out of his saddle, it was less likely to skewer his shield (and him) than the single pointed lance.

From the mid–14th century through the 15th century, armor and weapons for mounted combat in the tournaments became particularly specialized and it is some of these items which have given rise to many of the misperceptions about all medieval armor and fighting. As jousting with lances came to be the centerpiece of tournaments, armorers developed highly specialized pieces of armor solely for use in these contests. Armorers applied the same practical approach to designing tournament armors that they applied to creating combat armors. For example, the objective of jousting in the 15th century was to strike and break a lance against an opponent's shield. The shield was the only permissible target. There was no aiming at the head or below the belt nor was there striking at the opponent's back after the knight had passed by. Additionally, armorers factored in the limited range of movement required in jousting. Unlike actual combat which required being able to use a lance, swing a sword, and a host of other activities, jousting required only that the knight be able to control his horse on a short, straight course while couching his lance and aiming it at his opponent. Further, the knight did not need a complete range of movement. Unlike real combat, he could use mounting steps to get up on his horse and, if he was knocked out of the saddle, his attendants were on hand and would rush to help him get up and out of harm's way. Thus, with little regard for the weight of the armor, armorers designed suits that provided maximum protection to the arms, the chest, and the front of the head since these were the areas most at risk. Pieces could be made much larger and thicker than on suits of combat armor, even to the point that suits covering only from the waist up could weigh 95 pounds or more while severely restricting movement. For example, by the 15th century, the armor for the left arm usually rendered the arm immobile except for just enough articulation in the gauntlet for gripping the reins. Helmets and breast plates were made of great thickness in the front, sometimes with thicknesses of a half inch or more, while being left very thin in the back. Helmets were also made with very limited sight and ventilation holes to leave the front of the helmet as smooth and strong as possible to prevent a lance from penetrating. An extreme example is a type of helmet sometimes called a "frog-mouthed jousting helmet." This helmet was used in jousting throughout the 15th century and was bolted and strapped directly to the breastplate. Like the 14th century jousting helms from which it evolved (fig. 27), it had a vision slot and the top, front edge of the helmet that the knight could look through only if he leaned his entire upper body forward about 15 degrees. It did have small hatches that could be opened to facilitate seeing and breathing but these were securely sealed before the start of the joust. This seems very impractical but think about it for a moment: Bolting the helmet directly to the breastplate prevented the knight from tilting or turning his head but it also ensured that his neck could not be bent or twisted if a lance accidentally struck his head, thus preventing whiplash or, far worse, a broken neck. As for the vision slot, in the course of the jousting run, as with most horseback riding, the knight would naturally lean slightly forward in the saddle and so he could see out the vision slot and aim at his opponent. However, in the moment before impact, the knight would sit up straight in the saddle, thus moving his entire helmet, including the vision slot, up and back so that only the plain, smooth face of his helmet was exposed to his opponent's lance.

There were many other specialized pieces of armor for the joust and other tournament games, such as a gauntlet for the right hand that the user could lock shut to prevent losing his grip on his weapon (that great sportsman, Henry VIII, had at least one of these made despite the fact they were considered cheating and banned in most tournaments). The examples above demonstrate the differences between tournament armors and combat armors and these are important to keep in mind since tournament armors are the predominant form of armor which have survived to the present and are shown in books and displayed in museums. Unless the viewer recognizes what they are and how they differed from combat suits of armors, one could be easily misled as to the nature of medieval fighting by these specialty suits which were designed for sport and which were completely impractical in the fields of battle.

HEALING

The mere mention of medicine in the Middle Ages is enough to make most people cringe. The popular image of medieval medicine is filled with quack doctors applying leeches to hapless patients, plagues spreading unchecked across Europe, and peasants resorting to homebrewed concoctions and appealing to magical or divine intervention to heal their ills. And there is truth in these images, yet there was much more to the art and science of healing as it was practiced in the Middle Ages.

The state of the practice of medicine in the Middle Ages was certainly primitive by modern standards. Antibiotics, X-rays, and blood chemistry analysis are just a few of the medical tools which are now standard but which were unavailable during the Middle Ages and for centuries afterwards. Yet, in light of its place in history, medieval medical practice was not as backwards as it might appear. While there was some progress and innovation in medicine during the Middle Ages, most of the diagnostic and curative techniques associated with medieval physicians were developed by the Greeks and, to a lesser extent, the Romans.

The Classical Tradition

As with philosophy, architecture, and many other areas of art and science, medieval civilization inherited much from the classical Greek and Roman cultures. The works of Galen, Hippocrates, and a handful of other ancient experts on medicine were treasured and studied by medical students in the Middle Ages. While the true authorship of many of these texts remains dubious, these treatises were quite influential. The theories they expounded on topics such as anatomy, circulation, disease theory, and the medicinal uses of herbs and other substances remained the standards for centuries.

But, more than any other knowledge passed down from the Greeks and Romans, classical medicine was a mixed blessing. While it provided some useful and practical information, it also included much that was absurd and even potentially harmful such as the humoral theory and the practice of bloodletting. The problem of the uneven quality of this medical knowledge was compounded during the Middle Ages by a general tendency not to question the validity of information that had survived from the ancients. University medical curricula focused on studying the classic texts and assimilating their contents, not on weighing the merits of the theories and confirming or disproving the information presented as "facts." Though some doctors in each generation likely recognized disparities between the classical theories and their own firsthand experiences, open conflicts with classical medicine did not appear until late in the Middle Ages. Even then, these differences were usually styled as clarifications or reinterpretations of the classical teachings rather than as an outright rejection and replacement with new and better information. Thus, the practice of slavishly following classical medicine likely had a stifling effect on intellectual curiosity and the development of medicine during the Middle Ages.

THE HUMORAL THEORY

Among the medical theories inherited from the Greeks and Romans, one of the most fundamental and influential was the theory of bodily humors. This theory held that every person's health and temperament was governed by four bodily fluids or *humors*. These humors were blood, phlegm, yellow bile, and black bile and to each was attributed certain characteristics and influences on the human body:

• Blood — Hot and wet. Persons in whom this humor was dominant were said to be sanguine, from the Latin *sanguis* meaning blood. Under the humoral theory, sanguine people had ruddy,

healthy complexions and were cheerful, warm, and generous. In some medieval books on health, the illustration of the stereotypical sanguine person was a nobleman because the ideal noble was supposed to possess all these features.

• Phlegm — Cold and wet. Phlegmatic people were detached and cool. While this characteristic meant they were slow to anger, it also meant they were generally sluggish, dull, and slow to act on anything regardless of the motive. A cold and calculating merchant was often used as the illustration of stereotypical phlegmatic person.

• Yellow Bile — Hot and dry. An excess of yellow bile or *choler* was said to make a person irritable and prone to anger. On the plus side, choleric people were supposed to be thin, presumably as a result of their constant state of agitation. A belligerent knight was often the symbol for choleric complexions.

• Black Bile — Cold and dry. Too much black bile caused a person to be gloomy and depressed, in other words: melancholy. In fact, the word *melancholy* is derived from two Greek words that mean black (melanos) bile (chole). Besides depression, an excess of black bile made a person cowardly, pale, envious of others, and covetous of their possessions. A pasty-faced scholar was sometimes used as the personification of melancholy.

As these descriptions make clear, sanguine was the most desirable complexion and, under the humoral theory, humans were ideally hot and wet. However, the theory also stated that the three other humors besides blood were also present in everyone as well and that they were also vital to good mental and physical health. Besides the physical functions these fluids were thought to serve, their attributes of coolness, anger, and sadness all have a place in normal human behavior in *moderation*. Moderation was the key. While everyone had all four humors, each person was born with a different balance of fluids. After birth, environmental factors, from diet to the position of the stars, further altered that balance for better or worse. Thus, the physician's task was to analyze a patient's humoral balance and devise a regimen to adjust the balance to maintain or restore the patient's well being.

As part of the humoral theory, foods were determined to have specific characteristics of warmth, coolness, moistness and dryness in degrees ranging from the first through the fourth, with fourth being the highest level. For example, one health handbook from the early 15th century stated that oranges were both cold and moist in the third degree while marjoram was both warm and dry in the third degree. Applying this information, a physician might have advised a patient diagnosed as being phlegmatic (cold and wet) not to eat oranges and to eat foods flavored with marjoram as part of a diet designed to bring the patient's humors into a healthy balance.

Besides foods, certain objects and environmental conditions were also given humoral characteristics. Woolen clothing was warm and dry in the first degree while linen clothing was cold and dry in the second degree. Winds from the north were cold in the third degree and dry in the second degree while easterly winds were just warm in the second degree. Spring was moist in the second degree and winter was cold in the third degree and normally moist in the second degree. Medieval physicians duly took all these factors into account when advising patients on how to balance their humors.

While the humoral theory was largely absurd and lacked any apparent rational basis, it did have a few incidental benign if not beneficial aspects. For example, in pursuing a perfect balance of humors across an ever changing playing field of environmental factors, some physicians likely recommended varied diets to their patients and changed them with the seasons. This practice may have had the unintentional effect of encouraging more nutritionally balanced diets. The health handbooks that contained humoral information also often had some mundane but practical advice, such as:

• To mitigate the high degrees of cold and moisture encountered during winter, one should wear warm and dry heavy clothing.

• Cold, dry winds from the north often cause coughing and other afflictions of the chest. These dangers may be avoided by wearing warm, heavy clothing. Coughs and other discomforts caused by cold dry winds can be alleviated by taking warm baths.

Additionally, though the humors, or at least the attributes ascribed to them, were imaginary, the actual practice of humoral theory was based on some valid ideas which are still part of good medical practice today. For example, practitioners of humoral theory believed that it was better to look after one's health on a regular, on-going basis and try to prevent diseases rather than to ignore one's health and then try to cure the diseases that one contracted; in other words, they believed in preventive medicine. Further, a good medieval physician examined his patient's diet and surroundings as well as the patient's body to assess his or her health and the possible causes of any illnesses. Such an examination was patently inadequate when judged by modern medical standards and the humoral influences attributed to foods and the environment were usually quite fanciful, but a physician who conducted such an examination was trying to construct as complete a health profile of his patient as possible, something that good doctors still do today.

Medieval Ideas About the Transmission of Diseases

The existence of microbes was not discovered until the invention of the microscope by Anton van Leeuwenhoek in the late 17th century and the idea that some microbes carried infectious diseases, though developed in the 18th century, was not widely accepted until the 19th century. Physicians and others concerned with health care in the Middle Ages had to muddle through without the benefit of this knowledge. Thus, they came up with a number of theories for how diseases came into existence and spread. Some of these theories blamed supernatural causes such as God visiting His righteous wrath on sinful mankind or, conversely, witches, demons, and other agents of Satan inflicting suffering on the virtuous. For those schooled in astrology, supernatural causes also included malign configurations of the planets and other astronomical bodies creating unhealthy conditions on Earth. Other theories were more down to earth but just as fanciful. These included the spontaneous generation of any number of diseases by miasmas, clouds of noxious vapors emitted by the earth or formed in swamps or other places of decay and corruption, that contaminated the air and water. Just as fanciful but far more repugnant and dangerous was the belief that some people maliciously poisoned wells and took other actions to spread diseases. These charges were usually leveled at lepers and Jews, two groups that were excluded from the mainstream of society

in medieval Europe and were often viewed with fear, hate, and suspicion. When suddenly stricken by a lethal plague, communities panicked and all too often looked for scapegoats, resulting in mobs attacking and killing innocent Jews and lepers.

Not all medieval ideas about how diseases were spread and how they could be controlled were absurd. Though they did not know precisely how diseases such as the plague spread from one person to the next, medieval physicians did recognize that many diseases were contagious and that their spread could sometimes be controlled by limiting or avoiding contact with people who were infected with the disease. This idea led to the practice of requiring ships and their crews to anchor off-shore for a period of up to forty days before being allowed to land to ensure that they were not carrying any plagues. Known as *quarantine* from the Italian words for a period of forty days, this practice first developed in the ports of Italy and southern France in the late 14th century as part of efforts to combat recurrences of the bubonic plague or Black Death. There were also some instances in which sick people were shut up in their homes and quarantined until they either recovered or died as part of civic efforts to halt the spread of plagues. Since most efforts to isolate the sick failed and since avoiding contact with the sick was often very difficult in towns and cities, physicians also recommended that healthy people leave for the country if a plague appeared in their hometown or city. Such a flight from the city provided the setting for Boccaccio's *Decameron* and remained a common practice through the 17th century.

For those who could not leave town or otherwise avoid the sick, physicians often recommended carrying pomanders or censers filled with aromatic compounds or burning incense to neutralize the disease-filled air. Those physicians who were brave and devoted enough to stay on in town and treat their patients appear to have often used this method. Despite the fact that it did nothing to protect a physician from contracting diseases born by fleas or spread by airborne viruses and bacteria, some physicians continued to use this practice into the 18th century, by which time they used masks with large bird-like beaks filled with aromatic spices instead of pomanders.

Arabic Influences

Texts written by Arab medical scholars and practitioners were eagerly sought after by European physicians and medical students. The Arab texts were increasingly available in Latin translations starting around the 12th century and became quite influential on European medicine. Most of the Arab medical experts were Muslims but Jews and Christians who were natives of the Arab lands in the Middle East, North Africa, and Spain were also included in the numbers of noted Arab physicians.

Much of Arabic medical knowledge was drawn from Greek medical texts. These Greek texts had remained available to Arab scholars while they largely disappeared in Europe in the aftermath of the fall of Rome. Besides restating the original Greek information, the Arab scholars added their own contributions based on their experience, observations, and studies. However, even this additional information was still typically couched in terms of the humoral theory with cautery and bleeding as standard treatments. Still, both the Greek and Arabic materials provided fresh insights and sometimes valuable information to European physicians.

Medical Practitioners, Related Professions and Their Education and Training

Most people in the Middle Ages probably lived out their entire lives without ever seeing, let alone being treated by, a university trained physician. Physicians were in short supply and their services were usually quite expensive. Some cities in Italy and elsewhere retained physicians to oversee public health and to treat the poor but physicians primarily treated those who could afford to pay. Thus, in place of professional doctors, people turned to home remedies and a variety of health care providers who were not formally educated but had learned their trade through experience. These people ranged from family members and neighbors who helped tend the sick and injured to paid professionals such as midwives, itinerant surgeons, barbers, and empirics.

Though some of the unschooled healers appear to have been at least as effective and competent as their university trained counterparts, the lack of regulation and oversight of these medical practitioners meant that their patients had no guarantees of any minimum levels of training and experience. Thus, unless a patient went to a practitioner known to him or her either personally or by general good reputation, a patient often risked falling into the hands of a complete charlatan. While some formally educated medieval doctors were quacks, trained doctors had to undergo examination and licensing before being permitted to practice. Though the training these doctors received included medical theories and procedures that have long since been discredited, their training and examination guaranteed that they had some minimal level of medical knowledge, including some basic understanding of human anatomy. Further, physicians were clearly held accountable for the quality of their services under the licensing regulations and other legal obligations on their trade.

PHYSICIANS

Medieval physicians are often thought of as *leeches*, with the implication that their main form of "healing" was letting blood, usually by applying leeches to the patient to suck out his or her blood. While bleeding (also called *phlebotomy* or *venesection)* was a fairly common practice and is explained more below, the term *leech* is misleading. Though leeches were sometimes used for phlebotomy, simply cutting into a vein with a small knife was the most common technique by far for letting blood. Further, a doctor could be more certain of the amount of blood drawn by letting the blood flow from a cut or puncture into a bowl rather than by estimating how much a leech had absorbed. So why were doctors called leeches? In Old English, *lacnian* meant "to heal" and a *laece*, or *leche* in Middle English, was a "healer." These words were the origin for the Anglo-Saxon word *leech* meaning a physician. However, *laece* and *leche* came to be confused with two other Old English and Middle English words, *lyce* and *liche*, which referred to the blood-sucking worm. English is the only language in which this confusion occurred since it is the only European language in which the words for "healing" and for "leech" resembled each other. Thus, doctors in France, Germany, and elsewhere in Europe escaped this unflattering title.

As previously mentioned, the physician was set apart from other medical practitioners by his formal education in medicine, with emphasis on *his*. Medical training, like all other courses of education at medieval universities, was open only to men. In all universities, a working knowledge of Latin was a prerequisite for admission since the texts and lectures were all in Latin. Would-be students also needed a basic knowledge of logic and philosophy in order to comprehend their classes. The people who had the opportunity to acquire such knowledge were men who usually were either already members of the clergy or were in training to become clergymen. A few laymen from relatively wealthy families also had opportunities for such education and attended universities in increasing number over the course of the Middle Ages. On the other hand, very few women had the opportunity to learn Latin and other subjects required for admission to universities. Even if a woman possessed the requisite knowledge, she would still be denied entrance to a university. Medieval universities were typically founded as places to study Christian theology. Women were barred from becoming clergy in the medieval Christian church so the universities and their faculties saw no point in admitting women to the courses in philosophy and theology that formed the basic curriculum for all undergraduate students. And without a basic degree, no one, man or woman, was admitted to advanced studies such as medicine. The only significant exception to these limits was in Salerno, Italy, where women were allowed to teach and practice medicine. Despite the fame these women had for their medical skills, they disappeared by the end of the 12th century as medical training and the practice of medicine came to be monopolized, respectively, by the universities and their graduates.

Besides contributing to the exclusion of women, the central role of Christian theology in university curricula also served to exclude Jews from most universities. Some universities did admit those Jews willing to pay higher tuition fees than those paid by Christian students and a few universities, primarily those in Italy, recruited noted Jewish physicians for their faculties from time to time. Since they were generally excluded from the universities, Jewish physicians acquired their medical knowledge outside the university system. They likely learned much of this knowledge directly from Greek and Arabic texts, many of which were not available in Latin translations at the universities until late in the Middle Ages. Despite discrimination, Jewish physicians often achieved great reputations for their skill and were retained by royal and other noble Christian households.

Thus, the university system produced doctors who were Christian males and who were frequently members of the clergy as well. Having two careers sometimes caused conflicts. Clergymen, most notably monks, who had acquired medical training were routinely forbidden by the Church from engaging in the private practice of medicine. Such prohibitions weren't motivated by any inherent incompatibility between treating the sick and being a member of the clergy. In fact, caring for the sick and injured was a Christian duty which many monasteries and other religious institutions actively strove to perform. Rather, the prohibition was based on the Church's concern that medicine was such a lucrative occupation that clergymen who were medical practitioners would neglect their religious responsibilities while pursuing personal gain in treating patients privately. However, there were two common medical procedures, phlebotomy and surgery, that were often deemed unsuitable activities for clergymen-physicians for more fundamental moral reasons. Performing phlebotomy or surgery required the practitioner to shed blood which, regardless of its motive, was an action considered inim-

ical to the peaceful, nonviolent conduct expected of the Christian clergy.

After formal schooling, the physician underwent some period of supervised practice similar to a modern internship. Interestingly, the period of on-the-job training rarely included a tour of duty in a hospital. Hospitals in the Middle Ages were seldom used as teaching facilities for physicians though there are a handful of references to surgeons performing operations in hospitals and using these occasions to instruct students in surgery. Following the satisfactory completion of the supervised practice, the physician went on to an examination conducted by a group of practicing physicians. If successful, the physician was then licensed and ready to practice medicine on his own.

Guided by the humoral theory, his practice often involved advising patients on diet and environment to balance their humors to maintain their health or to cure their sicknesses. Routine health care for those wealthy enough to afford a physician also included bleeding to remove harmful excesses of humors and the physician would advise the patient when to be bled. Physicians also prescribed baths (hot, warm, or cold), rest, and exercise to assist a patient in balancing his or her humors. Regardless of the theory behind such activities, the benefits in comforting the patient and encouraging him or her to be more physically fit are readily apparent. Along with these treatments, physicians also often prescribed courses of medications. These drugs were intended to correct humoral imbalances but many were prescribed simply because of their reputed ability to cure or relieve certain ills. A large number of these drugs were compounded from vegetable matter, most commonly from herbs. Thus, despite their formal training, medieval physicians relied heavily on a pharmacopoeia that is now more commonly associated with folk medicine

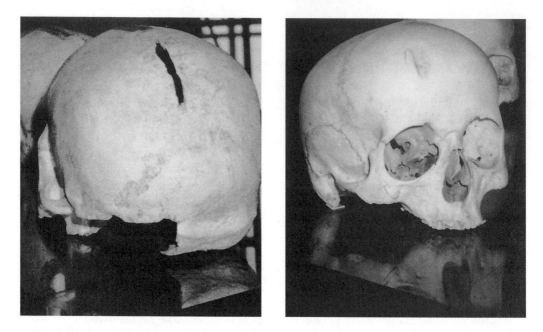

Figure 35. These two skulls were found at the site of a late 15th century battle in Switzerland. The skull on the left has a slot several inches long cut into it. This wound is believed to have been inflicted by a sword. Though such head wounds are quite serious and can prove fatal, these wounds were sometimes successfully treated in the Middle Ages as is shown by the skull on the right. The slight shadow high on the forehead of this skull is caused by a shallow groove a few inches long. This groove is a healed fracture which appears to have been caused by a sword cut similar to that suffered by the skull on the right. Thus, this healed skull belonged to a combat veteran who had survived and recovered from grievous wounds in previous battles prior to being slain in this battle. These skulls are currently in the Old Arsenal Museum, Solothurn, Switzerland (photographs by author).

than with professional medical care. Their use of these and other materials and techniques for healing is addressed further below.

SURGEONS

Today, all surgeons are medical doctors who have received the same advanced education as other physicians as well as additional training and practice in their particular fields of surgery. However, medieval surgeons were seldom educated as doctors. While a few doctors took up surgery, some doctors and university faculty appear to have held the practice of surgery in low esteem, if not outright con-

tempt. They purportedly based their disdain of surgery on its being manual work fit only for laborers and mechanics: A true doctor, in their estimation, healed by observing the patient and prescribing remedies rather than by intervening so directly and physically. In at least some instances, it's far more likely that these doctors recognized the high risks and liabilities involved in performing surgery and were just providing a rationalization for not doing it.

Regardless of anyone's opinion, surgery was a vital form of treatment and it was taught at many universities. Additionally, texts on surgery both in Latin and in vernacular languages became increasingly available over the course of the Middle Ages. These translations were studied by university students as well as by educated laymen outside the universities. Thus, some medieval surgeons were "learned" men though they were seldom fully trained and licensed as doctors. But the majority of skilled surgeons appear to have learned their art primarily by watching and assisting experienced surgeons and then practicing under these experts' direction. This apprenticeship gave the surgeons-in-training the practical and essential hands-on experience that they needed and which university lectures, books, and the occasional human anatomy dissection could not provide. Still, despite the rough way they learned their skills, these surgeons did not disdain academic methods; many eagerly sought out books on surgery and some appear to have routinely assisted in anatomy dissections at the universities.

Medieval surgeons and surgeons-in-training seldom lacked for opportunities to practice their profession. The physically demanding lives led by most people in the Middle Ages appears to have often resulted in broken bones, dislocations (fig. 36), sprains, animal bites, and, especially during any military conflicts, wounds inflicted by any number of weapons (fig. 35). Not unlike today, wars especially afforded surgeons many opportunities to practice and refine their skills. Further, service in war was often financially advantageous as well. If a surgeon achieved notoriety for his successes, he could expect to be offered valuable fees from noble households seeking to retain him to accompany and treat their members who were injured in battle. Some wealthy nobles retained surgeons as well as physicians on a full-time basis so that they could always be sure that competent treatment was near at hand: a rather expensive, early form of health insurance.

Starting in the 14th century, surgeons in Italy were employed for another medical specialty: autopsies. Along with physi-

Figure 36. An operation to reposition a dislocated shoulder. This mid–13th century physician or surgeon (on the right) is using both his hands and one of his feet to force the patient's left shoulder back into joint. Medieval medical books depict patients undergoing treatments such as this one and even more serious operations without anesthesia (J. Walker).

cians, surgeons were employed in Venice and elsewhere to examine bodies in instances of suspicious deaths or when the cause or nature of the death or injury was in dispute.

BARBERS, BARBER-SURGEONS, AND ITINERANT SURGEONS

The frequent need for surgical treatment and the scarcity of trained surgeons meant that desperate people often turned to anyone they thought could help them treat a wound or other injury. Common barbers sometimes filled this role. Besides shaving and cutting hair, many barbers performed routine bleedings for their patrons as well. (The practice of bleeding and the barber's other common sideline, dentistry, are discussed later in this chapter.) So, in addition to razors, lancets, and other sharp implements, these barbers possessed some basic knowledge about the locations of major veins and arteries and the techniques for controlling and stopping external bleeding. As part of their trade, such barbers likely kept a stock of bandages and styptics at hand so that they could provide these services when needed. Thus, when confronted with a serious injury, especially one that involved severe bleeding, people in the Middle Ages often turned to barbers for assistance.

The demand and compensation for urgent medical care must have been rather high in medieval Europe since some barbers found it desirable to specialize in the medical aspect of their profession. By the end of the 13th century, these specialists were known as barber-surgeons. Barber-surgeons rose from the ranks of common barbers and so had no university training in medicine or surgery. Instead, like other tradesmen, they received their training through apprenticeship with more senior barber-surgeons. Thus, their skills, or lack their of, were based exclusively on their own experiences. In this respect, they were similar to at least some of the learned surgeons but there was still a definite gulf between barber-surgeons and surgeons. Barber-surgeons remained members of the barbers' guild rather than becoming members of the surgeons' guild. Further, barber-surgeons in England and elsewhere actively resisted attempts by surgeons to merge the two guilds. The surgeons sought the merger so that they would gain authority to regulate the qualifications and conduct of the barber-surgeons. While they may have been attempting to control and limit competition by the barber-surgeons, the surgeons appear to have been motivated by a genuine desire to crack down on quacks preying on and harming the public.

As with surgeons, barber-surgeons were routinely hired to accompany armies and treat their wounded.

Another type of medieval medical tradesman was the itinerant surgeon. Like the barber-surgeon, the itinerant surgeon learned his trade only through hands-on experience rather than from university study. Some of these itinerant surgeons specialized in performing just one type of operation. The two most common specialties were "cutting for the stone" to remove stones from the bladder and lower urinary tract and "couching for cataract" to excise the clouded lens from a patient's eye. There were also traveling tooth-pullers. A few itinerant surgeons appear to have been quite proficient in performing these operations but one can't help but assume that the primary reason that these surgeons constantly traveled was so they would be long gone by the time a patient realized that an operation had failed. Having already received their pay at the time of the operation, these surgeons had little incentive to remain until a patient had either recovered from surgery or succumbed to complications.

EMPIRICS

Empirics were the largest group of health care providers in medieval Europe. Empirics were those healers who relied on cures supposedly derived from experience; that is, empirically, rather than from classical medical training. However, they appear to have relied more heavily on a mixture of traditional home remedies, incantations, or prayers than on their own experience. These practitioners never referred to themselves as empirics. Rather, this was a pejorative label given to them by the university-trained doctors. Instead, they were more commonly referred to simply as healers, wise men or women, and similar terms.

There is little evidence of how the empirics trained for their profession. Since it was not a formally recognized occupation, there were no established guilds or other organizations for educating them and verifying their qualifications to practice. Some empirics likely studied under those already practicing but many relied only on their own native intelligence and whatever medical information they could pick up. Thus, the quality of empirics' skills varied widely, though whether their skill levels varied more than other medical practitioners of the time remains open to debate.

Chronicles from across medieval Europe contain scattered references to empirics who had good reputations as healers but empirics appear more commonly in the written records as defendants in civil trials and criminal prosecutions. Most of these court actions were brought after the empiric's cures had failed but a few were brought by associations of physicians against successful empirics for practicing medicine without a license.

The ranks of empirics included both men and women. The men engaged in the same range of practice as their educated counterparts. Female empirics, as well, acted as general practitioners and as surgeons but many also practiced two specialties generally shunned by males: gynecology and obstetrics. These areas of medical care and the persons who engaged in them are discussed in the section on "Women and Medicine" below.

OTHER PRACTITIONERS

There was another group of medical practitioners that did not fit neatly into either of the two general categories of the university-trained or the illiterate empiric. These practitioners had some formal education but had not studied medicine at the universities. Besides many Jewish physicians who obtained their medical training outside of the Christian universities, this group included:

- Monks and nuns who learned Latin as part of the training for their religious orders and then went on and studied what medicine they could from the books in the libraries of their monasteries or convents. Such monks and nuns tended to ill and injured members of their orders in the infirmaries of their abbeys. On occasion, some of these monks and nuns provided medical care for sick lay people as well.

- Daughters of physicians or surgeons who were trained by their fathers. While these women were barred from the universities, some were taught the family trade and practiced medicine. As early as the 14th century, guilds of surgeons in some cities specifically allowed daughters as well as sons of guild members to be admitted to practice. Physicians' daughters do not appear to have received the same recognition. The sparse evidence about such female medical practitioners suggests that they did not offer their services publicly but only tended to persons who were acquainted with their families and knew to seek them out.

and

- Noble women who had received some formal education, including schooling in Latin, and then pursued additional medical learning from books and other sources as circumstances permitted. As with the daughters of physicians, these women did not offer their services to the public at large. Rather, they provided medical services for their own family and servants and for friends and acquaintances. In this respect, these women were the same as other women in medieval society who, noble or common, were expected to provide at least basic medical care to their families and friends. Some of these noble ladies appear to have been highly skilled but one cannot help but wonder how many women of lower social standing had comparable skill but whose deeds went unrecorded.

APOTHECARIES

While many medical practitioners, especially empirics, gathered the herbs and other common ingredients needed for remedies from local sources, physicians often required medicinal substances that had to be imported. For these items, they turned to the apothecary. Apothecaries were retailers of the ingredients for drugs and were the medieval forerunners of today's pharmacist. They traded in rare and expensive commodities such as ivory, gold, pearls, mummy dust, and ambergris from whales: all of which found their way into medicines in the Middle Ages. They also bought and sold spices such as saffron, ginger, and cinnamon that were used in medicines as well as in cooking. Along with spices, sugar was part of the apothecary's stock in trade and was often a key ingredient for making medicinal syrups and pills more palatable. Additionally, some apothecaries had a lucrative sideline in making and selling sugar pills or tablets which they sold to wealthy customers with a taste for candy.

As indicated above, the apothecary did more than just buy and sell raw ingredients; he also combined these ingredients to make ointments, pastes, syrups, and pills. Some of these products were custom-made in accordance with a physician's exact instructions, sometimes with the physician in attendance to supervise. Others were stock items apparently made up according to some generally agreed formula. Many of the apothecary's products were available only by prescription while others were available "over the counter."

Apothecaries were usually tradesmen who had learned their craft through apprenticeship rather than being physicians with a university education. And the practice of dispensing some common medicines without requiring a prescription sometimes caused conflicts between the physicians and the apothecaries, with occasional accusations by physicians that some apothecaries were diagnosing illnesses and prescribing drugs without a license to practice medicine. Further, in some jurisdictions, the apothecaries' wares were also subject to periodic inspections by the local physicians. As part of these inspections, the physicians could force an apothecary to throw out any drug ingredients or prepared medicines that they found to be stale, watered down, or otherwise defective. Yet despite these frictions, physicians and apothecaries generally appear to have worked well together; so well, in fact, that satirists in the Middle Ages routinely depicted them as co-conspirators in defrauding patients.

Diagnostic Techniques

When attempting to diagnose a patient's condition, medieval medical practitioners often turned to analyzing the patient's blood and urine. At first blush, this practice sounds very modern, but the technology for obtaining meaningful information from these bodily fluids were not developed until the 19th century. So, instead of chemically analyzing blood to determine its composition, its relative levels of antibodies, and other information relevant to assessing a patient's health, the medieval physician simply examined the smell, warmth, texture, and even the taste of the blood. Some physicians also observed the strength of the flow of blood from the patient as well as how the blood clotted afterwards. In the course of this analysis, the physician attempted to discern imbalances in the patient's humors or the presence of any impurities in the blood.

Examination of urine was even more a part of standard diagnostic procedures than analysis of blood. Uroscopy (examining the appearance of urine) was such a common and integral part of medieval medical practice that the glass containers for patients' urine became a symbol for the medical profession. These containers were called *jordans,* possibly after the River Jordan. They were made of clear, untinted glass so that the physician could view the urine to determine its exact color. To aid the physician, medieval medical texts frequently had full-color illustrations of the twenty recognized colors of urine. These ranged from very unhealthy shades of blue, black, and dark red through to healthier yellows and on again to less healthy pale yellow and clear. Besides color, the physician looked for any sediment or other solids in the urine. In addition to the visible qualities of the urine, its smell and texture (was it thin and watery or thick and greasy?) were also noted. As with blood analysis, the results of uroscopy were usually interpreted in the context of the humoral theory with the physician attempting to uncover the exact nature of the humoral imbalance afflicting the patient. However, the texts accompanying some uroscopy diagrams indicate that medieval practitioners did use uroscopy to ascertain information that a modern doctor would consider meaningful. For example, some of the texts noted that certain reddish discolorations of urine was a symptom of internal bleeding and that a gritty precipitate indicated that the patient might be suffering from kidney stones.

Besides examining bodily fluids, medieval physicians sometimes examined a patient's stool for clues or attempted to identify illnesses based on the strength and rapidity of the patient's pulse. Still others turned to astrological charts and calendars and sought to determine the nature and likely duration and outcome of the illness based upon the date of its onset. To help make these calculations and other diagnostic determinations, these physicians had small booklets containing calendars with astronomical annotations, urine color charts, and other information. These little reference books were small enough to fit into a leather bag or case on the physician's belt.

Medical Treatments

Physicians and other medical practitioners used a number of different treatments both in curing their patients' ills and in attempting to prevent illnesses. Some of these treatments, such as dietary guidance, bleeding, and cautery, were corrective measures designed to maintain or restore a patient's health by adjusting his or her humoral balances. Ingesting or applying herbs or other medicines were also used to correct humoral imbalances but they were more commonly used to directly treat and relieve specific illnesses. Because of its extreme risks, surgery was usually a treatment of last resort, used only for the most serious of conditions that would respond to no other form of treatment. And, finally, some treatments involved reciting prayers or incantations to appeal for divine or supernatural intervention.

DIET

Diet was an important part of medieval medicine. As mentioned before, diet was one of the factors deemed to affect a person's humors so the physician often reviewed his patient's diet when assessing his or her health. Then, to treat an existing illness or to keep the patient in good health, the physician prescribed a dietary regimen designed to restore or maintain a healthy balance of humors.

For example, to treat a specific illness such as colic and some other gastro-intestinal problems, physicians recommended consumption of foods that had moderate warm and dry qualities under the humoral theory such as dill and the meat of roosters. Presumably, the physicians believed that colic was caused by an excess of phlegm (the cold and damp humor) in the lower digestive tract and that it could be relieved by ingesting doses of warm, dry foods. While they couched their treatments in terms of balancing humors, it's interesting to see that, at least in this instance, the physicians were recommending foods which are still recognized today as providing some relief for these conditions: dill can relieve gas in the digestive tract while poultry, prepared plainly, is a nourishing and soothing food which is easy on the digestive tract. Thus, while the underlying theories of humors and the humoral qualities of foods lacked any scientific basis, physicians did at least occasionally develop beneficial treatments in their application of it.

This example also raises an interesting question: did the early physicians who originally assigned foods their humoral properties do so based solely on theoretical determinations of their nature and origin or did they first learn the beneficial and harmful properties of foods through practical experience and then work backwards, ascribing humoral qualities to the foods that made them "fit" the theory? Given the lack of any obvious similarities between dill and poultry, it certainly seems likely that the Greek and Roman originators of

the humoral theory based their classifications of at least some foods on their own observations of the effects these foods had on patients under various conditions. However, by the time the humoral theory reached medieval physicians, any evidence of an empirical basis for the dietary guidance was long forgotten, leaving only the charts and matrices that codified the foods' humoral qualities and recommended applications without any meaningful explanations. While some medieval physicians may have recognized the underlying beneficial properties of some foods regardless of their humoral labels, most physicians appear to have accepted the humoral theory at face value, learned the characteristics, and prescribed diets accordingly.

To maintain a patient in good health, a physician sought to keep the patient's humors in a balanced state: not too cold nor too hot, not too dry nor too wet; though tipping the balance slightly toward warmth and moisture, the healthy sanguine qualities, was ideal. Thus, if a person had a choleric complexion, that is, one that was hot and dry, he or she would typically be advised to eat more moist foods and fewer dry ones in order to bring his or her humors closer to the ideal balance. Also, depending on the degree of hotness he or she possessed, consumption of cooler foods might be recommended as well. This is a very simplified example. A skilled physician would also factor in external conditions such as the time of year, his patient's living conditions, and the position of the stars before determining precisely how and to what degree to balance the patient's humors. In some cases, the physicians appeared to have analyzed all these elements, both mundane and arcane, just to come up with the commonsense advice of eating a balanced diet, not eating too many rich foods, and going easy on alcoholic beverages. Though in other instances, the advice was more exotic and much less helpful, such as advising a patient with an excessively phlegmatic (cold and wet) complexion to avoid eating any fish since they are cold and wet by nature and would worsen the patient's condition. Still, regardless of the quality of the advice, this practice does show that even back in the Middle Ages good physicians were already concerned with helping their patients to maintain their health and avoid illness rather than simply treating them after they had already fallen ill.

BLEEDING

Bleeding is the medical practice most commonly associated with health care in the Middle Ages but, like the humoral theory of which it was a part, it was a practice that dated back as far as the heyday of the Roman Empire. As previously mentioned, bleeding was also called venesection or phlebotomy. It typically involved making a small incision in a vein in the patient's arm and draining off some of the patient's blood, though veins on the forehead and elsewhere were sometimes tapped for particular ailments. Illustrations of bleeding usually show the blood being caught in a small bowl so that it could be examined as well. Occasionally, leeches were used to suck out the blood but the most common technique was to simply have a surgeon, barber, or barber-surgeon slit the vein open with a small knife.

Cupping was an alternative technique for bleeding. In cupping, the surgeon did not apply leeches or cut open a vein. Instead, the surgeon, barber, or barber-surgeon made a number of small, shallow slashes in the patient's flesh at the appropriate location and then pressed a little glass or metal cup over the scarified flesh. The cup was heated over an open flame immediately before being applied and created a slight vacuum as it sealed against the patient's soft flesh. Despite its requiring both slashing the patient's skin and sticking hot glass or metal on to the bleeding flesh, contemporary practitioners appear to have considered cupping to have been less hazardous or discomforting than venesection for drawing blood since they thought that cupping was especially suitable for women, children, and the elderly.

Regardless of which technique was used to remove the blood, the theory behind the practice of bleeding was the same: that the balance of bodily humors could be adjusted and corrected by drawing off small quantities of blood that contained excessively high levels of humors. The location of the vein chosen for the incision was determined by traditional teaching on which parts of the body were served by which vein. In addition, some physicians used astrological charts and astronomical calendars to further guide their choice of veins and the time for the bleeding. This practice was based on the beliefs that the various signs of the zodiac governed specific parts of the human body and that the health of a patient was directly affected by the constellations. Thus, medieval physicians sometimes based their decisions on which veins to have bled and when to have the bleeding take place based upon whether the relevant astrological sign was ascending or descending.

While bleeding was certainly an unpleasant and, as we know today, pointless practice, the magnitude of its harm to the health of medieval Europeans has been exaggerated. As early as the 12th century, medical texts strongly advised that only a moderate amount of blood should be let, never so much as to cause the patient to pass out. Further, while some physicians did recommend the "gentler" form of bleeding by cupping for relatively weak patients, most practitioners recognized that some patients should not be bled at all. These patients included pregnant women, small children, the very old, and the very weak. Though there were some cases in which seriously ill patients were subjected to bleeding, these were likely the exception rather than the rule since the debilitating effects of bleeding appear to have been well recognized. For example, regulations for some monasteries indicate that monks were bled as part of their health care regimen and that they were routinely given light duties, extra time to relax, and additional rations of meat for several days after being bled. Other monastic records also shed some light on how often bleeding was undertaken. Monastic expense account records of payments to barbers or surgeons for their services show that bleeding was routinely performed on a monthly basis though bleeding only once every three months was also a common pattern. Thus, bleeding appears to have been practiced with a healthy measure of caution with only limited amounts of blood being drawn at intervals far enough apart to allow for the patient's complete recovery, not unlike the practice for modern blood donations.

Besides the limited frequency of bleedings and the relatively small amounts of blood that appear to have involved, the skills of the barbers, barber-surgeons, and surgeons that performed bleedings seems to have lessened the risks and harm of bleeding as well. Most of these practitioners must have known how and where to make the incisions with a minimum of injury to the patient; selecting the veins carefully, keeping the incisions small, and then controlling the blood flow from the incisions. And, despite their ignorance of antiseptics, they also must have known how to close the incisions so that they healed without infection. This conclusion is based on the fact that monks and many

other individuals survived repeated bleedings and that there are few records of people who were otherwise healthy dying or sustaining serious injuries from routine bleedings. Records of prosecutions and other legal actions suggest that most bleeding-related injuries, such as accidental severing of nerves, tendons, or major arteries, were inflicted by empirics and other unqualified people rather than by recognized professionals.

Leaving how it was practiced aside, the most important factor in mitigating the negative impact of bleeding on medieval society as a whole was that it was likely not part of most people's health care. Certainly, bleeding was a fundamental part of the humoral theory that dominated medieval medicine and nobles, clerics, and some other individuals across Europe routinely had themselves bled but, as with other areas of medicine, the majority of the population lacked access to such "state-of-the-art" health care. Some simply could not afford it while many others, such as those who lived and worked on farms, had limited opportunities to travel regularly to a town or city to seek the services of a professional phlebotomist. And, finally, regardless of its purported health benefits, some people likely forewent bleeding despite being able to afford it and having ready access to a practitioner. These were the forerunners of those people today who put off or avoid going to doctors or dentists because of inconvenience and time involved or because they fear or just dislike the experience even though they know that it's good for their health. Thus, while many people did undergo bleeding, most people probably lived out their entire lives without ever being bled.

CAUTERY

Over the last few centuries, surgeons have developed sophisticated techniques for removing diseased tissue, sterilizing wounds, and sealing them. One of these techniques is cautery in which either a chemical agent or a heated instrument is used to burn out diseased or severely damaged tissue along with any infection and then sear the wound shut. While this practice may sound crude, it is quite effective and is even practiced as part of modern microsurgery with surgeons using lasers to burn and seal blood vessels shut. Needless to say, the practice of cautery was far less developed in the Middle Ages. Further, while they did occasionally employ cautery for cleaning and sealing wounds, medieval medical practitioners more often used this technique for another purpose entirely. Cautery, like bleeding, was used to treat or prevent illnesses by correcting humoral imbalances. Medieval medical texts frequently included diagrams of human figures with spots marked where red-hot iron instruments were to be applied as sort of burning combination of acupuncture and acupressure. By applying a small, red-hot iron tool to the appropriate point, the physician believed that he could adjust the patient's humors and cure ailments ranging from headaches and pains in the joints to respiratory problems. Cautery was obviously painful and the illustrations of such operations often include depictions of bowls or cups that presumably contained sleep-inducing or pain-killing solutions administered to the patients.

As with bleeding, this use of cautery was not created in the Middle Ages. It was part of Roman medical practice from at least as early as the 2nd century A.D. Further, the practice of cautery was not limited to Europe. Arabic physicians adopted it as well as part of the medical knowledge they gleaned from their translations of classical Roman and Greek texts.

SURGERY AND WOUND CARE

Surgery was the riskiest form of treatment. Much like today, patients were loathe to undergo surgery unless it was the only means of saving their lives or correcting a serious condition such as blindness from cataracts. Medieval surgeons appear to have been hesitant as well. Some seem to have recognized the limitations of their skills and the relatively primitive tools and techniques available to them while others simply feared the liabilities they might incur if the operation failed. And this fear was not baseless. Though many jurisdictions had laws limiting the criminal and civil liabilities of accredited surgeons, distraught members of the patient's family might still take matters into their own hands.

Still, despite the risks, the complete lack of blood transfusions, and the very basic means of anesthesia then available, medieval surgeons undertook a surprising array of operations. Along with "cutting for the stone" and "couching for cataract" that were often the specialty of itinerant surgeons, surgeons in the Middle Ages also removed nasal polyps; excised hemorrhoids; restored dislocated shoulders and jaws to their proper positions (fig. 36); cleaned, stitched, and bandaged up wounds; treated hernias; amputated severely damaged limbs; and set broken bones, including even fractured skulls as shown in figure 35. There is insufficient evidence to determine how often surgeons performed these operations and how successful they were. Certainly, many patients likely died from infections and other post-operative complications which could be prevented today. However, the few accounts of the careers of individual surgeons that have survived indicate that at least some practitioners were highly competent and able to perform these operations with a good chance of success. Physical evidence in the form of skeletons of medieval people further supports this conclusion.

Human bones excavated from 14th and 15th century battlefields show that some warriors had sustained grave injuries in previous battles such as broken limbs or fractured skulls. The skulls (fig. 35) and other bones of some of these fighters even show signs of repeated injuries suffered in battles over the course of many years. Though the exact degree of healing varied depending upon how much time had elapsed between the time that the wounds were inflicted and the point at which the warrior received the final, fatal blows, many of these breaks were often completely mended. While some of the credit for this healing must go to the strength and natural regenerative abilities of the men who suffered these wounds, these men must have received significant medical treatment that helped both their bones and the surrounding flesh to heal. Particularly in cases of skull fractures which typically required the removal of bone fragments and careful treatment to avoid damaging the brain, medieval surgeons displayed amazing skill and, again based on the number of bones that show repeated injury and healing, were often successful in their operations.

The bones, however, provide little evidence of how well surgeons treated soft tissue injuries such as punctures in the abdomen or medical conditions such as tumors. Medical texts provided some guidance on treating tears or cuts in the lungs, bowels, and other organs as well as descriptions of various malignant growths and their symptoms. However, such wounds and illnesses were usually fatal, a point which some of the medieval texts mention as part of cautioning the surgeon against taking any action in such cases. A few accounts survive of surgeons who managed successfully to stitch up a perforated bowel or a torn lung or excise a tumor but these cases were recorded as rare examples of exceptional operations. More commonly, the less than antiseptic operating conditions, the lack of antibiotics, and the difficulties in completely stopping internal bleeding and removing all the corrupted tissue and other contaminants (such as the leaking contents of the digestive tract in cases where the intestines were damaged) meant that infection and death were inevitable in most cases. And these conditions continued to plague surgical practice and the health of the public for centuries after the Middle Ages.

Surgical Tools

Many of the instruments used by medieval surgeons remained unchanged for centuries and are even quite recognizable today. Among these were hacksaws for amputating limbs; devices for spreading apart and holding open wounds or incisions during operations; forceps, tweezers, and tongs for extracting foreign matter and repositioning tissue; knives and scalpels of various shapes and sizes; and needles for suturing. They even employed cannulae, which were small tubes, sometimes made of silver, for draining blood and other fluids from around internal wounds. However, cannulae served other purposes as well. One late 13th century Italian physician inserted a cannula into the esophagus of a patient who had an injured throat and used it as a feeding tube. In addition to these instruments, medieval surgeons did use some tools which have since fallen out of use such as the irons for performing cautery, mallets and chisels for opening the skull for trepanning, and the small knives used in bleeding, though these knives were the forerunners of the modern surgeon's lancet.

Other surgical tools that have mercifully disappeared are the cups and bowls used for administering anesthesia. Local anesthetics appear to have been completely unknown and so surgeons relied on general anesthesia. In many cases, general anesthesia likely came in the form of the patient passing out from the pain of his or her condition or injury prior to the commencement of surgery. Others less fortunate remained conscious during their operations; a terrifying ordeal but probably not an uncommon one, judging from the number of illustrations in which surgeons or their assistants were depicted restraining patients who were undergoing surgery. More fortunate patients either drank or inhaled anesthetics. These anesthetics were based on opiates and other sleep inducing herbs and compounds and either were mixed into wine for the patient to drink or were made into a liquid which was then soaked up in a sponge or rag and held over the patient's nose and mouth. Still, though these drugs could give the patient some relief from pain, they could also hurt or kill the patient as well. There was always a risk of accidentally poisoning the patient either by overdose or by mispreparation of the drugs regardless of which method of anesthesia was used.

Surgical Techniques and Wound Care

While medical practice in general was marked by the fanciful elements of astrology and the humoral theory, surgery in the Middle Ages, apart from cautery and bleeding, was far more basic and direct. The surgeon had little time for consulting the stars or for analyzing the humors of an injured or seriously ill patient who needed immediate care. Further, once the operation began, there was no time for such niceties: the lack of blood transfusions and the limited anesthesia available meant that completing an operation quickly was even more important than it is today. Thus, in those cases in which he believed that he could help the patient, the surgeon acted as quickly and directly as possible to correct the patient's condition, stop the bleeding, and complete the operation. To do this, he used some basic but effective techniques.

For broken bones, the surgeon realigned the ends of the bones and set them with splints and bandages. For more serious breaks such as skull fractures, he probed the wound to locate bone fragments and extracted them with tweezers or tongs before applying the bandages. For skull fractures, he also checked for dangerous accumulations of fluid and drained them off if possible. After cleaning such a wound to the skull, the surgeon inserted a light dressing of clean linen inside the opening in the skull to keep foreign matter out the wound. This dressing was replaced as needed and then removed before the opening in the skull healed shut. The surgeon also placed linen bandages soaked in egg white on top of the wound. As the egg white dried, these bandages contracted and pulled the patient's scalp together over the wound. This bandaging technique was used to treat less serious wounds as well.

For cuts and other open wounds to muscle tissue, the surgeon sought first to control the bleeding. Minor wounds were cleaned and then bandaged and or treated with styptics to stop the bleeding. More severe wounds such as those in which a weapon point was still lodged in the wound and or a major vein or artery had been severed required more extensive treatment. Depending upon the location of the wound and the volume of the blood flow, the surgeon used tourniquets, pressure, ligatures, or cautery to slow or halt the loss of blood from these serious wounds. Using forceps, tweezers, or tongs, the surgeon extracted any bone fragments or foreign matter, such as an arrowhead, from the wound. With a knife or scalpel, he would cut out any severely damaged surrounding tissue which he expected not to heal and which could cause infection if sealed inside the wound. In addition to this type of cleaning, there are occasional references in medieval accounts of medical operations to surgeons using solutions of wine to rinse out wounds. Since these solutions contained at least some alcohol, they may have helped clean out the wounds in relatively antiseptic fashion. After cleaning the wound, the surgeon sutured the wound shut using threads of linen or, if available, finer and stronger threads of silk.

While many of the medieval methods for treating wounds were basically sound, there was one rather peculiar and harmful method of treatment. In this treatment, instead of cleaning and then closing up the wound up entirely, the wound was kept at least partially open and was kept moist with unguents so that the wound would produce pus. This mode of treatment was based on the theory of "laudable pus." Under this theory of healing, a wound should produce pus before healing completely. This theory appears to have been based on a misunderstanding of the healing process. Wounds that are healing properly will sometimes exude pus but practitioners of the laudable pus theory believed that wounds must always produce pus as part of proper healing. Thus, these practitioners took additional and potentially very harmful steps to ensure that wounds in their care developed and secreted pus after initial dressing. Fortunately, before the end of the Middle Ages, proponents of dry healing won out over the adherents of the laudable pus theory. Under dry healing, wounds were usually completely cleaned, sealed, and dressed with dry bandages to keep the wound clean

and to keep out contamination. Of course, there were exceptions. Deep wounds and wounds to the abdomen were sometimes kept partially open or were fitted with cannulae to drain any fluids that accumulated.

MEDICINES

The compounding of plants and other materials into medicines for the sick is an ancient practice and medieval medical practitioners continued this tradition. The use of herbs, minerals, and other substances to create medicinal compounds was not limited to the unschooled empiric. University-trained doctors learned the medicinal applications of these items as part of their study of classical Greek and Roman medicine.

Medications were often used as part of a course of treatment that involved other practices such as changes in diet, bleeding, or cautery. Anesthetics and medicines that were believed to encourage healing or control bleeding were also sometimes used in conjunction with surgery. Regardless of the purpose of the medication, its composition was limited to those materials that were available to the apothecary and physician or empiric. And, to the best of their abilities, they tried to make these ingredients into medicines to cure every human ill. Not surprisingly, their products were seldom successful and, in some cases, were actually harmful to the patient.

Herbs and Other Vegetable-Based Ingredients

Herbs and other plant matter were the most common ingredients in medieval medicines. Many of these herbs such as rosemary, sage, marjoram, mint, and dill are still familiar to us today, but more for their culinary rather than medicinal applications. Other herbs used included squill, pimpinella, henbane, betony, pennyroyal, and dozens of others which are now seldom seen except in stores that specialize in herbal medicines. Besides herbs, many spices were believed to have curative properties. Thus, cumin, cardamom, ginger, cloves, and many other spices were often listed in recipes for medications. Some vegetables such as rhubarb and lettuce were also used in medicines as well in addition to other vegetable products including oils made from certain plants or their seeds and preparations made from the bark of various trees.

Some of these vegetable-based ingredients have been proven effective for the ailments which they have traditionally been used to treat. Yet, many herbal cures appear to have been at best inert while some were toxic and potentially lethal, especially if not prepared with the greatest care. Thus, despite their wide availability, herbal medicines were a mixed blessing for the sick. In most cases, their positive effects on a patient's health were likely derived from the patient's belief in their curative properties rather than from any actual physical benefits delivered by the medicine.

Non-Vegetable Ingredients

While herbs and other vegetable matter were the primary ingredients in many medicines, medieval *materia medica* did include substances more commonly associated with witches' brews than with prescription medications. For example, one medieval physician recommended applying pig dung to a patient's nose to stop a nosebleed. And raven droppings were listed as an ingredient in an ointment to relieve toothaches. Teeth, fat

or grease, and other parts of animals also found their way into some medieval medications.

Some other non-herbal ingredients were far more expensive than dung though were still just as worthless in curing or preventing illnesses. These included gold, powdered gemstones, ambergris from whales, and powder supposedly gathered from Egyptian mummies that was believed to contain rare and exotic materials used in their embalming. At least these ingredients were largely inert and did little if any harm to the patients, other than the financial damage of paying their high cost. In fact, some of these ingredients appear to have been included because the patients believed that the greater the expense then the greater the efficacy of the medicine. Other ingredients were not so harmless, such as mercury, whose extreme toxicity wasn't fully recognized until the 20th century. Fortunately for most medieval Europeans, medicines containing highly toxic exotic ingredients were usually available only to the wealthy.

Applying Medications

Medicines were typically made into liquid or solid forms that the patient drank or ate. These included syrups, cordials, pills, lozenges, and a paste called an *electuary*. To make these concoctions more palatable, they were usually sweetened with honey or sugar. In fact, some supposedly medicinal preparations appear to have contained nothing except sweeteners and flavorings. Given the dubious value of other medieval medicines, these placebos at least had the merit of not doing any harm to the patient.

Besides being ingested, medicinal compounds were administered in a number of ways even as they are today. Some medicines were applied topically, such as ointments for skin conditions. Others were ground into powders and inhaled either directly in powdered form or after being dissolved into water and heated into steam. Liquid medicines were sometimes applied to sponges or cloths which were held over the patient's mouth and nose so that he or she could inhale the medicinal vapors. This technique was most commonly used for anesthesia. Still other medicines were burnt in a process called fumigation. To protect themselves from contagion, physicians and others working amid epidemics sometimes fumigated the air around them by carrying portable incense burners filled with mixtures that were thought to counteract the noxious vapors of the plague. More commonly, fumigation involved having the patient inhale smoke, but the smoke in some fumigations was generated near orifices other than the mouth and nose with the intention of having the healing smoke enter the patient's body through these orifices. Finally, some medicines were also applied by means of enemas and suppositories as well.

MAGIC AND PRAYER

The distinction between magic and orthodox Christian practices was often blurry to people in the Middle Ages. Few were sufficiently educated in the intricacies of theology to clearly discern pre–Christian or distorted Christian practices from rites approved by the Church in Rome. Further confusion was added by the absorption of some pre–Christian religious traditions into early medieval Christianity. Thus, though some people appear to have sought help through means that they believed were occult, most people who wore charms or recited some seemingly innocuous and incomprehensible incanta-

tion in pursuit of good health did not believe that they were engaging in activities that were incompatible with being a good Christian.

Magic

Incantations and charms were the most common forms of magical healing and these methods appear to have been used most commonly by empirics. Incantations were seldom used by themselves. The empirics most often used incantations in conjunction with other treatments such as herbal medicines. Some empirics recited incantations while collecting the ingredients for the medicine and while compounding the medicine. Additional recitations sometimes accompanied the administering of a medicine as well. Many of the incantations that have survived in written form were gibberish. Some included words that appear to have originally been Latin but, through repeated mispronunciations, had been reduced to nonsense in the process of being passed down as an oral tradition. Some of these incantations also include words that appear to be references to persons and concepts associated with Christianity. The inclusion of these words suggests that these incantations may have originally been prayers whose form and meaning had been distorted over time by the problems of oral transmission in societies that were largely illiterate. Alternatively, the presence of these words may reflect an attempt to Christianize pre–Christian religious practices.

The use of charms also reflects a fusion of pre–Christian and Christian practices. In Rome during both the republic and the empire and in many other cultures in pre–Christian Europe, people had worn brooches and pins inscribed with phrases that supposedly protected them from specific dangers or illnesses. These phrases were often in the form of invocations of divine assistance from a god or goddess. This practice survived even after Christianity became the predominant religion in Europe though the names of pagan gods and goddesses were replaced with those of Christ and the saints. However, there were some medieval talismans that lacked even this veneer of Christianity such as small amulets filled with herbs, stones, and other materials that were believed to generate some supernatural power for healing or for warding off illness.

Though empirics likely resorted to magic more often than the university-educated physicians, physicians frequently did use magic in the form of astrology in diagnosing and treating their patients. Some physicians even used incantations and charms but such practices were not generally accepted by the educated medical community.

Prayer and Miracles

The Middle Ages is often referred to as the Age of Faith and this title is certainly borne out by the numerous instances in which people relied on prayer and divine intervention to heal illnesses, either mental or physical. Such faith healing was common for many reasons: Turning to religion is a common reaction to personal crises. Anyone can pray at any time, anywhere. It doesn't require any formal training. It doesn't cost anything to pray, though some people did spend considerable amounts on actions performed in conjunction with praying. And, given the limited efficacy of many medieval medical treatments, asking God for aid was often as helpful as any of the health care then available. Besides, unlike some of the treatments, praying at least did no harm to the patient.

While prayer was a common form of medical treatment, there is little evidence

that it was used to the exclusion of other treatments such as surgery or medication. Instead, prayer supplemented the efforts of the surgeon or physician. The cases in which prayer alone appears to have been relied were those in which the patient had been deemed beyond help by the medical practitioners.

At its most basic, healing through prayer simply involved the patient and family and friends praying to God to cure the patient's condition. The wording of many prayers indicate that the people praying petitioned God for help indirectly. The prayers were usually directed to a particular saint and asked the saint to intercede with God on behalf of the people offering the prayers. They apparently believed that asking in this way was more appropriate and effective than to audaciously approach God directly. However, they may have simply felt more comfortable addressing a saint, a person who had once been human like themselves, than in attempting to talk to omnipotent God Himself. This element of seeking a sympathetic and human aspect of God appears to have been one of the reasons that the Virgin Mary was one of the most popular saints of the Middle Ages and was often addressed in prayers to intercede with God on behalf of humanity.

While prayers to restore health were routinely directed through St. Mary, there were other saints who were asked to act as divine intermediaries as well. Some, in fact, were patron saints for various medical conditions. For example, St. Apollonia was the patron saint for toothaches and St. Lucy was the patron saint for eye problems. Patron saints were often martyrs and the connection between a saint and a particular condition was often based upon some aspect of the saint's martyrdom. St. Apollonia, for example, was reputed to have had her teeth knocked out and her jaw broken before her execution. Having suffered through this torment, she was believed to be especially sympathetic towards others who were suffering similar problems.

Saints also became affiliated with healing through the miraculous cures attributed to their relics. These relics were housed in special shrines in cathedrals and churches and sometimes attracted large numbers of pilgrims. If the saint was popular and the host church or cathedral had been successful in attracting donations, the shrine could be quite large and ornate and even be decorated in gold and gems. The shrine of St. Thomas à Becket, which was located in Canterbury Cathedral until its destruction in the time of Henry VIII and was the goal of the pilgrims in Chaucer's *Canterbury Tales*, was one example of such a shrine. Many people visited these shrines with no other purpose than as an expression of their devotion to God. Others came to express their devotion and also to ask or to give thanks for divine help in curing themselves or their loved ones.

As an expression of their sincerity and humility, those pilgrims who sought or were giving thanks for miraculous cures sometimes added additional hardships to their pilgrimages such as walking the entire way even though they could have afforded a horse or mule to ride. Besides undergoing the personal hardship and risks of traveling, pilgrims typically made financial sacrifices as well. In addition to the expense of undertaking a pilgrimage, pilgrims routinely made donations to the church or cathedral in which the shrine was housed. Some donations were in cash but, in some instances, pilgrims donated wax images either of the afflicted person or of the injured or diseased body part. These wax images likely served only as temporary decorations around the shrine. Wax was a valuable commodity and these images were probably melted down to make candles to illuminate the shrine.

Other decorations came in the form of crutches discarded by crippled people miraculously healed after visiting the shrine and of valuable ornaments from wealthy patrons.

Mental Illnesses

Mental illnesses were usually referred to as simple-mindedness, lunacy, idiocy, insanity, or — in extreme cases — demonic possession during the Middle Ages. These terms appear to have been applied to conditions ranging from learning disabilities and mental retardation to severe depression and schizophrenia. However, there were no psychologists or psychiatrists in the Middle Ages and the medieval physicians' understanding of the functioning of the human brain seems to have been even more limited than their understanding of the other organs. Thus, diagnosis of mental and emotional problems and the care provided were primitive at best.

Mental illnesses were typically interpreted either as being caused by physical conditions or by supernatural forces. If physical causes were suspected, a physician applied the humoral theory and treated the patient to restore him or her to a healthy balance both mentally and physically. For example, depression was attributed to an excess of that cold and dry humor, black bile, and so the physician would prescribe a diet and regimen to infuse the patient with more warmth and moisture. If supernatural causes were suspected, the patient's treatment was largely out of the hands of the physician. After all, the medical arts were of little use in combating and counteracting malign astrological alignments, demons, or acts of God. Though they were sometimes blamed for causing many physical ailments as well, these supernatural forces were routinely cited as the cause of mental disorders. While such diagnoses are absurd when judged by modern standards, medieval medical practitioners understood the causes of these disorders even less than they understood the causes of physical illnesses and so seem to have attributed them to the only other factors of which they knew. Thus, if a mental illness did not respond to changes in diet, bleeding, and other humor-based treatments, the patient's only hope for a cure was to turn to the Church and seek divine help. Through penance, prayer, and — in extreme cases — exorcism, the patient and the family sought relief through God from suffering.

If both medicine and divine aid failed to help the patient, the only remaining option was for the patient and the family to cope with the condition as best as they could. Many families could not afford to care indefinitely for an adult who could not work. The most fortunate of those suffering from serious and debilitating mental conditions were cared for either by their own families or in the few hospitals that admitted "idiots" or "lunatics." But such care required a compassionate and relatively wealthy family either to undertake the care themselves or to make the contributions often required to underwrite the patient's upkeep during permanent hospitalization. Those less fortunate were abandoned by their families and left to make their own way as best they could by begging.

Women and Medicine

Women in the Middle Ages appear both as patients and as medical practitioners. As patients, women received the same range of treatments as men, from dietary advice to bleeding and surgery. They also received specialized care in gynecology and obstetrics. As practitioners, women were technically barred from practicing most forms of medicine since they could not attend the universities and qualify for licenses to practice. But this did not stop many women from providing medical care, especially gynecological and obstetric care, two areas which were usually shunned by male doctors.

MIDWIVES AND NURSES

In one of few classical texts on gynecology that survived into the Middle Ages and became influential in the universities, a Roman author outlined the qualifications that a midwife should possess: physically robust, disciplined, sympathetic, sober, discreet, and calm with a good memory and knowledge of medicine. Besides listing the qualities she should possess, the author also clearly indicated that the midwife should be a subordinate to the physician. While medieval physicians shared this view, midwives routinely functioned independently of physicians. Midwives rarely had any formal education, but they typically possessed valuable experience which the physicians could not match. Thus, while doctors were sometimes called to wait upon noble ladies and other wealthy women when they were in labor, midwives were more routinely relied upon even by these privileged patients. For the less well-off, the midwife was usually the only medical professional available to help, though many such women likely delivered with only the help of their kinswomen and neighbors. Still, midwives were the most visible female medical practitioners in the Middle Ages. Except at cesarean births where she was displaced by the surgeon, the midwife always appeared in medieval illustrations of births.

Though lacking formal education, midwives were expected to have undergone some form of apprenticeship or similar hands-on training before practicing on their own. By the 14th century, cities in France, Germany, and elsewhere required midwives to be examined and licensed before being allowed to practice. The examinations were typically performed by physicians or clergymen but in at least one German city this responsibility was carried out by a group of the city's most respected women. Besides licensing the midwives and maintaining some control over the quality of their work, some civic authorities, most notably in Germany, retained midwives to assist any pregnant women in the city with their births, regardless of their ability to pay.

While midwives frequently practiced independently of the physicians, some other female medical practitioners did serve as adjuncts to physicians. In the hospitals, they acted as nurses and tended the sick. Many of these women belonged to religious orders, either as nuns or as lay sisters, and performed their nursing duties as part of their religious vocation. This aspect of the origin of nurses is still recalled today in England and Germany where nurses are still routinely called "sisters" (in German, "schwesters"). Nurses in the hospitals had to feed and bathe the patients and keep their clothing and bed linens clean, as well as provide them with medical care. The nurses also had to perform all the menial tasks required to keep the hospital functioning, from cooking the meals and washing the laundry to scrubbing the floors and keeping the fireplaces stoked.

In hospitals and in private practice, some nurses may have also worked with physicians in examining female patients since contemporary standards of modesty and morality deterred physicians from conducting these examinations themselves, even if they had possessed the requisite expertise. While records of this employment of nurses are virtually nonexistent, nurses as well as midwives were well suited and generally available to provide such assistance.

GYNECOLOGICAL AND OBSTETRICAL TREATMENTS

The same Roman text that outlined the qualifications for an ideal midwife also contained some practical information on gynecology as well. Unfortunately, it appears to have been largely disregarded by many medieval physicians. Most of the surviving medieval medical texts contain little material on gynecology and obstetrics and the information that they do include was often nonsense. For example, a woman's uterus was believed to be capable of moving around within her abdomen and causing various disorders depending upon where it stopped. This myth can be traced back to Roman times but it continued to be believed as fact by some medieval physicians who prescribed treatments such as having the woman inhale noxious fumes to drive her wayward uterus back to its proper position.

A few medieval texts did contain some useful information on women's health care mixed in with half-truths and myths. Among these is a medical manual attributed to the legendary Trotula who was one of the female physicians of Salerno. This manual addresses issues such as difficulties with menstruation and problems with giving birth. In the section on giving birth, it states that the placenta must be completely expelled from the uterus soon after the baby has been delivered. While this guidance is sound, the text then lists several different means for inducing the expulsion of the placenta, including burning the bones of salted fish, horses' hooves, or dung of a cat or lamb so that the smoke "fumigates the woman from below." Such fumigation, the text continues, can also be used for bringing on menstruation. Given that this is just one example of the absurd and distasteful treatments for women contained in the medical texts, it is not surprising that most women seem to have shunned treatment by male physicians, though personal modesty and the expense and scarcity of physicians were factors in their decisions as well. Thus, when they needed medical care, many women likely sought out other women within their own families or communities who had some reputation for medical skill. Since these female practitioners were not formally educated or licensed, few records survive to shed light on how they practiced. Like other empirics, their skills probably varied widely depending upon their experience as well as upon their own intelligence and common sense. These varying skill levels would account for the disparate reports of these practitioners' methods which ranged from simply reciting prayers or incantations to administering herbal compounds that had some proven effect in relieving the illness at hand.

Dentistry

Medieval Europeans performed only rudimentary dental hygiene such as rinsing their mouths out with vinegar, wiping their teeth and gums with cloths, picking their teeth to remove food particles, and chewing on soft sticks of wood or pieces of the mallow plant to stimulate their gums and remove some bits of food as well. Toothbrushes appear to have been unknown and remained a rarity until the second half of the 19th century, and flossing only caught on in the 20th century. Along with poor dental hygiene, many people in the Middle Ages suffered dietary condi-

tions that likely resulted in tooth and gum problems. For example, an inadequate intake of vitamin C caused by the scarcity of fresh fruits and vegetables during the late fall to early spring could cause several problems including weakening of the gums, while the consumption of coarse breads and other tough and fibrous foods caused excessive wear on the teeth. Thus, though their diet generally lacked the refined sugars and sticky treats responsible for many of today's dental problems, medieval Europeans suffered from tooth and gum diseases and often sought treatment to relieve their pain.

Toothaches and other mouth pains were routinely included in medieval lists of common ailments. Even decorative carvings in churches included images of people with their jaws bandaged, nursing an aching tooth along with other depictions of human suffering. So, what could they do to ease their suffering? Chewing or eating herbs and prayers appear to have been the most popular forms of treatment but often failed to provide relief. When the pain became too much, people finally turned to professional medical practitioners which, in most cases, meant a barber, a barber-surgeon, or a traveling tooth-pulling specialist.

Medieval dental treatment was rather primitive. Some practitioners followed the humoral theory in dentistry just as they did in other areas of medicine and attempted to correct problems through changes in diet, bleeding, and cautery. However, treatments appear to have more commonly focused directly on the tooth or part of the mouth that was in pain. This approach was pragmatic but it was also often motivated by the ancient belief that toothaches and other dental problems were caused by worms burrowing through the teeth and gums. (These so-called *toothworms* continued to be blamed for dental problems well into the 18th century.) Simply pulling out the aching tooth was the most common form of treatment but some practitioners carefully poured acid into the afflicted tooth. This treatment stopped the pain by destroying the nerve ending in the tooth but of course did nothing to correct the cavity or other problem that was causing the pain and left the tooth just a damaged shell. However, the use of acid may have entailed slightly lower risks to the patient's long term health since the bleeding gums left after extractions were highly susceptible to infection and since there was a chance that the patient's jaw might be broken during a particularly forceful extraction. In any event, patients turned to either extraction or the application of acid only when there was no other option since, besides the health risks, both operations were routinely performed without anesthetics.

Medieval barbers, barber-surgeons, and itinerant tooth-pullers removed some teeth that would have simply been filled if treated today but cavity sufferers had to wait until the late 18th century for the development of durable amalgams for filling teeth. Temporary fillings, often of lead, were used in the Middle Ages but these fillings were only served to keep a tooth from cracking apart while it was pulled. While fillings were unknown, crowns of gold for teeth were reported in the 15th century.

Once the tooth was removed, the gap was left unfilled. Egyptian and Roman dentists had fitted their patients with bridges and other arrangements of false teeth to fill in for lost teeth but this practice seems to have died out during the early Middle Ages and was not revived in Europe until the Renaissance.

Though most medieval dentistry was corrective, the surviving medical texts do show that some practitioners were aware of preventative measures as well. Scraping the calculus off the teeth was the most notable of these measures. This practice was likely first written about by a Greek medical scholar in the 7th century but it is more commonly attributed to an Arab physician in 10th century Spain whose works were translated into Latin and used throughout Europe by the 12th century. Despite the health benefits of such scraping, it does not appear to have become a common practice. Yet, medieval people should not be considered backward for not having embraced this form of teeth cleaning. After all, even today many people seek to avoid the inconvenience and potential pain of regular teeth cleaning and dental check-ups.

Hospitals

Institutions that were referred to as "hospitals" in the Middle Ages were not always "hospitals" in the modern sense of the word. Some medieval hospitals were actually almshouses and hospices. Almshouses were residences for people who were poor but not sick. The upkeep for these residences and their occupants was paid by charitable donations or *alms*. In return, the occupants were expected to offer prayers for the souls of the donors. Hospices were residences for transient people, particularly pilgrims, who needed shelter when traveling far from their homes. While some provided minor medical care for sick or injured travelers, the primary aim of these hospices was to provide food and shelter for pilgrims. But some medieval hospitals were actually specialized medical facilities. Some of these had evolved from earlier hospices and almshouse while others were medical centers from the start. The number of medical hospitals increased throughout Europe over the course of the Middle Ages and by the 15th century the term "hospital" usually referred only to a medical facility rather than a residence for travelers or for the poor. Regardless of the services provided, all these hospitals were usually staffed and managed by religious orders and many were adjuncts to monasteries and other religious institutions.

Medieval hospitals were small by modern standards. The largest hospital was in Florence and accommodated 200 to 300 patients. Most were far smaller and probably accommodated 50 patients at most. Hospitals generally took the form of large residential buildings that were similar to the dormitories of monasteries and convents. Along with wards for housing the patients, these hospitals typically had chapels, kitchens, laundry facilities, and domestic accommodations for the staff. The patients' wards were often depicted as long, open halls with rows of beds along the walls. In many hospitals, patients shared beds, usually with two patients per bed, though one account mentions that up to 12 children were sometimes packed into a single hospital bed. By the late 15th century, some hospitals provided their patients with private beds complete with curtains to further seclude themselves, just like patients in modern "semi-private" hospital rooms. Such amenities appear to have been more common in Italy than elsewhere in Europe.

One might question why patients accepted being placed in a bed with another sick person. In part, sharing beds was a common practice in the Middle Ages, in the home as well as in places of public accommodation such as inns. More importantly, the patients had no choice. Medieval hospitals were charitable institutions founded to treat people who could not afford medical services. Those people who could afford medical care were usually treated in their homes or else recovered in their homes after treatment at the physician's office. Thus, only the poor usually ended up in hospitals.

Medieval hospitals provided rather basic care that consisted primarily of regular meals, regular cleaning, and rest in an airy and sunny setting. Hospitals did provide medications and other treatments as much as their limited budgets allowed. Surprisingly, hospitals appear to have rarely employed physicians to examine and treat their patients. While references to hospitals retaining physicians increased sporadically over the course of the Middle Ages, most care and treatment appear to have been performed by the monks and, especially, the nuns who staffed the hospitals. They had presumably learned their skills both through experience and by reading medical texts in their orders' libraries.

Some hospitals appear to have specialized in or at least became noted for their treatment of pregnant women, especially unwed mothers. For those children whose mothers died in childbirth or who were abandoned after their birth, these hospitals also often served as orphanages. Another specialized type of hospital were Lazar houses. Called Lazar houses after the biblical Lazarus (the diseased beggar in one of Jesus' parables, not the Lazarus whom Jesus raised from the dead), these hospitals were refuges for lepers. These leprosariums provided room, board, some medical care, and spiritual support for the lepers as they lived out their lives isolated from the rest of society. Once admitted, a leper did not expect to ever leave the Lazar house and its grounds since leprosy was viewed as incurable and contagious. However, during the Middle Ages, the term "leprosy" was applied to any number of diseases that caused severe and unsightly skin conditions as well as to true leprosy. Thus, some forms "leprosy" did respond to the salves and ointments administered in the leprosariums while some patients may have recovered naturally after the "leprosy" had run its course.

APPENDIX: PLACES TO SEE MEDIEVAL ART AND ARTIFACTS IN THE U.S. AND CANADA

Finding fine examples of medieval art and architecture is quite easy if you are fortunate enough to be living in or traveling through Europe. Interesting museum collections and historic buildings, sites, and ruins are within easy reach of almost every town and city in Europe.

If you live in North America, getting to see medieval art and architecture firsthand takes more effort but doesn't require a trip to Europe. Across the U.S. and Canada (not just in New York City), there are many collections of art and other artifacts from the Middle Ages.

Though the size, quality, and range of these collections and sites vary greatly, they all provide opportunities for you to see genuine medieval objects for yourself. Some museums are worth the trip just to see their medieval objects, others are probably worth a side trip if you're already in the general vicinity.

United States

CALIFORNIA

Malibu   The J. Paul Getty Museum
The museum's collection includes Western art from the 13th to the 20th centuries.

San Francisco   The Fine Arts Museums of San Francisco, California Palace of the Legion
    Honor in Lincoln Park
The museum has a medieval collection as well as a tapestry collection.

CONNECTICUT

New London   The Lyman Allyn Museum
The museum has a collection of over 12,000 objects spanning 5,000 years, including
    medieval and Renaissance galleries.

FLORIDA

Miami   Vizcaya Museum and Gardens
Vizcaya is a museum of European decorative arts. The collection includes medieval pieces.

Also in the Miami area is a cloister from Segovia, Spain. The cloister dates from and was
    purchased and moved to the U.S. by William Randolph Hearst. It is now owned by
    a church.

Miami Beach   The Bass Museum of Art
A relatively small museum but its collections include medieval sculpture and tapestries.

ILLINOIS

Chicago   The Art Institute of Chicago
The institute has a collection of prints and drawings from the 15th century to the pres-
    ent. It also has reproductions in miniature that offer a study of interior design from
    the 13th to the 20th century. The decorative arts collection contains late medieval
    arms and armor.

Chicago   The Martin D'Arcy Gallery of Art at Loyola University, Lake Shore Campus
A small but growing collection, the D'Arcy Gallery contains only objects produced in
    Europe from the 12th through 18th centuries. They include decorative art pieces as
    well as manuscripts, paintings, and sculpture.

KANSAS

Lawrence   The Helen Foresman Spencer Museum of Art at the University of Kansas
The museum has a comprehensive collection of art, particularly noteworthy in the area
    of medieval art.

KENTUCKY

Louisville   The J. B. Speed Art Museum
This museum has European sculpture from the 13th century to the present as well as decorative arts from the 15th century to the present.

MARYLAND

Baltimore   The Walters Art Gallery
The Walters has an excellent collection of medieval decorative arts, including stained glass, sculptures in wood and stone, as well as arms and armor. Its most outstanding and exceptional collections are of carved ivory and illuminated manuscripts, though — as with most collections — only a few of the manuscripts are on display at any one time.

MASSACHUSETTS

Boston   The Museum of Fine Arts
Among the museum's holdings are European paintings dating back to the 12th century and prints back to the 15th century. There is also a large selection of textiles, including French and Flemish tapestries.

Gloucester   The Hammond Museum
The museum is a "medieval castle" built by John Hays Hammond, Jr., an inventor. The museum contains Hammond's collection of medieval European furniture, tapestries, sculpture, and stained glass.

Worcester   The Worcester Art Museum
This museum's collection of medieval art features a 12th century Romanesque chapter house from a monastery near Poitiers, 13th century frescoes from Spoleto, and 14th and 15th century Italian paintings. The collection also includes medieval stained glass, ivories, and sculpture.

Worcester   The Higgins Armory
In addition to the art museum, Worcester is also home to the Higgins Armory, a museum devoted entirely to medieval and Renaissance arms and armor.

MICHIGAN

Ann Arbor   The University of Michigan Museum of Art
The museum's collections include paintings, graphics, sculpture and decorative arts from medieval times to the present.

Detroit   The Detroit Institute of Art
The institute has a fine collection of arms and armor as well as sculptures, stained glass, and other decorative arts from the Middle Ages.

Missouri

Kansas City   The Nelson-Atkins Museum of Art
This museum has European decorative arts dating back to the 13th century. The collection includes arms and armor.

St. Louis   The St. Louis Art Museum
The museum's collections include armor and other decorative art objects from the Middle Ages.

New York

New York City   The Cloisters
Part of the Metropolitan Museum of Art, the Cloisters is completely dedicated to medieval art, containing tapestries, ivory carvings, architectural elements, and many more splendid pieces of medieval craftsmanship.

New York City   The Metropolitan Museum of Art
While the Cloisters houses much of the museum's medieval collection, the Metropolitan Museum itself displays arms and armor as well as decorative art pieces from the Middle Ages.

New York City   The Pierpont Morgan Library
Many of the finest illuminated medieval manuscripts and Renaissance manuscripts in the world are in this collection, but only a handful are usually on display.

Brooklyn   The Brooklyn Museum of Art
Probably one of the lesser known major museums in the metropolitan area, the Brooklyn Museum of Art's collections include painting and sculpture from medieval Europe.

Rochester   The Memorial Art Gallery at the University of Rochester
The museum has an extensive general art collection which includes medieval art.

Ohio

Cleveland   The Cleveland Art Museum
Cleveland has one of the best medieval collections in the U.S., including reliquaries, illuminated books and manuscripts, sculpture, tapestries, a recently reinstalled collections of arms and armor with many pieces on loan from major European collections, and an extremely rare example of a table fountain of the type that graced the tables of noble feasts in the later Middle Ages.

Toledo   The Toledo Museum of Art
The museum has a medieval cloister assembled from various monasteries in the south of France as well as sculpture and other decorative art items.

PENNSYLVANIA

Philadelphia   The Philadelphia Museum of Art
The museum has an armory filled with a superb collection of arms and armor from across
Europe. In addition to the arms and armor, there is a large gallery of medieval European arts, including part of a cloister, domestic furniture, and many other rare
objects.

VERMONT

Burlington   The Robert Hull Fleming Museum at the University of Vermont
The museum's collections include medieval sculpture and manuscripts.

VIRGINIA

Richmond   The Virginia Museum of Fine Arts
The permanent collection includes a small but choice selection of gothic ivory carvings,
reliquaries, and other medieval art.

WASHINGTON, D.C.

Washington   The National Cathedral
Completed in 1990, the Cathedral is the newest gothic building in the world, constructed
with the same techniques of load-bearing arches and flying buttresses used in cathedrals throughout western Europe in the late Middle Ages.

Canada

ONTARIO

Toronto   The Royal Ontario Museum
The museum has a fine decorative arts collection that includes arms, armor, and other
medieval pieces.

BIBLIOGRAPHY

General

Aries, Philippe, and Georges Duby, general editors. *Revelations of the Medieval World. A History of Private Life*. Vol. 2. Trans. by Arthur Goldhammer from the French. Cambridge: Belknap Press. 1988.

Backhouse, Janet. *The Luttrell Psalter*. London: The British Library. 1989.

Basing, Patricia. *Trades and Crafts in Medieval Manuscripts*. New York: New Amsterdam Books. 1990.

Bautier, Robert-Henri. *The Economic Development of Medieval Europe*. Trans. by Heather Karolyi from the French. London: Thames and Hudson Ltd. 1971.

Colling, Marie, and Virginia Davis. *A Medieval Book of Seasons*. New York: HarperCollins. 1992.

Martin, Janet. *Medieval Russia, 980–1584*. Cambridge: Cambridge University Press. 1995.

Paterson, Linda M. *The World of the Troubadours, Medieval Occitan Society, c.1100–c.1300*. Cambridge: Cambridge University Press. 1993.

Pognon, Edmond. *Les Tres Riches Heures du Duc De Berry*. Trans. by David Macrae from the French. Geneva: Productions Liber S.A. 1987.

Riche, Pierre. *Daily Life in the World of Charlemagne*. Trans. by Jo Ann McNamara from the French. Philadelphia: University of Pennsylvania Press. 1978.

Shahar, Shulamith. *Childhood in the Middle Ages*. Trans. by Chaya Galai from the Hebrew. New York: Routledge. 1992.

Eating and Cooking

Adshead, Samuel Adrian Miles. *Salt and Civilization*. New York: St. Martin's Press. 1992.

Arano, Luisa Cogliati. *The Medieval Health Handbook, Tacuinum Sanitatis*. Trans. from the Italian by Oscar Retti and Adele Westbrook. New York: George Braziller. 1976.

Bayard, Tania, editor and translator. *A Medieval Home Companion.* New York: Harper-Collins. 1991.

Black, Maggie. *The Medieval Cookbook.* New York: Thames & Hudson. 1992.

Cosman, Madeleine Pelner. *Fabulous Feasts: Medieval Cookery and Ceremony.* New York: George Braziller. 1989.

Dyer, Christopher. *Standards of Living in the Later Middle Ages, Social Change in England c. 1270–1520.* Cambridge: Cambridge University Press. 1990.

Hieatt, Constance B., and Sharon Butler. *Pleyn Delit: Medieval Cookery for Modern Cooks.* Toronto: University of Toronto Press. 1985.

Pearson, Kathy L. "Nutrition and the Early-Medieval Diet." *Speculum* 72 (1997), 1–32.

Radford, C. A. Raleigh. *Dover Castle.* London: Her Majesty's Stationery Office. 1959.

Scully, Terence. *The Art of Cookery in the Middle Ages.* Woodbridge, Suffolk: Boydell Press. 1995.

Strong, L. A. G. *The Story of Sugar.* London: George Weidenfeld and Nicolson, Ltd. 1954.

Thorne, Stuart. *The History of Food Preservation.* Totowa, N.Y.: Barnes & Noble. 1986.

Building and Housing

Anderson, William. *Castles of Europe.* New York: Random House. 1970.

Ball, Katharine. *Notre-Dame de Paris: The Stained Glass.* Paris: Association Maurice de Sully. 1987.

Binski, Paul. *Medieval Craftsmen: Painters.* Toronto: University of Toronto Press. 1991.

_____. *The Painted Chamber at Westminster.* London: Society of Antiquaries of London. 1986.

Brown, R. Allen. *Castles: A History and Guide.* Poole, Dorset: Blandford Press Ltd. 1980.

Brown, Sarah. *Stained Glass: An Illustrated History.* Avenel, N.J.: Crescent Books. 1992.

Calkins, Robert G. *Medieval Architecture in Western Europe.* Oxford: Oxford University Press. 1998.

Clark, Helen. *The Archaeology of Medieval England.* London: British Museum Publications, Ltd. 1984.

Coldstream, Nicola. *Medieval Craftsmen: Masons and Sculptors.* London: British Museum Press. 1991.

Coppack, Glyn. *Fountains Abbey.* London: B. T. Batsford Ltd./Historic Buildings and Monuments Commission for England. 1993.

Eames, Elizabeth. *English Medieval Tiles.* London: British Museum Publications. 1985.

Eames, Penelope. "Furniture in England, France and the Netherlands from the Twelfth to the Fifteenth Century." *Furniture History* XIII (1977), 1–303.

Erlande-Brandenburg, Alain. *Cathedrals and Castles: Building in the Middle Ages.* Trans. by Rosemary Stonehewer from the French. New York: Harry N. Abrams. 1995.

Gilyard-Beer, R. *Fountains Abbey.* London: Historic Buildings and Monuments Commission for England. 1970 (1986 edition).

Harris, Richard. *Discovering Timber-Framed Buildings.* Aylesbury, Buckinghamshire: Shire Publications Ltd. 1989.

Higham, Robert, and Philip Barker. *Timber Castles.* Mechanicsburg, Pa.: Stackpole Books. 1995.

Hindley, Geoffrey. *Great Buildings of the World: Castles of Europe.* Feltham, Middlesex: Paul Hamlyn Ltd. 1968.

Kerr, Nigel, and Mary Kerr. *A Guide to Medieval Sites In Britain*. London: Grafton Books. 1988.

_____. *A Guide to Norman Sites in Britain*. London: Granada Publishing Ltd. 1988.

MacMahon, K. A. *Beverley Minster*. London: Pitkin Pictorials Ltd. 1975.

Magi, Giovanni. *All Avignon*. Firenze: Casa Editrice Bonechi. 1988.

McIntyre, Anthony Osler. *Medieval Tuscany and Umbria*. London: Penguin Books. 1993.

The National Trust Handbook. London: The National Trust. 1990.

Platt, Colin. *The Architecture of Medieval Britain*. New Haven and London: Yale University Press. 1990.

Rouse, E. Clive. *Longthorpe Tower*. London: Historic Buildings and Monuments Commission for England. 1987.

Taylor, A. J. *Beaumaris Castle*. Cardiff: Welsh Historic Monuments. 1980.

Viollet-le-Duc, Eugene Emmanuel. *Military Architecture*. Trans. by M. MacDermott from the French. London: Lionel Leventhal Ltd. 1990 (reproduction of the third edition by James Parker and Co. 1907).

Wilcox, R. P. *Timber and Iron Reinforcement in Early Buildings*. London: Society of Antiquaries of London. 1981.

Williamson, Paul. *Gothic Sculpture, 1140–1300*. New Haven: Yale University Press. 1995.

Wood, Margaret. *The English Mediaeval House*. New York: Harper & Row. 1983.

Yarwood, Doreen. *The Architecture of Europe: The Middle Ages 650–1550*. London: B. T. Batsford Ltd. 1992.

Clothing and Dressing

Bradfield, Nancy. *900 Years of English Costume*. London: Peerage Books. 1987.

Crowfoot, Elisabeth, Francis Pritchard, and Kay Staniland. *Medieval Finds from Excavation in London: (4) Textiles and Clothing*. London: Her Majesty's Stationery Office. 1992.

Cunnington, C. William, and Phillis Cunnington. *The History of Underclothes*. New York: Dover Publications. 1992.

Grew, Francis, and Margrethe de Neergaard. *Medieval Finds from Excavation: (2) Shoes and Pattens*. London: Her Majesty's Stationery Office. 1988.

Owen-Crocker, Gale R. *Dress in Anglo-Saxon England*. Manchester: Manchester University Press. 1986.

Piponnnier, Françoise, and Perrine Mane. *Dress in the Middle Ages*. Trans. by Caroline Beamish from the French. New Haven: Yale University Press. 1997.

Cleaning

Cavitch, Susan Miller. *The Soapmaker's Companion*. Pownal, Vt.: Storey Publishing. 1997.

Goepfert, Yvette. *Pont du Gard*. Trans. by Candice Richards and Catherine Ungar from the French. Le Cannet (France): Editions AIO. 1982.

Sabine, Ernest L. "City Cleaning in Mediaeval London." *Speculum* 12 (1937), 19–43.

_____. "Latrines and Cesspools of Mediaeval London." *Speculum* 9 (1934), 303–321.

Thorndike, Lynn. "Sanitation, Baths, and Street-Cleaning in the Middle Ages and Renaissance." *Speculum* 3 (1928), 192–203.

Wright, Lawrence. *Clean and Decent*. Toronto: University of Toronto Press. 1967.

Relaxing and Playing

Barber, Richard, and Juliet Barker. *Tournaments.* New York: Weidenfeld and Nicolson. 1989.

Cummins, John. *The Hound and the Hawk: The Art of Medieval Hunting.* New York: St. Martin's Press. 1988.

Flower, Raymond. *The History of Skiing and Other Winter Sports.* New York: Methuen. 1976.

Fraser, Antonia. *A History of Toys.* New York: Weidenfeld and Nicolson. 1966.

Fritzch, Karl Ewald, and Manfred Bachmann. *An Illustrated History of Toys.* Trans. by Ruth Micheals-Jena from the German. London: Abbey Library. 1966.

Green, Robert. *The Illustrated Encyclopedia of Golf.* London: CollinsWillow. 1995.

Grunfeld, Frederic V., ed. *Games of the World.* New York: Holt, Rinehart and Winston. 1975.

Hargrave, Catherine Perry. *A History of Playing Cards: And a Bibliography of Cards and Gaming.* New York: Dover Publications. 1966.

Hoffman, Richard C. "Fishing for Sport in Medieval Europe: New Evidence." *Speculum* 60 (1985), 877–902.

Montagu, Jeremy. *The World of Medieval and Renaissance Musical Instruments.* Woodstock, N.Y.: Overlook Press. 1980.

Murray, H. J. R. *A History of Board Games Other Than Chess.* Oxford: Clarendon Press. 1952.

Nagler, A. M. *The Medieval Religious Stage.* New Haven: Yale University Press. 1976.

Nelson, Alan H. *The Medieval English Stage.* Chicago: University of Chicago Press. 1974.

Parlett, David. *The Oxford Guide to Card Games.* Oxford: Oxford University Press. 1990.

Pelham, David. *The Penguin Book of Kites.* Harmondsworth, Middlesex, UK: Penguin Books Ltd. 1976.

Quennell, Marjorie, and C. H. B. Quennell. *A History of Everyday Things in England, Volume I: 1066–1499.* London: B. T. Batsford Ltd. 1938 (third edition).

Sachs, Curt. *World History of the Dance.* Trans. from the German by Bessie Schonberg. New York: Norton. 1937.

Schimmelpfennig, Wolfgang. *Making and Flying Kites.* Secaucus, N.J.: Castle (Hamlyn Publishing Group Ltd.) 1989.

Sorrell, Walter. *Dance in Its Time.* Garden City, NY: Anchor Press. 1981.

Southern, Richard. *The Medieval Theatre in the Round.* London: Faber and Faber Ltd. 1975.

Squires, Dick. *The Other Racquet Sports.* New York: McGraw-Hill. 1978.

Wickham, Glynne. *The Medieval Theatre.* New York: St. Martin's Press. 1974.

Fighting

Alm, Josef. *European Crossbows: A Survey.* Trans. by H. Bartlett Wells from the Swedish. London: Trustees of the Royal Armouries. 1994.

Arms and Armour in Britain. London: Her Majesty's Stationery Office. 1986.

Blair, Claude. *European Armour.* London: B. T. Batsford Ltd. 1979.

Bradbury, Jim. *The Medieval Archer.* Woodbridge: Boydell Press. 1985.

Contamine, Philippe. *War in the Middle Ages.* Trans. by Michael Jones from the French. Oxford: Basil Blackwell Ltd. 1990.

Crossbows. Treasures of the Tower. London: Her Majesty's Stationery Office. 1981.

Davis, R. H. C. *The Medieval Warhorse.* London: Thames and Hudson. 1989.

Dean, Bashford. *Helmets and Body Armor in Modern Warfare.* Tuckahoe, N.Y.: Carl J. Pugliese. 1977.

Edge, David. *European Arms and Armour.* London: Trustees of the Wallace Collection. 1992.

_____, and John Miles Paddock. *Arms and Armour of the Medieval Knight.* London: Guild Publishing. 1988.

Hardy, Robert. *Longbow: A Social and Military History.* Sparkford, Somerset: Patrick Stephens Ltd. 1992.

Hooper, Nicholas, and Matthew Bennett. *The Cambridge Illustrated Atlas: Warfare: The Middle Ages, 768–1487.* Cambridge: Cambridge University Press. 1996.

Mann, Sir James. *Wallace Collection Catalogues: European Arms and Armour.* Two Volumes. London: The Trustees of the Wallace Collection. 1962.

Neillands, Robin. *The Hundred Years War.* London: Routledge. 1990.

Norman, A. V. B. *The Medieval Soldier.* New York: Barnes & Noble. 1993.

_____. *Wallace Collection Catalogues: European Arms and Armour — Supplement.* London: The Trustees of the Wallace Collection. 1986.

_____, and Don Pottinger. *English Weapons & Warfare, 449–1660.* New York: Dorset Press. 1985.

Oakeshott, R. Ewart. *The Archaeology of Weapons.* New York: Barnes & Noble. 1994.

_____. *The Sword in the Age of Chivalry.* London: Lutterworth Press. 1964.

Pfaffenbichler, Matthias. *Medieval Armourers.* Toronto: University of Toronto Press. 1992.

Upton-Ward, J. M. *The Rule of the Templars.* Woodbridge: Boydell Press. 1992.

The Wallace Collection Guide to the Armouries. London: Trustees of the Wallace Collection. 1982.

Healing

Amt, Emilie, editor. *Women's Lives in Medieval Europe: A Sourcebook.* New York: Routledge. 1993.

Friedman, Meyer, and Gerald W. Friedland. *Medicine's 10 Greatest Discoveries.* New Haven: Yale University Press. 1998.

Gordon, Benjamin Lee. *Medieval and Renaissance Medicine.* New York: Philosophical Library, Inc. 1959.

Jones, Peter Murray. *Medieval Medicine in Illuminated Manuscripts.* London: The British Library. 1998.

Rawcliffe, Carole. *Medicine and Society in Later Medieval England.* Stroud, Gloucestershire: Alan Sutton Publishing. 1995.

Ring, Malvin E. *Dentistry: An Illustrated History.* New York: Abradale Press. 1992.

Siraisi, Nancy G. *Medieval and Early Renaissance Medicine: An Introduction to Knowledge and Practice.* Chicago: University of Chicago Press. 1990.

Travers, Bridget, and Fran Locher Freiman, editors. *Medical Discoveries: Medical Breakthroughs and the People Who Developed Them.* Detroit: UXL. 1997.

INDEX